The Aspen Instit Guide to Socially Responsible MBA Programs: 2008–2009

THE ASPEN INSTITUTE
Center for Business Education

BK

Berrett–Koehler Publishers, Inc.
San Francisco
a BK Business book

Berrett-Koehler Publishers, Inc.
235 Montgomery Street, Suite 650
San Francisco, CA 94104-2916
Tel: (415) 288-0260   Fax: (415) 362-2512   www.bkconnection.com

Ordering Information
Quantity sales. Special discounts are available on quantity purchases by corporations, associations, and others. For details, contact the "Special Sales Department" at the Berrett-Koehler address above.
Individual sales. Berrett-Koehler publications are available through most bookstores. They can also be ordered directly from Berrett-Koehler: Tel: (800) 929-2929; Fax: (802) 864-7626; www.bkconnection.com
Orders for college textbook/course adoption use. Please contact Berrett-Koehler: Tel: (800) 929-2929; Fax: (802) 864-7626.
Orders by U.S. trade bookstores and wholesalers. Please contact Ingram Publisher Services, Tel: (800) 509-4887; Fax: (800) 838-1149; E-mail: customer.service@ingrampublisherservices.com; or visit www.ingrampublisherservices.com/Ordering for details about electronic ordering.

Berrett-Koehler and the BK logo are registered trademarks of Berrett-Koehler Publishers, Inc.

Printed in the United States of America

ISBN 978-1-57675-765-9 (print edition)
ISBN 978-1-57675-666-9 (PDF e-book)

First Edition/2

The information in this book was gathered and prepared by
Business and Society Program
The Aspen Institute
271 Madison Avenue, Suite 606
New York, NY 10016

Introduction

School Profiles

Resources

About the Aspen Institute and Center for Business Education

The Aspen Institute, founded in 1950, is an international nonprofit organization dedicated to fostering enlightened leadership and open-minded dialogue. Through seminars, policy programs, conferences, and leadership development initiatives, the Institute and its international partners seek to promote nonpartisan inquiry and an appreciation for timeless values. The Institute is headquartered in Washington, DC, and has campuses in Aspen, Colorado, and on the Wye River on Maryland's Eastern Shore. Its international network includes partner Aspen Institutes in Berlin, Rome, Lyon, Tokyo, New Delhi, and Bucharest, and leadership programs in Africa, Central America, and India. www.aspeninstitute.org

The Aspen Institute Center for Business Education (CBE) equips business leaders for the 21st century with a new management paradigm—the vision and knowledge to integrate corporate profitability and social value. To that end, it provides business educators with cutting edge-classroom resources and creates peer networks to incorporate social and environmental stewardship into teaching, research, and curriculum development. CBE websites draw over 75,000 visits monthly and its events and networks attract over 1,000 participants each year. www.CasePlace.org and www.beyondgreypinstripes.org are the leading sources of innovative curriculum in top business schools around the world.

CBE is a part of the **Aspen Institute Business and Society Program** (**BSP**), which is dedicated to developing leaders for a sustainable global society. Through dialogues and groundbreaking research, we create opportunities for executives and educators to explore new pathways to sustainability and values-based leadership.

The Aspen Institute Guide to Socially Responsible MBA Programs: 2008-2009

This *Guide to Socially Responsible MBA Programs (The Aspen Institute Guide)* provides an overview of how global MBA programs bring social impact management into their curricular and extracurricular programs. Social impact management, which includes environmental, ethical, and corporate governance issues, is the field of inquiry at the intersection of business needs and wider societal concerns that reflects the complex interdependency between these two realities. It is a critical part of contemporary business-without an understanding of this interdependency, neither business nor the society in which it operates can thrive.

Aspen CBE strives to promote and celebrate innovation in business school education. Every two years we conduct a major survey and alternative ranking as part of our Beyond Grey Pinstripes (BGP) project. Over the years the number of schools participating and the amount of information collected has increased dramatically. While all detailed survey information is available at www.BeyondGreyPinstripes.org, we felt that the business education community—both students and faculty—would find a user-friendly format helpful. And so *The Aspen Institute Guide* was born.

The Aspen Institute Guide provides MBA program highlights drawn from data collected for the 2007-2008 BGP survey, and covers information pertaining to academic years 2005-2006 and 2006-2007. Surveys consist entirely of self-reported data from each school, and were filled out online by MBA school faculty or administrators. Please visit the survey website (www.BeyondGreyPinstripes.org) for a more detailed account of content, methodology, and process.

Each year business schools strive to differentiate themselves and attract the best and the brightest future business leaders, while prospective MBAs are looking for a program that will equip them with effective management skills to succeed in the ever-changing world of business. The bottom line in business is no longer exclusively dedicated to financial returns. Rather, business leaders must also consider the environmental and social impacts of their decisions in order to compete in the global marketplace. The MBA schools that participate in our survey, and are therefore highlighted in *The Aspen Institute Guide,* are leaders in integrating these issues into their curricula.

The Aspen Institute Guide can be used to review a single school's dedication to environmental and social impact management or to compare several schools based on a variety of topics such as size, course offerings, geographic area, diversity, etc. Our hopes for *The Aspen Institute Guide* are threefold:, First, prospective MBA students who care about these issues will consult this guide for an overview of each school's dedication to social and environmental impact management. Second, the business education community will use *The Aspen Institute Guide* as a resource for best practices in teaching, research, and extracurricular activities and continue to challenge themselves and one another to offer the most relevant and innovative curriculum. And finally, employers and recruiters will use *The Aspen Institute Guide* as a window into how individual MBA programs prepare managers to lead businesses in a financially, socially, and environmentally conscious manner.

> *"I believe that the* Beyond Grey Pinstripes *program has been one of the most important information initiatives of the past decade for the emerging field of sustainable and socially responsible business. It enables prospective MBA students from all over the world to identify and focus on those business schools that are most responsive to their needs and aspirations when it comes to fusing societal contribution with business competitiveness. It turns out that these prospective students also happen to be the highest possible caliber applicants on the market."–Stuart Hart, S.C. Johnson Chair of Sustainable Global Enterprise, Johnson Graduate School of Management, Cornell University*

Schools Featured in *The Aspen CBE's Alternative Guide to Socially Responsible MBA Education Programs: 2008-2009*

As with the Beyond Grey Pinstripes survey, *The Aspen Institute Guide* profiles only full-time, accredited, on-campus MBA programs. Due to resource constraints, we do not collect data about Executive MBA, part-time MBA, undergraduate, Ph.D., or other programs.

Working with international MBA accrediting bodies, we assembled a roster of close to 700 MBA programs around the world. Each school was then invited to participate in the 2007 survey. A total of 111 schools from over 20 countries submitted more than 40,000 pages of data.

Schools collectively submitted information on over 2,500 courses, 800 speakers and conferences, 340 institutes and centers, 320 student clubs, and 130 MBA student competitions related to environmental and social impact management. Also submitted were almost 3,000 names of faculty who have a research interest in social, environmental, or ethical issues. Due to space limitations, only a sampling of each school's information is presented in *The Aspen Institute Guide*. Almost all of the collected information for 2007 and previous years can be found at http://www.beyondgreypinstripes.org. Each profile in *The Aspen Institute Guide* provides a link to the school's own program website for further information.

Student Perceptions of Their MBA Program

While student contributions and feedback are a critical part of the execution of a successful environmental and social impact management MBA curriculum, *The Aspen Institute Guide* presents relevant information disclosed directly from the business schools; student opinions were not solicited.

For the student perspective, we encourage readers to learn more about Net Impact (www.netimpact.org), "an international nonprofit organization whose mission is to make a positive impact on society by growing and strengthening a community of new leaders who use business to improve the world." Net Impact conducts an annual survey of Net Impact student chapter leaders and members at business programs around the world to share student perspectives of their own business schools regarding social and environmental initiatives. *The 2007 Net Impact Student Guide to Graduate Business Programs* is a great resource to gain the student perspective on MBA programs, while using the profiles in this Guide.

"Beyond Grey Pinstripes is an invaluable resource for the increasing number of MBA students who place a high value on learning how to work with social and environmental issues in their business careers. For current MBA students, the database of courses and syllabi provide a benchmark against which they can measure their curriculum. The work that we do at Net Impact on curriculum change is helped substantially by Beyond Grey Pinstripes" –Liz Maw **,** *Executive Director , Net Impact*

Navigating *The Aspen Institute Guide*
School profiles are ordered alphabetically, and specific schools and page numbers can easily be located in the table of contents. Additional information relevant to an interest in socially and environmentally minded MBA programs is available in the appendix.

In order to make The Aspen Institute Guide informative, yet manageable, we chose to highlight a sample of each school's most innovative offerings. While we wanted to include all of the remarkable curriculum and program information from every school, a 4,000-page guide would have been very difficult to lift! So, taking into account the quantity and quality of each school's self-reported data provided for the 2007-2008 BGP survey covering academic years 2005-2006 & 2006-2007, we constructed a standard outline to best highlight each MBA program. If any specific section is absent from an individual school profile, that information was unavailable or not applicable:

- WHAT THE SCHOOL SAYS – A summary describing the business school's self-reported approach to preparing MBA students to manage social and environmental issues inherent in mainstream business. (Verbatim descriptions are available in their entirety at www.BeyondGreyPinstripes.org)

- A QUICK LOOK

    o COURSES – Combined number of all relevant core and elective courses offered in each department that include social impact and/or environmental management issues.
    o KEY CONCENTRATIONS – 1-2 selected specializations or concentrations offered by the business school that provide MBA students an opportunity to study social impact and/or environmental management. (A comprehensive list of self-reported concentrations/specializations offered by the school is available in the appendix.)
    o KEY JOINT DEGREES – 1-2 selected innovative joint degrees offered by the business school that provide MBA students an opportunity to study social impact and/or environmental management. (A comprehensive list of self-reported joint degrees offered by the school is available in the appendix.)
    o ACTIVITIES – Combined number of all self-reported activities and programs at the school that include social impact and/or environmental management issues.

- CORE/REQUIRED COURSES – 1-2 selected MBA core/required courses that include social impact and/or environmental management issues.

- ELECTIVE COURSES – 1-2 selected MBA elective courses that include social impact and/or environmental management issues.

INSTITUTES AND CENTERS – 1-2 selected institutes or centers at the business school that focus most directly on social impact and/or environmental management. The institute or center may be housed in the business school or sponsored in partnership with another school.

- QUESTIONS TO CONSIDER – Standardized questions for quick reference regarding relevant curriculum and student programs. (For more information on Net Impact, visit www.netimpact.org.)

- ANNUAL EVENTS – 1-3 selected events that occur on an annual basis at or in affiliation with the school, such as an innovative speaker series, seminars and conferences, orientation activities, internship and consulting programs, and MBA student competitions related to social impact and/or environmental management.

- OTHER PROGRAMS – 1-2 additional selected activities/programs offered by the school that include social impact and/or environmental management issues.

- STUDENT CLUBS AND PROGRAMS – 1-2 selected MBA student clubs that are related to social impact and/or environmental management.

- FACULTY PIONEER –Aspen CBE's Faculty Pioneer Awards recognize exceptional faculty who are leaders in integrating social and environmental issues into their research and teaching both on and off-campus. If a Faculty Pioneer is teaching at a school, we note it here. (A comprehensive list of all Faculty Pioneers since 1999 is available in the appendix.)

- SCHOOL DEMOGRAPHICS – Self-reported statistics on the student body.

- THE BOTTOM LINE – We applied a statistical analysis to determine the relative strength of each school along a with few select criteria. We assess both the number of courses reported to us, and the proportion of those courses that address mainstream, for-profit business issues, as opposed to public policy or nonprofit themes. We then make qualitative remarks using the following terms to reflect precise statistical scores:

  o Truly Extraordinary – given to schools that scored more than one standard deviation above average
  o Excellent – given to schools that scored between average and one standard deviation above average
  o Good – given to schools that scored between one standard deviation below average and average

Thank You

Thank you for your interest in *The Aspen Institute Guide to Socially Responsible MBA Programs: 2008-2009*; please enjoy and use it as a resource however it will best fit your needs. For further information or for questions and feedback, please visit www.AspenCBE.org or email us at AspenCBE@AspenInstitute.org.

A Closer Look at:
Ashridge Business School
Hertfordshire, United Kingdom
http://www.ashridge.org.uk/

WHAT THE SCHOOL SAYS:
Central to the Ashridge MBA is the belief that business leaders require a broad, integrated and transferable portfolio of skills. The Ashridge MBA aims to develop individuals with the capabilities to achieve both personal and organizational success.

A QUICK LOOK

NOTE: All information is self-reported data submitted to the Center for Business Education

COURSES*

CSR/Business Ethics (1)
General Management (1)

ACTIVITIES*

Speakers/Seminars (1)
Orientation Activities (1)
Internship/Consulting (2)
Student Competitions (1)
Career Development (1)
Institutes/Centers (2)

* Figures in parentheses indicate the number of courses/activities that, in whole or in part, integrate social, environmental, or ethical perspectives

NOTABLE FEATURES

CORE COURSES:
▦ *Business in Society*
This module raises students' awareness of the changing social pressures and legislative requirements redefining the role of business in society. The symbiotic relationship between business and society is explored, including the impact of this relationship on corporate governance and the implications for students' leadership roles. The module provides students with tools and frameworks to integrate corporate responsibility into mainstream business practices and demonstrates how leading companies respond to these challenges to build sustainable business strategies.

▦ *Live Consulting Project*
This project gives MBA students an opportunity to apply the skills they have acquired at Ashridge by delivering a strategic consulting assignment for an organization. Students can elect to undertake this eight-week consulting project with an organization involved in social/environmental management. About 24 percent of students provide research/internship/consulting projects on CSR and/or for not-for-profit organizations.

INSTITUTES AND CENTERS:
▦ *Ashridge Center for Business and Society*
The Ashridge Centre for Business and Society is a leading authority on relations between business, government, and civil society. It aims to further the debate on how issues of corporate governance, employee relations, supplier alliances, business values, environmental responsibility, community investment, and government relations impact the long-term viability of business.

▦ *Ashridge Public Leadership Centre*
The Ashridge Public Leadership Centre is the innovative window on the world of business for leaders and managers in the public sector. Its vision is to be the leading developer of public sector managers. This is inspired by Ashridge's drive to seek excellence and improve the services it offers to students and members of the business community. The center helps clients to make better decisions in development initiatives and to reach higher levels of quality with improved mechanisms for quality research and better evidence leading to more informed delivery.

QUESTIONS TO CONSIDER:

Does any required course contain some element of Social Impact Management? **YES**

Is any required course entirely dedicated to social, environmental, or ethical issues? **YES**

Is there a Net Impact chapter on campus? **NO**

All information in this profile is drawn and/or adapted from the self-reported data of the Center for Business Education's Beyond Grey Pinstripes 2007 MBA survey. The Center for Business Education is housed within the Business and Society Program at the Aspen Institute. For more info, visit www.AspenCBE.org.

13

A Closer Look at:
Ashridge Business School
Hertfordshire, United Kingdom

THE ASPEN INSTITUTE
Center for Business Education

ANNUAL EVENTS:

▪ Outside Speakers

Ashridge MBA students regularly have the opportunity to meet and listen to senior businesspeople from external organizations. A number of speakers from breweries, manufacturing organizations, and airlines have spoken on subjects that include corporate social responsibility and sustainability.

▪ Ashridge Best European MBA Essay Award

Ashridge presents an award for the most thought-provoking MBA student essay on the changing role of business in society. The award exists to further debate about the role of business in society and to bring this discussion to a wider audience, particularly business leaders and public policy -makers. It also aims to raise awareness about these issues in mainstream management education.

OTHER PROGRAMS:

▪ MBAid

MBAid is an opportunity open to all Ashridge alumni and students to be involved in voluntary consultancy projects in the charity and not-for-profit sector.

SCHOOL DEMOGRAPHICS	
Number of Full-Time Students	23
International Students	81%
Female Students	40%
Pre-MBA Employment:	

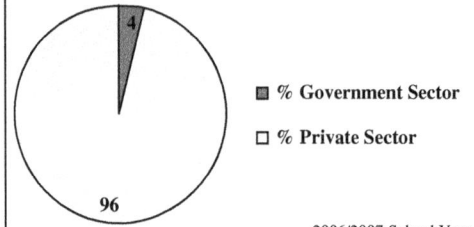

- ▪ % Government Sector
- ☐ % Private Sector

4
96

2006/2007 School Year

THE CENTER FOR BUSINESS EDUCATION'S BOTTOM LINE ON ASHRIDGE BUSINESS SCHOOL:
Compared to other business schools in our survey, Ashridge Business School does a good job in relevant courses explicitly addressing how mainstream business improves the world. Ashridge Business School requires 2 core courses featuring relevant content.

A Closer Look at:
Asian Institute of Management

Washington SyCip Graduate School of Business / Makati City, Philippines
http://www.wsgsb.aim.edu/

THE ASPEN INSTITUTE
Center for Business Education

WHAT THE SCHOOL SAYS:

AIM's mission has been to make "a difference in sustaining the growth of Asian societies by developing professional, entrepreneurial, and socially responsible leaders and managers." We have a responsibility to produce managers who possess integrity and high ethical standards and who will endeavor to humanize the corporation, understand the ethical implications of every management decision, and feel personal responsibility for their workers.

A QUICK LOOK

NOTE: All information is self-reported data submitted to the Center for Business Education

COURSES*

Business & Government (1)
CSR/Business Ethics (1)
Economics (1)
Entrepreneurship (5)
Finance (9)
HR Management (5)
International Management (2)
General Management (2)
Marketing (6)
Organizational Behavior (1)
Operations Management (1)
Strategy (2)

KEY CONCENTRATIONS

Development Management

Social & Development Entrepreneurship

ACTIVITIES*

Speakers/Seminars (57)
Orientation Activities (1)
Internship/Consulting (3)
Clubs & Programs (1)
Career Development (1)
Institutes/Centers (6)
Concentrations (3)

* Figures in parentheses indicate the number of courses/activities that, in whole or in part, integrate social, environmental, or ethical perspectives

NOTABLE FEATURES

CORE COURSES:

CSR in Asia
This course starts with a presentation on "The Changing Role of Business in Society," focusing on why CSR is important today. Students are then given an overview of what CSR: what it is, what drives companies to do CSR work, where different countries are in the evolution of CSR, the different types of CSR activities, and what and how its performance is measured.

Economics
This is a macro- and microeconomics foundations course with a special focus on contemporary Asian issues. It seeks to involve noneconomists in the formulation and implementation of public policies that impact the economy and people's welfare. Topics covered include central banking and monetary policy; unemployment; growth, development, and policy; and basic elements of supply and demand.

ELECTIVE COURSES:

Banking with the Poor
In this course, students will grapple with the opportunities, challenges, and issues in providing financial services to low-income groups, small entrepreneurs, and other so-called high-risk groups. Students will review different models and approaches that have emerged and will be exposed to day-to-day issues such as delinquency management, price setting, and managing financial and operational performance.

Social Entrepreneurship
Social Entrepreneurship addresses the theory and practice of wealth creation with a triple bottom line– financial, social, and environmental. This course examines creating space for the poor and marginalized sectors of society to participate more effectively in the economy, not only as beneficiaries but also as owners and managers of enterprises.

INSTITUTES AND CENTERS:

Ramon V. del Rosario Sr. (RVR) Center for Corporate Responsibility
The RVR Center for Corporate Responsibility promotes corporate responsibility through casewriting, research, surveys, investigative research, program development, executive education, and conferences. The RVR Center is one of the first research centers in the region concentrating on corporate responsibility issues and is in the process of establishing its own network in the fields of CSR and corporate governance, connecting and collaborating with counterpart organizations throughout the region.

AIM-Mirant Center for Bridging Societal Divides
The AIM-Mirant Center aims to develop Bridging Leaders who understand the societal divides, engage critical stakeholders to take ownership of the problem and its solutions, and work with them to facilitate program interventions that will bridge the divides. The center provides capacity-building activities through the academic curricula of AIM and through public offerings and customized programs to meet the needs of particular groups.

QUESTIONS TO CONSIDER:

Does any required course contain some element of Social Impact Management? **YES**

Is any required course entirely dedicated to social, environmental, or ethical issues? **YES**

Is there a Net Impact chapter on campus? **NO**

A Closer Look at:
Asian Institute of Management
Washington SyCip Graduate School of Business / Makati City, Philippines

ANNUAL EVENTS:

■ *Asian Forum on Corporate Social Responsibility*

The Asian Forum on Corporate Social Responsibility provides viewpoints from distinguished speakers on new trends and challenges, while special interest sessions highlight the major topics with CSR insights, experiences, and best practices of specific companies and industries. The forum also offers a pre-conference workshop; senior executives from several nations representing government, corporate, and NGOs are workshop speakers at the event.

■ *State of Philippine Competitiveness National Conference*

As a prospective measure for boosting national competitiveness, this conference focuses on the creative industries as a way forward for the country, with presentations from government agencies and the private sector on what the Philippines can take advantage of vis-à-vis individual creativity, skills, and talents that have a potential for wealth and job creation through the generation and exploitation of intellectual property.

OTHER PROGRAMS:

■ *United Nations Forum on Millennium Plus Five Summit*

As part of the UN 60th anniversary celebration, AIM hosted this forum, which drew close to 600 representatives from the diplomatic community, government, civil society, business sector, academia, and media. Some points raised:
(1) Resolve global partnership issues related to debt, trade, and governance.
(2) Strengthen existing treaty-monitoring bodies to ensure a more effective system to monitor state compliance with human rights commitments/obligations.

SCHOOL DEMOGRAPHICS	
Number of Full-Time Students	179
International Students	51%
Female Students	30%
Pre-MBA Employment:	

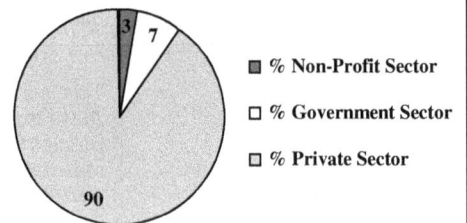

■ % Non-Profit Sector
□ % Government Sector
□ % Private Sector

2006/2007 School Year

■ *Exchange agreement between Copenhagen Business School and AIM*

The European Union funds an exchange agreement between the Copenhagen Business School (CBS) and AIM. Candidates from AIM and CBS must focus on corporate social entrepreneurship.

STUDENT CLUBS AND PROGRAMS:

■ *Philanthropic Activities Society*

The Philanthropic Activities Society is dedicated to serving underprivileged Asians. It conducts fundraising, blood drives, and visits to the different charities it sponsors.

THE CENTER FOR BUSINESS EDUCATION'S BOTTOM LINE ON ASIAN INSTITUTE OF MANAGEMENT:
Compared to other business schools in our survey, Asian Institute of Management offers an excellent number of courses featuring relevant content and does an excellent job in those courses explicitly addressing how mainstream business improves the world. Asian Institute of Management requires 12 core courses featuring relevant content.

A Closer Look at:
Audencia Nantes
School of Management / Nantes, France
http://www.audencia.com

WHAT THE SCHOOL SAYS:
Given their involvement in the global economy, MBA students need to be specifically exposed to global social responsibility and business ethics issues. Our aim at Audencia is to train MBA participants to become conscious of the importance of acting as socially and environmentally responsible leaders.

A QUICK LOOK

NOTE: All information is self-reported data submitted to the Center for Business Education

COURSES*

Business & Government (**1**)
CSR/Business Ethics (**1**)
International Management (**1**)
General Management (**2**)

KEY CONCENTRATIONS

Business Development

ACTIVITIES*

Speakers/Seminars (**4**)
Orientation Activities (**2**)
Internship/Consulting (**1**)
Clubs & Programs (**3**)
Career Development (**1**)
Institutes/Centers (**2**)
Concentrations (**2**)

* Figures in parentheses indicate the number of courses/activities that, in whole or in part, integrate social, environmental, or ethical perspectives

NOTABLE FEATURES

CORE COURSES:

▪ *Business Ethics*
This course seeks to enhance one's ability to master ethical dilemmas, to refine the knowledge of one's value system and to connect the various levels of the ethical issues in management. In this way, students discover the importance of the role played by a manager's ethics in business, review the U.S. approach to business ethics, analyze new European approaches to the question, and discuss a criticism of business ethics ideology.

▪ *International Business*
This course is designed to assist students in understanding the global environment in which international business takes place. Topics addressed include key global policy issues plus environmental and ethical concerns and the dynamics of the global economy.

INSTITUTES AND CENTERS:

▪ *Center for Global Responsibility*
Audencia's Center for Global Responsibility is comprised of researchers, students, companies, non-governmental organizations, and unions. The center analyzes the latest international research in the field, defines and launches future research projects, and examines data collected. The center has launched its own global responsibility trophy awards for the region's companies and regularly organizes conferences on key responsibility questions.

▪ *LESMA (laboratory for research and strategy in the food industry)*
LESMA's multidisciplinary team of researchers performs research generally concentrated on the enhancement of foodstuffs, nutritional claims, consumer perception and risks, etc. This research allows for the creation of certain practical recommendations that contribute to the prevention and anticipation of food scares while addressing the concerns of those involved in marketing and innovation for the agribusiness sector.

QUESTIONS TO CONSIDER:

Does any required course contain some element of Social Impact Management? **YES**

Is any required course entirely dedicated to social, environmental, or ethical issues? **YES**

Is there a Net Impact chapter on campus? **NO**

All information in this profile is drawn and/or adapted from the self-reported data of the Center for Business Education's Beyond Grey Pinstripes 2007 MBA survey. The Center for Business Education is housed within the Business and Society Program at the Aspen Institute. For more info, visit www.AspenCBE.org.

17

A Closer Look at:
Audencia Nantes
School of Management / Nantes, France

ANNUAL EVENTS:

▣ *Global Responsibility Conference and Awards*

During this conference, researchers from Audencia's Center for Global Responsibility present studies in order to promote global responsibility and business ethics among students and local managers. Also, speakers of selected companies share their experiences in roundtables organized on a regular basis at Audencia. For the Global Responsibility Awards, students evaluate the economic, social, and environmental performances of the participating companies through interviews with different stakeholders.

▣ *Microfinance Conference*

Each year, Axé Sud, one of Audencia's student clubs aiming to promote microfinance, organizes a conference on the subject. It is open to all students and the general public. These conferences are organized in partnerships with banks and NGOs.

OTHER PROGRAMS:

▣ *Community Tutoring*

Audencia students take part in a joint initiative of Audencia and an engineering school that aims to promote higher business education among pupils from high schools in underprivileged areas of Nantes. Audencia students work as tutors for these pupils, helping them to learn the general culture and correct approach needed to access business school education.

STUDENT CLUBS AND PROGRAMS:

▣ *EIDOS*

One of Audencia's student clubs organizes an annual film festival on global responsibility and sustainable development. The first film festival took place in 2006 and formed p0art of the National Sustainable Development Conference organized in Nantes. The students were sponsored by companies and local officials to organize this two-day festival and to give free access to all the films. After viewing the films, those in attendance had the opportunity to discuss them with the filmmakers.

▣ *Axé Sud*

This student club aims to promote microfinance. It allows certain students to spend several months in India and other developing countries in order to become involved in microfinance projects. The club also organizes an annual conference at Audencia to promote microfinance.

SCHOOL DEMOGRAPHICS	
Number of Full-Time Students	**36**
International Students	**65%**
Female Students	**25%**
Pre-MBA Employment:	

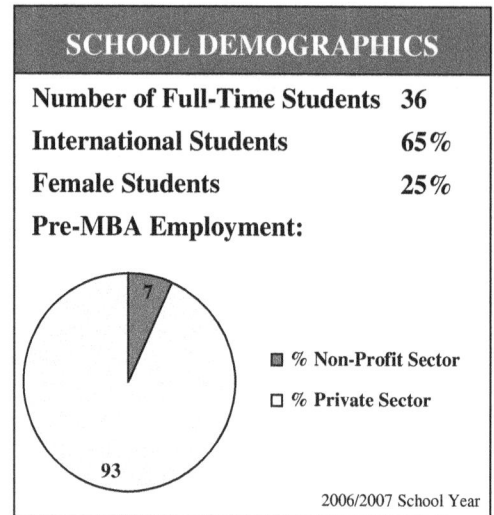

7
93

■ % Non-Profit Sector
□ % Private Sector

2006/2007 School Year

THE CENTER FOR BUSINESS EDUCATION'S BOTTOM LINE ON AUDENCIA NANTES:
Compared to other business schools in our survey, AUDENCIA Nantes offers a good number of courses featuring relevant content, and requires 5 core courses featuring relevant content.

A Closer Look at:
Babson College
School of Management / Babson Park, MA
http://www3.babson.edu/mba/

THE ASPEN INSTITUTE
Center for Business Education

WHAT THE SCHOOL SAYS:

Central to entrepreneurial thought and action at Babson are social venturing, global development and civic engagement, all of which are essential to preparing students to be social and environmental stewards. Babson's philosophy is that entrepreneurship requires attention to global economic and social issues.

A QUICK LOOK

NOTE: All information is self-reported data submitted to the Center for Business Education

COURSES*

Accounting (2)
Business & Government (1)
Business Law (2)
CSR/Business Ethics (2)
Economics (3)
Entrepreneurship (11)
Finance (2)
General Management (4)
Marketing (4)
Organizational Behavior (1)
Operations Management (1)
Strategy (2)

ACTIVITIES*

Speakers/Seminars (5)
Clubs & Programs (3)
Institutes/Centers (3)

* Figures in parentheses indicate the number of courses/activities that, in whole or in part, integrate social, environmental, or ethical perspectives

NOTABLE FEATURES

CORE COURSES:

▨ Business Law
The business law core covers the legal issues that "every MBA needs to know" in a fashion that is typically integrated with other disciplines and raises social and ethical issues. Students examine the duties of loyalty and proper care that the law requires of every manager, including the duty to avoid illegal activity.

▨ Ethics and Social Responsibility
Ethics and Social Responsibility is a yearlong course that is integrated throughout the first-year curriculum. The course addresses managers' ethical decision making and business' responsibilities in society. The course's main goal is to provide students with a set of tools and frameworks that will allow the students to evaluate and determine which course of action will lead to the most ethical and sustainable outcome.

ELECTIVE COURSES:

▨ 21st Century Entrepreneurship
Through cases, projects, and present-day examples, this course challenges students to understand the impact of business on society. In addition, it offers new frameworks for entrepreneurial ventures that capitalize on social responsibility to gain competitive advantage and increase valuation.

▨ Macroeconomics and the Monetary System
From GDP growth accounting, this course examines the environmental consequences of failing to distinguish between gross and net domestic product, where, for example, strategic sales of a country's hardwood forests treat the receipts as income, while wealth is diminished and the environment degraded. Also discussed are the social costs and economic underpinnings of larger macro failures, such as the debt, hyperinflation, and balance of payments crises experienced in the developing world.

INSTITUTES AND CENTERS:

▨ The Arthur M. Blank Center for Entrepreneurship
The Arthur M. Blank Center for Entrepreneurship is the hub for entrepreneurial activity at Babson. The center's mission is to lead the global advancement of entrepreneurship education and practice through the development of academic, research, and outreach initiatives that inspire entrepreneurial thinking and cultivate entrepreneurial leadership in all organizations and society.

▨ The William F. Glavin Center for Global Management at Babson
The William F. Glavin Center for Global Management at Babson leads the college's international initiatives and contributions to the advancement of its global management education. The Glavin Center brings Babson to the world, extending the college's global reach and leadership through a network of partner institutions. Just as importantly, the Glavin Center brings the world to Babson, providing an international orientation to all facets of the college and ensuring that students receive the preparation they need to succeed as entrepreneurial leaders in the global economy.

QUESTIONS TO CONSIDER:

Does any required course contain some element of Social Impact Management? **YES**

Is any required course entirely dedicated to social, environmental, or ethical issues? **YES**

Is there a Net Impact chapter on campus? **YES**

A Closer Look at:
Babson College
School of Management / Babson Park, MA

ANNUAL EVENTS:

■ *Socially Responsible Business Panel at the Babson Forum on Entrepreneurship and Innovation*

This panel, organized by Net Impact at the annual Babson Forum on Entrepreneurship and Innovation, focuses on building a business through social responsibility. The panel provides the opportunity for forum attendees to explore the benefits of embracing socially responsible business practices to grow a new venture.

OTHER PROGRAMS:

■ *The Solution - Energy Debate*

The Babson Energy Club sponsored a debate entitled "The Solution," which dealt with the topic of climate change. Industry leaders discussed the future of energy and opportunities in the alternative and traditional energy industries with particular attention paid to global warming, energy legislation, and energy issues beyond U.S. borders.

SCHOOL DEMOGRAPHICS	
Number of Full-Time Students	446
International Students	34%
Female Students	27%
	2006/2007 School Year

STUDENT CLUBS AND PROGRAMS:

■ *Babson Energy and Environmental Club*

The Babson Energy and Environmental Club is dedicated to identifying, publicizing, and educating others on the facts and opportunities present in the rapidly evolving energy industry in order to enable entrepreneurial action. "We realize the importance that oil and coal have played in shaping our world and, like the early adopters of that technology, we represent the early adopters in cleaner and renewable energy forms." To this end the club sponsors events relating to energy topics to promote issues among the student body.

■ *Babson Global Outreach through Entrepreneurship*

Babson Global Outreach through Entrepreneurship (BGOE) is a student-led, nonprofit organization that exists for the purpose of enriching talented and motivated people worldwide with the knowledge of entrepreneurship. BGOE offers an opportunity for current business students to travel to a developing country and work directly with the local entrepreneurs in order to create sustainable business models that will contribute to the economic health of the region. Through this work, business students will take an active part in helping people outside of their normal scope while gaining experience in applying entrepreneurial tools in a real-world setting.

THE CENTER FOR BUSINESS EDUCATION'S BOTTOM LINE ON BABSON COLLEGE:
Compared to other business schools in our survey, Babson College offers an excellent number of courses featuring relevant content, and does a truly extraordinary job in those courses explicitly addressing how mainstream business improves the world. Babson College requires 7 core courses featuring relevant content.

A Closer Look at:
Bainbridge Graduate Institute
Bainbridge Island, WA
http://www.bgiedu.org/edu

THE ASPEN INSTITUTE
Center for Business Education

WHAT THE SCHOOL SAYS:
The hallmark of the BGI program is the infusion of sustainability considerations into every single course, including the traditional MBA core. Our goal is to produce graduates who will lead their organizations to a more sustainable future. Toward that end, what is emphasized is systems thinking, entrepreneurship and intrapreneurship, management and leadership, sustainability and social justice, as well as the traditional functional business disciplines.

A QUICK LOOK

NOTE: All information is self-reported data submitted to the Center for Business Education

COURSES*

Accounting (**1**)
CSR/Business Ethics (**2**)
Economics (**2**)
Entrepreneurship (**2**)
Environmental (**1**)
General Management (**4**)
Marketing (**1**)
Operations Management (**1**)
Quantitative Methods (**1**)
Strategy (**1**)

KEY CONCENTRATIONS
Industry Concentrations

ACTIVITIES*

Speakers/Seminars (**1**)
Orientation Activities (**1**)
Internship/Consulting (**1**)
Clubs & Programs (**2**)
Career Development (**1**)
Concentrations (**1**)

* Figures in parentheses indicate the number of courses/activities that, in whole or in part, integrate social, environmental, or ethical perspectives

NOTABLE FEATURES

CORE COURSES:
- *Social Justice and Business*

This course examines the role of business in community and society. Topics covered in this course include globalization, stakeholder analysis, community economic development, public-private partnerships, and social entrepreneurship.

- *Foundations of Sustainable Business*

This course examines the business case for sustainability, considering current conceptual frameworks, measurement systems, and reporting initiatives, and also sustainability as a driver of strategy, innovation, and profit. The course is the beginning of a yearlong action learning project.

QUESTIONS TO CONSIDER:

Does any required course contain some element of Social Impact Management? **YES**

Is any required course entirely dedicated to social, environmental, or ethical issues? **YES**

Is there a Net Impact Chapter on campus? **YES**

A Closer Look at:
Bainbridge Graduate Institute
Bainbridge Island, WA

ANNUAL EVENTS:
- *In-Residence Programs*

Each monthly intensive weekend, we invite three different types of individuals to spend the weekend in community with us, sharing both personal and professional stories in both formal and informal settings. Our Entrepreneurs-in-Residence are people who have successfully built business that embody environmental and/or social values. Our Executives-in-Residence are business leaders in larger firms who have helped to integrate sustainability into the operation of their firms. And our Acitivists-in-Residence are thought leaders, advocates, and social entrepreneurs who have made a difference in their communities and the wider world.

- *Orientation Retreat*

Each school year begins with a four-day retreat on Cortes Island, British Columbia. Our students travel there in groups of 30 to live in sustainable comfort off-the-grid and begin building the learning community that will support them in their studies and throughout their working life.

STUDENT CLUBS AND PROGRAMS:
- *Diversity and Social Justice Committee*

This is a standing committee of students, faculty, and administration who work together in three areas: recruitment, institutional structure, and culture. This student-led group is the largest and most established of our formal student committees.

SCHOOL DEMOGRAPHICS	
Number of Full-Time Students	62
International Students	11%
Female Students	11%

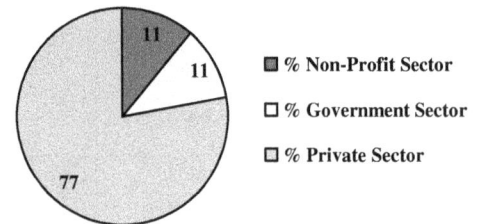

- % Non-Profit Sector
- % Government Sector
- % Private Sector

11
11
77

2006/2007 School Year

THE CENTER FOR BUSINESS EDUCATION'S BOTTOM LINE ON BAINBRIDGE GRADUATE INSTITUTE:
Compared to other business schools in our survey, Bainbridge Graduate Institute offers a good number of courses featuring relevant content, and does a good job in those courses explicitly addressing how mainstream business improves the world. Bainbridge Graduate Institute requires 16 core courses featuring relevant content.

A Closer Look at:
Baruch College-The City University of New York

The Zicklin School of Business / New York, NY

http://zicklin.baruch.cuny.edu/

THE ASPEN INSTITUTE
Center for Business Education

WHAT THE SCHOOL SAYS:

The Zicklin School of Business at Baruch College educates leaders committed to global awareness, ethical practice, and responsible management. Issues of corporate governance and responsibility are woven throughout the curriculum and are reflected in the activities of our academic centers and students.

A QUICK LOOK

NOTE: All information is self-reported data submitted to the Center for Business Education

COURSES*

Accounting (1)
Business Law (1)
CSR/Business Ethics (1)
International Management (1)
Marketing (2)

ACTIVITIES*

Speakers/Seminars (11)
Orientation Activities (1)
Student Competitions (1)
Clubs & Programs (2)
Institutes/Centers (5)

* Figures in parentheses indicate the number of courses/activities that, in whole or in part, integrate social, environmental, or ethical perspectives

NOTABLE FEATURES

CORE COURSES:

▨ The Societal and Governmental Environment of Business

This course is intended to explain the environment of business decision making. Emphasis is on government regulation as a growing dimension of business decision making in regard to environmental protection, occupational health and safety, and consumer regulation. The course will also address traditional topics such as antitrust regulations. The impact of social problems and the ethical dilemmas of today's business manager will be considered.

▨ Marketing Management

In this course, students are encouraged to consider marketing management issues from two perspectives: from that of the marketing manager and from the consumer. In this way, ethical issues are discussed in terms of active decision making and passive receiving of products and promotions. Recent ethics debates have included targeting minority consumers with high-alcohol-content malt liquors, the use of potentially deceptive infomercials, privacy issues in an online environment, and the use of mouseprint disclosures in marketing materials and advertisements.

ELECTIVE COURSES:

▨ Intensive Survey of Business Contracts and Law of Corporations

This course covers contract law and explores in depth what types of promises are legally enforceable and what it means for a promise to be legally enforceable. With respect to the sale of both goods and services, students discuss not only the legal responsibilities of the parties but also other constraints on behavior, including market forces, social or business norms, and personal moral beliefs. The course also focuses on agency law and the legal regulation of business organizations such as general partnerships and corporations.

▨ International Comparative Management

International Comparative Management is an international elective that seeks to introduce students to issues, theories, strategies, and practices in a cross-national context. Examples of topics discussed include comparison of managerial goals, structures, functions, processes, and behavior cross-nationally; multiculturalism as it relates to the multinational corporation; country-specific comparative/competitive advantages and disadvantages; and ways to accomplish business and social objectives internationally.

INSTITUTES AND CENTERS:

▨ Robert Zicklin Center for Corporate Integrity (ZCCI)

ZCCI is a forum for discussing corporate reporting and governance, ethical behavior, accountability, responsible global business development, and the role of governmental regulation. Throughout the year, the center brings together leaders in business, government, and NGOs to increase the impact of discussions of ethics in the classroom.

▨ The International Center for Corporate Accountability (ICCA)

The ICCA is a not-for-profit organization founded to promote good corporate citizenship worldwide. Its mission is to urge multinational corporations to create voluntary codes of conduct regarding issues such as wages and working conditions, protection of human rights, and sustainable development. ICCA also provides independent external monitoring to verify compliance by companies with their voluntarily created codes of conduct.

QUESTIONS TO CONSIDER:

Does any required course contain some element of Social Impact Management? **YES**

Is any required course entirely dedicated to social, environmental, or ethical issues? **YES**

Is there a Net Impact chapter on campus? **YES**

A Closer Look at:
Baruch College-The City University of New York
The Zicklin School of Business / New York, NY

ANNUAL EVENTS:

- *Mitsui & Company Lunch-Time Forums*

The Mitsui & Company Lunch-Time Forums is a series of six forums over the course of the year that focus on current topics in international business and the global economy. The sessions provide value-added education in global business for students, provoke campus dialogue, and stimulate faculty. The series has featured many prominent experts from the worlds of business, government, and academia.

- *The Baruch College Merrill Lynch IPO® Challenge*

For this challenge, teams submit concepts for new ventures- real ideas for real businesses. Over the course of two semesters, they develop their concepts into full-blown business plans leading to the launch of their businesses. The competition includes a social entrepreneurship track for students who are interested in utilizing business skills to achieve social goals. These businesses must have a clear focus on social benefits and a plan for achieving financial viability, rather than being profit-making enterprises.

OTHER PROGRAMS:

- *Globalization and the Good Corporation*

The International Center for Corporate Accountability holds a semiannual international conference examining globalization and implications for human rights and corporate social accountability. Other issues discussed include corporate citizenship, the role of NGO's, sustainable private equity funds, and environmental protection and sustainable growth.

STUDENT CLUBS AND PROGRAMS:

- *Corporate Responsibility, Ethics, and Governance Association (CREGA)/Net Impact*

CREGA is the Baruch College chapter of Net Impact. It creates its own programming on topics related to corporate social responsibility and ethics and makes corporate site visits to see CSR in action. Programming includes a seminar on social responsibility and social entrepreneurship programs and the value-add to MBA programs.

- *Baruch Legacy Project*

The Baruch Legacy Project is a student-devised, student-run project in which each incoming class chooses a community-based or other NGO to work with during the two-year MBA program. The work may include fundraising, capital projects, or strategic consulting.

FACULTY PIONEER:

- *2003 – External Impact Award, S. Prakash Sethi*

For over thirty years Dr. S. Prakash Sethi has been a pioneer in the nascent field of corporate social responsibility. A prolific researcher and author, Professor Sethi is recognized as an advocate who applies theory to practice through his work with corporations. His activities have induced multinational corporations to become more accountable for their activities and their impacts on poorer workers in developing countries, on child labor practices, environmental degradation, sweatshop-like working conditions, and human rights violations.

SCHOOL DEMOGRAPHICS

Number of Full-Time Students	**84**
International Students	**61%**
Female Students	**54%**

Pre-MBA Employment:

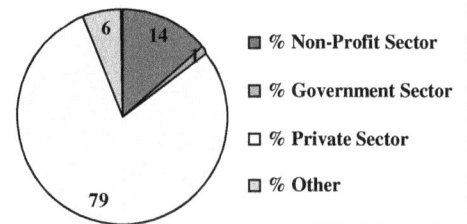

- ■ % Non-Profit Sector
- ■ % Government Sector
- □ % Private Sector
- □ % Other

2006/2007 School Year

THE CENTER FOR BUSINESS EDUCATION'S BOTTOM LINE ON BARUCH COLLEGE -THE CITY UNIVERSITY OF NEW YORK:
Compared to other business schools in our survey, Baruch College-The City University of New York offers a good number of courses featuring relevant content, and requires 2 core courses featuring relevant content.

A Closer Look at:
Bentley College

McCallum Graduate School of Business / Waltham, MA

http://www.bentley.edu/graduate/

THE ASPEN INSTITUTE
Center for Business Education

WHAT THE SCHOOL SAYS:

Bentley College has continually promoted a sense of ethics and social responsibility through teaching, research, and corporate and community relations. The Bentley Alliance for Ethics and Social Responsibility was created to amplify and extend the work of the autonomous centers and initiatives on campus, supporting and encouraging greater awareness of, respect for, and commitment to ethics, service, and social responsibility in our research, curricula, and campus culture.

A QUICK LOOK

NOTE: All information is self-reported data submitted to the Center for Business Education

COURSES*

Accounting (2)
Business Law (2)
CSR/Business Ethics (5)
Finance (2)
General Management (5)
Marketing (1)
Organizational Behavior (2)
Strategy (1)

ACTIVITIES*

Speakers/Seminars (13)
Orientation Activities (1)
Student Competitions (1)
Clubs & Programs (4)
Career Development (1)
Institutes/Centers (6)
Concentrations (1)

* Figures in parentheses indicate the number of courses/activities that, in whole or in part, integrate social, environmental, or ethical perspectives

NOTABLE FEATURES

CORE COURSES:

Leadership, Ethics and Corporate Responsibilities

This ethics course examines the role of managers as ethical thought leaders and problem solvers. The challenges of leading change in an ethical and socially responsible manner in a rapidly changing, international, diverse, and information-based environment are emphasized. Through discussion, case analysis, role playing, decision making simulations, and experiential exercises, students explore the responsibilities of contemporary business and the complex issues of leading organizations in a turbulent environment.

Team Effectiveness: Theory and Skills

This course develops the ability to lead and work effectively in teams and to know when teams are and are not the best way to reach organizational goals. Emphasis is placed on identifying competing values and beliefs as they influence differing perceptions of ethical dilemmas. Focus is placed on different ethical frameworks and the need for teams to identify when conflict is value based and the need to discuss values and beliefs as a way to work through the conflict.

ELECTIVE COURSES:

Ethical Issues in Corporate Life

This course introduces principles of ethical thinking and applies them to situations and models for business decision making. It explores and analyzes business ethics issues relating to the nature of the corporation, work in the corporation, the corporation and society, and the development of the corporate culture.

Managing Ethics in Organizations

This course provides practical advice and theoretical tools for creating an effective ethics and compliance program. The primary objective of the course is to achieve the Ethics and Compliance Officer Association's (ECOA) educational mission by providing more of the fundamental, theoretical knowledge and general skills that ECOA members themselves have discovered would facilitate carrying out their responsibilities.

INSTITUTES AND CENTERS:

Bentley Alliance for Ethics and Social Responsibility

The Bentley Alliance supports and encourages collaborative and interdisciplinary applied research that has the potential to significantly affect current practice; influences curriculum development and pedagogical innovations intended to make our students more ethically sensitive and socially aware; works to ensure a broader application of these principles and ideals in campus life; attempts to foster lifelong civic engagement among our students; and seeks to work closely with external organizations, academic and professional associations, and corporations in pursuit of these goals.

Bentley Service-Learning Center (BSLC)

The BSLC has built a national reputation as an innovator in integrating meaningful community service into the curriculum. The main objectives of BSLC are to promote the academic learning of Bentley students, to assist community partners in reaching their full potential as providers of services within the community, and to nurture in Bentley students a commitment to lifelong civic engagement.

QUESTIONS TO CONSIDER:

Does any required course contain some element of Social Impact Management? **YES**

Is any required course entirely dedicated to social, environmental, or ethical issues? **YES**

Is there a Net Impact chapter on campus? **NO**

All information in this profile is drawn and/or adapted from the self-reported data of the Center for Business Education's Beyond Grey Pinstripes 2007 MBA survey. The Center for Business Education is housed within the Business and Society Program at the Aspen Institute. For more info, visit www.AspenCBE.org.

A Closer Look at:
Bentley College
McCallum Graduate School of Business / Waltham, MA

ANNUAL EVENTS:

■ Raytheon Lectureship in Business Ethics

The Center of Business Ethics hosts the Raytheon Lectureship in Business Ethics, highlighting respected corporate leaders of companies that have a manifest and deep-rooted commitment to doing business in the right way. These individuals share their insights and ideas and engage in discussion about how the business community can and should achieve ethical excellence.

■ Bentley Leadership Forum in cooperation with TIME Magazine

The forum "The Business of Healing Our World" brings together leaders from business, technology, arts and entertainment, and philanthropy to explore critical issues in our global business world.

■ Bentley Business Bowl (BBB) Case Competition

The BBB is a one-day, college-wide case competition held annually and open to all students—graduate and undergraduate. A panel of judges drawn from the professional and corporate community evaluates each team's presentation. Students work on a case that requires critical thinking and the application of a team's knowledge of ethics, business, accounting, and information technology.

OTHER PROGRAMS:

■ Orientation Workshop

This 12-day orientation emphasizes an integrated perspective on business fundamentals. As part of this orientation, students participate in workshops on valuing diversity, ethical decision making, and academic integrity. A team project supports this effort; students deliver a written analysis of an ethics case by the end of orientation. The orientation's day long ethical decision making workshop exposes students to ethical theory (e.g., Kantian ethics, utilitarianism, Aristotelian ethics) and the idea of ethical leadership and social responsibility.

STUDENT CLUBS AND PROGRAMS:

■ Graduate Management Association (GMA)

The GMA is a group of diverse individuals with the goal of helping to build the foundation needed for students to eventually assume roles in the arena of executive management. The goals of the GMA are focused on career development and community service. The GMA provides a diverse assortment of extracurricular, career, and community development activities to fulfill its mission.

■ Academic Integrity Council

The Academic Integrity Council is a student-led organization dedicated to upholding the highest standards of academic integrity throughout the Bentley community. The council organizes educational activities, hosts events, and performs local outreach to raise awareness and facilitate communication surrounding academic integrity.

SCHOOL DEMOGRAPHICS	
Number of Full-Time Students	176
International Students	12%
Female Students	44%

Pre-MBA Employment:

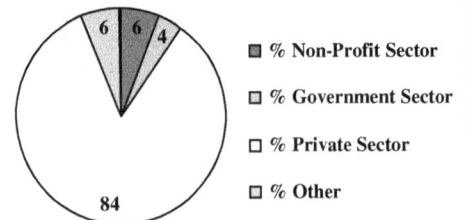

Pie chart values: 6, 6, 4, 84

- ■ % Non-Profit Sector
- ■ % Government Sector
- □ % Private Sector
- □ % Other

2006/2007 School Year

THE CENTER FOR BUSINESS EDUCATION'S BOTTOM LINE ON BENTLEY COLLEGE:
Compared to other business schools in our survey, Bentley College offers an excellent number of courses featuring relevant content, and does a good job in those courses explicitly addressing how mainstream business improves the world. Bentley College requires 2 core courses featuring relevant content.

Boston College

Carroll School of Management / Chestnut Hill, MA

http://www.bc.edu/schools/csom/mba/home.html

THE ASPEN INSTITUTE
Center for Business Education

WHAT THE SCHOOL SAYS:

The Carroll School of Management at Boston College possesses a unique combination of resources and assets that position it at the forefront of the emerging emphasis on corporate citizenship and business involvement in social issues.

A QUICK LOOK

NOTE: All information is self-reported data submitted to the Center for Business Education

COURSES*

Accounting (1)
Business Law (2)
Finance (1)
Information Technology (1)
General Management (3)
Marketing (1)
Organizational Behavior (2)
Operations Management (2)
Strategy (2)

KEY CONCENTRATIONS

Leadership for Change

ACTIVITIES*

Speakers/Seminars (8)
Orientation Activities (1)
Internship/Consulting (3)
Student Competitions (2)
Clubs & Programs (4)
Career Development (1)
Institutes/Centers (5)
Concentrations (1)

* Figures in parentheses indicate the number of courses/activities that, in whole or in part, integrate social, environmental, or ethical perspectives

NOTABLE FEATURES

CORE COURSES:

Information Management

This course includes discussions about the ethical issues related to information technology—at what point should managers draw the line in customer data collection or in prescreening employees? When does technology become too intrusive?

Operations Management

This course integrates topics such as environmentally responsible manufacturing, green supply chain management, and green manufacturing requirements planning.

ELECTIVE COURSES:

African Business

This course is a survey of political, economic, physical, legal, cultural, and religious influences that affect the ability of foreign corporations to do business in Africa. North-South dialogue, development questions, nationalization, strategic concerns, economic treaties, and import-export regulations will be examined.

Managing Corporate Responsibility

This course explores how companies can develop responsibility management systems that implement corporate citizenship to meet growing demands. Topical coverage includes systems thinking, responsibility management approaches, vision setting and leadership commitment processes, integration of systemic approaches to responsibility management, and innovation, improvements, and indicators (measurement and assessment systems). Students will undertake a hands-on (work-based or action) learning project in an organization of their choice.

INSTITUTES AND CENTERS:

The Center for Corporate Citizenship

The Center for Corporate Citizenship provides global thinking and leadership in establishing corporate citizenship as a business essential so that all companies are able to act as economic and social assets to the communities they impact. The center aims to develop the leadership capacity of its 300 plus corporate members by providing education, training, research, and consulting on corporate citizenship issues. Additionally, the center closely collaborates with the MBA student community, providing research assistant and internship positions and sponsoring an annual Best MBA Paper Competition.

Center for Work and Family

The Center for Work and Family is a research unit that aims to enhance the quality of life of today's workforce by providing leadership for the integration of work and life, an essential for business and community success. It has been a national leader in helping organizations create effective workplaces that support and develop healthy and productive employees. The center has provided a bridge linking the academic community to the world of employees balancing worklife issues.

QUESTIONS TO CONSIDER:

Does any required course contain some element of Social Impact Management? **YES**

Is any required course entirely dedicated to social, environmental, or ethical issues? **NO**

Is there a Net Impact chapter on campus? **YES**

A Closer Look at:
Boston College
Carroll School of Management / Chestnut Hill, MA

ANNUAL EVENTS:

Chief Executives Club of Boston
Named as the nations top speaking forum, the CEO Club is the premier forum for the exchange of ideas on business and management issues. The club works in partnership with Boston College's Carroll School of Management to foster management excellence, leadership, and good corporate citizenship. The club sponsors seven luncheons a year at which some of the world's leading CEOs offer views on a wide variety of topics. A select number of graduate students are invited to attend each luncheon. The speakers address topics such as the evolution of the telecom industry, the implications of the Sarbanes-Oxley Act, and embracing environmental, technological, and social change.

Clough Colloquium
This speaker series brings together accomplished professionals, public intellectuals, and Boston College faculty to participate in and reflect upon structured conversations related to leadership and ethics. The events help executives, students, and faculty gain special insight into the challenges of ethical leadership in contemporary culture.

SCHOOL DEMOGRAPHICS	
Number of Full-Time Students	169
International Students	22%
Female Students	36%
	2006/2007 School Year

OTHER PROGRAMS:

Corporate Citizenship Graduate Internships
Funded by Boston College, the Carroll School supports graduate internships to assist project-based assignments related to corporate citizenship sustainability at The Center for Corporate Citizenship at Boston College. The center engages with companies to redefine business success as creating measurable gains for business and society.

Community Service Requirement
The Carroll School is committed to instilling a strong sense of community service in its MBA students. In an effort to align this commitment with the program, all MBA students must fulfill a requirement to serve others through meaningful volunteer work. Students may choose to serve as mentors, role models, and academic tutors to children in surrounding communities. Students may also choose to provide pro bono consulting or other professional services to benefit a range of nonprofit organizations and off-campus programs.

STUDENT CLUBS AND PROGRAMS:

Invest 'n Kids
Invest 'n Kids provides tutoring for Boston grade school students while exposing them to a college environment. MBA students volunteer as tutors and meet with their students weekly to work on a variety of academic subjects. The program provides a valuable service to the grade school students as it serves to support and develop the students' skills in math, reading, and science.

Net Impact
As the Carrolll School's chapter of Net Impact, the group promotes a full spectrum of progressive business practices, hosting speakers on campus, attending the national Net Impact conference, and generally helping students to expand their vision of the role of business in society.

FACULTY PIONEER:

2005 – External Impact Award, Sandra Waddock
Professor Waddock is a pioneer in the field of social investing and corporate citizenship; her work has had a lasting impact on management scholarship, practice, and education. She has published path-breaking books on corporate citizenship and currently serves as the editor of the *Journal of Corporate Citizenship*. As a leader among peers, she has chaired the Social Issues division of the Academy of Management.

THE CENTER FOR BUSINESS EDUCATION'S BOTTOM LINE ON BOSTON COLLEGE:
Compared to other business schools in our survey, Boston College offers a good number of courses featuring relevant content and does a good job in those courses explicitly addressing how mainstream business improves the world. Boston College requires 10 core courses featuring relevant content.

A Closer Look at:
Boston University
School of Management / Boston, MA
http://management.bu.edu/gpo/fulltime/mba/

WHAT THE SCHOOL SAYS:

Boston University's School of Management recognizes that often it's not the profit motive that drives students into management. During the past several years the Graduate School of Management at Boston University has expanded its activities, curriculum, research, and support for corporate social responsibility, social impact management, business ethics, social entrepreneurship, and environmental stewardship.

A QUICK LOOK

NOTE: All information is self-reported data submitted to the Center for Business Education

COURSES*

Business & Government (1)
CSR/Business Ethics (3)
Economics (1)
Entrepreneurship (2)
Finance (1)
HR Management (1)
Information Technology (1)
International Management (2)
Marketing (1)
Organizational Behavior (2)
Operations Management (1)
Strategy (1)

KEY CONCENTRATIONS

**Public and Nonprofit
  Management**

ACTIVITIES*

Speakers/Seminars (8)
Orientation Activities (1)
Internship/Consulting (4)
Student Competitions (1)
Clubs & Programs (6)
Career Development (4)
Institutes/Centers (3)
Concentrations (1)

* Figures in parentheses indicate the number of courses/activities that, in whole or in part, integrate social, environmental, or ethical perspectives

NOTABLE FEATURES

CORE COURSES:

Current Topics in Law and Ethics

This course develops a framework for analyzing ethical issues. Students then apply this framework throughout the course as ethical issues arise in discussions of legal issues. For example, no discussion of corporate governance would be complete without a consideration of a manager's ethical obligations to shareholders and stakeholders.

Managing Individuals and Organizations

Emphasis in this course is on behavioral science concepts and research findings related to the major challenges that managers face—how to organize individuals in order to fulfill the objectives and strategies of the firm. Topics to be examined include the nature and dynamics of the organization, the elements of individual leadership and personal development, managing change within organizational contexts, and the relationships between the firm and the external environment in which it operates.

ELECTIVE COURSES:

Global Social Enterprise Field Seminar-Brazil

This intensive 10-day seminar in Brazil provides students with a broad understanding of the ways in which business strategies can create value at the base of the economic pyramid. Students gain firsthand experience of how businesses, NGOs, and government are using models of social enterprise to address social and economic issues in the fields of health, education, and the environment in the context of an emerging market. Topics covered include renewable energy, sustainable development, ecotourism, micro-enterprise, corporate social responsibility, and public/private partnerships.

Competitive Environmental Strategy

This course explores the critical and complex drivers of contemporary corporate environmental strategies and actions; individual, organizational, and broader institutional level action strategies that are or can be implemented in response to the drivers; and some emerging issues that will likely shape corporate environmental strategy in the future.

INSTITUTES AND CENTERS:

Center for Energy and Environmental Studies

The Center for Energy and Environmental Studies engages in education, research, and professional training in the fields of energy and environmental analysis. The multidisciplinary, systems-oriented approach underlies the center's research programs that investigate some of the planet's most challenging environmental problems.

The Center for the Advancement of Ethics and Character

The center focuses on bringing the issues of ethics and character into the lives of leaders at the early stages of development through existing educational infrastructure. It serves as a resource for administrators, teachers and parents as they seek to fulfill their responsibilities as moral educators, and it fosters research initiatives and publications on moral and character education by students, faculty, scholars, and researchers from around the world.

QUESTIONS TO CONSIDER:

Does any required course contain some element of Social Impact Management? **YES**

Is any required course entirely dedicated to social, environmental, or ethical issues? **NO**

Is there a Net Impact chapter on campus? **YES**

A Closer Look at:
Boston University
School of Management / Boston, MA

ANNUAL EVENTS:

Lunch and Learn
Open to the entire MBA community, eight Lunch and Learn seminars are held each year focusing on topics of interest to students. Executive leaders from a variety of fields offer their insight and lead students in a discussion. Topics have included careers in corporate social responsibility, the role of advocacy in nonprofit organizations, managing in the global NGO, careers in nonprofit finance, successful leaders of nonprofit organizations, and more.

Link Day
Link Day is an opportunity for small- to medium-sized nonprofit organizations to access effective managerial expertise. This one-day intensive workout, organized and managed by MBA students, is designed to bring together nonprofits, MBA students, faculty, and alumni to analyze a specific problem facing an organization and to develop a work plan to address the challenges. Teams of up to six MBA students work alongside faculty and alumni to address the needs of the nonprofit organizations.

Boston University Net Impact Case Competition
Each year the Boston University Net Impact club sponsors a case competition that challenges MBA students to consider a current issue regarding social responsibility in the corporate sector. Twelve teams of three to four students have one week to analyze a complex case study and present their recommendations to a panel of judges consisting of Boston business executives and university faculty.

SCHOOL DEMOGRAPHICS	
Number of Full-Time Students	279
International Students	33%
Female Students	38%
	2006/2007 School Year

OTHER PROGRAMS:

Public and Nonprofit Summer Internship Program
Every student enrolled in the Public and Nonprofit Management concentration completes a paid internship between Year I and Year II in a nonprofit organization or in a for-profit company engaged in social enterprise, corporate social responsibility, or social impact activities. The majority of students maintain their internship during their second year of school.

The Feld Career Center
The Feld Career Center has made a significant commitment to broadening the scope of the industries and opportunities for those students interested in the nonprofit and public sectors, as well as for those with an interest in international development and corporate social responsibility. Information sessions have included topics such as careers in nonprofit financial management and careers in international development, and careers in nonprofit accounting and finance. In addition to hosting guest speakers, the Feld Career Center has created new relationships with partner institutions to increase the opportunities available to those seeking to join the nonprofit industry.

STUDENT CLUBS AND PROGRAMS:

Arts Management Association
The Arts Management Association was founded to establish a channel through which Boston University MBA students could provide business consulting services to local arts organizations in need and gain real-world experience in the process. The association seeks to also make MBA students more aware of the arts through educational events, with the hope that these future business leaders will help support and encourage arts organizations in the future.

BU Energy Club
The BU Energy Club focuses on innovations in energy commercialization. Members have interests in the energy sector, particularly in the field of renewable energy. Students at BU hope to grow the club into a consortium of programs in the Boston area.

THE CENTER FOR BUSINESS EDUCATION'S BOTTOM LINE ON BOSTON UNIVERSITY:
Compared to other business schools in our survey, Boston University offers a good number of courses featuring relevant content, and does an excellent job in those courses explicitly addressing how mainstream business improves the world. Boston University requires 2 core courses featuring relevant content.

A Closer Look at:
Brandeis University

THE ASPEN INSTITUTE
Center for Business Education

Heller School for Social Policy and Management / Waltham, MA

http://heller.brandeis.edu/

WHAT THE SCHOOL SAYS:

A new generation of managers is needed to lead organizations in the effective pursuit of social missions in the non-profit, for-profit, and public sectors. The Heller School's high standards for management education and its history of excellent policy research and activism are important assets for people contemplating careers as leaders of organizations with a social mission.

A QUICK LOOK

NOTE: All information is self-reported data submitted to the Center for Business Education

COURSES*

Accounting **(2)**
Business & Government **(1)**
Business Law **(2)**
CSR/Business Ethics **(3)**
Economics **(1)**
Entrepreneurship **(1)**
Finance **(3)**
HR Management **(1)**
International Management **(2)**
General Management **(4)**
Marketing **(1)**
Organizational Behavior **(1)**
Operations Management **(1)**
Public/Nonprofit Mgt **(1)**
Strategy **(2)**

KEY CONCENTRATIONS

Sustainable Development

Health Care Policy and Management

ACTIVITIES*

Speakers/Seminars **(16)**
Orientation Activities **(1)**
Internship/Consulting **(1)**
Student Competitions **(2)**
Clubs & Programs **(1)**
Career Development **(1)**
Institutes/Centers **(8)**
Concentrations **(4)**
Joint Degrees **(4)**

* Figures in parentheses indicate the number of courses/activities that, in whole or in part, integrate social, environmental, or ethical perspectives

NOTABLE FEATURES

CORE COURSES:

Economics

This course introduces various economic concepts. The concepts are useful in understanding markets and also some key management decisions. The course examines how the manager of an organization with a social mission must also work with revenues and costs as basic factors in decisions.

Social Justice, Management and Policy

This module provides MBA students with the opportunity to explore the management implications of "knowledge advancing social justice." Students examine historical and contemporary thinkers, explore justice issues and management activities, and actively grapple with the daily management dilemmas faced by managers and change agents both inside and outside organizations.

ELECTIVE COURSES:

Assets and Social Policy

This course is focused on understanding the emerging field of asset building as a key social policy for reducing poverty and addressing wealth inequalities. This course examines the institutional and structural conditions that limit the ability of many to accumulate wealth resources and explores opportunities for promoting asset building among those at the bottom of the social structure. This course lays a foundation for taking a new look at the sources and solutions to poverty through an asset-focused lens.

Community Building for Managers

Community building has emerged as an important approach to rebuilding urban and rural communities through comprehensive strategies. This movement of civil society organizations working in partnership with donors and local policy makers uses a bottom-up approach to create an economic base, reduce poverty and improve the well-being of citizens in particular places. The purpose of this course is to learn from these experiences and review the context that has given rise to the call for community in so many settings.

INSTITUTES AND CENTERS:

Institute on Assets and Social Policy

The mission of the Institute on Assets and Social Policy is to help broaden wealth, reduce inequality, and improve the social and economic well-being of American households by fostering the adoption of an asset policy framework through research, analysis, education, and public engagement. The institute's research, analysis, teaching, and technical assistance enable organizations and policy makers to evaluate and advance asset-based social and economic policies.

Center for Youth and Communities (CYC)

CYC has established a reputation as one of the nation's leading research centers and professional development and policy organizations in youth and community development. CYC's ultimate goal is to "make knowledge productive"; it does so by connecting the knowledge gained from scholarly research and practical experience in ways that help both policy makers and practitioners.

QUESTIONS TO CONSIDER:

Does any required course contain some element of Social Impact Management? **YES**

Is any required course entirely dedicated to social, environmental, or ethical issues? **YES**

Is there a Net Impact chapter on campus? **YES**

Brandeis University

Heller School for Social Policy and Management / Waltham, MA

ANNUAL EVENTS:

■ Team Consulting Projects

Non-profit, community-based, and other mission-driven organizations are offered the opportunity to work with a team of Heller MBA students on a project that addresses an important management need. Working under the supervision of a faculty advisor, teams of students provide management consulting services and work with staff to resolve a management problem in areas such as strategy, marketing, human resource management, operations management, information systems, accounting, or financial management.

■ Orientation Workshop-Exploring Social Justice

In order for managers to be effective social and organizational change agents and prepared to manage in environments with value conflicts and diversity, they must first understand what social justice means to them and how these meanings and values have been formed. During orientation, students read a short selection about social justice and engage in a compelling discussion regarding their views on social justice.

OTHER PROGRAMS:

■ Bailis Family Social Justice Award

The Bailis Family Social Justice Award is offered yearly to students who have made the most significant social impact at the Heller School for Social Policy and Management in the previous year.

■ Managing Your Mission-Driven Career

Managing Your Mission-Driven Career is a series of career workshops that begin with orientation and continue until the end of the MBA program. Whether students plan to work in the non-profit, forprofit or public sector and whether they plan to be a manager, a consultant, or a social entrepreneur, this series is designed to prepare them to build rewarding careers with high levels of social impact.

STUDENT CLUBS AND PROGRAMS:

■ NetImpact

The Brandeis Heller/International Business School (IBS) Net Impact chapter has strengthened a network of social leaders on campus. The Brandeis chapter upholds Net Impact's mission to improve the world by creating new business, NGO, and CSR models to impact societal problems.

SCHOOL DEMOGRAPHICS

Number of Full-Time Students	77
International Students	11%
Female Students	62%

Pre-MBA Employment:

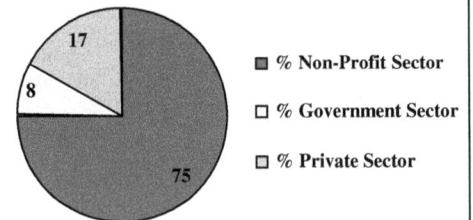

- ■ % Non-Profit Sector
- □ % Government Sector
- □ % Private Sector

2006/2007 School Year

THE CENTER FOR BUSINESS EDUCATION'S BOTTOM LINE ON BRANDEIS UNIVERSITY:
Compared to other business schools in our survey, Brandeis University offers an excellent number of courses featuring relevant content, and does a truly extraordinary job in those courses explicitly addressing how mainstream business improves the world. Brandeis University requires 13 core courses featuring relevant content.

California State University, Chico

College of Business / Chico, CA
http://www.cob.csuchico.edu/

THE ASPEN INSTITUTE
Center for Business Education

WHAT THE SCHOOL SAYS:

The College of Business at California State University, Chico has integrated ethics and sustainable business practice issues into the curriculum in several of the required courses. Our goal is to provide MBA students with a foundation that includes social and environmental issues in the business decision making process.

A QUICK LOOK

NOTE: All information is self-reported data submitted to the Center for Business Education

COURSES*

General Management (1)

ACTIVITIES*

Speakers/Seminars (2)
Clubs & Programs (1)
Institutes/Centers (1)

* Figures in parentheses indicate the number of courses/activities that, in whole or in part, integrate social, environmental, or ethical perspectives

NOTABLE FEATURES

CORE COURSES:

▪ *Management of People and Organizations*

The learning objectives for this course are to understand the basic management roles of mentor, facilitator, monitor, coordinator, director, producer, broker, and innovator; to know personal strengths and weaknesses in each of these roles; to understand what integrity means as a manager and how to manage according to personal integrity; and, to become aware of how American and international business practices are affecting climate change and what steps organizations can take to decrease their impact on the natural environment.

INSTITUTES AND CENTERS:

▪ *Center for Corporate Governance and Values Based Leadership*

The Center for Corporate Governance and Values Based Leadership houses the social entrepreneurship, sustainability, and ethics programs, with a sustainable business practices component to be added in the future.

ANNUAL EVENTS:

▪ *Sustainability Conference*

The college cosponsors the annual CSU, Chico Sustainability Conference.

▪ *Ethics Speaker Series*

The college sponsors an ethics speaker series with three to four speakers each semester on topics including social and environmental issues.

STUDENT CLUBS AND PROGRAMS:

▪ *Students for the Advancement of Global Entrepreneurship*

Students for the Advancement of Global Entrepreneurship (SAGE) is actively involved in both social entrepreneurship and sustainability initiatives.

SCHOOL DEMOGRAPHICS

Number of Full-Time Students	**50**
International Students	**32%**
Female Students	**32%**

Pre-MBA Employment:

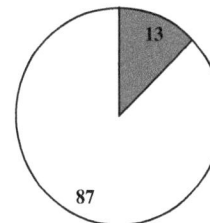

■ % Government Sector
□ % Private Sector

13
87

2006/2007 School Year

QUESTIONS TO CONSIDER:

Does any required course contain some element of Social Impact Management? **YES**

Is any required course entirely dedicated to social, environmental, or ethical issues? **NO**

Is there a Net Impact chapter on campus? **YES**

THE CENTER FOR BUSINESS EDUCATION'S BOTTOM LINE ON CALIFORNIA STATE UNIVERSITY, CHICO:
By participating in the Center for Business Education's Beyond Grey Pinstripes 2007 MBA survey, California State University, Chico demonstrates great dedication to integrating environmental and social impact management issues into its teaching and research. California State University, Chico requires 1 core course featuring relevant content.

A Closer Look at:
Carnegie Mellon University
Tepper School of Business / Pittsburgh, PA
http://www.tepper.cmu.edu/

WHAT THE SCHOOL SAYS:

The Tepper School of Business annually evaluates how to best integrate business ethics, values and corporate responsibility into its curriculum. The Tepper School's academic format encourages that leadership, diversity, and ethics be integrated throughout all courses to educate students on the various dimensions that apply to different disciplines, topics, and situations.

A QUICK LOOK

NOTE: All information is self-reported data submitted to the Center for Business Education

COURSES*

Accounting (3)
Business & Government (1)
Business Law (1)
Economics (2)
Entrepreneurship (1)
Finance (2)
Information Technology (2)
General Management (3)
Marketing (3)
Organizational Behavior (3)
Operations Management (5)
Strategy (3)

KEY CONCENTRATIONS

Global Enterprise Mgmt

Biotechnology

KEY JOINT DEGREES

MBA & Public Policy

MBA & Civil and Environmental Engineering

ACTIVITIES*

Speakers/Seminars (10)
Orientation Activities (5)
Internship/Consulting (1)
Student Competitions (4)
Clubs & Programs (7)
Institutes/Centers (4)
Concentrations (4)
Joint Degrees (4)

* Figures in parentheses indicate the number of courses/activities that, in whole or in part, integrate social, environmental, or ethical perspectives

NOTABLE FEATURES

CORE COURSES:

Business Law and Ethics
This course addresses the difference between a company's responsibility to its "stakeholders" and its stockholders. A major part of the course is focused on the environment, especially air pollution and global climate change. Students consider the benefit-cost analysis of the 1970 Clean Air Act as an illustration of benefit-cost analysis, cost-effectiveness, analysis, risk-benefit analysis, and other frameworks for managing social risks.

Production Operations Management
The focus of this class includes a case study with numerous implications for how the global community will handle the explosive growth in auto demand and the role of major stakeholders. The class discussion ties concepts from several functional areas in the extended value chain in the auto industry and raises many questions about whether the US is lagging behind in managing the value chain from an environmental impact standpoint.

ELECTIVE COURSES:

Quality Design and Analysis
This course discusses ISO 9000 and ISO 14000 standards, the reasons for certifiication—including the implicit benefits of working for a company that is recognized as being concerned with the environment, in addition to marketing benefits. The class discusses not only the professional obligations and liabilities involved in manufacturing, but also ethical decisions and the human and societal obligations involved.

Business Intelligence Tools and Techniques
This course uses short scenarios to discuss and analyze ethical dilemmas. Students propose and argue for an appropriate course of action for scenario participants. Students discuss social impacts and potential ethical dilemmas arising from broad and inappropriate use of IT (invasion of privacy, misuse of private data, etc.). Environmental issues, including scarce resources, are also discussed.

INSTITUTES AND CENTERS:

Green Design Institute
The Green Design Institute is a major interdisciplinary research effort created to impact environmental quality through green design. The institute does this by forming partnerships with companies, government agencies, and foundations to develop pioneering design, management, manufacturing, and regulatory processes that can improve environmental quality and product quality while enhancing economic development.

Center for International Corporate Responsibility
The Center for International Corporate Responsibility researches cultural differences and investigates business ethics from a global perspective. The center organizes conferences; sponsors ethics-related courses; publishes scholarly books and articles on international business ethics; organizes a speaker series for students and faculty; and provides teaching materials to faculty for integration into existing courses.

QUESTIONS TO CONSIDER:

Does any required course contain some element of Social Impact Management? **YES**

Is any required course entirely dedicated to social, environmental, or ethical issues? **NO**

Is there a Net Impact chapter on campus? **YES**

A Closer Look at:
Carnegie Mellon University
Tepper School of Business / Pittsburgh, PA

THE ASPEN INSTITUTE
Center for Business Education

ANNUAL EVENTS:

▦ *India Business Conference*

Tepper India Business Conference is a regional event for students, faculty, and regional business leaders to discuss the many issues surrounding the expanding Indian economy, including outsourcing, wages, labor issues, etc.

▦ *Tepper Service Days*

Two Saturdays, one prior to orientation and one during orientation provide students with opportunities to connect with Pittsburgh through service.

OTHER PROGRAMS:

▦ *Pro Bono Consulting*

A Tepper student group provides pro bono consulting for local Pittsburgh nonprofit organizations.

STUDENT CLUBS AND PROGRAMS:

▦ *Operations Club*

The Tepper Operations Club is a proud sponsor of the long-running International Operations Case Competition; the group also has a speaker series, an internal case competition, workshops, and faculty presentations on operations and manufacturing. Issues of responsibility, sustainability, renewable resources, and developing nations are main focuses for the group.

▦ *Net Impact: Tepper Chapter*

Net Impact: Tepper sponsors internal and external speakers and has sponsored both student and faculty debates about timely issues. The group has also worked with the director of the Master's programs to increase the number of ethics-related cases used in the curriculum and the amount of time spent on ethics during orientation.

FACULTY PIONEER:

▦ *1999 – Lester B. Lave*

With expertise in economics and political economy, especially in environmental issues, Professor Lester Lave has special interest in applied economics, particularly identification and structuring of public policy issues; deregulation of the electricity industry (market power, transmission, and ancillary services); environmental regulation; designing products and processes for the environment; nanotechnology; the value of information in testing toxic chemicals; rethinking regulation; automobile safety, emissions, and fuel economy; and pollution prevention.

SCHOOL DEMOGRAPHICS	
Number of Full-Time Students	302
International Students	27%
Female Students	20%

2006/2007 School Year

THE CENTER FOR BUSINESS EDUCATION'S BOTTOM LINE ON CARNEGIE MELLON UNIVERSITY:

Compared to other business schools in our survey, Carnegie Mellon University offers an excellent number of courses featuring relevant content, and does a good job in those courses explicitly addressing how mainstream business improves the world. Carnegie Mellon University requires 6 core courses featuring relevant content.

A Closer Look at:
Case Western Reserve University
Weatherhead School of Management / Cleveland, OH
http://weatherhead.case.edu/

THE ASPEN INSTITUTE
Center for Business Education

WHAT THE SCHOOL SAYS:

At the Case Weatherhead School of Management, we believe that management is a matter of world affairs, a noble profession, and that every global and social issue of our day is a business opportunity. The school has been an early pioneer bringing social entrepreneurship and sustainability into its core curriculum and throughout the entire fabric of the school's learning environment.

A QUICK LOOK

NOTE: All information is self-reported data submitted to the Center for Business Education

COURSES*

Accounting (4)
CSR/Business Ethics (1)
Economics (1)
Finance (1)
HR Management (1)
Information Technology (1)
General Management (3)
Organizational Behavior (7)
Operations Management (2)
Public/Nonprofit Mgt (4)
Strategy (2)

KEY CONCENTRATIONS

Health Care Management
Nonprofit Management

KEY JOINT DEGREES

MBA & Nonprofit Organization

MBA & Science and Social Administration

ACTIVITIES*

Speakers/Seminars (6)
Orientation Activities (3)
Internship/Consulting (1)
Student Competitions (4)
Clubs & Programs (3)
Career Development (1)
Institutes/Centers (7)
Concentrations (4)
Joint Degrees (3)

* Figures in parentheses indicate the number of courses/activities that, in whole or in part, integrate social, environmental, or ethical perspectives

NOTABLE FEATURES

CORE COURSES:

Information Design and Management
This class discusses the impact society experiences from the introduction of new information technology in corporations and industries.

Leadership Assessment and Development
This course requires students to develop their leadership through an examination of their values, purpose, and ideals. It encourages them to see themselves as agents for positive change in the world. In their term reports about their personal leadership values, students must include their approach to both social and environmental responsibility as future leaders.

ELECTIVE COURSES:

Social Ethics and Taxes
This course engages students as tax compliance volunteers for lower-income people in the Greater Cleveland area. This hands-on experience provides a means for future managers to better understand the concerns of "rank-and-file" employees who may be affected by corporate action.

Executive Leadership
This course discusses topics including how executive leadership must be redefined in the context of contemporary society; the social and global impact of the decisions of senior executives; corporate mission statements and stakeholder issues; the leadership tension of balancing stockholder return and social responsibility; and moving to a higher standard of leadership—the social global impact of moral leadership.

INSTITUTES AND CENTERS:

Case Center for Business as an Agent of World Benefit
The Case Center for Business as an Agent of World Benefit is a global forum for research, leadership education, and engagement in management innovation to advance the creation of sustainable value. The center is committed to advancing the premise that "every global and social issue of our day is a business opportunity." The center forms long-term, innovation-centered partnerships with businesses devoted to sustainable value creation and bringing MBA students, leading faculty, and executives together in a design lab environment called the "Sustainable Design Factory."

The Mandel Center for Nonprofit Management
The Mandel Center for Nonprofit Management aims to enhance the effectiveness of nonprofit leaders and managers. Acting as a university-wide multidisciplinary academic center for education, research, and community service, the Mandel Center is an important resource for current and potential students, nonprofit managers and leaders, faculty members, researchers, and anyone who works in, supports, or studies the nonprofit/non-governmental sector.

QUESTIONS TO CONSIDER:

Does any required course contain some element of Social Impact Management? **YES**

Is any required course entirely dedicated to social, environmental, or ethical issues? **YES**

Is there a Net Impact chapter on campus? **YES**

All information in this profile is drawn and/or adapted from the self-reported data of the Center for Business Education's Beyond Grey Pinstripes 2007 MBA survey. The Center for Business Education is housed within the Business and Society Program at the Aspen Institute. For more info, visit www.AspenCBE.org.

Case Western Reserve University
Weatherhead School of Management / Cleveland, OH

ANNUAL EVENTS:

Weatherhead Tax Assistance Program
The Weatherhead Tax Assistance Program (TAP) is an initiative annually coordinated by the Community Service Committee. TAP works with over 20 Cleveland-area agencies to provide tax preparation and assistance to low-income individuals and families. TAP teaches Weatherhead students, faculty, staff, and alumni volunteers how to prepare taxes, then those volunteers work with agencies to provide tax assistance to those in need.

Net Impact Case Bowl
The annual Net Impact Case Bowl explores two sides of a corporate social responsibility issue by pitting teams of professors against each other in a battle of skill, wit, and humor. Weatherhead's Net Impact chapter uses the event to raise money for various charities.

SCHOOL DEMOGRAPHICS	
Number of Full-Time Students	142
International Students	29%
Female Students	32%
	2006/2007 School Year

OTHER PROGRAMS:

The Career Development Center
The Career Development Center partners with the Mandel Center for Nonprofit Management to provide students with career education, panels, and opportunities that help them to prepare and pursue opportunities relevant to social impact and environmental management.

The Colloquium Series on Business as an Agent of World Benefit
The world's leading thinkers on sustainability and social entrepreneurship are brought together for this powerful learning and discussion environment for MBA students, executives, and faculty. The event focuses on businesses leading sustainable and socially conscious practices.

STUDENT CLUBS AND PROGRAMS:

Multicultural MBA Student Association
The Multicultural MBA Student Association works with Weatherhead administration to enhance exposure to minority and diversity issues, as well as concerns relevant to the general body. The Multicultural MBA Student Association works with the National Black MBA Association and the National Society of Hispanic MBAs to host joint programs and network with leaders in the Greater Cleveland community.

Community Service Committee
The Weatherhead Community Service Committee promotes awareness of, involvement in, and commitment to service in our community for Weatherhead students, faculty, staff, and alumni. The organization links MBA students with service opportunities. Weatherhead also has a Community Service certificate program, which recognizes those students who participate in 180 or more community service hours.

FACULTY PIONEER:

2007 – External Impact Award, David Cooperrider
Professor David Cooperrider is the pioneer and co-originator of Appreciative Inquiry (AI), which is a whole-system, multistakeholder approach to creating sustainable value. AI is being used worldwide to advance sustainability in leading corporations. In 2005, through his vision and leadership, "The Global Forum for Business as an Agent of World Benefit," brought together the leaders and companies of the UN Global Compact with faculty and students associated with the Academy of Management. Professor Cooperrider is the founder of Weatherhead's Case Center for Business as an Agent of World Benefit and has written 16 books and over 60 articles and chapters.

THE CENTER FOR BUSINESS EDUCATION'S BOTTOM LINE ON CASE WESTERN RESERVE UNIVERSITY:
Compared to other business schools in our survey, Case Western Reserve University offers an excellent number of courses featuring relevant content, and does a good job in those courses explicitly addressing how mainstream business improves the world. Case Western Reserve University requires 6 core courses featuring relevant content.

A Closer Look at:
Chapman University

The George L. Argyros School of Business and Economics / Orange, CA
http://www.chapman.edu/argyros/programs/gradprograms.asp

WHAT THE SCHOOL SAYS:
The Argyros School of Business develops business leaders who create value for their organizations by blending the capacity for sound economic reasoning and global perspectives with the qualities of individual initiative, accountability, effective communication, and integrity.

A QUICK LOOK

NOTE: All information is self-reported data submitted to the Center for Business Education

COURSES*

CSR/Business Ethics (**1**)
Economics (**1**)

ACTIVITIES*

Speakers/Seminars (**2**)
Orientation Activities (**1**)
Student Competitions (**2**)
Career Development (**1**)
Institutes/Centers (**2**)

* Figures in parentheses indicate the number of courses/activities that, in whole or in part, integrate social, environmental, or ethical perspectives

NOTABLE FEATURES

ELECTIVE COURSES:

Corporate Governance

This course is a study of the constraints designed to make managers and directors act in their shareholders' interest. Topics covered include choice of legal form of organization, ownership structure, corporate charter provisions including voting rules, antitakeover measures, stakeholders and corporate social responsibility, board of directors, CEO performance evaluation, boundaries of the firm, and international corporate governance. Emphasis is placed on how optimal practices vary across industry, strategy, and country and how they evolve.

Environmental and Natural Resource Economics

In this course, theories of environmental and natural resource economics will be examined both for allocative efficiency and for impacts on growth. The theories of public choice and market failure will be studied. Theory will be applied to topics of renewable and nonrenewable resources and the pollution of air, water, and land.

INSTITUTES AND CENTERS:

Roger Hobbs Institute for Real Estate, Law and Environmental Studies

This institute differentiates itself from other programs with the belief that today's real estate professionals require much more than business and financial acumen. Responsible real estate development also involves an understanding of increasingly complex legal and environmental issues.

Leatherby Center for Entrepreneurship and Business Ethics

The goal of this center is to foster entrepreneurship among students and to promote principled entrepreneurship and the interests of entrepreneurs.

ANNUAL EVENTS:

Distinguished Speaker Series

Each month the school hosts a dinner and invites senior executives to campus to speak to the MBA students. Discussions cover a wide range of topics including business ethics and responsibility of companies to their communities.

OTHER PROGRAMS:

Dinner for Eight

The school provides 8-10 students with the opportunity to dine with a CEO. Since this is an informal discussion, topics include whatever the students' interests, including ethics and environmental issues.

QUESTIONS TO CONSIDER:

Does any required course contain some element of Social Impact Management? **NO**

Is any required course entirely dedicated to social, environmental, or ethical issues? **NO**

Is there a Net Impact chapter on campus? **NO**

SCHOOL DEMOGRAPHICS

Number of Full-Time Students	**51**
International Students	**11%**
Female Students	**55%**

2006/2007 School Year

THE CENTER FOR BUSINESS EDUCATION'S BOTTOM LINE ON CHAPMAN UNIVERSITY:
By participating in the Center for Business Education's Beyond Grey Pinstripes 2007 MBA survey, Chapman University demonstrates great dedication to integrating environmental and social impact management issues into its teaching and research.

All information in this profile is drawn and/or adapted from the self-reported data of the Center for Business Education's Beyond Grey Pinstripes 2007 MBA survey. The Center for Business Education is housed within the Business and Society Program at the Aspen Institute. For more info, visit www.AspenCBE.org.

A Closer Look at:
Columbia University
Columbia Business School / New York, NY
http://www.gsb.columbia.edu/

THE ASPEN INSTITUTE
Center for Business Education

WHAT THE SCHOOL SAYS:

Columbia Business School's philosophy is to provide a framework for students to think in broader terms about their role in business and society, and prepare them with the skills, knowledge, and experience to respond to the challenges of a rapidly changing world. The school ensures that environmental and social issues are woven throughout the core curriculum, elective courses, extracurricular activities, and in academic research.

A QUICK LOOK

NOTE: All information is self-reported data submitted to the Center for Business Education

COURSES*

Accounting (3)
Business & Government (1)
Business Law (2)
CSR/Business Ethics (1)
Economics (5)
Entrepreneurship (4)
Finance (6)
HR Management (1)
International Management (3)
General Management (8)
Marketing (6)
Operations Management (3)
Public/Nonprofit Mgt (2)
Quantitative Methods (2)

KEY CONCENTRATIONS

Social Enterprise
International Business

KEY JOINT DEGREES

**MBA & Master of Science in
    Earth Resources Engineering**
**MBA & Master of
    International Affairs**

ACTIVITIES*

Speakers/Seminars (4)
Orientation Activities (3)
Internship/Consulting (4)
Student Competitions (3)
Clubs & Programs (6)
Career Development (1)
Institutes/Centers (5)
Concentrations (4)
Joint Degrees (3)

* Figures in parentheses indicate the number of courses/activities that, in whole or in part, integrate social, environmental, or ethical perspectives

NOTABLE FEATURES

CORE COURSES:

▪ Managerial Economics
This course focuses on the problem of business decisions, making extensive use of cases. The emphasis throughout is on the use of economic reasoning to solve actual business decision problems. Social impact issues include externalities, property rights, and private versus social cost; predatory pricing; and whether a monopoly is ever socially optimal and the reasons for antitrust policies.

▪ Marketing Strategy
This course emphasizes the role of marketing in creating value for customers, which in turn leads to value for other stakeholders in a firm (e.g., owners, shareholders, employees, and society at large). Trade-offs exist when considering what to sell, how to sell it, who to sell it to, and what customers do with it once they have it. Truth in advertising, use of customer information, and pricing and price discrimination (e.g., on the basis of ability to pay for pharmaceuticals) are all issues of how to (or not to) sell.

ELECTIVE COURSES:

▪ Economics of Health Care and Pharmaceuticals
This course considers the efficiency of alternative health care delivery systems; analyzes incentives and organizational structure of the health care system; and assesses the roles of physicians, hospitals, pharmaceutical and device manufacturers, and HMOs and other contractual networks.

▪ Finance and Sustainability
This course will explore the theories and practical applications that financial professionals can leverage to simultaneously earn a profit and have a positive impact on society. Some specific areas examined are capital markets (to address environmental issues including emissions, climate change, and renewable energy) and commercial banking (to reduce poverty and create sustainable development).

INSTITUTES AND CENTERS:

▪ The Social Enterprise Program
The Social Enterprise Program aims to inspire and prepare leaders who create social value in business, nonprofit, and government organizations locally, nationally, and internationally. The program supports a broad range of activities that help expose students to the breadth and depth of social enterprise.

▪ Sanford C. Bernstein Center for Leadership and Ethics
Using teaching, practical experience, and research, the Sanford C. Bernstein Center for Leadership and Ethics—the umbrella for leadership and ethics activities at the school—ensures that these issues are an integral aspect of training the next generation of global business leaders.

QUESTIONS TO CONSIDER:

Does any required course contain some element of Social Impact Management? **YES**

Is any required course entirely dedicated to social, environmental, or ethical issues? **NO**

Is there a Net Impact chapter on campus? **YES**

All information in this profile is drawn and/or adapted from the self-reported data of the Center for Business Education's Beyond Grey Pinstripes 2007 MBA survey. The Center for Business Education is housed within the Business and Society Program at the Aspen Institute. For more info, visit www.AspenCBE.org.

Columbia University
Columbia Business School / New York, NY

ANNUAL EVENTS:
■ *Annual Social Enterprise Conference*
The Social Enterprise Conference brings together industry leaders, students, academics, and practitioners to share best practices and engender new ideas surrounding the intersection of business and society. Panels feature speakers from all sectors to challenge and deepen current understanding of topics such as global health and business, community development finance, and bottom-of-the-pyramid business strategies.

■ *Corporate Social Responsibility and Sustainability paper awards*
The Social Enterprise Program organizes the CSR and Sustainability paper awards, which encourage students doing projects or internships with companies to examine how the organization addresses CSR, sustainability, corporate citizenship, or social impact management issues.

OTHER PROGRAMS:
■ *CORPS Fellowship Program and Social Venture Internship Fund*
The CORPS Fellowship supports Columbia MBA students who take summer internships in the public or nonprofit sector or with nongovernmental organizations. The program makes it possible for MBA students to contribute analytical and management skills to organizations that could not otherwise afford to hire them. The Social Venture Internship Fund supports students with summer internships at early-stage nonprofit or for-profit social ventures.

■ *International Development Consulting Projects*
The Social Enterprise Program supports students and the International Development Club in creating pro bono consulting opportunities with nonprofits, nongovernmental organizations, small businesses, and entrepreneurial ventures in developing countries.

STUDENT CLUBS AND PROGRAMS:
■ *Bernstein Student Leadership and Ethics Board*
The Bernstein Student Leadership and Ethics Board aims to foster a culture and safeguard a tradition of principled leadership throughout the Columbia Business School community. The board fulfils its purpose by developing, implementing, and monitoring programs that cultivate leadership, build character, and promote ethical decision making.

■ *Community Action Rewards Everyone (CARE)*
CARE is the umbrella organization for community service and philanthropic activities for the business school. CARE also sponsors schoolwide initiatives that bring together faculty, students, and staff in community service.

FACULTY PIONEER:
■ *2006 – Rising Star Award, Ray Fisman*
Dr. Fisman is the research director at Columbia's Social Enterprise Program, where he aims to expand the scope of CSR research in conjunction with the business community. His areas of research expertise include corruption, developing economies, and credit markets. His influence on the practice of social enterprise is steadily expanding; he has been leading executive education seminars for nonprofit leaders for a number of years and his recent writings have appeared in *Forbes* and the *Financial Times*.

SCHOOL DEMOGRAPHICS	
Number of Full-Time Students	**1410**
International Students	**38%**
Female Students	**34%**
Pre-MBA Employment:	

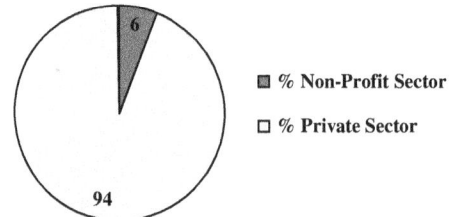

- ■ % Non-Profit Sector
- □ % Private Sector

6
94

2006/2007 School Year

THE CENTER FOR BUSINESS EDUCATION'S BOTTOM LINE ON COLUMBIA UNIVERSITY:
Compared to other business schools in our survey, Columbia University offers a truly extraordinary number of courses featuring relevant content, and does a truly extraordinary job in those courses explicitly addressing how mainstream business improves the world. Columbia University requires 13 core courses featuring relevant content.

A Closer Look at:
Concordia University
John Molson School of Business / Montreal, Canada
http://www.johnmolson.concordia.ca/mba/

THE ASPEN INSTITUTE
Center for Business Education

WHAT THE SCHOOL SAYS:

The mission of John Molson School of Business is to "graduate employable students who are responsible community citizens." We offer a wide array of opportunities for MBAs from not-for-profit organizations and make a concerted effort to integrate corporate social responsibility into core and elective courses.

A QUICK LOOK

NOTE: All information is self-reported data submitted to the Center for Business Education

COURSES*

Accounting (2)
CSR/Business Ethics (3)
Economics (2)
Finance (2)
Information Technology (4)
General Management (6)
Marketing (2)
Public/Nonprofit Mgt (1)

KEY CONCENTRATIONS

Corporate Governance
Global Business

ACTIVITIES*

Speakers/Seminars (10)
Orientation Activities (2)
Internship/Consulting (4)
Student Competitions (1)
Clubs & Programs (3)
Career Development (1)
Institutes/Centers (3)
Concentrations (3)

* Figures in parentheses indicate the number of courses/activities that, in whole or in part, integrate social, environmental, or ethical perspectives

NOTABLE FEATURES

CORE COURSES:

Seminar in Business Ethics
The objective of this course is to provide students with the opportunity to explore the value and relevance of ethical theory as it relates to business. By utilizing the case method, current newspaper articles, and videos, this course will provide students with a hands-on approach to understanding opposing views when it comes to the ethical implications of business decisions.

Financial Management
This course focuses on the investment and financing decisions of financial managers in the framework of identifying and undertaking business opportunities that maximize the value of the enterprise. This course emphasizes one of the vital functions of the financial manager, which is incorporating social responsibility with the objective to maximize shareholder wealth. This is elaborated with examples in the context of "bad social responsibility" and "good social responsibility."

ELECTIVE COURSES:

Management Information Systems for Not-for-Profit Organizations
This course is designed for students of management and administration in not-for-profit, arts, cultural, sport, para-public, and public organizations. Its focus is to provide these students with an understanding of the impact of information systems on their effectiveness as managers and users.

Health Care Economics and Finance
The objectives of this course are to develop health care managers and administrators skilled in the economics and finance of health care and to enhance their productivity so as to improve market strategies and raise quality of services. Students learn how to make better capital investment and financial decisions to develop more effective policies for enhancing access and managed-case care.

INSTITUTES AND CENTERS:

The Entrepreneurship Institute for the Development of Minority Communities (EIDMC)
The mission of the EIDMC is to provide opportunities for members of minority communities to acquire the knowledge and skills necessary to better their situation and thus improve the economic and social conditions in their communities. The EIDMC achieves its mission by developing, promoting, and delivering noncredit customized courses and certificate programs that will assist aspiring businesspersons, professionals, and leaders from minority communities in becoming successful entrepreneurs and decision makers.

Centre for Small Business and Entrepreneurial Studies (CSBES)
The mission of the CSBES is threefold: to develop and conduct both undergraduate- and graduate-level courses as well as training programs designed to prepare individuals for an entrepreneurial career; to sponsor and promote research geared to the needs of small businesses; and to provide support to Montreal entrepreneurs, small businesses, NGOs, and entrepreneurial and small business associations. The CSBES also provides consulting and training to entrepreneurs.

QUESTIONS TO CONSIDER:

Does any required course contain some element of Social Impact Management? **YES**

Is any required course entirely dedicated to social, environmental, or ethical issues? **YES**

Is there a Net Impact chapter on campus? **NO**

Concordia University
John Molson School of Business / Montreal, Canada

ANNUAL EVENTS:

■ *Sustainable Business Conference (SBC)*

Concordia's SBC seeks to challenge the conventional models of business management. The SBC brings together representatives from private, public, and non-governmental organizations as well as JMSB students and faculty members. It highlights renowned leaders who have implemented sustainable practices in business decisions and provides a unique forum for discussing the obstacles, strategies, and advantages surrounding sustainable companies.

■ *The John Molson International Case Competition*

The John Molson International Case Competition is the oldest, largest, and most respected international case competition in the world. Organized by the MBA students, the competition brings together top MBA students from 30 business schools around the world and dedicates at least one of its cases to ethical/social responsibility issues.

OTHER PROGRAMS:

■ *Community Experience Initiative*

JMSB participates in the Community Experience Initiative, a summer internship program that develops community-minded business leaders of tomorrow and strengthens the capacity of Canada's community sector. The goal is to transform the business school and graduates into active supporters in the creation of a more socially responsible and environmentally sustainable society.

■ *The Concordia Small Business Consulting Bureau*

The Concordia Small Business Consulting Bureau is a consulting service staffed by MBA and other graduate students. It provides quality, professional business consulting services at little or no cost to nonprofit organizations and small- to medium-sized businesses in the Greater Montreal area.

SCHOOL DEMOGRAPHICS	
Number of Full-Time Students	215
International Students	11%
Female Students	30%

2006/2007 School Year

STUDENT CLUBS AND PROGRAMS:

■ *Colors of Concordia University—Bicycle Marathon*

Students from different ethnic backgrounds tour the city on bicycles, highlighting the multicultural nature of both Montreal and Concordia's student population while raising funds for charity.

■ *MBA Society*

The MBA Society works to enhance the MBA experience by providing opportunities for professional growth outside of the classroom. Through an integrated framework of curricular and extracurricular services and activities, the MBA Society encourages greater interaction between students, alumni, recruiters, guest speakers, and the business community.

THE CENTER FOR BUSINESS EDUCATION'S BOTTOM LINE ON CONCORDIA UNIVERSITY:

Compared to other business schools in our survey, Concordia University offers an excellent number of courses featuring relevant content, and does a good job in those courses explicitly addressing how mainstream business improves the world. Concordia University requires 6 core courses featuring relevant content.

A Closer Look at:
Copenhagen Business School
Fredericksburg, Denmark
http://uk.cbs.dk/

WHAT THE SCHOOL SAYS:

Our ambition is to make a difference in society. We believe that managers can only create true value for their companies when their management knowledge is leveraged by personal competencies. Developing competencies is a natural part of the quality assurance of CBS programs. The education environment at Copenhagen Business School focuses on reflective learning and developing individual talent.

A QUICK LOOK

NOTE: All information is self-reported data submitted to the Center for Business Education

COURSES*

Accounting (3)
Business & Government (1)
Economics (2)
Finance (1)
HR Management (1)
International Management (1)
Organizational Behavior (3)
Strategy (7)

ACTIVITIES*

Speakers/Seminars (7)
Clubs & Programs (2)
Institutes/Centers (6)

* Figures in parentheses indicate the number of courses/activities that, in whole or in part, integrate social, environmental, or ethical perspectives

NOTABLE FEATURES

CORE COURSES:

Management Accounting

This course discusses the following topics: accounting for sustainability, the triple bottom line, and environmental costing.

Managing Communications and Political Processes

This course discusses new communication challenges to companies and where the role of communication becomes increasingly strategic. This course will cover recent research areas such as corporate branding, stakeholder relations, CSR, and the development and communication of company values.

ELECTIVE COURSES:

Humanitarian Operations and Supply Chain Logistics

The aim of this course is to provide students with an understanding of humanitarian operations by introducing the context in which they take place, the organizations (UN humanitarian agencies, NGOs, public and private sector), and the activities and challenges in the supply chain for the procurement, delivery, warehousing and distribution of the aid. It will also introduce arguments from corporate social responsibility to highlight the role of the private sector.

Sustainable Accounting and Finance

The aim of the course is to introduce markets, investments, reporting techniques, and analytical methods used by entities (governments, nongovernmental organizations, firms, and individuals) to support sustainability. Course content includes topics such as external financial reporting of environmental liabilities, sustainability reporting based on Global Reporting Initiative Guidelines; Green House Gas Accounting and Reporting Standard and Guidance, the impact of environmental costs on product pricing, and Social Return on Investment (SROI).

INSTITUTES AND CENTERS:

Center for Corporate Values and Responsibility (CVR)

The general purpose of CVR is to bring into focus the new conditions of business operations in society when questions of values, ethics, and social responsibility are integrated into the way business and management is conducted. It is our mission to conduct research and teaching of high international standards regarding companies' work with values and social responsibility. CVR aims to attract and work with existing research groups in Denmark and to encourage and develop new research talents and nurture strong international networks.

International Center for Business and Politics (CBP)

The CBP is open to research from political science, sociology, economics, and media studies and to a variety of theoretical and methodological approaches. Of special interest are orientations that focus on institutions associated with business, politics, and the media, and that are responsible for political economic governance and their relationship to globalization past and present, Europeanization, and other important political and economic developments.

QUESTIONS TO CONSIDER:

Does any required course contain some element of Social Impact Management? **YES**

Is any required course entirely dedicated to social, environmental, or ethical issues? **NO**

Is there a Net Impact chapter on campus? **YES**

All information in this profile is drawn and/or adapted from the self-reported data of the Center for Business Education's Beyond Grey Pinstripes 2007 MBA survey. The Center for Business Education is housed within the Business and Society Program at the Aspen Institute. For more info, visit www.AspenCBE.org.

Copenhagen Business School
Fredericksburg, Denmark

PROGRAMS:

Conference on CSR in SMEs

Because most of the research to date addresses CSR in large businesses and considerably less attention has been directed at the CSR activities within small- and medium-sized enterprises (SMEs), this conference was organized as a forum for academics, practitioners, and policy makers to come together in order to identify business case opportunities of CSR activities in SMEs, identify best practices of strategic engagement in CSR activities among SMEs, and, discuss research on strategic CSR in SMEs.

Broadening the Scope of CSR Research in Europe

This workshop aimed at exploring some of the barriers and opportunities for broadening the scope of CSR research in discussion with leading scholars specializing in these areas, as well as those from applied business disciplines and fundamental disciplines from Europe and around the world. Academics from various disciplines participated; the discussion also benefited from the presence of practitioners.

STUDENT CLUBS AND PROGRAMS:

WELL

WELL is a nonprofit student organization that promotes Corporate Social Responsibility. The objectives of WELL are to arrange and execute knowledge-based activities revolving around multiple aspects of CSR, to maintain a high level of visibility among students, to create partnerships with relevant institutions and organizations in order to strengthen and maintain access to knowledge creation and distribution, and to secure constant improvement of the content of our activities by enhancing internal knowledge about CSR.

Develop

Develop is a student organization committed to supporting development through involvement of the private sector. Develop hosts various projects every year and organizes seminars, conferences, and other events. Develop covers a wide range of topics such as investments in developing countries, private sector development in developing countries, microfinancing, CSR related to developing countries, innovations for developing countries and "bottom of the pyramid" marketing, social entrepreneurship, and trade and development.

SCHOOL DEMOGRAPHICS	
Number of Full-Time Students	99
International Students	75%
Female Students	25%
	2006/2007 School Year

THE CENTER FOR BUSINESS EDUCATION'S BOTTOM LINE ON COPENHAGEN BUSINESS SCHOOL:
Compared to other business schools in our survey, Copenhagen Business School offers an excellent number of courses featuring relevant content, and does an excellent job in those courses explicitly addressing how mainstream business improves the world. Copenhagen Business School requires 9 core courses featuring relevant content.

A Closer Look at:
Cornell University

Samuel Curtis Johnson Graduate School of Management / Ithaca, NY
http://www.johnson.cornell.edu

WHAT THE SCHOOL SAYS:

"Sustainability in the Age of Global Development" is a cornerstone of Cornell University's strategy. Consistent with this vision, the Johnson School takes an innovative approach to sustainable enterprise management education by framing social and environmental challenges as unmet market needs that can be addressed through innovation and enterprise development.

A QUICK LOOK

NOTE: All information is self-reported data submitted to the Center for Business Education

COURSES*

Accounting (2)
Business Law (3)
Economics (4)
Entrepreneurship (8)
Environmental (1)
Finance (4)
Information Technology (3)
International Management (13)
General Management (13)
Marketing (4)
Organizational Behavior (3)
Operations Management (1)
Quantitative Methods (1)
Strategy (5)

KEY JOINT DEGREES

MBA & Industrial and Labor Relations

MBA & Asian Studies

ACTIVITIES*

Speakers/Seminars (34)
Orientation Activities (7)
Student Competitions (2)
Clubs & Programs (36)
Career Development (2)
Institutes/Centers (28)
Joint Degrees (4)

* Figures in parentheses indicate the number of courses/activities that, in whole or in part, integrate social, environmental, or ethical perspectives

NOTABLE FEATURES

CORE COURSES:

Marketing Management
This course is designed to introduce students to marketing strategy and management and to improve their skills in analytical thinking and effective communication. Specific social issues discussed in this course include new product development, behavioral pricing, international marketing, and sustainability. An entire lecture is devoted to "ethical vignettes" in marketing management.

Sustainable Global Enterprise Immersion
The Sustainable Global Enterprise immersion focuses on the competitive business opportunities stemming from social and environmental issues across a number of industries. Students spend much of their time gaining valuable firsthand experience in field projects that require them to address real problems currently being faced by companies that expect to receive practical, operational solutions.

ELECTIVE COURSES:

Global Corporate Social Responsibility
This course provides an introduction to the various practices developed by multinational corporations in their attempt to redefine their role on a world stage as "global citizens"—actively participating in creating a safer, more humane, sustainable world. Students discuss in detail and debate the various manifestations of corporate citizenship.

Sustainability as a Driver for Innovation in the Entrepreneurial Organization
Students in this course will gain an understanding of how entrepreneurial business professionals use sustainability principles as drivers for innovation and how to incorporate this strategic thinking into their own career paths. Students will also learn that in addition to traditional strategic financial analysis, business decisions do benefit from taking into account the impacts of social and ecological capital.

INSTITUTES AND CENTERS:

Northeast Sun Grant Institute of Excellence
The Sun Grant Initiative is a concept to address America's energy needs and revitalize rural communities with land-grant university research, education, and extension programs on renewable energy and bio-based, non-food industries. The initiative partners are making important strides in industrial biotechnology, agricultural biotechnology, and the development of bio-based "green" products.

Center for Sustainable Global Enterprise
The Center for Sustainable Global Enterprise conducts innovative research and helps design teaching programs to generate and disseminate cutting-edge ways for private enterprises to achieve unparalleled financial success by addressing social and environmental issues through innovation and entrepreneurship.

QUESTIONS TO CONSIDER:

Does any required course contain some element of Social Impact Management? **YES**

Is any required course entirely dedicated to social, environmental, or ethical issues? **NO**

Is there a Net Impact chapter on campus? **YES**

A Closer Look at:
Cornell University

Samuel Curtis Johnson Graduate School of Management / Ithaca, NY

ANNUAL EVENTS:

Sustainable Global Enterprise/Net Impact Career Symposium

The Center for Sustainable Global Enterprise and Net Impact collaborate on an annual event focused on careers in sustainability. A recent event considered the relevance of the MBA in a millennial age and included panel discussions on New competencies for next-generation leaders of multinational corporations; unique management capabilities leadership competencies for emerging energy and technology markets; and government, NGO, and private sector opportunities in sustainable global development.

HABLA Marketing Case Competition

The Marketing Case Competition sponsored by the Hispanic American Business Leaders of America (HABLA) judges strength of business analysis, recommendations, and presentation skills. This is an annual competition held at the Johnson School in the fall term. HABLA's mission is to educate the Johnson School community about the significant impact on business resulting from Latinos becoming the largest ethnic minority in the U.S. and to provide educational and career resources for Latino students and members.

OTHER PROGRAMS:

Base of the Pyramid Learning Laboratory

The Base of the Pyramid Learning Lab (BoPLL) program is a membership-based consortium of multinationals, non-profits, multilateral organizations, entrepreneurs, and academics. The consortium works together to develop and implement initiatives among firms, communities, and individuals that create value and alleviate poverty. The BoPLL encourages learning and the creation of new knowledge related to the exploration of new business opportunities for low-income communities that mutually benefit both the companies and communities involved.

SCHOOL DEMOGRAPHICS	
Number of Full-Time Students	617
International Students	35%
Female Students	30%
	2006/2007 School Year

Business, Engineering, and Sustainability Workshop

The Business, Engineering, and Sustainability Workshop was organized together with World Resources Institute, Penn State, and Engineers for a Sustainable World. The event brought together leading academics in engineering and business—as well as practitioners from industry, NGOs, and government—interested in exploring the potential linkages and opportunities for programmatically bridging these disciplines within the context of sustainable enterprise curriculum development, research, and technology commercialization.

STUDENT CLUBS AND PROGRAMS:

Entrepreneurship and Venture Capital Club (EVC)

The Entrepreneurship and Venture Capital Club's goal is to foster thinking and discussion regarding entrepreneurship and the funding of entrepreneurship through venture capital. EVC and Net Impact collaborate on an annual symposium focused on entrepreneurship, venture capital, and sustainable enterprise.

Community Impact

Community Impact is a 150+ member student organization at the Johnson School committed to strengthening the community through volunteering, understanding, and learning from the relationships among the for-profit, non-profit, and public sectors, and promoting socially responsible business.

FACULTY PIONEER:

1999 – Stuart Hart

Professor Stuart Hart is one of the world's top authorities on the implications of sustainable development and environmentalism for business strategy. He has consulted or served as management educator for many corporations and organizations throughout the world and has published over 50 papers and authored or edited five books. With C. K. Prahalad, Hart wrote the path-breaking 2002 article, "The Fortune at the Bottom of the Pyramid," which provided the first articulation of how business could profitably serve the needs of the four billion poor in the developing world.

THE CENTER FOR BUSINESS EDUCATION'S BOTTOM LINE ON CORNELL UNIVERSITY:
Compared to other business schools in our survey, Cornell University offers a truly extraordinary number of courses featuring relevant content, and does a truly extraordinary job in those courses explicitly addressing how mainstream business improves the world. Cornell University requires 6 core courses featuring relevant content.

A Closer Look at:
Cranfield University

School of Management / Bedford, United Kingdom
http://www.som.cranfield.ac.uk/som/

THE ASPEN INSTITUTE
Center for Business Education

WHAT THE SCHOOL SAYS:

Cranfield's School of Management motto is "knowledge into action" and on the Cranfield MBA a sense of shared responsibility—personal, professional, ethical, environmental—is an intrinsic part of the learning experience, both intellectually (acquiring new knowledge) and pragmatically (translating this knowledge into responsible action).

A QUICK LOOK

NOTE: All information is self-reported data submitted to the Center for Business Education

COURSES*

Finance (2)
HR Management (1)
International Management (1)
General Management (5)
Organizational Behavior (2)

ACTIVITIES*

Speakers/Seminars (8)
Orientation Activities (2)
Internship/Consulting (2)
Career Development (1)
Institutes/Centers (3)

* Figures in parentheses indicate the number of courses/activities that, in whole or in part, integrate social, environmental, or ethical perspectives

NOTABLE FEATURES

CORE COURSES:

▣ Supply Chain Management

This program is designed to introduce students to the emerging area of sustainable supply chain management. On completion of this course, students will have an understanding of the emerging field of sustainable development in the context of supply chain management, be able to define sustainable development and sustainable supply chain management, and have an understanding of the various models for evaluating sustainability. Another part of the program addresses emerging areas of producer responsibility and reverse logistics systems.

▣ International Business Experience

All Cranfield MBAs travel to a variety of different destinations across the world as part of their program . The School of Management believes that the International Business Experience is unique – with 2007 destinations ranging from Brazil, China, Cuba, India, Japan, South Africa and the USA. The program goes to the heart of environmental and social impact issues in requiring students to see and feel how the world looks different from another perspective.

ELECTIVE COURSES:

▣ Globalization and Society

Within globalization there is a strong societal dimension, so a large part of this module is related to social impact and environmental management concerns. Numerous sessions focus on responsibility issues, including presentations on CSR. The purpose of this course is to critically examine the process of globalization from the triple perspective of economic growth, ecological sustainability, and social development.

▣ Managing International Mergers and Acquisitions (MMA)

In addition to the traditionally covered financial aspects of M&A transactions, the MMA course explores in detail the human consequences of M&A activity, including issues of acculturative stress and the increased rate of executive turnover (departure) in acquired businesses.

INSTITUTES AND CENTERS:

▣ Doughty Centre for Corporate Responsibility

This recently established centre will look at all aspects of business in society, including corporate social responsibility, corporate governance, sustainability and environmental management, community involvement, and stakeholder activity.

▣ Centre for Research into the Management of Expatriation (CRÈME)

CREME has the following aims: to conduct innovative, rigorous, and relevant research into international Human Resource Management (HRM), management of global assignments, and intercultural management; to use academic and professional insights to inform the strategies, structures, and processes of leading-edge multinational corporations; to enable the exchange of ideas and well-informed opinions on international HRM between company and academic experts; and to disseminate research findings worldwide.

QUESTIONS TO CONSIDER:

Does any required course contain some element of Social Impact Management? **YES**

Is any required course entirely dedicated to social, environmental, or ethical issues? **NO**

Is there a Net Impact chapter on campus? **NO**

Cranfield University
School of Management / Bedford, United Kingdom

ANNUAL EVENTS:

International Studying Leadership Conference
Papers were presented by both academics and practitioners and the aim was for all participants to leave with new understandings of the field of leadership and with practical ideas for developing leadership and that these should lead to actionable resolutions for 2007.

Compulsory Projects
Due to the one-year length of the program, students undertake intensive projects rather than internships. Many of these projects are in the nonprofit sector and are concerned with social and environmental issues.

OTHER PROGRAMS:

Cranfield Centipede in the London Marathon
Cranfield Centipede marathon runners raise money for Whizz-Kidz, a UK-based charity that provides mobility equipment for permanently disabled children. A team of 16 MBA students runs in the now-famous Cranfield Centipede costume, a distinctive purple and orange outfit, in the London Marathon.

Cranfield Trust
The Cranfield Trust is an independent national charity that provides free consultancy to small and medium sized charities tackling poverty, disability, or social exclusion across the UK. The Trust works in a variety of management areas using a register of 600 volunteers from the commercial sector, all of whom hold professional qualifications such as MBAs, many of them Cranfield MBAs. Projects with client charities typically take 5 to 15 days of a volunteer's time, spread over several months, and Trust volunteers carry out approximately 150 projects each year.

SCHOOL DEMOGRAPHICS	
Number of Full-Time Students	113
International Students	70%
Female Students	24%

Pre-MBA Employment:

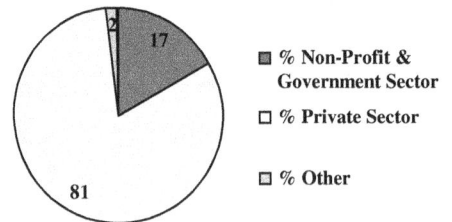

- ■ % Non-Profit & Government Sector
- □ % Private Sector
- □ % Other

2006/2007 School Year

THE CENTER FOR BUSINESS EDUCATION'S BOTTOM LINE ON CRANFIELD UNIVERSITY:
Compared to other business schools in our survey, Cranfield University offers a good number of courses featuring relevant content, and does a good job in those courses explicitly addressing how mainstream business improves the world. Cranfield University requires 6 core courses featuring relevant content.

A Closer Look at:
Curtin University of Technology
Curtin Business School / Perth, Western Australia
http://www.cbs.curtin.edu.au/

THE ASPEN INSTITUTE
Center for Business Education

WHAT THE SCHOOL SAYS:
Social and environmental issues are addressed in the curricula of many of the subjects offered at the Curtin Business School. Several of these subjects have modules within the unit that focus on triple bottom line activity and sustainable business practices.

A QUICK LOOK

NOTE: All information is self-reported data submitted to the Center for Business Education

COURSES*

Economics (1)
Environmental (1)
Finance (1)
General Management (1)
Operations Management (1)

KEY CONCENTRATIONS

Human Services

KEY JOINT DEGREES

MBA & Natural Resources Management

ACTIVITIES*

Speakers/Seminars (1)
Orientation Activities (1)
Internship/Consulting (1)
Career Development (1)
Institutes/Centers (1)
Concentrations (1)
Joint Degrees (1)

* Figures in parentheses indicate the number of courses/activities that, in whole or in part, integrate social, environmental, or ethical perspectives

NOTABLE FEATURES

CORE COURSES:

Environmental Management Strategy

This unit focuses on how businesses have approached the diverse and increasingly complex agenda of environmental management, evaluating the degree of influence that environmental issues have on business activities. It offers comprehensive grounding in environmental management issues, including strategies, accountability, policies, auditing, and reporting. Given appropriate tools and an exposure to international and local environmental and ethical issues, students will use real-life business industry situations to formulate environmental management policy.

Financial Management

This course provides a broad understanding of the financial accounting area, including accounting regulations, business structures, the use of cash flows, the scope and content of financial statements, environmental issues in accounting, corporate accountability, and triple bottom line (TBL) reporting. Students will be better able to interpret financial statements to ascertain the financial position of an organization regarding its liquidity, profitability, and financial backing and its corporate, social, and environmental performance.

INSTITUTES AND CENTERS:

Governance and Corporate Social Responsibility

The Governance and Social Responsibility research unit is a cross-disciplinary group of researchers and Ph.D. students who are funded to produce original work in the areas of governance and corporate social responsibility. Its primary focus is the study of social and environmental impacts of businesses on the wider community. The unit conducts academic and contract research with a particular focus on the development of leadership and management practice. The unit incorporates issues of governance with not only financial accountability but also the environmental and community challenges increasingly experienced by business and government.

QUESTIONS TO CONSIDER:

Does any required course contain some element of Social Impact Management? **YES**

Is any required course entirely dedicated to social, environmental, or ethical issues? **NO**

Is there a Net Impact chapter on campus? **NO**

All information in this profile is drawn and/or adapted from the self-reported data of the Center for Business Education's Beyond Grey Pinstripes 2007 MBA survey. The Center for Business Education is housed within the Business and Society Program at the Aspen Institute. For more info, visit www.AspenCBE.org.

51

A Closer Look at:
Curtin University of Technology
Curtin Business School / Perth, Western Australia

ANNUAL EVENTS:

▩ *Business Leaders Seminar Series*

Curtin Business School hosts a regular series of speakers who give seminars on a variety of topics. Recently speakers discussed social and environmental issues.

OTHER PROGRAMS:

▩ *Orientation Speakers*

In the orientation for MBA students, the alumni and Toastmasters organizations introduce themselves. Both organizations provide links to social and environmental management organizations outside of the university. This is primarily done through networking activities, but each organization also holds regular seminars at which business leaders discuss various topics.

▩ *TBD and LEDGE 620*

These two classes provide students with the experience of consulting in a global environment. The TBD class allows students the opportunity to work with socially responsible firms on consulting projects and projects that have significant social impact.

SCHOOL DEMOGRAPHICS	
Number of Full-Time Students	47
International Students	10%
Female Students	48%

2006/2007 School Year

THE CENTER FOR BUSINESS EDUCATION'S BOTTOM LINE ON CURTIN UNIVERSITY OF TECHNOLOGY:
Compared to other business schools in our survey, Curtin University of Technology offers a good number of courses featuring relevant content, and does a good job in those courses explicitly addressing how mainstream business improves the world. Curtin University of Technology requires 5 core courses featuring relevant content.

A Closer Look at:
Dalhousie University
Faculty of Management / Halifax, Canada
http://management.dal.ca/

WHAT THE SCHOOL SAYS:

All units of the Faculty of Management maintain a genuine commitment to students' understanding of the social and ecological impacts of their future employment choices. As a result, our graduates are equipped to exercise this thinking whether they pursue careers in business, in the public sector, in civil society organizations, or all three.

A QUICK LOOK

NOTE: All information is self-reported data submitted to the Center for Business Education

COURSES*

Accounting (1)
Business & Government (5)
Business Law (6)
CSR/Business Ethics (2)
Environmental (16)
HR Management (3)
Information Technology (4)
International Management (1)
General Management (3)
Operations Management (2)
Public/Nonprofit Mgt (4)
Strategy (2)

KEY CONCENTRATIONS

Environmental Management

Public Policy

KEY JOINT DEGREES

MBA & MA International Affairs

ACTIVITIES*

Speakers/Seminars (16)
Orientation Activities (1)
Student Competitions (1)
Clubs & Programs (2)
Career Development (1)
Institutes/Centers (2)
Concentrations (3)
Joint Degrees (4)

* Figures in parentheses indicate the number of courses/activities that, in whole or in part, integrate social, environmental, or ethical perspectives

NOTABLE FEATURES

CORE COURSES:

Management Without Borders
A major public issue in the minds of business executives, politicians, scientists, and others is the effect of industrial, agribusiness, and other human activities on the bio-physical environment. This course examines questions that pointedly and forcefully confront multinational enterprises and explore the choices decision makers must make within a complex array of different economies, markets, cultures, social systems, and that perhaps most important, regulatory regimes.

Accounting
This course introduces the principles and practices necessary to process and communicate an organization's financial information to different user groups. The emphasis is on financial statement accounting, reporting, analysis, and management information needs. Each section of this course examines ethical considerations.

ELECTIVE COURSES:

Corporate Responsibility
This seminar explores ways to unify economic, social, and environmental objectives with standard managerial objectives. It examines the dynamics of globalization and the role of civil society and the private and public sectors in forging strategies that can increase the positive effects of business on society and ameliorate the negative consequences.

International Environmental Law
The progression of international environmental law from "customary" coexistence to "conventional" cooperation is explored through several topics, some of which includestate responsibility and liability for transboundary pollution; the legal waterfront of marine environmental protection; the international law of the atmosphere: climate change, ozone depletion; and polar regions and the environment: the Arctic and Antarctica.

INSTITUTES AND CENTERS:

Eco-Efficiency Centre
The Eco-Efficiency Centre is a not-for-profit agency that brings an important message to small and medium sized businesses: "There can be both ecological and economical advantages to making the right environmental choices. By supporting cooperation between businesses, the centre works to improve the efficiency of individual companies, while encouraging an "eco-systemic" perspective." MBA students regularly take internship positions with the centre.

RBC Centre for Risk Management
The goal of the centre is to be a catalyst for interdisciplinary knowledge transfer between the various disciplines that study risk. Risk is obviously a subject that has an impact on many fields of study, and the RBC Centre for Risk Management aims to be a unique hub of research and ideas and a focal point for stimulating growth in analysis, measurement, and management of risk. The centre accomplishes its mission by sponsoring workshops, conferences, a working paper series, and graduate faculty research.

QUESTIONS TO CONSIDER:

Does any required course contain some element of Social Impact Management? **YES**

Is any required course entirely dedicated to social, environmental, or ethical issues? **YES**

Is there a Net Impact chapter on campus? **COMING SOON**

A Closer Look at:
Dalhousie University
Faculty of Management / Halifax, Canada

ANNUAL EVENTS:

■ *Dalhousie Dump and Run*

The Dalhousie Dump and Run is a community garage sale/waste-diversion project and environmental fair. Used items are collected from the community and the student residences at Dalhousie and then resold at a community yard sale. The event includes exhibits and displays from local environmental organizations to inform and educate the public about important environmental issues. All proceeds from the sale are donated to charities and nonprofit groups.

■ *HSBC Bank Canada—Business and the Environment Lectures*

The HSBC Bank Canada Business and the Environment Lecture Series explores the relationship between the environment that provides the ecological life support systems and the resources on which businesses depend and the businesses that extract and transform those resources into products and services. In particular this series highlights business leaders and companies that have recognized that business is inextricably linked to the environment and that their sustainability ultimately depends on a healthy environment.

■ *Dalhousie Business Ethics Case Competition (DBECC)*

The DBECC is a student-run competition in which each team is given four weeks to prepare a 20-minute presentation on the issue at hand, upon which they are to present their findings to a panel of judges composed of ethics professors and executives from across Canada. The judges evaluate the teams and determine the three best presentations. Six out of ten teams are chosen to advance and are given an additional case for which they have four hours to evaluate and present their findings.

OTHER PROGRAMS:

■ *Social and Environmental Responsibility Graduation Pledge*

In 2002, Dalhousie University became the first university in Canada to offer the Social and Environmental Responsibility Graduation Pledge. The purpose of the pledge is to give students an opportunity to make a commitment to social and environmental responsibility in their future careers.

STUDENT CLUBS AND PROGRAMS:

■ *The Society for Corporate Environmental and Social Responsibility (CESR)*

CESR members have a shared interest in promoting and acting on issues related to social justice, peace, sustainable development, corporate responsibility, ethics, democracy, environmentalism, good governance, and human rights. CESR is active on campus and in the community. Members are united in the realization that people must come together and work with each other to address problems of environmental degradation and social disparity.

SCHOOL DEMOGRAPHICS

Number of Full-Time Students	147
International Students	19%
Female Students	35%

Pre-MBA Employment:

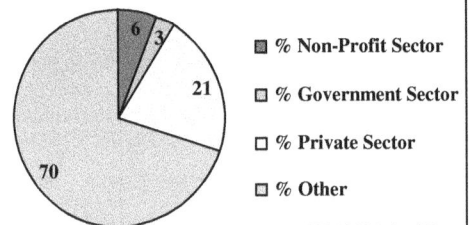

- ■ % Non-Profit Sector
- □ % Government Sector
- □ % Private Sector
- □ % Other

2006/2007 School Year

THE CENTER FOR BUSINESS EDUCATION'S BOTTOM LINE ON DALHOUSIE UNIVERSITY:

Compared to other business schools in our survey, Dalhousie University offers a truly extraordinary number of courses featuring relevant content, and does a truly extraordinary job in those courses explicitly addressing how mainstream business improves the world. Dalhousie University requires 4 core courses featuring relevant content.

A Closer Look at:
Dartmouth College
Tuck School of Business / Hanover, NH
http://www.tuck.dartmouth.edu/

THE ASPEN INSTITUTE
Center for Business Education

WHAT THE SCHOOL SAYS:
The Tuck School of Business was founded in 1900 to provide "training commensurate with the larger meaning of business." The school maintains that goal of preparing its graduates to be principled business leaders who understand the broad social and environmental effects of their decisions and use their knowledge to better the world.

A QUICK LOOK

NOTE: All information is self-reported data submitted to the Center for Business Education

COURSES*

Accounting (4)
Business Law (1)
CSR/Business Ethics (2)
Economics (5)
Entrepreneurship (1)
Finance (5)
International Management (2)
General Management (9)
Marketing (5)
Organizational Behavior (2)
Operations Management (1)
Public/Nonprofit Mgt (2)
Strategy (6)

KEY JOINT DEGREES

MBA & Environmental Law

ACTIVITIES*

Speakers/Seminars (10)
Orientation Activities (3)
Internship/Consulting (3)
Student Competitions (1)
Clubs & Programs (5)
Career Development (4)
Institutes/Centers (1)
Joint Degrees (3)

* Figures in parentheses indicate the number of courses/activities that, in whole or in part, integrate social, environmental, or ethical perspectives

NOTABLE FEATURES

CORE COURSES:
First-Year Project
In teams, first-year students complete an entrepreneurial or consulting project. Projects can be either proposed by students themselves or can be sponsored by an outside business or organization. All projects will involve a real opportunity or issue that is significant to the business and have the support of the organization's management. Almost half of the projects during the past two years have involved either non-profits or focused on environmental or social impact issues.

Managerial Economics
In this course, students examine the principles of microeconomics and how they apply to managerial decision making. Sessions dealing with social impact or environmental issues include the discussion of allocation of landing slots at Logan Airport, clean air and supply and demand in the oil industry, and externalities and property rights as they relate to global warming and sulfur dioxide emissions trading.

ELECTIVE COURSES:
Corporate Social Responsibility
This course examines the responsibilities of business corporations and corporate executives to shareholders and other constituencies as they are manifested in the day-to day issues faced by senior managements. It explores the rationale behind the proposition that business has a responsibility to society beyond that of wealth creation.

Transformative Marketing
The object of this course is to show how marketing and consumer research, frameworks, and processes can be applied to social issues. Three social issues are selected as illustrations: retirement savings, museum management, and health. Class members will apply what they have learned from the three examples to meeting the marketing challenges of various social service or governmental agencies.

INSTITUTES AND CENTERS:
Allwin Initiative for Corporate Citizenship
The Allwin Initiative aims to prepare Tuck students for leadership in this increasingly complex, interconnected world. The Allwin Initiative focuses on enhancing the Tuck MBA experience through education, cocurricular activities, career support, and outreach to alumni, the local community, and the broader business community. In addition to programming for students, the Allwin Initiative supports case writing and faculty research.

QUESTIONS TO CONSIDER:

Does any required course contain some element of Social Impact Management? **YES**

Is any required course entirely dedicated to social, environmental, or ethical issues? **NO**

Is there a Net Impact chapter on campus? **YES**

All information in this profile is drawn and/or adapted from the self-reported data of the Center for Business Education's Beyond Grey Pinstripes 2007 MBA survey. The Center for Business Education is housed within the Business and Society Program at the Aspen Institute. For more info, visit www.AspenCBE.org.

Dartmouth College
Tuck School of Business / Hanover, NH

ANNUAL EVENTS:
Business and Sustainability Conference
Sustainable business practices are necessary to remain competitive and ensure that future generations will benefit from the world's resources. This annual conference held at Tuck is organized by a committee of students and sponsored by the Allwin Initiative for Corporate Citizenship and the Thayer School of Engineering. It addresses key aspects of sustainability: environmental, economic, and social.

Managing Consumer Data: Improving Service and Protecting Privacy
This daylong event examines how firms make decisions about the types of consumer data they collect and use to enhance their products or services and how to do so securely and ethically.

OTHER PROGRAMS:
Loan Forgiveness or Subsidy Program
This program is designed to offer financial, mentoring and networking support to Tuck graduates working at nonprofit or public sector organizations. It provides high caliber-management and analytical support to organizations that could not otherwise attract such talent. While separately funded, this program extends the internship support provided by Tuck GIVES and complements Tuck's programmatic and course work in this area.

SCHOOL DEMOGRAPHICS	
Number of Full-Time Students	490
International Students	30%
Female Students	25%
	2006/2007 School Year

The Ethics of Executive Compensation
Hosted by the Allwin Initiative for Corporate Citizenship, this Tuck case competition focuses on the ethics of executive compensation. Teams of Tuck students prepare a presentation based on a case, then compete against each other in front of visiting experts who judge their cases on financial, strategic, and ethical arguments.

STUDENT CLUBS AND PROGRAMS:
Tuck Student Consulting Services (TSCS)
TSCS is a free student-managed and -staffed, free consulting service for local nonprofit organizations, entrepreneurs, and small businesses. Its goal is to increase student understanding of nonprofit and small business issues, broaden awareness of opportunities using business consulting skills, and to improve Tuck outreach in local communities.

Business and Sustainability Club
The Business and Sustainablility Club explores areas such as socially responsible investing, renewable energy, sustainable sourcing, microfinance, and fair labor practices, among others. In fulfilling its mission of promoting sustainable business practices, the club hosts speakers and engages companies to generate recruiting opportunities.

FACULTY PIONEER:
2001 – Rising Star Award, Andrew King
Andrew King is an associate professor of strategy at the Tuck School of Business. He is the recipient of numerous honors including the Industrial Ecology Fellowship from AT&T and the Zannetos Prize for Scholarly Excellence. He currently directs an NSF/EPA-funded research effort on industry self-regulation.

THE CENTER FOR BUSINESS EDUCATION'S BOTTOM LINE ON DARTMOUTH COLLEGE:
Compared to other business schools in our survey, Dartmouth College offers a truly extraordinary number of courses featuring relevant content, and does an excellent job in those courses explicitly addressing how mainstream business improves the world. Dartmouth College requires 9 core courses featuring relevant content.

A Closer Look at:
Duke University

The Fuqua School of Business / Durham, NC
http://www.fuqua.duke.edu/

THE ASPEN INSTITUTE
Center for Business Education

WHAT THE SCHOOL SAYS:

In recent years, Duke's Fuqua School of Business has dedicated significant resources to several new initiatives that exemplify the school's commitment to social and environmental impact and ethics, a commitment that is integral to our mission to educate thoughtful business leaders worldwide—leaders with an outrageous ambition to make a difference.

A QUICK LOOK

NOTE: All information is self-reported data submitted to the Center for Business Education

COURSES*

Accounting (1)
CSR/Business Ethics (2)
Economics (4)
Entrepreneurship (1)
Finance (3)
International Management (1)
General Management (13)
Marketing (3)
Operations Management (3)
Public/Nonprofit Mgt (1)
Quantitative Methods (1)
Strategy (2)

KEY CONCENTRATIONS

Social Entrepreneurship

Health Sector Management

KEY JOINT DEGREES

MBA & Public Policy

MBA & Environmental Sciences

ACTIVITIES*

Speakers/Seminars (6)
Orientation Activities (4)
Internship/Consulting (3)
Student Competitions (5)
Clubs & Programs (7)
Career Development (1)
Institutes/Centers (4)
Concentrations (3)
Joint Degrees (2)

* Figures in parentheses indicate the number of courses/activities that, in whole or in part, integrate social, environmental, or ethical perspectives

NOTABLE FEATURES

CORE COURSES:

Marketing Management

This class delves into the "4 Ps" of marketing (Price, Promotion, Product, Place) through a case discussion focusing on how managers in the health care industry have to be especially cognizant of their decisions because they may directly affect human lives. Students also view and debate a thought-provoking video documentary about the ethics surrounding the marketing and pricing of a drug for human cancer treatment that was originally created for use in sheep.

Operations Management

This course discusses issues relating with ISO 14000, Environmental Management Systems, European laws promoting remanufacturing, Internet and IT impact on supply chain management, and product recovery and remanufacturing to reduce waste and make money.

ELECTIVE COURSES:

Corporate Social Impact Management

In this course, we will examine how corporations can become more effective at managing their social impact, improving the relationships they have with all of their stakeholders in the process. Recent debates about issues such as obesity, tobacco and alcohol marketing, immigration, and gasoline prices will receive special attention.

Global Academic Travel Experience (GATE) - India

In this course, students study the business, culture, economy, and politics of a country or region for six weeks before traveling to that area. Duke's Center for the Advancement of Social Entrepreneurship is collaborating on the India GATE program. Classroom sessions include speakers and discussions on topics of social entrepreneurship, social enterprise, and Base of the Pyramid business. Site visits include trips to local social entrepreneurs, microfinance institutions, and economic development initiatives.

INSTITUTES AND CENTERS:

Center for the Advancement of Social Entrepreneurship (CASE)

CASE is a research and education center dedicated to promoting the entrepreneurial pursuit of social impact through the thoughtful adaptation of business expertise. CASE provides individuals and organizations with the knowledge and skills they need to address social needs effectively. CASE provides courses, service-learning opportunities, speakers, career planning support, and financial aid for Duke MBA students, including two $25,000 competitive scholarships annually for incoming students who intend to pursue careers in the social sector.

Nicholas Institute for Environmental Policy Solutions

The Nicholas Institute's mission is to become the nation's leading source of effective solutions to critical environmental problems—by providing policy makers in the public and private sectors with unbiased, science-driven evaluations of policy risks and rewards and innovative, practical ideas for meeting complex challenges.

QUESTIONS TO CONSIDER:

Does any required course contain some element of Social Impact Management? **YES**

Is any required course entirely dedicated to social, environmental, or ethical issues? **NO**

Is there a Net Impact chapter on campus? **YES**

A Closer Look at:
Duke University
The Fuqua School of Business / Durham, NC

THE ASPEN INSTITUTE
Center for Business Education

ANNUAL EVENTS:

CASE Brown Bag Lunch Series

Throughout the academic year, Duke provides opportunities for students to gain access to leaders in the social sector. Through the Brown Bag Lunch Series, sponsored by the Center for the Advancement of Social Entrepreneurship, students hear from recognized leaders who are making social impacts and are able to interact with them in a small group setting.

Footprints: Professionals Forging a Social Impact

This annual conference includes interactive workshops, thought-provoking debates, engaging speakers, and panel discussions on integrating business professionals—no matter their field—into the social fabric of our society, both professionally and personally. Participants engage with recognized thought leaders in the fields of corporate social responsibility, cause marketing, environmental sustainability, and social entrepreneurship.

OTHER PROGRAMS:

Fuqua on Board

Fuqua on Board matches Duke MBA students with local nonprofits to serve as nonvoting board members during the academic year. Students work closely with a board mentor, participate in board meetings, attend relevant committee meetings and complete a consulting project for the nonprofit organization.

CaseBowl

CaseBowl pits teams of first-year students against each other in a two-stage competition that allows students the chance to display their academic acumen and business savvy. Before the sustainability-focused case is given out, Duke MBA faculty train competitors in case analysis, resolution, and presentation. Second-year mentors then work with the teams to guide the framing of analysis and recommendations. The competition is judged by Duke faculty, alumni, and local business leaders.

STUDENT CLUBS AND PROGRAMS:

The Duke Microfinance Group

The Duke Microfinance Group brings together students in business, public policy, law, and other departments interested in the power of microfinance to make a real difference in the world. The club aims to stimulate an exchange of ideas and information about microfinance with activities such as a speaker series featuring leaders in microfinance and connecting members with internship and job opportunities within the industry.

Student Entrepreneurs Program (STEP)

STEP is a partnership between Duke's Fuqua School of Business and Durham, NC, high schools to enrich the business learning experience for at-risk students. The goal of the program is to provide meaningful hands-on business learning experiences and increase awareness of entrepreneurial career options. The program partners Duke MBA students with high school juniors and seniors who must formulate business plans and "pitch" them to panels of judges.

SCHOOL DEMOGRAPHICS

Number of Full-Time Students	**833**
International Students	**37%**
Female Students	**30%**

Pre-MBA Employment:

- ■ % Non-Profit Sector
- □ % Government Sector
- □ % Private Sector

4
5
91

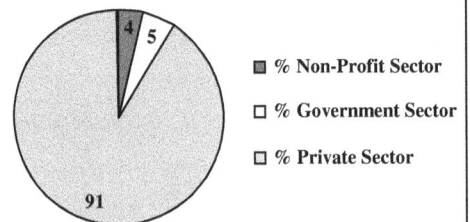

2006/2007 School Year

THE CENTER FOR BUSINESS EDUCATION'S BOTTOM LINE ON DUKE UNIVERSITY:

Compared to other business schools in our survey, Duke University offers an excellent number of courses featuring relevant content, and does a good job in those courses explicitly addressing how mainstream business improves the world. Duke University requires 8 core courses featuring relevant content.

A Closer Look at:
Duquesne University

John F. Donahue Graduate School of Business / Pittsburgh, PA
http://www.business.duq.edu/grad/

WHAT THE SCHOOL SAYS:

The Donahue Graduate School of Business at Duquesne University strives to develop strategic, ethical, and multidisciplined leaders who are capable of managing in an uncertain global economy. The focus of the program is on formulating responsive strategies to serve all stakeholders—customers, shareholders, employees, communities, and society—with integrity.

A QUICK LOOK

NOTE: All information is self-reported data submitted to the Center for Business Education

COURSES*

Accounting (2)
Business & Government (1)
Business Law (1)
CSR/Business Ethics (9)
Economics (2)
HR Management (1)
Information Technology (3)
General Management (6)
Marketing (7)
Operations Management (3)
Strategy (1)

KEY CONCENTRATIONS

Environmental Management

Business Ethics

KEY JOINT DEGREES

MBA & MS Environmental Sciences

MBA & MA Social and Public Policy

ACTIVITIES*

Speakers/Seminars (3)
Orientation Activities (1)
Student Competitions (1)
Clubs & Programs (2)
Institutes/Centers (1)
Concentrations (2)
Joint Degrees (11)

* Figures in parentheses indicate the number of courses/activities that, in whole or in part, integrate social, environmental, or ethical perspectives

NOTABLE FEATURES

CORE COURSES:

Applied Business Ethics
This course examines basic ethical decision making skills necessary to recognize, evaluate and resolve ethical conflicts. The course also examines the organizational influences affecting ethical decision making and behavior. An emphasis on technological and global issues will be incorporated throughout the course. Using articles from current periodicals and newspapers, students will identify ethical and social issues that could impact business.

Public Affairs Management
In this course, students identify and evaluate key external and internal organizational forces and environments impacting the organization. Students will contrast the origins of corporate social responsibility and corporate citizenship, review the current state of the regulatory business environment, conduct an organizational ecological audit, and explore the international views and perspectives of a global public issue.

ELECTIVE COURSES:

Global Marketing Management
This course provides a conceptual framework for a managerial approach to global marketing. It presents the performance of a marketing function within the context of social, environmental, public policy, and ethical issues as it pertains to the international, global environment.

Strategic Supply Chain Management (SCM)
The focus of this course is on the impact of effective SCM on all organization's productivity and competitiveness. Social and environmental factors are inherent to understanding the value chain. For example, ethical issues critical in making purchasing decisions relate to bribery and fair treatment of suppliers. Also, critical environmental factors must be considered in the packaging, design, and disposal of products. Field research combined with Duquesne SCM software will provide students with experience in SCM strategic development and integration.

INSTITUTES AND CENTERS:

Beard Center for Leadership in Ethics
The Beard Center for Leadership in Ethics seeks to become a nationally recognized resource for businesses, not-for-profit organizations, professional associations, and universities interested in promoting applied business ethics or compliance programs or ethics education. The Beard Center strives to be at the leading edge in providing materials and delivering these materials in the form of ethics and compliance programs, forums discussing critical business ethics issues, and effective, innovative learning techniques used in business ethics instruction.

QUESTIONS TO CONSIDER:

Does any required course contain some element of Social Impact Management? **YES**

Is any required course entirely dedicated to social, environmental, or ethical issues? **YES**

Is there a Net Impact chapter on campus? **YES**

A Closer Look at:
Duquesne University

John F. Donahue Graduate School of Business / Pittsburgh, PA

ANNUAL EVENTS:

■ *Ethics Luncheon Forum*

Tri-annual event featuring speakers or panelists addressing important ethical issues, including those impacting society and the environment.

OTHER PROGRAMS:

■ *Donahue Sustainability Speaker Series*

Lecture series on advancing global business sustainability that is designed to promote an understanding of economic prosperity through management of financial, human, and natural resources. The lecture series allows the Donahue School to introduce a forum for distinguished scholars to visit the university to speak on topics related to sustainability.

SCHOOL DEMOGRAPHICS	
Number of Full-Time Students	146
International Students	8%
Female Students	39%
	2006/2007 School Year

STUDENT CLUBS AND PROGRAMS:

■ *Donahue Business Society*

The Donahue Business Society serves as a student advocacy group that works with both students and faculty to improve the student experience of earning a Duquesne MBA, strengthen alumni relations and networking, improve career placement before and after graduation, and work with local charities to build leadership and character within the business and local communities.

■ *Duquesne University Net Impact*

Donahue Net Impact is involved in community and sustainability activities such as stocking stuffer drives for the community, campus greening initiatives, and cell phone recycling.

THE CENTER FOR BUSINESS EDUCATION'S BOTTOM LINE ON DUQUESNE UNIVERSITY:
Compared to other business schools in our survey, Duquesne University offers an excellent number of courses featuring relevant content, and does an excellent job in those courses explicitly addressing how mainstream business improves the world. Duquesne University requires 14 core courses featuring relevant content.

A Closer Look at:
Durham University
Durham Business School / Durham, United Kingdom
http://www.dur.ac.uk/dbs/

THE ASPEN INSTITUTE
Center for Business Education

WHAT THE SCHOOL SAYS:
Durham Business School has developed an integrated approach to the development of MBAs for social and environmental stewardship.

A QUICK LOOK

NOTE: All information is self-reported data submitted to the Center for Business Education

COURSES*

Business & Government (**1**)
CSR/Business Ethics (**1**)
Finance (**1**)
HR Management (**1**)
Strategy (**1**)

ACTIVITIES*

Student Competitions (**1**)

* Figures in parentheses indicate the number of courses/activities that, in whole or in part, integrate social, environmental, or ethical perspectives

NOTABLE FEATURES

CORE COURSES:

▪ *Managing in the Competitive Environment*
This course covers strategy, marketing, and operations management. The strategy discussions include a specific element on the purpose of business, which concentrates on the stakeholder/shareholder debate. Ecological and environmental issues are also included.

▪ *Managing in the Global Environment*
This module covers the role of markets and business in society, the economic and social consequences of the abuse of market power and the challenges and difficulties of regulating market power, agency problems in the cooperation between stakeholders of the firm, the economic and social consequences of changes in the macroeconomic environment, and social impact of international trade policies.

ELECTIVE COURSES:
▪ *Business Ethics*
This module addresses leadership and management ethics, ethics and trust, global ethics, ethical accounting, ethical decision making, and consumer and financial ethics.

QUESTIONS TO CONSIDER:

Does any required course contain some element of Social Impact Management? **YES**

Is any required course entirely dedicated to social, environmental or ethical issues? **NO**

Is there a Net Impact Chapter on campus? **NO**

SCHOOL DEMOGRAPHICS

Number of Full-Time Students 73
International Students 81%
Female Students 26%
Pre-MBA Employment:

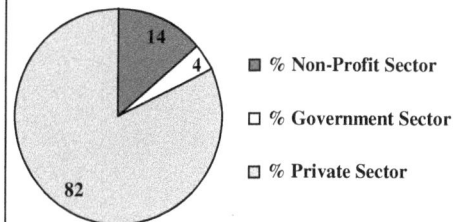

- ▪ % Non-Profit Sector
- ☐ % Government Sector
- ☐ % Private Sector

2006/2007 School Year

THE CENTER FOR BUSINESS EDUCATION'S BOTTOM LINE ON DURHAM UNIVERSITY:
Compared to other business schools in our survey, Durham University offers a good number of courses featuring relevant content and requires 4 core courses featuring relevant content.

A Closer Look at:
EADA—Escuela de Alta Dirección y Administración

THE ASPEN INSTITUTE
Center for Business Education

Barcelona, Spain
http://www.eada.edu/

WHAT THE SCHOOL SAYS:

EADA is an institution built upon a long-standing tradition of training business leaders with a highly developed "human touch"; we consider a concern for social and environmental issues an integral part of decisions made by corporate leaders. This concern is part of the genetic code of the institution and permeates the courses, projects, group work, and personal development that comprise the activities undertaken throughout the MBA program.

A QUICK LOOK

NOTE: All information is self-reported data submitted to the Center for Business Education

COURSES*

CSR/Business Ethics (1)
Economics (1)
HR Management (1)
Strategy (1)

ACTIVITIES*

Speakers/Seminars (3)
Orientation Activities (2)
Student Competitions (3)
Institutes/Centers (3)

* Figures in parentheses indicate the number of courses/activities that, in whole or in part, integrate social, environmental, or ethical perspectives

NOTABLE FEATURES

ELECTIVE COURSES:

- *Buddha in the Company*

This course is highly experiential and is aimed at developing the personal effectiveness that is essential to executives operating in demanding environments and situations. Topics explored include living a life of plentitude and abundance; self-assurance and authenticity; being more effective in the things we do; achieve our objectives with peace and tranquility; alternatives to the tyranny of management by objectives; Neuro Linguistic Programming and creating change; superficial versus profound change; and a personal plan for change.

- *Globalization: National, Regional and Management Aspects*

This course analyzes factors that have an impact on competitive power of countries and applies the concept of competitive advantage at the national level. This concept is basic to analyzing foreign markets and predicting their development. A key strategy in order to improve competence is the creation of a commercial block. There are several on all continents: the European Union, NAFTA, and Mercosur are only a few. Advantages and disadvantages for companies and for consumers are discussed at different levels of integration.

INSTITUTES AND CENTERS:

- *Corporate Social Responsibility Centre*

- *Centre for Creative Leadership*

SCHOOL DEMOGRAPHICS

Number of Full-Time Students	143
International Students	90%
Female Students	36%
Pre-MBA Employment:	

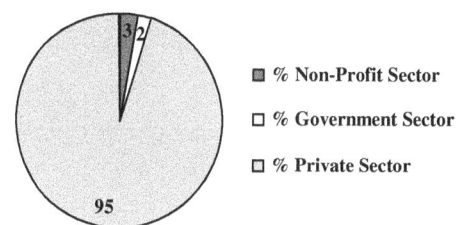

- ▣ % Non-Profit Sector
- ☐ % Government Sector
- ☐ % Private Sector

3 2
95

2006/2007 School Year

QUESTIONS TO CONSIDER:

Does any required course contain some element of Social Impact Management? **YES**

Is any required course entirely dedicated to social, environmental, or ethical issues? **YES**

Is there a Net Impact chapter on campus? **NO**

THE CENTER FOR BUSINESS EDUCATION'S BOTTOM LINE ON EADA—ESCUELA DE ALTA DIRECCIÓN Y ADMINISTRACIÓN:
By participating in the Center for Business Education's Beyond Grey Pinstripes 2007 MBA survey, EADA - Escuela de Alta Dirección y Administración demonstrates great dedication to integrating environmental and social impact management issues into its teaching and research.

A Closer Look at:
Emory University
Goizueta Business School / Atlanta, GA
http://www.goizueta.emory.edu/

WHAT THE SCHOOL SAYS:

At the Goizueta Business School at Emory University, we educate students to be "principled leaders for global enterprise." To support this mission and our brand, we have a set of seven core values that direct what we do on a daily basis: Courage • Integrity • Accountability • Rigor • Diversity • Team • Community.

A QUICK LOOK

NOTE: All information is self-reported data submitted to the Center for Business Education

COURSES*

Accounting (4)
Economics (2)
Entrepreneurship (1)
Finance (3)
General Management (4)
Marketing (6)
Organizational Behavior (3)
Operations Management (2)
Quantitative Methods (1)
Strategy (4)

KEY CONCENTRATIONS

Sustainability

Nonprofit Management

KEY JOINT DEGREES

MBA & Masters of Public Health Administration

ACTIVITIES*

Speakers/Seminars (12)
Orientation Activities (4)
Internship/Consulting (1)
Student Competitions (2)
Clubs & Programs (9)
Institutes/Centers (1)
Concentrations (3)
Joint Degrees (2)

* Figures in parentheses indicate the number of courses/activities that, in whole or in part, integrate social, environmental, or ethical perspectives

NOTABLE FEATURES

CORE COURSES:

▣ *Managerial Accounting*
Managerial Accounting focuses on managing and reporting on performance metrics, including the balanced scorecard (BSC). Discussions include issues such as ethical leadership, the necessity of stakeholder engagement, and the importance of considering triple-bottom-line measures.

▣ *Marketing Management*
This course includes readings from C.K. Prahalad and casework on how to target emerging markets with products and services.

ELECTIVE COURSES:

▣ *Customer Behavior*
In this course, students create a social marketing project that requires them to design a marketing campaign for a social marketing initiative or sensitive issue. Students read a case about AIDs and the failure to curb the spread of the disease and then the success of ad campaigns promoting condom use for the prevention of AIDs. Students must think about who they might offend, who might be opposed, and how they can gain "buy in" from these groups.

▣ *Global Macroeconomic Perspectives*
This course covers topics including globalization, international trade, foreign direct investment, development of emerging economies, basics of international finance and global investing, the Asian financial crisis and recovery, balance of payments, and global demographic trends. This course helps students develop their own global perspective and is enhanced by numerous global leaders who serve as guest speakers.

INSTITUTES AND CENTERS:

▣ *The Center for Entrepreneurship and Corporate Growth*
The focus of the Center for Entrepreneurship and Corporate Growth has been to understand the challenges of organic growth in very large public companies and managing high growth in private, entrepreneurial companies. Both of these areas raise important strategy, marketing, and organizational research questions about the identification of opportunities, the basis of advantage in competitive settings, and the organizational processes that are central to generating and managing high rates of growth. The center is fully engaged in various research, teaching and corporate outreach activities.

QUESTIONS TO CONSIDER:

Does any required course contain some element of Social Impact Management? **YES**

Is any required course entirely dedicated to social, environmental, or ethical issues? **NO**

Is there a Net Impact chapter on campus? **YES**

A Closer Look at:
Emory University
Goizueta Business School / Atlanta, GA

ANNUAL EVENTS:

■ *Lead Week*

Goizueta students took the initiative to organize a Lead Week based on servant leadership and giving back to the community. To culminate the event, students write papers on their experience and what they learned about servant leadership.

■ *Net Impact Speech Competition*

This competition is a new event focused on using Goizueta students' communication skills to motivate and influence the audience regarding a social or environmental topic.

OTHER PROGRAMS:

■ *Microfinance, Access to Markets and Poverty— A Discussion*

This event was attended by students, alumni, and officers/professionals from non-profits and businesses. Some topics addressed included implementing microfinance to address poverty and grassroots projects in India and the role of civil society. With an active Q&A lasting over an hour, students gain valuable insights into the fast-growing area of microfinance, the imperatives for rural development, and the role of the private sector in alleviating poverty through providing economic opportunities.

■ *Scholarship for Nonprofit Internships*

This scholarship provides roughly $6,000 in a living stipend to one Goizueta student to enable him/her to take an internship in the nonprofit sector.

STUDENT CLUBS AND PROGRAMS:

■ *Net Impact*

Net Impact is for students who are committed to using the power of business to improve the world. Members believe that business can earn a profit and create positive social change.

■ *Goizueta Gives*

Goizueta Gives is a club with a focus on responsible business, social issues, ethics, and related business challenges.

SCHOOL DEMOGRAPHICS

Number of Full-Time Students	345
International Students	33%
Female Students	33%

Pre-MBA Employment:

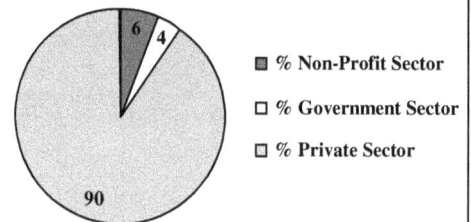

- ■ % Non-Profit Sector
- □ % Government Sector
- □ % Private Sector

2006/2007 School Year

THE CENTER FOR BUSINESS EDUCATION'S BOTTOM LINE ON EMORY UNIVERSITY:

Compared to other business schools in our survey, Emory University offers an excellent number of courses featuring relevant content, and does a good job in those courses explicitly addressing how mainstream business improves the world. Emory University requires 7 core courses featuring relevant content.

A Closer Look at:

ESADE— Escuela Superior de Administration y Direccion de Empressa

Business School / Barcelona, Spain

WHAT THE SCHOOL SAYS:

Facing today's major economic and social challenges of the world, ESADE Business School aims to move society toward respect for individual dignity, pluralism, and human rights. ESADE intends to achieve these goals by educating leaders and managers, generating and disseminating knowledge, and facilitating social debate.

A QUICK LOOK

NOTE: All information is self-reported data submitted to the Center for Business Education

COURSES*

Business & Government (2)
CSR/Business Ethics (3)
Economics (7)
Entrepreneurship (1)
Environmental (1)
Finance (11)
HR Management (10)
Information Technology (1)
General Management (4)
Marketing (7)
Operations Management (5)
Strategy (3)

ACTIVITIES*

Speakers/Seminars (13)
Orientation Activities (2)
Internship/Consulting (5)
Student Competitions (2)
Clubs & Programs (2)
Career Development (1)
Institutes/Centers (7)

* Figures in parentheses indicate the number of courses/activities that, in whole or in part, integrate social, environmental, or ethical perspectives

NOTABLE FEATURES

CORE COURSES:

Geopolitics, Society and Culture

This course analyzes the social changes produced or accentuated by the impact of new technologies and economic globalization, and places considerable emphasis on the key role played by the economic system. Attention is given to phenomena such as increasing inequalities in many countries (the "disappearing middle class"), different ways of understanding development and each method's difficulties, and the increasing importance of natural resources as a key element affecting political and social dynamics.

Operations Strategy

This course encourages students to look for synergies between the search for competitive advantages and the adoption of decisions that respect the natural and human environment. Participants study the way in which these values and new product development may be combined within the same strategy, fostering collaboration between operations management, the marketing team, and the research and development team.

ELECTIVE COURSES:

International Finance

This course seeks to transcend the aseptic accounts of the world of finance to examine the implications these accounts have on the real lives of people around the world. Students should understand that the capital transactions a company may make at an international level require strong ethical self-regulation with respect to both social and environmental considerations.

Social Entrepreneurship

The main goal of this course is to explore the key issues of high performance in established nonprofit social enterprises through the prism of the top managers and leaders of these institutions. The objective is to acquire the skills and knowledge necessary to build and lead high-performing social enterprises, which are dealing with some of the most challenging problems facing societies around the globe.

INSTITUTES AND CENTERS:

Institute for Social Innovation

The Institute for Social Innovation is intended to bring together and lead all training, research and knowledge dissemination in the scope of social responsibility and business ethics. The institute will also address themes related to leadership and management of non-governmental organizations and collaboration between enterprise and the third sector.

Institute for the Individual, Corporations and Society (IPES)

IPES promotes research and activities within the areas of business ethics, Corporate Social Responsibility, and organizational values. IPES also fosters the development of research lines geared toward improving knowledge of the social context in which business operates and encourages social debate regarding to the challenges posed to business by the new social, political, and economic transformations.

QUESTIONS TO CONSIDER:

Does any required course contain some element of Social Impact Management? **YES**

Is any required course entirely dedicated to social, environmental, or ethical issues? **YES**

Is there a Net Impact chapter on campus? **NO**

A Closer Look at:
ESADE
Business School / Barcelona, Spain

ANNUAL EVENTS:

■ *Vicens Vives Program*

This is an innovative management training program designed for young executives who want to develop a global vision of the environment, integrating into their professional specialization an interest in and sensitivity for the problems (scientific, economic, sociological and cultural) that currently affect our world.

■ *Human Resources Forum on Diversity and Equality*

Topics discussed include the main challenges faced by human resources Departments: the internationalization of the labor market and the introduction of measures to promote the hiring of women; and the importance of women, immigrants, and people over age 55 in the Spanish economy.

SCHOOL DEMOGRAPHICS	
Number of Full-Time Students	**182**
International Students	**76%**
Female Students	**25%**
2006/2007 School Year	

OTHER PROGRAMS:

■ *New Ventures CSR Project—Alternative*

Alternative is an ecotourism project that seeks to create social and ecological conditions that function in harmony. Alternative is developing new routes for the European market; students will work on development of new routes/packages for the European routes; analysis of the market and competitors; and marketing research/recommendations (considering CSR factors).

■ *Seminar: Tools for Companies to Evaluate Their Human Rights Practices*

ESADE's Institute for the Individual, Corporations and Society and Universitat Autònoma de Barcelona's School of Peace Culture present a Spanish version of Quick Check, a practical tool via the Internet that lets companies evaluate their corporate strategy on human rights. The tool is based on the rights listed in the Universal Declaration on Human Rights and other international agreements in this field.

STUDENT CLUBS AND PROGRAMS:

■ *ESADE Corporate Social Responsibilty (CRS) Club*

The Corporate Social Responsibility club seeks to strengthen sustainability-oriented knowledge and entrepreneurship among MBA students. Through service to the global community, collaborative research, and attention to current issues in the field of CSR, the club encourages students to develop into responsible business and community leaders who see themselves and business as an important part of the solution to a better and more sustainable world.

■ *Public Management and Politics (Alumni Club)*

The Public Management and Politics Club provides an opportunity for debates and exchange of experiences among ESADE Graduates working in the management of public or semipublic organizations or in jobs with political responsibility. The debates and activities are often related to social and environmental concerns, in order for attendess to share experiences in management and public policy making that improve organizations in society and contribute to creating and maximizing public value.

THE CENTER FOR BUSINESS EDUCATION'S BOTTOM LINE ON ESADE:
Compared to other business schools in our survey, ESADE offers a truly extraordinary number of courses featuring relevant content, and does a truly extraordinary job in those courses explicitly addressing how mainstream business improves the world. ESADE requires 23 core courses featuring relevant content.

A Closer Look at:
Free University of Brussels
Solvay Business School / Brussels, Belgium
http://www.solvay.edu/EN/Programmes/mba/

THE ASPEN INSTITUTE
Center for Business Education

WHAT THE SCHOOL SAYS:

Solvay Business School transforms theory into practice. From the first day, students integrate knowledge gained across subjects and apply insights to real business situations. In that way students will draw from the core courses, electives, and other experiences provided by the MBA to secure competence in assessing the economic, social, and environmental dilemmas in business and the complex choices managers face.

A QUICK LOOK

NOTE: All information is self-reported data submitted to the Center for Business Education

COURSES*

General Management (1)

ACTIVITIES*

Speakers/Seminars (1)
Orientation Activities (1)
Internship/Consulting (1)
Career Development (1)
Institutes/Centers (1)

*Figures in parentheses indicate the number of courses/activities that, in whole or in part, integrate social, environmental, or ethical perspectives

NOTABLE FEATURES

ELECTIVE COURSES:
▣ *MBA Governance and Managing CSR*
This course addresses a range of recent, current, and emerging issues in corporate governance and the management of corporate responsibility. The course introduces key concepts in corporate governance and considers the success of different approaches to corporate governance in balancing the interests of managers and the variety of stakeholder groups.

INSTITUTES AND CENTERS:
▣ *The Emile Bernheim Centre for Research*
The school conducts research through the structure of the Emile Bernheim Centre for Research. This centre provides a base for the development of knowledge and ideas on management issues, including managing corporate social responsibility and issues of the contribution of companies to human sustainable development through their activities in developing and emerging economies.

PROGRAMS:
▣ *Business Field project*
The Business Field Project includes work experience in an economic think tank and research group to examine public policy in relation to economic development and change, ecology and demographics in the European Union. The idea of the project is to expose students to the work of integrating complex ideas and developing responses to present and future issues of importance to Europe and European business.

FACULTY PIONEER:
▣ *2006 – European Award, Nigel Roome*
Professor Roome has widely published on corporate responsibility topics, developed a pioneering module on sustainability at the Rotterdam School of Management, and helped establish sustainability and CSR programs at Manchester Business School, Schulich Business School, and Tilburg University. Professor Roome has consistently generated an outstanding body of research, embodied excellence in leading curriculum development initiatives, and shown a deep commitment to advancing corporate responsibility knowledge, learning, and training.

SCHOOL DEMOGRAPHICS

Number of Full-Time Students	**28**
International Students	**63%**
Female Students	**42%**
Pre-MBA Employment:	

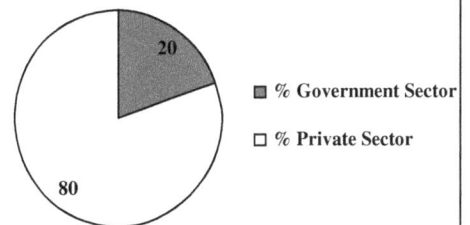

- ▣ % Government Sector
- ☐ % Private Sector

20
80

2006/2007 School Year

QUESTIONS TO CONSIDER:

Does any required course contain some element of Social Impact Management? **NO**

Is any required course entirely dedicated to social, environmental, or ethical issues? **NO**

Is there a Net Impact chapter on campus? **NO**

THE CENTER FOR BUSINESS EDUCATION'S BOTTOM LINE ON FREE UNIVERSITY OF BRUSSELS:
By participating in the Center for Business Education's Beyond Grey Pinstripes 2007 MBA survey, Free University of Brussels demonstrates great dedication to integrating environmental and social impact management issues into its teaching and research.

All information in this profile is drawn and/or adapted from the self-reported data of the Center for Business Education's Beyond Grey Pinstripes 2007 MBA survey. The Center for Business Education is housed within the Business and Society Program at the Aspen Institute. For more info, visit www.AspenCBE.org.

A Closer Look at:
Fundacao Getulio Vargas

Brazilian School of Public and Business Administration—EBAPE / Rio de Janeiro, Brazil
http://www.ebape.fgv.br/english/comum/asp/index.asp

WHAT THE SCHOOL SAYS:

At the Brazilian School of Public and Business Administration, students are encouraged to engage in faculty research projects related to social and environmental issues.

A QUICK LOOK

NOTE: All information is self-reported data submitted to the Center for Business Education

COURSES*

CSR/Business Ethics (3)

KEY CONCENTRATIONS

Public Administration

ACTIVITIES*

Speakers/Seminars (3)
Orientation Activities (1)
Internship/Consulting (1)
Institutes/Centers (1)
Concentrations (1)

Figures in parentheses indicate the number of courses/activities that, in whole or in part, integrate social, environmental, or ethical perspectives

NOTABLE FEATURES

CORE COURSES:

■ *Ethics in Management*
This course provides a general overview of business ethics.

ELECTIVE COURSES:

■ *Corporate Social Responsibility and Sustainability*
This course discusses the emerging concepts of corporate social responsibility and sustainability. It examines how companies have responded to demands for more ethical behavior and social and environmental responsibilities. The course aims at studying the economic and political forces that drive changes toward more socially responsible behavior and identifies the main obstacles to change.

■ *Business and Social Responsibility*
This course uses cases to guide a general overview of the debates on corporate social responsibility.

INSTITUTES AND CENTERS:

■ *The International Center for Sustainable Development*
The center's objective is to study, reflect upon, promote, and publicize the concept of sustainable development. The Center seeks to spread the notion of sustainability, helping to integrate the concept into the developmental process, in the management of public policies, within the business culture and social practices of participatory democracy according to the principles of Agenda 21, the main document of the United Nations Conference on the Environment and Development.

ANNUAL EVENTS:

■ *Consulting for Slum Development Programs*
Students can intern with an NGO, Caritas, which develops projects for low-income communities in the slums of Rio de Janeiro. Students prepare projects and help community groups to identify funding opportunities for their projects.

SCHOOL DEMOGRAPHICS

Number of Full-Time Students	**40**
International Students	**30%**

2006/2007 School Year

OTHER PROGRAMS:

■ *Environmental and Social Management in Petrobras*
Students visit the oil and gas terminal of Petrobras, a Brazilian oil company, where they hear a lecture about the measures Petrobras has taken to improve its social and environmental performance and how it could enter in the Dow Jones Sustainability Index.

■ *Upgrading Clusters: Experiences of Asia and Latin America*
The objective of this seminar/workshop is to discuss the experiences of clusters of firms in less developed countries in Asia and Latin America that are being competitive while simultaneously searching for innovations, better environmental and labor standards,and imporoved health and safety and social responsibilities practices. The workshop seeks to understand what factors may lead these firms to organize themselves to manage those issues and how they are able to both overcome obstacles to collective action and be competitive.

QUESTIONS TO CONSIDER:

Does any required course contain some element of Social Impact Management? **YES**

Is any required course entirely dedicated to social, environmental, or ethical issues? **YES**

Is there a Net Impact chapter on campus? **NO**

THE CENTER FOR BUSINESS EDUCATION'S BOTTOM LINE ON FUNDACAO GETULIO VARGAS:
Compared to other business schools in our survey, Fundacao Getulio Vargas does a good job in relevant courses explicitly addressing how mainstream business improves the world. Fundacao Getulio Vargas requires 1 core course featuring relevant content.

A Closer Look at:
Georgetown University

Robert Emmett McDonough School of Business / Washington, DC

http://msb.georgetown.edu/

THE ASPEN INSTITUTE
Center for Business Education

WHAT THE SCHOOL SAYS:

The McDonough School of Business at Georgetown takes seriously the preparation of our students for managing social and environmental issues and having a positive impact on business's social environment. We believe a manager's training is incomplete without an understanding of this important aspect of business.

A QUICK LOOK

NOTE: All information is self-reported data submitted to the Center for Business Education

COURSES*

General Management (6)
Marketing (1)
Strategy (3)

KEY JOINT DEGREES

MBA & Public Policy

ACTIVITIES*

Speakers/Seminars (21)
Orientation Activities (2)
Internship/Consulting (5)
Student Competitions (1)
Clubs & Programs (4)
Career Development (1)
Institutes/Centers (3)
Joint Degrees (1)

* Figures in parentheses indicate the number of courses/activities that, in whole or in part, integrate social, environmental, or ethical perspectives

NOTABLE FEATURES

CORE COURSES:

Global Experience

This course has two components: on-campus classes in the third module during spring semester followed by a nine-day foreign residency between the third and fourth modules in March in one of five locations abroad. The centerpiece of the course is consulting projects conducted by five-person MBA teams with organizations located at the site of the foreign residency.

Social Enterprise

This module focuses on the special challenges of business leaders working with the nonprofit sector through board memberships, volunteering, cause partnerships, and corporate philanthropy. Teaching methods include cases, discussions, and a number of high-profile guest speakers. Among the topics covered are increased interpenetration of corporate and nonprofit sectors, venture philanthropy, cause marketing, and the use of business models in the social sector.

ELECTIVE COURSES:

Community Reinvestment

This course addresses how to promote investment, entrepreneurial actions, and creative development in inner cities and other communities undergoing structural dislocation or experiencing long-term stagnation. This course provides a chance to complete a consulting assignment, and produce a strategic study that can add value, be implemented, and make a lasting tangible difference in a growing business.

Social Marketing

This course gives students a set of frameworks and tools valuable in bringing about socially desirable behavioral outcomes beyond the economic marketplace. The need for structural change is considered as well as behavioral changes in those carrying out undesirable practices. Class discussion includes the challenges of raising issues on the public, media, and political agendas, and developing strategies to influence legislators, community leaders, and the media to bring about social change.

INSTITUTES AND CENTERS:

Georgetown Business Ethics Institute

The Georgetown Business Ethics Institute fosters the creation and dissemination of significant conceptual, empirical, and applied knowledge in business ethics. The research results of its members and associates are disseminated in places of national and international repute. The practical implications, methods, and techniques that derive from these research results are used to advance the ethical understanding and activities of students and practitioners in business at the local, national, and international levels.

Center for Business and Public Policy

The purpose of the center is to engage scholars, business people, and policy makers in relevant inquiries and dialogue on key business, economic, and ethical policy issues confronting American and international businesses today.

QUESTIONS TO CONSIDER:

Does any required course contain some element of Social Impact Management? **YES**

Is any required course entirely dedicated to social, environmental, or ethical issues? **NO**

Is there a Net Impact chapter on campus? **YES**

A Closer Look at:
Georgetown University
Robert Emmett McDonough School of Business / Washington, DC

ANNUAL EVENTS:

Georgetown MBA Net Impact Career Day

Georgetown MBA Net Impact Career Day is a conference on management careers in the social and environmental fields. Panels of leading speakers discuss topics such as what social issues are important to their businesses and how these issues are addressed, their career path and what advice would they offer to MBA students who have similar interests, and their firm's approach to nonprofit consulting and the career opportunities within this segment.

International Impact Georgetown MBA Case Competition

The Georgetown MBA Net Impact Chapter teamed with the Emerging Markets Network club to organize an International Impact Case Competition, focusing on improving the sustainable growth of small businesses in foreign markets. This event brings together students from international and MBA programs to compete against each other in case analysis, strategy development, and presentation skills.

OTHER PROGRAMS:

Foundation for International Community Assistance (FINCA).

In this internship opportunity with FINCA, students lead an in-depth analysis of Private sector client survey techniques. Students also document current survey practices at FINCA and evaluate existing survey tools. They draw on best practices identified through their external and internal research to develop a FINCA template for client entrance and exit surveys, a framework for analyzing existing clients, and a tool to compile client data and identify potential new financial products and services sought by clients.

SCHOOL DEMOGRAPHICS	
Number of Full-Time Students	478
International Students	40%
Female Students	31%

2006/2007 School Year

Career Services

Career Services helps students to identify CSR-related learning activities, identify speakers, and connect with companies that have commitments to CSR. Activities have included international development and CSR treks in San Francisco and Chicago, Net Impact Career Day, speakers series, and the nonprofit internship fund in which students support their peers financially so they can afford to accept summer internships at nonprofit organizations.

STUDENT CLUBS AND PROGRAMS:

MBA Volunteers

MBA Volunteers provides a link between the Georgetown University MBA program and the Washington, DC, community. Providing a central location for community information and coordination of volunteer events, the MBA Volunteers strives to offer a variety of opportunities for students to become involved in the local community.

Emerging Markets Network (EMN)

The EMN focuses on social impact issues within the emerging markets. It co-sponsors the International Impact Georgetown MBA Case Competition (with Net Impact), leveraging cases that incorporate sustainable, capacity-building enterprises within the developing world. It also hosts guest speakers as they address issues of concern in developing nations.

FACULTY PIONEER:

2006 – Academic Leadership Award, Pietra Rivoli

Pietra Rivoli teaches finance and international business in the undergraduate, graduate, and executive programs at the McDonough School of Business at Georgetown University. Professor Rivoli has special interests in social justice issues in international business and in China, and she regularly leads MBA residencies to China. Her academic research has been published in numerous leading journals and her recent book, *The Travels of a T-Shirt in the Global Economy*, has been widely acclaimed by both the popular press and the academic community as a path-breaking study of globalization.

THE CENTER FOR BUSINESS EDUCATION'S BOTTOM LINE ON GEORGETOWN UNIVERSITY:
Compared to other business schools in our survey, Georgetown University offers a good number of courses featuring relevant content, and does an excellent job in those courses explicitly addressing how mainstream business improves the world. Georgetown University requires 4 core courses featuring relevant content.

A Closer Look at:
The George Washington University
School of Business / Washington, DC

http://mba.gwu.edu/

THE ASPEN INSTITUTE
Center for Business Education

WHAT THE SCHOOL SAYS:

The George Washington University School of Business is proud to be an active part of the emerging movement of businesses and business schools that are paying increasing attention to environmental and social issues in business. Washington, D.C., with its numerous public and nonprofit organizations and its international community, provides the ideal setting for students to increase their awareness of and interactions with organizations and individuals who have broad and deep experience in these important areas.

A QUICK LOOK

NOTE: All information is self-reported data submitted to the Center for Business Education

COURSES*

Accounting (4)
Business & Government (5)
CSR/Business Ethics (3)
Economics (1)
Environmental (4)
HR Management (3)
Information Technology (5)
International Management (11)
General Management (9)
Marketing (7)
Operations Management (1)
Public/Nonprofit Mgt (5)
Strategy (7)

KEY CONCENTRATIONS

Environmental Policy & Management

Nonprofit Organization Management

KEY JOINT DEGREES

MBA & MA International Affairs

ACTIVITIES*

Speakers/Seminars (5)
Orientation Activities (1)
Internship/Consulting (2)
Student Competitions (2)
Clubs & Programs (1)
Career Development (1)
Institutes/Centers (7)
Concentrations (5)
Joint Degrees (2)

* Figures in parentheses indicate the number of courses/activities that, in whole or in part, integrate social, environmental, or ethical perspectives

NOTABLE FEATURES

CORE COURSES:

Business and Public Policy
This course is dedicated to the topic of business stakeholder management and includes attention to multiple business stakeholders. Other relevant topics include ethics and morality, environmentalism, antitrust, facilities location, global trade, public affairs management, corporate social responsibility, strategic philanthropy, and sustainability.

Strategic Formulation and Implementation
This course includes attention to both social and environmental issues, primarily through the use of case studies that involve various stakeholders and natural resource-consuming industries. Specific topics include Corporate Social Responsibility and Environmental Strategy and strategic planning of corporations in response to these issues.

ELECTIVE COURSES:

Environmental Policy
This course focuses on global, domestic, and local environmental policy with attention to multiple environmental issues: climate change, biodiversity, water resources, food resources, and poverty. Environmental ethics, legislation, regulation, and advocacy, are all topics of discussion.

Emerging Technologies
This course focuses on the assessment of social impacts, technological change and society, natural resources and events, environmental limits, social systems evolution, local and virtual communities, "spiritual technology," energy alternatives, and ethical issues of bioengineering.

INSTITUTES AND CENTERS:

Institute for Corporate Responsibility
The Institute for Corporate Responsibility was established to advance scholarship on the topic of corporate responsibility and on peace through commerce, environmental sustainability, corporate governance, and global stakeholder management.

GW International NGO Team (INGOT)
GW INGOT brings together faculty, researchers, and doctoral students from multiple disciplines across the University to discuss research and progress related to the international development of NGOs.

QUESTIONS TO CONSIDER:

Does any required course contain some element of Social Impact Management? **YES**

Is any required course entirely dedicated to social, environmental or ethical issues? **NO**

Is there a Net Impact Chapter on campus? **YES**

All information in this profile is drawn and/or adapted from the self-reported data of the Center for Business Education's Beyond Grey Pinstripes 2007 MBA survey. The Center for Business Education is housed within the Business and Society Program at the Aspen Institute. For more info, visit www.AspenCBE.org.

75

A Closer Look at:
The George Washington University
School of Business / Washington, DC

ANNUAL EVENTS:

■ *Nonprofit Case Competition*

Each March, up to 25 MBA teams from around the world are invited to compete. Working from faculty-created cases, teams develop strategic analyses and recommendations for a large, well-known nonprofit organization.

■ *WRI (The World Resources Institute) Environmental Enterprise Corps*

MBA students work with faculty and business entrepreneurs to promote sustainability and the triple bottom line for businesses in developing countries.

OTHER PROGRAMS:

■ *Implementing Solutions to Climate Crises*

This action-oriented conference focuses on business, government, NGO's, and consumer/citizen solutions to climate crises. Representatives from each of these sectors are invited to provide expert insights on how participants can develop and commit to these actions. Breakout sessions and networking opportunities reinforce these commitments.

■ *Environmental and Social Sustainability Initiative*

This initiative focuses on environmental and social sustainability research, teaching, and service. Current research topics include environmental entrepreneurship, voluntary environmental programs, environmental information systems, and corporate and community sustainability programs.

STUDENT CLUBS AND PROGRAMS:

■ *GW Net Impact*

This student organization has more than 70 members, mostly GW MBA students, who attempt to advance socially and environmentally responsible businesses and business practices. The organization conducts meetings and socials and recruits executive guest speakers to address the entire student body.

FACULTY PIONEER:

■ *2003 – Academic Leadership Award, Timothy L. Fort*

Timothy Fort was awarded the Academic Leadership Award while a professor at the University of Michigan, Ross School of Business. Professor Fort co-led a Corporate Governance and Peace Initiative through the William Davidson Institute; developed two programs with the World Bank designed to provide an interactive, Internet-based dialogue and education program concerning the extent to which businesses can contribute to sustainable peace; and currently continues his work along these lines.

SCHOOL DEMOGRAPHICS

Number of Full-Time Students	165
International Students	35%
Female Students	45%

Pre-MBA Employment:

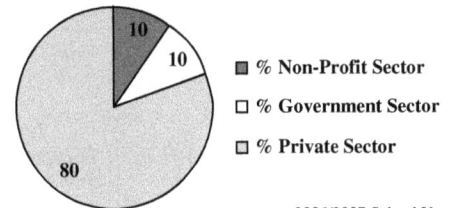

- ■ % Non-Profit Sector
- □ % Government Sector
- □ % Private Sector

2006/2007 School Year

THE CENTER FOR BUSINESS EDUCATION'S BOTTOM LINE ON THE GEORGE WASHINGTON UNIVERSITY:

Compared to other business schools in our survey, The George Washington University offers a truly extraordinary number of courses featuring relevant content, and does a truly extraordinary job in those courses explicitly addressing how mainstream business improves the world. The George Washington University requires 9 core courses featuring relevant content.

A Closer Look at:
Georgia Institute of Technology
College of Management / Atlanta, GA

http://mgt.gatech.edu/programs/mba

THE ASPEN INSTITUTE
Center for Business Education

WHAT THE SCHOOL SAYS:

Georgia Tech College of Management is developing a strong emphasis on social responsibility and sustainable, environmentally friendly business practices, aiming to incorporate these concepts into all aspects of students' education. With the right people and programs in the right place, Georgia Tech is creating a new standard in business education—one emphasizing that doing right is just as important as doing well.

A QUICK LOOK

NOTE: All information is self-reported data submitted to the Center for Business Education

COURSES*

Accounting (1)
Business & Government (2)
CSR/Business Ethics (1)
Marketing (3)
Organizational Behavior (2)
Operations Management (2)
Strategy (1)

KEY JOINT DEGREES

MBA & Public Policy

MBA & Environmental Sciences

ACTIVITIES*

Speakers/Seminars (2)
Student Competitions (1)
Clubs & Programs (1)
Institutes/Centers (2)
Joint Degrees (3)

* Figures in parentheses indicate the number of courses/activities that, in whole or in part, integrate social, environmental, or ethical perspectives

NOTABLE FEATURES

CORE COURSES:

Ethical Environment of Business

This course is a survey of ethical issues with which the manager must be familiar in order to adequately understand the business environment in which the modern company operates. The course is designed to teach and foster discussion about important topics in ethics (moral problems and ethical duties) and will give the student a formal experience in analyzing how the ethical environment creates a structure for commercial activity at the firm level.

Leadership and Organizational Behavior

The primary emphasis of this course is on developing an understanding of how to effectively manage and lead in business. Given the increasingly global nature of business, it is essential that the approach taken include an explicit emphasis on social and ethical issues.

ELECTIVE COURSES:

International Marketing

Issues in this course are specifically addressed in the cultural and political-legal environment, essentially cross-cultural comparisons between what ethics means in the U.S. versus in China, and how international marketers deal with the differences and similarities in this regard. Social, environmental, and ethical issues across international markets, their effect on cross-cultural consumer behavior, and the implications for international marketing strategy and implementation are examined throughout the course.

Business and the Environment

This course takes a holistic view of the interaction of businesses with the environment. It outlines reasons why businesses would want to care about environmental issues, introduces environmental assessment and management tools, and addresses topics from various business functions. Main topics include the science underlying environmental issues relevant domestic and international environmental legislation, environmental operations, and sustainable development.

INSTITUTES AND CENTERS:

Institute for Sustainable Technology and Development (ISTD)

The ISTD serves as the advocate for sustainability and guides the implementation of a 20-year strategy for institutional transformation in education, research, and campus management practices. The goal of the ISTD is to incorporate concepts of sustainable technology and development into every academic program, to promote innovation through research and development programs, and to model sustainable practices managing the environment of the campus.

Institute for Leadership and Entrepreneurship (ILE)

The ILE bridges units across and beyond campus to increase and enhance the learning opportunities available to those who aspire to become effective leaders in a complex global arena. Through increased class offerings and coordinated activities, ILE empowers students and others from every industry and discipline to consider the economical, social, and environmental impacts of their actions when making everyday business decisions.

QUESTIONS TO CONSIDER:

Does any required course contain some element of Social Impact Management? **YES**

Is any required course entirely dedicated to social, environmental, or ethical issues? **YES**

Is there a Net Impact Chapter on campus? **YES**

Georgia Institute of Technology

College of Management / Atlanta, GA

ANNUAL EVENTS:

▣ *IMPACT Speaker Series*

The IMPACT Speaker Series brings highly successful business leaders from a variety of industries to campus to share their experiences and give advice to students and other entrepreneurs on topics ranging from building a venture around intellectual capital to successful entrepreneurship in large organizations. The weekly series provides Georgia Tech students, alumni, and the Atlanta community an opportunity to network and learn from high-tech entrepreneurs, venture capitalists, and notable business leaders.

▣ *Georgia Tech Product Re-X Conference*

Georgia Tech recently hosted the first Georgia Tech Product Re-X (recover, recycle, remanufacture, and reuse) Conference.
This event is a great opportunity for students to hear researchers and representatives from major companies and public agencies discuss innovative environmental solutions and business opportunities.

▣ *Georgia Tech Business Plan Competition (BPC)*

The BPC begins in the fall with a mentoring program and workshops designed to help students refine their venture ideas, create and establish their teams, and develop their business plans. The BPC culminates in February with the competition's preliminary and final events. A cash award is presented to the team whose business plan best incorporates concepts of social and/or environmental sustainability.

STUDENT CLUBS AND PROGRAMS:

▣ *Net Impact at Georgia Tech*

Current activities include speaker series, dinners and socials, student awareness events such as Net Impact Day, and field trips to local businesses that include social and environmental values into their daily operations.

SCHOOL DEMOGRAPHICS

Number of Full-Time Students	**138**
International Students	**24%**
Female Students	**25%**

Pre-MBA Employment:

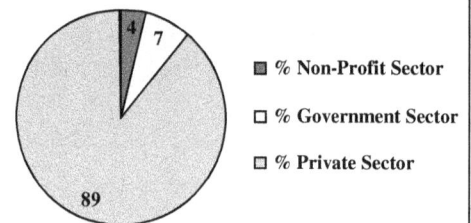

- ▣ % Non-Profit Sector
- ☐ % Government Sector
- ☐ % Private Sector

4
7
89

2006/2007 School Year

THE CENTER FOR BUSINESS EDUCATION'S BOTTOM LINE ON GEORGIA INSTITUTE OF TECHNOLOGY:
Compared to other business schools in our survey, Georgia Institute of Technology offers a good number of courses featuring relevant content, and does a good job in those courses explicitly addressing how mainstream business improves the world. Georgia Institute of Technology requires 4 core courses featuring relevant content.

Harvard University

Graduate School of Business Administration / Boston, MA
http://www.hbs.edu/

THE ASPEN INSTITUTE
Center for Business Education

WHAT THE SCHOOL SAYS:

In keeping with its core mission to educate leaders who make a difference in the world, Harvard Business School exposes MBA students to the principles and practices of social enterprise, corporate governance, ethics, and values throughout the curriculum, and offers a host of related activities and opportunities.

A QUICK LOOK

NOTE: All information is self-reported data submitted to the Center for Business Education

COURSES*

Accounting (1)
Business & Government (3)
Business Law (2)
CSR/Business Ethics (3)
Economics (2)
Entrepreneurship (8)
Environmental (1)
Finance (5)
HR Management (2)
International Management (2)
General Management (16)
Marketing (3)
Organizational Behavior (4)
Operations Management (1)
Strategy (5)

KEY JOINT DEGREES

MD/MBA
JD/MBA
MBA and Public Policy

ACTIVITIES*

Speakers/Seminars (9)
Orientation Activities (4)
Internship/Consulting (4)
Student Competitions (4)
Clubs & Programs (8)
Career Development (10)
Institutes/Centers (11)
Joint Degrees (3)

* Figures in parentheses indicate the number of courses/activities that, in whole or in part, integrate social, environmental, or ethical perspectives

NOTABLE FEATURES

CORE COURSES:

▪ *Negotiation*
The course offers a prescriptive approach to analyzing and engaging in negotiations effectively and ethically. It provides an understanding of negotiations in a variety of organizations and markets and the effect of negotiations on those organizations and markets.

▪ *Leadership and Corporate Accountability*
The course examines the economic, legal, and ethical responsibilities of business leaders. In each case discussed in the course, students are challenged to make decisions and devise action plans that meet the relevant economic, legal, and ethical requirements.

ELECTIVE COURSES:

▪ *Energy*
The course is devoted to a broad range of energy-related topics. It consists of short modules exploring the energy value chain and the distribution of economic surplus, the basic economics of the energy industry, innovations in management of risk, energy supplies, and energy conservation. Examples of cases include upstream pipeline and crude transportation projects in Africa, a large coal-fired power plant in China, corn-based ethanol in the U.S., and energy conservation opportunities in the building sector.

▪ *Entrepreneurship in Education Reform*
This course is devoted to social entrepreneurship with a focus on efforts to transform public education in the U.S. The course is organized around four compelling entrepreneurial opportunities that exist due to the appallingly low levels of performance in U.S. schools, particularly in urban areas.

INSTITUTES AND CENTERS:

▪ *Harvard Humanitarian Initiative (HHI)*
The HHI is a university-wide center involving multiple entities within the Harvard academic and medical community. The initiative combines expertise in public health, medicine, social science, and humanities to advance research, practice, and policy in the field of humanitarian assistance to populations affected by war and disaster.

▪ *Corporate Social Responsibility Initiative*
The Corporate Social Responsibility Initiative at the Kennedy School of Government is a multidisciplinary and multi stakeholder program that seeks to study and enhance the public role of the private enterprise. It explores the intersection of corporate responsibility, corporate governance, and strategy, public policy, and the media.

QUESTIONS TO CONSIDER:

Does any required course contain some element of Social Impact Management? **YES**

Is any required course entirely dedicated to social, environmental, or ethical issues? **YES**

Is there a Net Impact Chapter on campus? **YES**

A Closer Look at:
Harvard University
Graduate School of Business Administration / Boston, MA

ANNUAL EVENTS:

- *Social Enterprise Conference*

The annual student-led conference brings together over 1,000 students, faculty, and practitioners from across the country. The 2007 conference focused on the theme of "Engage. Your Value. Your Work. Your World." and included two keynote addresses, 18 panels ranging from CSR and climate change, to innovations in microfinance, a career fair, practitioner lunches, and a pitch-for-change business plan contest.

- *Professional Development Training*

The Harbus Foundation and Volunteer Consulting Organization together offer a number of professional development sessions that support the work of their club members and also open to the broader student body.

- *Leadership and Values Initiative (LVI) Speaker Series*

The LVI is where the mission of the school—to educate leaders who make a difference in the world—and community values meet. The speaker series included "Leading with Integrity During Times of Change" with Rick Wagoner, Chairman/CEO, General Motors; "Coming Out on Ford: An Insider's Perspective on Leadership, Diversity and American Automobile Industry" with Allan Gilmour, Former Vice Chairman/CFO, Ford Motor Company; "A Changing Business Climate" with Al Gore.

OTHER PROGRAMS:

- *Green Team*

The Harvard Business School Green Team is led by the Operations Department to establish a sense of environmental awareness throughout the HBS community. The Green Team's goal is to influence behavioral change through communication and education so that HBS realizes a reduction in waste, water, and energy consumption. The Green Team hosts a speaker series and an annual energy competition.

SCHOOL DEMOGRAPHICS	
Number of Full-Time Students	907
International Students	32%
Female Students	34%
Pre-MBA Employment:	

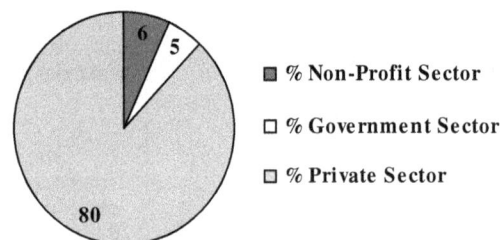

Pie chart values: 6, 5, 80

- % Non-Profit Sector
- % Government Sector
- % Private Sector

2006/2007 School Year

- *Leadership and Ethics Forum*

The Leadership and Ethics Forum challenges the HBS Community to confront, consider, and debate leadership and ethical issues. Annual events include the Harvard-Yale Debate and a speaker series.

STUDENT CLUBS AND PROGRAMS:

- *Business and Environment Club*

The mission of the club is to educate future business leaders on the important relationship between business and the environment through exposure to careers, industries, organizations, leaders, and business models.

- *Social Enterprise Club*

The Social Enterprise Club serves as the main student focal point for social enterprise. Its mission is to inspire, enable, and support students to use leadership and management skills to achieve social impact. The club recognizes that students may do this through personal and professional pursuits in nonprofit, public, and for-profit organizations.

FACULTY PIONEER:

- *2006 – Lifetime Achievement, Max Bazerman*

Bazerman is the Jesse Isidor Straus professor of business administration at Harvard Business School and his research focuses on decision making in negotiation and improving decision making in organizations, nations, and society. He has written or coauthored more than 180 research articles and chapters, and is the author, coauthor, or co-editor of 15 books.

- *2003 – Institutional Leadership, James E. Austin*

Professor Austin's work on social enterprise focuses on organizations and partnerships created by business and social sector leaders to mobilize their collective capabilities to address social issues and problems facing their communities. Under his skillful leadership, social enterprise topics have been integrated into mainstream research, teaching, and programs at the Harvard Business School. He has encouraged the growth of social enterprise research and teaching at graduate schools around the world, including the establishment of the Social Enterprise Knowledge Network in Latin America.

THE CENTER FOR BUSINESS EDUCATION'S BOTTOM LINE ON HARVARD UNIVERSITY:

Compared to other business schools in our survey, Harvard University offers a truly extraordinary number of courses featuring relevant content, and does a truly extraordinary job in those courses explicitly addressing how mainstream business improves the world. Harvard University requires 9 core courses featuring relevant content.

A Closer Look at:
HEC School of Management—Paris (École des Hautes Études Commerciales)

Jouy-en-Josas, France
http://www.mbahec.edu

WHAT THE SCHOOL SAYS:

The HEC MBA takes a proactive, holistic approach in training leaders with a high degree of ethical awareness. Given the diversity of our student body—55 nationalities are represented among approximately 180 participants for each graduating class—our approach starts with the intrinsic values and traditions of each individual.

A QUICK LOOK

NOTE: All information is self-reported data submitted to the Center for Business Education

COURSES*

CSR/Business Ethics (5)
Environmental (2)
HR Management (2)
Marketing (2)
Public/Nonprofit Mgt (1)

KEY CONCENTRATIONS

Mission and Action Project

KEY JOINT DEGREES

MBA & Environmental Law
MBA & Environmental Economics

ACTIVITIES*

Speakers/Seminars (13)
Orientation Activities (2)
Internship/Consulting (1)
Student Competitions (1)
Clubs & Programs (3)
Career Development (1)
Concentrations (1)
Joint Degrees (2)

* Figures in parentheses indicate the number of courses/activities that, in whole or in part, integrate social, environmental, or ethical perspectives

NOTABLE FEATURES

CORE COURSES:

Sustainable Development Seminar

This seminar introduces sustainable development to MBA students. This event features high-level executives, key industry decision makers and outstanding HEC faculty members in the field of sustainable development, corporate social responsibility, and the environment. Discussions focus on sustainable financial concepts, including the importance of ecologically and socially responsible investments and changes in investment criteria for the world's largest financial institutions.

Introduction to Marketing

Concepts that will be covered in this course include marketing strategy; consumer and business behavior; market segmentation, targeting, and positioning, branding, new products and product life cycle strategies; pricing; distribution channels; integrated marketing communications; advertising; consumer and trade promotion; direct marketing; Internet marketing; public relations; international marketing; and marketing ethics and social responsibility.

ELECTIVE COURSES:

Business Ethics: The Individual, Business and Society

The purpose of this course is to explore ethical issues in a rational, pragmatic, responsible, and decisive manner in order to best prepare students to resolve these when facing them in their personal and professional lives. Vigorous discussions involving all participants and perspectives will explore values integration and ethical reasoning processes through studying real cases. Participants challenge themselves through both individual and group projects and analyses.

Business, the Natural Environment, and the Global Economy

Through short lectures, videos, guest speakers, and group exercises, this course addresses business strategies that affect the natural environment and the ways business strategies and practices can produce "win-win" outcomes that are both good for the environment and good for business.

QUESTIONS TO CONSIDER:

Does any required course contain some element of Social Impact Management? **YES**

Is any required course entirely dedicated to social, environmental, or ethical issues? **NO**

Is there a Net Impact Chapter on campus? **YES**

HEC School of Management—Paris (École des Hautes Études Commerciales)

Jouy-en-Josas, France

THE ASPEN INSTITUTE
Center for Business Education

ANNUAL EVENTS:

■ *Equation Forum*

The Equation Forum is an innovative forum that brings together students from 15 schools with the aim of increasing awareness about the main issues concerning sustainable development. Workshops and debates conducted by students and company representatives allow for a realistic introduction to the opportunities created by greater awareness.

■ *HEC – ESADE Roundtable on CEO Board CSR*

Corporate governance and social responsibility are key issues for European companies. The founding meeting of the ESADE--HEC CEO Board Forum aims at identifying key challenges and appropriate answers at Board level regarding these issues. This forum brings together an elite group of directors, CEOs, and business experts from ESADE and HEC faculty and is orientated toward the exchange of corporate experiences, joint research endeavors, and the formulation of educational proposals regarding corporate governance and social responsibility.

OTHER PROGRAMS:

■ *HEC Net Impact*

The HEC Net Impact club researches issues regarding corporate sustainability to promote awareness and facilitate their integration into core business teaching. By organizing internal debates, inviting prominent outside speakers, and involving the HEC community at large, Net Impact plays a fundamental role in promoting those causes implicitly related in social impact as well as environmental management.

STUDENT CLUBS AND PROGRAMS:

■ *HEC Women in Leadership*

The HEC Women in Leadership club promotes the pivotal role that women leaders can play in today's global world. Ongoing club activities include conferences by outside female speakers and informational sessions and partnerships with leading women's groups; activities are open to all MBA students.

■ *The Sustainable Development Committee*

The Sustainable Development Committee was created with the mission of helping the group define and put in place a concrete policy of social and environmental responsibility, by making everyone within the group aware of the role they play. The committee has numerous focuses such as teaching and research, campus life, and communication. MBA students work with the committee and are primarily concerned with improving awareness of sustainability issues within the school.

SCHOOL DEMOGRAPHICS	
Number of Full-Time Students	370
International Students	80%
Female Students	27%
Pre-MBA Employment:	

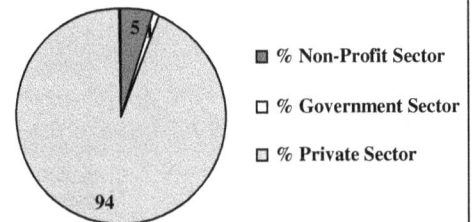

■ % Non-Profit Sector
□ % Government Sector
□ % Private Sector

2006/2007 School Year

THE CENTER FOR BUSINESS EDUCATION'S BOTTOM LINE ON HEC SCHOOL OF MANAGEMENT-PARIS:
Compared to other business schools in our survey, HEC School of Management-Paris offers a good number of courses featuring relevant content, and does a good job in those courses explicitly addressing how mainstream business improves the world. HEC School of Management-Paris requires 3 core courses featuring relevant content.

A Closer Look at:
IE Business School
Business School / Madrid, Spain
http://www.ie.edu/

WHAT THE SCHOOL SAYS:
Since its inception, IE Business School's commitment to society has permeated every aspect of the school. This commitment culminated in the creation of a dedicated department, Social Impact Management at IE, which now plays a pivotal role in the day-to-day fabric of the school.

A QUICK LOOK

NOTE: All information is self-reported data submitted to the Center for Business Education

COURSES*

Accounting (8)
Business & Government (1)
Business Law (5)
Economics (6)
Entrepreneurship (9)
Finance (8)
HR Management (9)
Information Technology (3)
General Management (5)
Marketing (7)
Operations Management (8)
Strategy (10)

KEY CONCENTRATIONS

Social Entrepreneurship

ACTIVITIES*

Speakers/Seminars (12)
Orientation Activities (1)
Internship/Consulting (3)
Student Competitions (2)
Clubs & Programs (3)
Career Development (1)
Institutes/Centers (4)
Concentrations (1)

* Figures in parentheses indicate the number of courses/activities that, in whole or in part, integrate social, environmental, or ethical perspectives

NOTABLE FEATURES

CORE COURSES:

Strategy and Marketing Plan
This course stresses the growing importance of social responsibility in the corporate environment. Companies should pay increased attention to issues such as balanced development and growth of host countries where they operate and to environmental concerns, particularly in less developed countries. In the marketing arena, special attention is focused on matters such as ethical behavior regarding misleading communications and advertising, and bribery practices.

Country Economic Analysis
This course addresses the issues of development and sustainability by exploring paths of economic development and higher human welfare and the limitations of current growth models in terms of their environmental and social impact. The role of institutions, corruption, and income equality in economic success is discussed in the context of specific country cases.

ELECTIVE COURSES:

Customer Relationship Management (CRM)
The course looks at CRM not as a software program that must be installed and run in order to turn the firm into a customer-centric one, but as a radical change in philosophy that affects every person in every department, supported by software. Social impact management topics covered in this course include ethical implications of customer valuation techniques and corporate social responsibility as a competitive tool.

Strategy, Culture, and Ethics
This course will provide the means to help the student identify incoherencies between the organization's "official" values and the implicit values in the organizational culture. This course will underline the nature of the inherent ethical dilemmas in modern organizations, their causes and possible solutions.

INSTITUTES AND CENTERS:

PwC & IE Centre for Corporate Responsibility
The PwC & IE Centre for Corporate Responsibility (CR) is a joint initiative of IE and PriceWaterhouseCoopers that focuses on research, training, and the dissemination of CR material in three basic areas: good governance and transparency, environment and sustainability, and society and diversity.

Centre for Diversity in Global Management
The Centre for Diversity in Global Management's mission is to promote diversity management of gender, culture, personality, and age as a competitive advantage in the corporate world, through reflection, creation of knowledge, and the dissemination of know-how.

QUESTIONS TO CONSIDER:

Does any required course contain some element of Social Impact Management? **YES**

Is any required course entirely dedicated to social, environmental, or ethical issues? **NO**

Is there a Net Impact Chapter on campus? **YES**

A Closer Look at:
IE Business School
Business School / Madrid, Spain

ANNUAL EVENTS:

Corporate Responsibility Tribune

The Corporate Responsibility Tribune is a joint initiative by IE Business School, PriceWaterhouseCoopers, and Expansión, whose main aim is to bring the CR discussion to the highest levels of European companies, ranging from board members, CEOs, and top management, to high government officers, NGOs, and other social representatives together with academia. It is intended to serve as a catalyst between all the different stakeholders and thus bring input from all ends, enriching the CR discussion while adding value to all participants.

Eco-Intelligent Management Conferences

Eco-intelligent innovations go well beyond the incremental improvements sought by standard environmental management and eco-efficiency. Achieving eco-intelligence requires altering product design criteria, renegotiating relationships with suppliers, developing new human resources skills, changing the company's technology and manufacturing processes, and developing new relationships with customers.

The Social Entrepreneurship Business Plan Competition

The Social Entrepreneurship Business Plan Competition has been created to foster projects that have social impact as a central component of the enterprise; this while being both economically and socially sustainable, and having strong potential for implementation in other countries.

OTHER PROGRAMS:

Internship—Fundación Bip-Bip

IE students spend a year long internship working as volunteers at Bip-Bip in Spain. Bip-Bip is an NGO that focuses on integrating people through technology. It offers spaces equipped with internet-enabled computers from which people without resources or at risk of exclusion receive social integration and labor insertion education.

STUDENT CLUBS AND PROGRAMS:

DiversitIE Club

This club serves as a platform for women studying at IE by pursuing two main objectives. First, addressing issues that are of common interest, and second to making them known to other IE students, alumni, prospective students, and recruiters.

Entrepreneurship Club

The mission of the IE Entrepreneurship Club is to continuously provide its members with access to knowledge and experiences from professors, alumni, students, and other professionals. The main objective of the entrepreneurship club is to foster the creation and development of new businesses by IE students and alumni while raising awareness and promotion of social entrepreneurship and corporate responsibility.

SCHOOL DEMOGRAPHICS

Number of Full-Time Students	823
International Students	76%
Female Students	36%

Pre-MBA Employment:

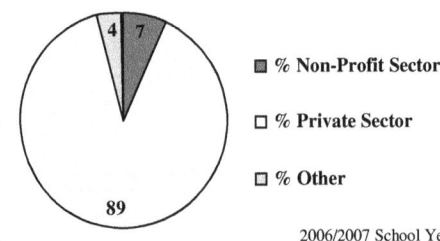

- ■ % Non-Profit Sector
- □ % Private Sector
- □ % Other

4 | 7 | 89

2006/2007 School Year

THE CENTER FOR BUSINESS EDUCATION'S BOTTOM LINE ON IE BUSINESS SCHOOL:
Compared to other business schools in our survey, IE Business School offers a truly extraordinary number of courses featuring relevant content, and does a truly extraordinary job in those courses explicitly addressing how mainstream business improves the world. IE Business School requires 40 core courses featuring relevant content.

A Closer Look at:
IESA

Instituto de Estudios Superiores de Administracion / Caracas, Venezuela
www.iesa.edu.ve/

WHAT THE SCHOOL SAYS:

To prepare MBA students to manage social and environmental issues, contribute to societal development, and instill social responsibility values, IESA combines academic and extracurricular inputs that build on its mission: "To prepare individuals capable of assuming leadership positions in business, management, and the professions; and contribute to the success of public, private, and not-for-profit organizations."

A QUICK LOOK

NOTE: All information is self-reported data submitted to the Center for Business Education

COURSES*

Business & Government (1)
CSR/Business Ethics (2)
Economics (3)
HR Management (2)
General Management (1)
Organizational Behavior (3)
Public/Nonprofit Mgt (2)
Strategy (1)

KEY CONCENTRATIONS

Organizations

KEY JOINT DEGREES

**MBA & Masters in
  International Business**

ACTIVITIES*

Speakers/Seminars (9)
Orientation Activities (1)
Internship/Consulting (1)
Student Competitions (1)
Career Development (1)
Institutes/Centers (12)
Concentrations (4)
Joint Degrees (1)

* Figures in parentheses indicate the number of courses/activities that, in whole or in part, integrate social, environmental, or ethical perspectives

NOTABLE FEATURES

CORE COURSES:

Enterprise, State and Society
The state, the market, and the not-for-profit private sector play different roles in society, but inter-relations among the three sectors are inevitable. Thus, this course stresses the importance of understanding that the borders of each sector are becoming increasingly blurred and the use of inter-sector cooperation mechanisms are increasingly frequent and essential for society's well-being, that effective management of these interrelations is crucial for success in business, and that governments face severe limitations to ensuring the common good on their own.

Personal Development
Personal Development is a series of workshops the Ethics workshop aims to make students aware of the ethical dimension of their decisions; the Tasks to Attend session encourages students to reflect on the country's social, economic, and political realities; and the Social Responsibility workshop examines corporate social initiatives and competitive advantages obtained by firms able to generate social as well as economic value.

ELECTIVE COURSES:

Social Responsibility in Latin America
In this course, students are expected to become acquainted with diverse conceptualizations of corporate social responsibility and the debate over the scope of CSR and its features in Latin America. Students willl also examine the impact of CSR on local communities, the relevance of partnership strategies in CSR, the relation between CSR and sustainable development, and the use of intervention strategies for local development.

Business with Low Income Sectors (LIS)
This course discusses how market initiatives focused on LIS generate social value in addition to profit. Promoting business ventures that draw on LIS as consumers, suppliers, or business partners invites reflection on isues such as the role of private enterprise in fighting poverty and promoting social development.

INSTITUTES AND CENTERS:

IESA International Center for Energy and Environmental Studies (CIEEA)
CIEEA promotes the generation of, reflection on, and dissemination of knowledge on energy and the environment, together with the preparation of managers with leadership skills for the local, regional, and international context. CIEEA undertakes applied research on relevant issues that feature major social impact and promote investment and development in ways that are sustainable from an economic, financial, environmental, and political standpoint.

The IESA Marketing Center
The IESA Marketing Center seeks to contribute to the understanding and development of the Venezuelan market by stimulating management capacity; updating concepts, approaches, and methods; and managing of relevant information for marketing decisions. The Marketing Center is also conducting important research on low income consumers/bottom of the pyramid.

QUESTIONS TO CONSIDER:

Does any required course contain some element of Social Impact Management? **YES**

Is any required course entirely dedicated to social, environmental, or ethical issues? **YES**

Is there a Net Impact Chapter on campus? **NO**

A Closer Look at:
IESA

Instituto de Estudios Superiores de Administracion / Caracas, Venezuela

ANNUAL EVENTS:

■ *Competition on Social Responsibility—Sumaq Alliance*
The goal of IESA's first Competition on Social Responsibility is to show students how social responsibility and social enterprises can also be profitable.

OTHER PROGRAMS:

■ *SEKN (Social Enterprise Knowledge Network) - IESA Chapter*
The SEKN is an association of business schools in Latin America and Spain. Its purpose is to develop intellectual capital focused on social initiatives within each school's area of influence. The SEKN-IESA chapter features an advisory board made up of distinguished business leaders representing major multinational and local companies and leaders of noted NGOs. Projects managed over two-year cycles center around issues such as social initiatives led by private enterprise and not-for-profit organizations and business-led market initiatives that improve the living conditions of low income sectors. Biannual SEKN meetings take place where faculty gather to share results of their research in the field and to discuss administrative issues of the alliance.

■ *Leaders in Action Seminar: "The Challenge of Turning Health Care into a Mass Market Product"*
In this seminar, IESA presents the case of a very successful social initiative of in Caracas, which unites the basics of a business with the goal of social responsibility projects: profit and social care.

SCHOOL DEMOGRAPHICS	
Number of Full-Time Students	69
International Students	6%
Female Students	42%
	2006/2007 School Year

THE CENTER FOR BUSINESS EDUCATION'S BOTTOM LINE ON IESA:
Compared to other business schools in our survey, IESA offers a good number of courses featuring relevant content, and does a good job in those courses explicitly addressing how mainstream business improves the world. IESA requires 6 core courses featuring relevant content.

A Closer Look at:
Illinois Institute of Technology

Stuart Graduate School of Business / Chicago, IL

http://www.stuart.iit.edu/programs_mba/

WHAT THE SCHOOL SAYS:

The Stuart School of Business at the Illinois Institute of Technology provides students an enhanced MBA curriculum that prepares them for managing in the "Next Economy." The "Next Economy" is driven by globalization, demographics, technology, and the environment. The program focuses in strategic competitiveness, which is best exemplified by the concepts of innovation, creativity, sustainability, leadership, and entrepreneurship.

A QUICK LOOK

NOTE: All information is self-reported data submitted to the Center for Business Education

COURSES*

Accounting (2)
CSR/Business Ethics (1)
Economics (1)
Environmental (11)
Information Technology (1)
International Management (1)
General Management (1)
Marketing (2)
Organizational Behavior (1)
Operations Management (1)
Strategy (1)

KEY CONCENTRATIONS

Sustainable Enterprise

KEY JOINT DEGREES

MBA & MS in Environmental Management

ACTIVITIES*

Speakers/Seminars (10)
Orientation Activities (1)
Internship/Consulting (5)
Student Competitions (1)
Clubs & Programs (1)
Career Development (1)
Institutes/Centers (1)
Concentrations (1)
Joint Degrees (2)

* Figures in parentheses indicate the number of courses/activities that, in whole or in part, integrate social, environmental, or ethical perspectives

NOTABLE FEATURES

CORE COURSES:

▓ *Managerial Accounting*

This course is an introduction to the basic financial and managerial accounting topics: GAAP, major financial statements, accrual accounting, financial reporting alternatives, financial statement analysis, cost behavior, cost systems, short- and long-term decision making and product costing, and a review of environmental accounting.

▓ *Marketing*

This course is an introduction to marketing concepts, processes, function, and institutions. Topics include economic, cultural, and behavioral foundations of marketing, market segmentation, product positioning, green marketing, marketing mix, the product life cycle, and linkages with the company's other functional areas.

ELECTIVE COURSES:

▓ *Legal, Ethical, and Political Issues in Business*

This course is an exploration of the social foundations of law and ethics and selected topics of law and public policy. It covers topics in commercial law (traditional and emerging), legal and social control mechanisms of corporations (antitrust, securities, regulation, corporate responsibilities), and classic and emerging legal issues (employment, environmental, and international law).

▓ *Business Strategy: The Sustainable Enterprise*

This course integrates environmental management issues with the use of strategic planning tools for assessing and responding to competitive and social forces. Emphasis will be on the company's ability to build and sustain a competitive advantage utilizing traditional management concepts as and new sustainability practices.

INSTITUTES AND CENTERS:

▓ *Center for Sustainable Enterprise (CSE)*

The CSE serves as a resource center where business, academic, government agency, and NGO communities collaborate to identify, develop, communicate, and help implement practical and equitable business strategies to advance the ecological and economic sustainability of the Greater Chicago area. The center is engaged in the research of a unique prototype wind turbine in Chicago, the only one of its kind in the world. Research also includes projects for carbon footprint reduction, life-cycle analyses for a company's new product, developing the next-generation product for carbon emission reduction, and a remote lighting system operating totally off the grid. The CSE also hosts several conferences and seminars throughout the year.

QUESTIONS TO CONSIDER:

Does any required course contain some element of Social Impact Management? **YES**

Is any required course entirely dedicated to social, environmental, or ethical issues? **NO**

Is there a Net Impact Chapter on campus? **NO**

Illinois Institute of Technology

Stuart Graduate School of Business / Chicago, IL

ANNUAL EVENTS:

■ *Networking Event*

Every December, IIT-Stuart hosts a reunion for all of its students or alumni who either graduated with an MBA and a concentration in sustainable enterprise or graduated with an MS in environmental management. This reunion is held at the school in conjunction with the holiday reception of the Air & Waste Management Association, the most active environmental trade organization in the Chicago area. This event gives the students/alumni an excellent opportunity to network with professionals in the various industries in the Greater Chicago area.

■ *MidWest Audit Roundtable*

This event brings together environmental auditors and Stuart students to listen to speakers who discuss various topics in the areas of environmental management, remediation, auditing, and sustainability.

OTHER PROGRAMS:

■ *Illinois Environmental Protection Agency (IL EPA) Internship*

Illinois corporations submit proposals for environmental projects to be funded jointly by the company and IL EPA. The agency then solicits applications from IIT-Stuart students to work on these projects. A representative of IL EPA then interviews IIT-Stuart students every spring to work on these pollution-prevention projects during the summer.

■ *Chicago Sustainable Business Alliance*

Once a month, IIT-Stuart's Center for Sustainable Enterprise hosts an event for members of the Chicago Sustainable Business Alliance to meet for breakfast, network, and listen to a speaker. The alliance consists of SMEs, large corporations, NGOs, government and individuals all interested in furthering sustainability in their organization and the Greater Chicago community. Students are invited to attend this event as a learning experience and for career enhancement.

STUDENT CLUBS AND PROGRAMS:

■ *Stuart Consulting Club*

The Stuart Consulting Club is a student-driven organization that aims to provide students with valuable consulting experience on business projects as well as planning a speaker session for all Stuart students. It is through this organization that students volunteer for the Innovate Illinois competition, where companies in the environmental, service, and manufacturing sectors compete for monetary awards to be used by the company for its growth; students from various schools volunteer to assist an assigned company with its study and presentation.

SCHOOL DEMOGRAPHICS	
Number of Full-Time Students	86
International Students	68%
Female Students	42%

Pre-MBA Employment:

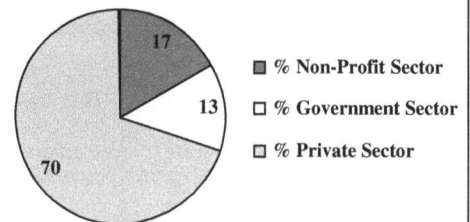

- ■ % Non-Profit Sector
- □ % Government Sector
- □ % Private Sector

17
13
70

2006/2007 School Year

THE CENTER FOR BUSINESS EDUCATION'S BOTTOM LINE ON ILLINOIS INSTITUTE OF TECHNOLOGY:

Compared to other business schools in our survey, Illinois Institute of Technology offers an excellent number of courses featuring relevant content, and does a truly extraordinary job in those courses explicitly addressing how mainstream business improves the world. Illinois Institute of Technology requires 5 core courses featuring relevant content.

A Closer Look at:

IMD—International Institute for Management Development

Lausanne, Switzerland
http://www.imd.ch/programs/mba/index.cfm

THE ASPEN INSTITUTE
Center for Business Education

WHAT THE SCHOOL SAYS:

The IMD MBA program is focused on leadership. Social responsibility is a key program element and social and ethical issues are integrated to both daily classroom discussions and specific elements of the program. Representing more than 40 nationalities, participants have the opportunity to explore social responsibility issues from multiple perspectives, providing for a rich classroom experience.

A QUICK LOOK

NOTE: All information is self-reported data submitted to the Center for Business Education

COURSES*

Accounting (2)
Business & Government (1)
CSR/Business Ethics (3)
Economics (2)
Entrepreneurship (3)
Information Technology (1)
International Management (1)
General Management (2)
Marketing (1)
Organizational Behavior (4)
Strategy (1)

ACTIVITIES*

Clubs & Programs (2)
Career Development (1)
Institutes/Centers (2)

* Figures in parentheses indicate the number of courses/activities that, in whole or in part, integrate social, environmental, or ethical perspectives

NOTABLE FEATURES

CORE COURSES:

Accounting

This course addresses issues of environmental sensitivity and remediation; contract risk; bribery and corruption in overseas operations; hubris, greed, and remuneration policies; tax evasion and transfer pricing; transparency; corporate failure; and international taxation. Some of these topics are covered in classes on internal controls and risk management; others are covered as they arise in relation to M&A activities.

Stakeholder Management and Ethics

This ethics module discusses ethical, social, and business issues from different ethical perspectives (not from an underlying, presumed dominant view) by challenging students to discuss which perspectives are relevant for a viable global business world, using case studies and workshop exercises. It takes place within a module on stakeholder management where students discuss the relationship with NGOs, government, the investment community, the press, and employees and how effective leaders must work closely with all constituencies.

ELECTIVE COURSES:

Meeting Global Challenges in the 21st Century

The objectives of this course are to address the key challenges of the global environment and the means for business to be more effective in solving them. Emphasis is given especially to the business executive as a global citizen and leader. Students will develop a better understanding of the structures, strategies, and methods of some of the key international organizations and NGOs.

Entrepreneurship

This elective on addresses the following issues through case studies and speakers: entrepreneurship evolution over generations in the context of societal and environmental changes; connecting entrepreneurship with corporate social responsibility; and ethical, environmental, and societal benefits for suppliers in developing countries.

INSTITUTES AND CENTERS:

Forum for Corporate Sustainability Management

The Forum for Corporate Sustainability Management is IMD's corporate sustainability research initiative. Corporations participate in the forum to build a sustainable business advantage through social and environmental strategic action.

Evian Group

The Evian Group is an international coalition of corporate, government, and opinion leaders committed to fostering an open, inclusive, equitable, and sustainable global market economy in a rules-based multilateral framework. The Evian Group advocates trade liberalization to achieve growth and sustain the momentum of globalisation. The Evian Group believes that international trade and investment has the great potential of uniting people through greater mutual understanding and common interest across countries, continents, cultures, and generations, rather than dividing them.

QUESTIONS TO CONSIDER:

Does any required course contain some element of Social Impact Management? **YES**

Is any required course entirely dedicated to social, environmental, or ethical issues? **YES**

Is there a Net Impact Chapter on campus? **YES**

A Closer Look at:
IMD - International Institute for Management Development
Lausanne, Switzerland

ANNUAL EVENTS:

■ *Discovery Expedition*

The Discovery Expedition is a trip to a developing country (previously Argentina, Bosnia-Herzegovina, and South Africa) where students meet with leaders from business, government, and civil society to learn what it takes to do business in a difficult business environment and how business can make a difference in leading a country forward. Each year following the Discovery Expedition trips, students organize fund-raising efforts to benefit specific educational organizations in those countries.

OTHER PROGRAMS:

■ *Career Services*

IMD's extensive career services helps participants find their next career step. This may include positions in industry, NGOs, consulting, or financial services. When participants identify social impact and/or environmental management as their career goal, career services works with them to identify potential companies through on-campus recruiting, the IMD alumni network, and the IMD learning network companies.

STUDENT CLUBS AND PROGRAMS:

■ *Net Impact*

IMD participants have started a Net Impact chapter to share their experiences and interests in corporate social responsibility and NGO work.

SCHOOL DEMOGRAPHICS

Number of Full-Time Students   **90**

International Students   **98%**

Female Students   **18%**

Pre-MBA Employment:

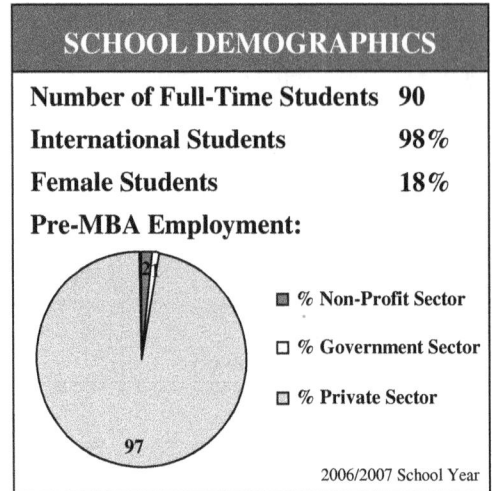

■ % Non-Profit Sector

□ % Government Sector

□ % Private Sector

2006/2007 School Year

THE CENTER FOR BUSINESS EDUCATION'S BOTTOM LINE ON IMD—INTERNATIONAL INSTITUTE FOR MANAGEMENT DEVELOPMENT:
Compared to other business schools in our survey, IMD offers an excellent number of courses featuring relevant content, and does a good job in those courses explicitly addressing how mainstream business improves the world. IMD requires 13 core courses featuring relevant content.

A Closer Look at:
INSEAD (Institut Européen d'Administration des Affaires)
Fontainebleau, France / Singapore
http://www.insead.edu/mba/

WHAT THE SCHOOL SAYS:
We encourage participants in each core course to address social and environmental issues within that discipline. Outside the classroom, student clubs (together with the INSEAD research centers) organize regular sessions and conferences that include alumni and outside speakers.

A QUICK LOOK

NOTE: All information is self-reported data submitted to the Center for Business Education

COURSES*

Accounting (1)
Business & Government (2)
Business Law (1)
CSR/Business Ethics (2)
Economics (3)
Entrepreneurship (3)
Environmental (1)
Finance (2)
Organizational Behavior (2)
Public/Nonprofit Mgt (1)
Quantitative Methods (1)
Strategy (4)

ACTIVITIES*

Speakers/Seminars (7)
Internship/Consulting (2)
Clubs & Programs (4)
Career Development (1)
Institutes/Centers (2)

*Figures in parentheses indicate the number of courses/activities that, in whole or in part, integrate social, environmental, or ethical perspectives

NOTABLE FEATURES

CORE COURSES:

▣ Management, Culture and Values
This introductory module presents issues related to the role of business in society, such as ethical dilemmas in business, the role of values, and inequality.

▣ Macroeconomics in the Global Economy
This course provides an overview of the macroeconomic environment in which companies operate. Class discussions include topics such as economic development, the role of economic policies and the influence of the private sector, and income inequality.

ELECTIVE COURSES:

▣ Environmental Management and Corporate Responsibility in a Global Economy
This class explores a number of the most important challenges firms face in integrating growing public expectations for improved environmental performance with a successful competitive strategy. It also explores the relationship between environmental management and corporate social responsibility and critically examines the risks, opportunities, and challenges associated with managing a "responsible" global corporation in a highly competitive global economy.

▣ Economics and Management in Developing Countries
The objective of this course is to provide future managers with a set of tools for understanding the political economy of development and to apply these tools to a number of challenges—economic, political, managerial, and ethical—that investors, and in particular foreign investors, confront in the developing world. Students learn an analytical framework for studying issues of poverty, inequality, and economic development and growth, and examine important managerial and ethical dilemmas facing multinational firms in the developing world.

INSTITUTES AND CENTERS:

▣ INSEAD Business in Society (IBiS)
Within INSEAD, IBiS provides the focal point for activities aimed at creating a sustainable business environment that encompasses the millions of people now left largely outside the market economy. IBiS has incorporated the Centre for the Management of Environmental and Social Responsibility and has enlarged its portfolio of activities.

▣ Healthcare Management Initiative (HMI)
HMI aims to encourage and support innovative and rigorous management research on challenges facing the healthcare sector and to diffuse new knowledge through publication, MBA teaching, executive education, and stakeholder consultation. The intent is to make INSEAD an international point of reference in healthcare management.

QUESTIONS TO CONSIDER:

Does any required course contain some element of Social Impact Management? **YES**

Is any required course entirely dedicated to social, environmental, or ethical issues? **YES**

Is there a Net Impact Chapter on campus? **YES**

A Closer Look at:

INSEAD (Institut Européen d'Administration des Affaires)

Fontainebleau, France / Singapore

ANNUAL EVENTS:

INSEAD Sustainability Executive Roundtable

The INSEAD Sustainability Executive Roundtable is a quarterly event organized by INSEAD Business in Society. The roundtable brings together senior INSEAD alumni to discuss the business impact of sustainable development. These meetings attract senior executives who, via the roundtable, can share their experiences and debate the challenges related to sustainability. Keynote speakers highlight the major issues of a given topic, leaving the majority of the roundtable meeting time open for discussion.

Executive Program on Humanitarian Operations

The Executive Program on Humanitarian Operations is a five-day program that addresses the management issues specific to the humanitarian sector. This program also provides participants with a common management framework through which they can share their experienced-based knowledge.

OTHER PROGRAMS:

INSEAD-Lewa Challenge in Kenya

The INSEAD-Lewa Challenge is designed to give MBAs the opportunity to make a difference in a challenging work environment. Selected students spend 10 days on the Lewa Wildlife Conservancy, a 65,000-acre property located in Kenya's Rift Valley. Students assist the organization in achieving its ultimate goal of finding ways of generating revenue through for-profit businesses while preserving the integrity of the wildlife and nature. Projects have included a microfinancing bank, a potential bottled water business, housing projects, and an electricity project.

INSEAD's Career Services (CS)

INSEAD's CS has one dedicated representative for not-for-profit and CSR-related employment opportunities. CS provides one-on-one advising sessions, conducts career panels and workshops, and actively assists student groups in organizing peer-to-peer sessions and speaker events. INSEAD's CS works closely with numerous Not-for-profit organizations, Consulting firms that operate in not-for-profit or development sectors, and for-profit companies that pursue socially responsible business practices.

SCHOOL DEMOGRAPHICS	
Number of Full-Time Students	1790
International Students	89%
Female Students	25%
Pre-MBA Employment:	

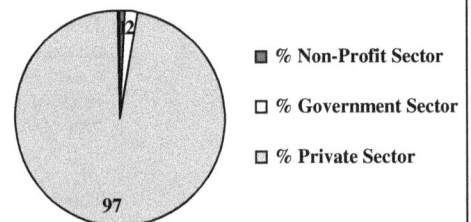

- ■ % Non-Profit Sector
- □ % Government Sector
- □ % Private Sector

2006/2007 School Year

STUDENT CLUBS AND PROGRAMS:

INSEAD International Development Organization (INDEVOR)

INDEVOR serves as a forum for those interested in social, environmental, and ethical issues, often bridging the gap between business and the social sector. It seeks to channel student aspirations in the areas of international development, non-profit, social entrepreneurship, and socially responsible businesses into practical activities that benefit its participants and the community at large.

INSEAD Energy Club

The INSEAD Energy Club aims to be a forum for discussion and networking on energy-related issues for all the entire INSEAD community. It promotes awareness on campus of the issues faced by the energy economy and its political, social, and environmental impact within the context of balanced debate on energy needs and usage. The Energy Club leverages the alumni network and INSEAD's existing corporate relationships in order to provide career services and to support future entrepreneurs in nascent industries such as alternative energy sources, new technologies, and energy trading.

THE CENTER FOR BUSINESS EDUCATION'S BOTTOM LINE ON INSEAD:
Compared to other business schools in our survey, INSEAD offers an excellent number of courses featuring relevant content, and does a good job in those courses explicitly addressing how mainstream business improves the world. INSEAD requires 9 core courses featuring relevant content.

A Closer Look at:
Iowa State University
College of Business / Ames, IA
http://www.bus.iastate.edu/mba/

WHAT THE SCHOOL SAYS:
The Iowa State MBA provides students with an understanding of the values of business and society and the ethical and legal consequences of business decisions and practices.

A QUICK LOOK

NOTE: All information is self-reported data submitted to the Center for Business Education

COURSES*

Accounting (**2**)
CSR/Business Ethics (**1**)
HR Management (**2**)
Information Technology (**2**)
General Management (**1**)
Marketing (**1**)
Organizational Behavior (**1**)
Operations Management (**1**)
Strategy (**3**)

KEY CONCENTRATIONS

Sustainable Agriculture

ACTIVITIES*

Speakers/Seminars (**4**)
Student Competitions (**1**)
Clubs & Programs (**1**)
Institutes/Centers (**1**)
Concentrations (**1**)

* Figures in parentheses indicate the number of courses/activities that, in whole or in part, integrate social, environmental, or ethical perspectives

NOTABLE FEATURES

CORE COURSES:
Business Ethics and Corporate Social Responsibility
This course is designed to provide students with an understanding of the values of business and society to present some ethical models used to make decisions. The course examines ethics in a business context, focusing on dilemmas that managers encounter when dealing with employees and other stakeholders. Decisions affecting customers, the community, government/society, and other countries also reflect the values and ethics of the corporation; thus the course examines some important decisions arising in these relationships.

Management Information Systems
Course content relates to social issues pertaining to ethical and privacy issues with Information Technolody (IT). Numerous topics are discussed related to social and ethical management, security management, socially responsible use of technology, etc. Topics include ethics, privacy, use of technology for social good, misuse of technology, issues related to the digital divide, management responsibility related to IT resources, and applications of IT in developing countries.

ELECTIVE COURSES:
Corporate Governance and Leadership
This course deals with the control functions and managerial issues surrounding the board of directors and CEOs of firms. It examines the work of top managers and corporate boards of directors in terms of roles, responsibilities, and tasks. Some of the topics include CEO tenure and compensation, board monitoring and composition, CEO and board roles in strategic management, shareholder and stakeholder representation, corporate social responsibility, ethics and corporate governance, international governance, and executive leadership style.

International Accounting
Differential accounting standards and potential conflicts in reporting standards in global business are major themes of this course. The course explicitly considers international accounting patterns, culture, and development. The constructs of professional responsibility, ethical development, and culture are examined. The course considers the relationship between governments and multinational corporations, especially with respect to taxation.

INSTITUTES AND CENTERS:
Iowa State University Pappajohn Center for Entrepreneurship
The Pappajohn Center for Entrepreneurship is the catalyst that brings together the people and ideas necessary for launching or growing successful enterprises. The Center works to help grow the economy in Iowa by helping launch new companies or organizations, assisting existing enterprises in their growth strategies, encouraging successful businesses to tap into global markets, and providing students with the opportunity to learn by actively working side-by-side with entrepreneurs.

QUESTIONS TO CONSIDER:

Does any required course contain some element of Social Impact Management? **YES**

Is any required course entirely dedicated to social, environmental, or ethical issues? **YES**

Is there a Net Impact Chapter on campus? **NO**

A Closer Look at:
Iowa State University
College of Business / Ames, IA

ANNUAL EVENTS:

■ *Iowa State University MBA Case Competition*

Iowa State MBA students compete in an internal case competition at the conclusion of their first year of study. Teams are given one day to analyze a strategic management case and then present their findings and recommendations to a panel of judges composed of faculty and business executives. Students are expected to consider social and environmental implications when analyzing the case and preparing recommendations. Team and individual awards are presented to the top performers.

■ *Contemporary Issues in Accounting Conference*

This conference includes a plenary session on ethics followed by breakout sessions.

STUDENT CLUBS AND PROGRAMS:

■ *MBA Association*

The MBA Association, a student-led organization, works with the local United Way to conduct workshops for directors and staff employed in various human services agencies throughout the county. A sample of workshop topics includes accounting for non-profits, developing a marketing plan, strategic planning, creating an effective Web presence, team-building, and managing human resources. Teams of MBA students prepare and present these workshops under the guidance of MBA faculty.

SCHOOL DEMOGRAPHICS	
Number of Full-Time Students	67
International Students	41%
Female Students	44%
	2006/2007 School Year

THE CENTER FOR BUSINESS EDUCATION'S BOTTOM LINE ON IOWA STATE UNIVERSITY:

Compared to other business schools in our survey, Iowa State University offers a good number of courses featuring relevant content, and requires 5 core courses featuring relevant content.

ITESM (EGADE Monterrey)

EGADE (Graduate School of Business Administration and Leadership)

San Pedro Garza Garcia, Mexico

http://www.mty.itesm.mx/rectoria/pi/internacional/

THE ASPEN INSTITUTE
Center for Business Education

WHAT THE SCHOOL SAYS:

Tecnológico de Monterrey's EGADE is increasingly becoming a leadership school whose academic and research work has a positive impact on the private, public, and social sectors. EGADE is a leading-edge education institution interested in contributing to environmental conservation and in addressing the complex social issues from an integral perspective.

A QUICK LOOK

NOTE: All information is self-reported data submitted to the Center for Business Education

COURSES*

CSR/Business Ethics (2)
Economics (2)
Entrepreneurship (5)
Environmental (1)
Finance (5)
HR Management (1)
Information Technology (1)
International Management (4)
Marketing (6)
Organizational Behavior (5)
Operations Management (1)
Quantitative Methods (1)
Strategy (8)

ACTIVITIES*

Speakers/Seminars (24)
Orientation Activities (1)
Internship/Consulting (1)
Institutes/Centers (5)

* Figures in parentheses indicate the number of courses/activities that, in whole or in part, integrate social, environmental, or ethical perspectives

NOTABLE FEATURES

CORE COURSES:

▣ *Leadership for Sustainable Development*

This course discusses environmental impact management topics that include environmental policies and standards and voluntary programs, product responsibility, toxics release inventory, and the life cycle of products and the role of suppliers in the life cycle. Social impact management topics discussed include integrity and accountability in reporting systems; potential conflicts of reporting standards in global business; and operating in economically disadvantaged areas and emerging markets.

▣ *Field Project*

The Field Project course is an opportunity for students to demonstrate core competencies developed in their studies. Project opportunities address social and environmental concerns such as consulting to green or social entrepreneurs, research on leadership traits for sustainability, development of educational materials for sustainable consumption, and community engagement initiatives.

ELECTIVE COURSES:

▣ *Corruption and Corporate Governance in Latin American Business*

This course examines the most significant social issue and ethical problem in Latin America: corruption. The inability of Latin American governments to enforce health, safety, and environmental regulation throughout the region has had a tremendous human and environmental cost. The course analyzes the economic, cultural, and institutional roots of the problem and examines proposed solutions based on public administration reform, business policy, and technological innovation.

▣ *Integral Marketing Communications*

This course discusses labor practices in foreign countries and the diffusion of these practices in the media as an example of brand image deterioration. Students read an article on democratic inclusion of all stakeholders in corporate governance as a means to solve these types of social conflicts between economic goals of the company and community interests.

INSTITUTES AND CENTERS:

▣ *Faculty Chair in Sustainable Development*

This faculty group has the purpose of developing relevant research related to new business models for the creation of sustainable enterprises in an international context. The group carries out research on topics such as product life- cycle management, competitive advantage, new sustainable business models, eco-efficiency, and inter-sector alliances. Through this group, EGADE promotes the creation of new sustainable business as one of its principal research and academic strategies in order to contribute to the social, economic, and environmental development of the region.

▣ *Base of the Pyramid (BOP) Circle*

The BOP Circle is an initiative to join EGADE with New Ventures Mexico and the World Resources Institute. The circle gathers representatives from business, academia, and nongovernmental organizations involved in the base of the pyramid market with the intention of facilitating development of new business in this sector.

QUESTIONS TO CONSIDER:

Does any required course contain some element of Social Impact Management? **YES**

Is any required course entirely dedicated to social, environmental, or ethical issues? **YES**

Is there a Net Impact Chapter on campus? **NO**

A Closer Look at:
ITESM (EGADE Monterrey)
EGADE (Graduate School of Business Administration and Leadership)
San Pedro Garza Garcia, Mexico

ANNUAL EVENTS:

▪ *Technological Based Business Development Program*

This program focuses on technological firms and entrepreneurs. Its focus is the development of businesses with a technological base and the investigation of best practices and successful business models. There is emphasis on the creation of businesses with a high value-add in the society.

▪ *Transcendent and Successful Women: Building Leadership*

This forum aims for the development of executive and entrepreneurial women in our community. It includes the participation of leading women working in private and social organizations, who share their experience and knowledge about different professional paths and careers and the challenges related to achieving a balanced life.

SCHOOL DEMOGRAPHICS	
Number of Full-Time Students	37
International Students	69%
Female Students	24%
	2006/2007 School Year

OTHER PROGRAMS:

▪ *Corporative Citizenship Seminar*

The Corporative Citizenship Seminar is an online program in collaboration with the World Bank, Tecnológico de Monterrey Virtual University, and COPARMEX (Chamber of Commerce). This program provides examples of firms that have succeeded in their local business environment in order to compete in international markets and the incorporation of sustainable development and corporate responsibility.

THE CENTER FOR BUSINESS EDUCATION'S BOTTOM LINE ON TECNOLÓGICO DE MONTERREY, CAMPUS MONTERREY:
Compared to other business schools in our survey, Tecnológico de Monterrey, Campus Monterrey offers an excellent number of courses featuring relevant content, and does a good job in those courses explicitly addressing how mainstream business improves the world. Tecnológico de Monterrey, Campus Monterrey requires 13 core courses featuring relevant content.

A Closer Look at:
Lamar University
College of Business / Beaumont, TX
http://info.cob.lamar.edu/

WHAT THE SCHOOL SAYS:

The Lamar MBA seeks to prepare students for service to the Southeast Texas region, the nation, and the world through active participation in experiential learning, professional involvement, and civic/cultural activities that impact economic development and societal values.

A QUICK LOOK

NOTE: All information is self-reported data submitted to the Center for Business Education

COURSES*

Business Law (3)
Economics (1)
General Management (2)
Organizational Behavior (1)
Strategy (1)

KEY CONCENTRATIONS

Experiential Business & Entrepreneurship

ACTIVITIES*

Speakers/Seminars (1)
Orientation Activities (1)
Student Competitions (1)
Clubs & Programs (1)
Career Development (1)
Institutes/Centers (1)
Concentrations (1)

*Figures in parentheses indicate the number of courses/activities that, in whole or in part, integrate social, environmental, or ethical perspectives

NOTABLE FEATURES

CORE COURSES:

■ *Business Environment and Ethics*

This course examines the performance of an efficient market. Major market failures, including monopoly power, public goods, externalities, and lack of knowledge, are discussed with respect to how they impede the attainment of free-market benefits. Articles and cases in ethics conclude the course.

■ *Principles of Management*

Students discuss issues related to social responsibility and managerial ethics, particularly regarding managerial decision making. Additionally, students discuss the implications of business ethics in an international and cross-cultural context.

ELECTIVE COURSES:

■ *Environmental Law*

This course emphasizes environmental, health, and safety laws and their impact on business. Topics include social policy and legal framework, administrative and enforcement agencies, and judicial interpretation. Students become aware of the positive aspects of "green" business and businesses, social responsibility toward the environment, in addition to the potential civil and criminal liability for noncompliance with the law.

■ *Employment Law*

This course covers the universe of federal laws dealing with workplace issues, with special emphasis on federal antidiscrimination statutes, and also issues such as labor law, wage and hour law, ERISA, and OSHA. It discusses the evolution of these laws and examines how they were designed to respond to social ills.

INSTITUTES AND CENTERS:

■ *Institute for Entrepreneurial Studies*

The Institute for Entrepreneurial Studies stimulates economic development and diversification in Southeast Texas by addressing the needs of current entrepreneurs and small businesses, while simultaneously enhancing the education of tomorrow's entrepreneurs.

QUESTIONS TO CONSIDER:

Does any required course contain some element of Social Impact Management? **YES**

Is any required course entirely dedicated to social, environmental, or ethical issues? **NO**

Is there a Net Impact Chapter on campus? **NO**

A Closer Look at:
Lamar University
College of Business / Beaumont, TX

ANNUAL EVENTS:

■ *ExxonMobil Executive in Residence Program*

One speaker is chosen by the College of Business each year to discuss social impact and/or environmental management. The executive will present a public lecture, hold discussions with smaller groups, and conduct one session addressing only MBA students.

■ *MBA Exit Exam*

All MBA students are required to complete a written and oral case analysis. Faculty attending, the oral presentation are asked to complete a rubric that measures the students coverage of social responsibility, ethical leadership, ethical decision making, and corporate government issues. This assessment will be used by the College of Business to revise curriculum and other programs.

STUDENT CLUBS AND PROGRAMS:

■ *Cohort MBA*

This group of students has many extracurricular activities on which to focus including the Board of Directors luncheon, the ExxonMobil Executive in Residence luncheon, Meet Your Mentor, Shadowing an Executive, and Study Abroad.

SCHOOL DEMOGRAPHICS	
Number of Full-Time Students	187
International Students	22%
Female Students	47%

2006/2007 School Year

THE CENTER FOR BUSINESS EDUCATION'S BOTTOM LINE ON LAMAR UNIVERSITY:
Compared to other business schools in our survey, Lamar University offers a good number of courses featuring relevant content, and does a good job in those courses explicitly addressing how mainstream business improves the world. Lamar University requires 3 core courses featuring relevant content.

A Closer Look at:
Loyola University Chicago
School of Business Administration / Chicago, IL
http://www.luc.edu/gsb/

THE ASPEN INSTITUTE
Center for Business Education

WHAT THE SCHOOL SAYS:

Loyola University Chicago's School of Business Administration has a long history of alignment with principles of business ethics and social justice. The School of Business Administration develops responsible leaders in an MBA program that combines theory with practice and focuses on effective communication, critical thinking and good judgment, global awareness, and social responsibility.

A QUICK LOOK

NOTE: All information is self-reported data submitted to the Center for Business Education

COURSES*

CSR/Business Ethics (**5**)
Environmental (**2**)
HR Management (**1**)
General Management (**1**)

KEY CONCENTRATIONS

Business Ethics

ACTIVITIES*

Speakers/Seminars (**6**)
Internship/Consulting (**1**)
Clubs & Programs (**1**)
Career Development (**1**)
Institutes/Centers (**2**)
Concentrations (**2**)

* Figures in parentheses indicate the number of courses/activities that, in whole or in part, integrate social, environmental, or ethical perspectives

NOTABLE FEATURES

CORE COURSES:

Business Ethics

This course examines the ethical aspects of individual and corporate decision making in business and provides resources for making ethical decisions within the context of managerial practice. Students will be acquainted with the concepts and principles of ethical reasoning that have been developed in ethical theory,be aware of the specific ethical issues that arise in management and of the ways in which these issues are commonly analyzed, and be able to make sound ethical and managerial decisions and to implement those decisions within the context of an organization in a competitive marketplace.

ELECTIVE COURSES:

Global Environmental Ethics

This course develops an understanding of the ethical issues and responsibilities arising from human interaction with the nonhuman natural environment. Perspectives from various religious traditions, Western philosophy, and the science of ecology are considered. Through this course, students will be able to demonstrate ethical awareness, reflection, and application of ethical principles in decision making.

Microenterprise Consulting

In this course, students utilize and improve their business knowledge and skills by meeting the real-life business consulting needs of individual entrepreneurial and not-for-profit clients starting up or operating businesses in economically distressed communities.

INSTITUTES AND CENTERS:

Center for Ethics and Social Justice

The Center for Ethics and Social Justice at Loyola University Chicago offers ethics education to individuals and organizations within and outside the university, as well as to organizations, to provide them with the specialized skills for greater ethical awareness and judgment that will lead to making better decisions.

Center for Integrated Risk Management and Corporate Governance

The Center for Integrated Risk Management and Corporate Governance integrates a variety of core competencies, including economics, finance, information systems, law, ethics, philosophy, psychology, environmental science, and leadership. Promoting research, teaching, and outreach activities both nationally and internationally, the center's activities lead to the creation of a knowledgeable and effective workforce capable of addressing the increasing complexities and uncertainties that organizations face today.

QUESTIONS TO CONSIDER:

Does any required course contain some element of Social Impact Management? **YES**

Is any required course entirely dedicated to social, environmental, or ethical issues? **YES**

Is there a Net Impact Chapter on campus? **NO**

All information in this profile is drawn and/or adapted from the self-reported data of the Center for Business Education's Beyond Grey Pinstripes 2007 MBA survey. The Center for Business Education is housed within the Business and Society Program at the Aspen Institute. For more info, visit www.AspenCBE.org.

Loyola University Chicago
School of Business Administration / Chicago, IL

ANNUAL EVENTS:

■ *Corporate Values Breakfast Series*
The Corporate Values Breakfast Series was established by the Center for Ethics at Loyola University as a series of talks presented by business and civic leaders from the Chicago area on ethical issues of contemporary importance. The mission of this series is to bring provocative ideas to an audience of prominent professionals with the purpose of stimulating dialogue and encouraging a deeper understanding of ethical issues and ways to advance ethical behavior in the corporate sphere.

OTHER PROGRAMS:

■ *Business Career Center*
The Business Career Center fosters the career development process through comprehensive career services and resources. The Business Career Center hosts a number of events geared toward social responsibility; recent events included a presentation on ethics in accounting, a panel on corporate sustainability, and a presentation on integrity in the consulting field.

SCHOOL DEMOGRAPHICS	
Number of Full-Time Students	153
International Students	20%
Female Students	49%
	2006/2007 School Year

■ *The Biennial Organizational Ethics in Health Care Conference*
This conference has acquired national stature as a forum for health care ethics specialists working in organizational ethics within hospitals and health systems and in the academy. The focus of this year's conference was on administrators at the highest level of organizational decision making, the ethical challenges they face, and the resources available to them for making sound ethical decisions.

STUDENT CLUBS AND PROGRAMS:

■ *The Loyola Strategic Consulting Group (SCG)*
The SCG is a hybrid of both an information-focused and project-oriented consulting club. The mission of the SCG is to create a mutually beneficial relationship among the university, the business community, and the students through the implementation of strategic consulting services to businesses and nonprofit organizations. The SCG benefits businesses and the local community by providing these services at low or no cost. The group also promotes student interaction with faculty sponsors and advisors to foster ongoing relationships that contribute to increased business knowledge.

THE CENTER FOR BUSINESS EDUCATION'S BOTTOM LINE ON LOYOLA UNIVERSITY CHICAGO:
Compared to other business schools in our survey, Loyola University Chicago offers a good number of courses featuring relevant content, and does an excellent job in those courses explicitly addressing how mainstream business improves the world. Loyola University Chicago requires 1 core course featuring relevant content.

A Closer Look at:
Massachusetts Institute of Technology
Sloan School of Management / Cambridge, MA
http://mitsloan.mit.edu/

THE ASPEN INSTITUTE
Center for Business Education

WHAT THE SCHOOL SAYS:

MIT Sloan's mission is to "develop principled, innovative leaders who improve the world and to generate ideas that advance management practice," and we take this quite seriously. Our emphasis on immersing students in topics of managing social and environmental issues is part of educating and preparing these leaders, which is accomplished both inside and outside the classroom.

A QUICK LOOK

NOTE: All information is self-reported data submitted to the Center for Business Education

COURSES*

Business & Government (1)
CSR/Business Ethics (4)
Economics (1)
Entrepreneurship (2)
International Management (2)
Organizational Behavior (1)
Public/Nonprofit Mgt (2)

KEY CONCENTRATIONS

Sustainability

KEY JOINT DEGREES

MBA & Public Policy

ACTIVITIES*

Speakers/Seminars (5)
Orientation Activities (3)
Internship/Consulting (2)
Student Competitions (1)
Clubs & Programs (3)
Career Development (1)
Institutes/Centers (3)
Concentrations (1)
Joint Degrees (2)

* Figures in parentheses indicate the number of courses/activities that, in whole or in part, integrate social, environmental, or ethical perspectives

NOTABLE FEATURES

ELECTIVE COURSES:

Literature, Ethics, and Authority
This course examines management ethics and problems of leadership. It stresses the relevance of classic works of literature to various ethical dilemmas facing management executives. Works by authors such as Sophocles, Shakespeare, Ibsen, Dostoyevsky, Orwell, and G. B. Shaw are connected to philosophy by Plato, Hobbes, and Machiavelli, and to pertinent business case studies. The course also uses short fiction, novels, plays, and feature films to examine the development of professional ethics and leadership skills.

Sustainability, Trade, and the Environment
This course explores the many dimensions of sustainability and the use of national, multinational, and international political and legal mechanisms to further sustainable development.

INSTITUTES AND CENTERS:

Center for Energy and Environmental Policy Research
This research center draws on resources from MIT Sloan, the MIT Department of Economics, and the MIT Energy Laboratory. For almost 30 years, the center has supplied research to inform domestic and international energy and environmental policy making. Current projects are organized into emissions trading, electricity markets, energy-based derivatives, and productivity improvement in the supply of energy.

Institute for Work & Employment Research
This research center studies the full range of issues related to work, labor-employment relations, human resource management, labor market theory, and public policy analysis. Faculty and graduate students research technology's relation to organizational and industrial structure. They also explore dispute resolution, employment policy for disadvantaged workers, training, and health and safety.

QUESTIONS TO CONSIDER:

Does any required course contain some element of Social Impact Management? **NO**

Is any required course entirely dedicated to social, environmental, or ethical issues? **NO**

Is there a Net Impact Chapter on campus? **YES**

All information in this profile is drawn and/or adapted from the self-reported data of the Center for Business Education's Beyond Grey Pinstripes 2007 MBA survey. The Center for Business Education is housed within the Business and Society Program at the Aspen Institute. For more info, visit www.AspenCBE.org.

A Closer Look at:

Massachusetts Institute of Technology

Sloan School of Management / Cambridge, MA

THE ASPEN INSTITUTE
Center for Business Education

ANNUAL EVENTS:

■ *Global Entrepreneurship Laboratory*

The Global Entrepreneurship Laboratory places teams of students to work full-time, for three to four weeks, on-site, with socially motivated entrepreneurs, primarily in developing countries. The lab seeks to teach students about entrepreneurship in non-US contexts while also providing real advice and assistance to entrepreneurs.

■ *$100K Entrepreneurship Competition*

The MIT $100K Entrepreneurship Competition is designed to encourage students and researchers in the MIT community to act on their talent, ideas and energy to produce tomorrow's leading firms. The competition has two parallel tracks: Venture Competition and the Social Impact Prize. Venture Competition is for high technology value/risk products with a targeted market and the Social Impact Prize focuses on business plans targeting low-income communities in developed and developing countries.

OTHER PROGRAMS:

■ *Sustainability@Sloan Speakers Series*

This year, Sloan launched a new speakers series that brings to campus leaders in various areas of sustainability.

■ *Laboratory for Sustainable Business*

The Laboratory for Sustainable Business seeks to teach students about various sustainability issues (climate change, energy, labor/social standards, poverty and public health, etc.); provide students with the analytical tools to understand and impact (technically/professionally) these issues, and to work with various organizations (profit and not for profit) that are seeking to either develop new sustainable business models or reform existing business practices to render them more sustainable.

STUDENT CLUBS AND PROGRAMS:

■ *MIT Sloan Net Impact Chapter*

The MIT Sloan Net Impact chapter focuses its mission on the community at MIT to give Sloanies the best education, experience, and connections to improve the social and environmental consciousness of tomorrow's businesses and communities.

SCHOOL DEMOGRAPHICS	
Number of Full-Time Students	752
International Students	33%
Female Students	31%
Pre-MBA Employment:	

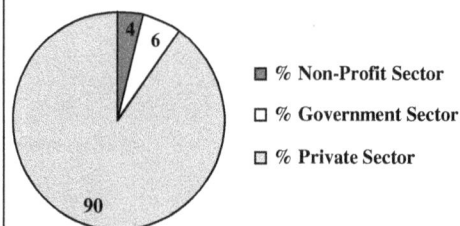

■ % Non-Profit Sector
□ % Government Sector
□ % Private Sector

2006/2007 School Year

■ *Sloan Entrepreneurs for International Development (SEID)*

SEID is a group of Sloan MBA students who have a desire to use their skills and experience to assist with the sustainable global development process through entrepreneurship, as well as raise awareness of the issues faced by emerging economies and how students can make substantial contributions.

FACULTY PIONEER:

■ *2005 – Academic Leadership Award, Richard M. Locke*

Professor Locke has been a consistent voice for integrating social and economic concerns into curriculum and research. He is an acclaimed teacher who has won multiple teaching awards and supervised countless Ph.D. and master's students whose research interests focus on how business practices intersect with economic and social policy concerns. Professor Locke has also created an innovative global entrepreneurship teaching program for MBAs and midcareer executives called (Global E-Lab) which now attracts over 150 students. Locke's current research focuses on economic development in two regions: southern Italy and northeast Brazil.

■ *1999 – Lifetime Achievement Award, John Ehrenfeld (Retired)*

Dr. Ehrenfeld, the (retired) director of the MIT Program on Technology, Business, and Environment, an interdisciplinary educational, research, and policy program, has focused on industrial ecology and sustainability. Ehrenfeld's research examined the way businesses manage environmental concerns. He is author or coauthor of over 200 papers, books, reports, and other publications.

THE CENTER FOR BUSINESS EDUCATION'S BOTTOM LINE ON MASSACHUSETTS INSTITUTE OF TECHNOLOGY:
Compared to other business schools in our survey, Massachusetts Institute of Technology offers a good number of courses featuring relevant content, and does a good job in those courses explicitly addressing how mainstream business improves the world.

A Closer Look at:
McGill University

Desautels Faculty of Management / Montreal, Canada
http://www.mcgill.ca/mba/

WHAT THE SCHOOL SAYS:

Personal responsibility is a core value in the MBA program at McGill's Desautels Faculty of Management. The MBA core is being redesigned for 2008 to bridge functional silos in ways that will include integrative aspects of social and environmental issues.

A QUICK LOOK

NOTE: All information is self-reported data submitted to the Center for Business Education

COURSES*

CSR/Business Ethics (1)
Economics (1)
Entrepreneurship (2)
HR Management (2)
International Management (1)
General Management (3)
Marketing (2)
Organizational Behavior (5)
Operations Management (1)
Strategy (9)

KEY CONCENTRATIONS

Management for Development

KEY JOINT DEGREES

MBA & International Masters in Health Leadership

ACTIVITIES*

Speakers/Seminars (5)
Orientation Activities (1)
Internship/Consulting (2)
Clubs & Programs (1)
Career Development (1)
Institutes/Centers (2)
Concentrations (1)
Joint Degrees (3)

*Figures in parentheses indicate the number of courses/activities that, in whole or in part, integrate social, environmental, or ethical perspectives

NOTABLE FEATURES

CORE COURSES:

▨ *Global Leadership: Redefining Success*

The Global Leadership seminar is designed to prepare people for leadership at the intersection of business and society. It is created out of concern for the future of humanity and the earth, and recognizes that how we respond today to global ecological and economic change will reverberate across generations well into the future. The seminar examines how to unite the strengths of business with the most compelling challenges facing the world today.

▨ *Organizational Behavior*

This course provides an introduction to some of the ethical issues students might encounter in their careers. This course examines many issues that influence the management of people in complex organizations. Students explore and discuss leadership, power and ethics, social influence and diversity, and cross-cultural management.

ELECTIVE COURSES:

▨ *Strategies for Sustainable Development*

This course will explore sustainability from an organizational perspective. While the core material of the course deals with traditional business corporations, it also looks at social sector organizations and emerging "fourth sector" organizations, which combine business structures with social goals.

▨ *Creating Wealth and Prosperity*

This course examines issues such as, Why and how do some countries prosper and others fall behind? What are the implications for financing and managing companies in various countries? How are these issues linked to governments' and central banks' monetary, exchange rate, fiscal, and immigration policies? How do some companies create wealth while others destroy it?

INSTITUTES AND CENTERS:

▨ *Centre for Strategy Studies in Organizations*

The Centre for Strategy Studies in Organizations' goal is to promote the execution and dissemination of insightful research on issues central to organizations, especially the formation of strategic direction, the coordination of organizational activities, and the relationship between organizations and society.

▨ *McGill Finance Research Centre*

The McGill Finance Research Centre is pioneering research on emerging markets, international asset pricing, governance issues, global asset management, and risk management.

QUESTIONS TO CONSIDER:

Does any required course contain some element of Social Impact Management*?* **YES**

Is any required course entirely dedicated to social, environmental, or ethical issues? **YES**

Is there a Net Impact *Chapter on campus?* **YES**

McGill University
Desautels Faculty of Management / Montreal, Canada

ANNUAL EVENTS:

■ *The Global Leadership Seminar*

The Global Leadership Seminar is an intensive orientation workshop with follow-up panels on work/life balance, sustainable development, and governance. The seminar examines how to unite the strengths of business with the most compelling challenges facing the world today. A fundamental premise of the seminar is that a healthy world depends on the evolution of great organizations, and great organizations don't exist without great leadership.

OTHER PROGRAMS:

■ *Leadership and Social Change Internship and Career Fair*

Net Impact McGill cosponsors with the Community Experience Initiative the Leadership and Social Change Internship and Career Fair.

STUDENT CLUBS AND PROGRAMS:

■ *Net Impact McGill*

Net Impact McGill is the first Canadian Net Impact chapter and has organized events and activities that align with the vision of the Net Impact organization. Net Impact McGill has been an active participant within the Montreal business community, and the network of Net Impact chapters across North America and around the world. Net Impact McGill has endeavored to promote social responsibility thinking among MBA students within and outside the Desautels Faculty of Management. A number of Net Impact McGill graduates are spearheading important social responsibility initiatives.

SCHOOL DEMOGRAPHICS	
Number of Full-Time Students	182
International Students	45%
Female Students	30%

2006/2007 School Year

THE CENTER FOR BUSINESS EDUCATION'S BOTTOM LINE ON MCGILL UNIVERSITY:

Compared to other business schools in our survey, McGill University offers an excellent number of courses featuring relevant content, and does a good job in those courses explicitly addressing how mainstream business improves the world. McGill University requires 7 core courses featuring relevant content.

A Closer Look at:
Michigan Technological University
School of Business and Economics / Houghton, MI
http://sbe.mtu.edu/

THE ASPEN INSTITUTE
Center for Business Education

WHAT THE SCHOOL SAYS:

In addition to introducing students to the core business disciplines, the objectives of our MBA program include developing decision making skills, communicating results clearly, and an awareness of and appreciation for the relationships between business and technology within their social, political, and economic contexts. Our philosophy is to embed social and environmental issues in our core courses while also offering electives that cover these issues in more depth.

A QUICK LOOK

NOTE: All information is self-reported data submitted to the Center for Business Education

COURSES*

CSR/Business Ethics (1)
General Management (1)
Operations Management (1)

ACTIVITIES*

Speakers/Seminars (1)
Institutes/Centers (1)

* Figures in parentheses indicate the number of courses/activities that, in whole or in part, integrate social, environmental, or ethical perspectives

NOTABLE FEATURES

CORE COURSES:

▦ *Management and Organizational Behavior*
This course covers leadership; negotiations, which includes conflict management; sustainability; and social and global issues.

▦ *Operations and Quality Management*
This course discusses issues associated with Environmental Management practices, ISO 14001 certification, and lean practices (with emphasis on waste reduction in product, process, and service).

ELECTIVE COURSES:

▦ *Corporate Social Responsibility and Business Ethics*
This course explores corporate social responsibility, business ethics, and corporate governance. Topics include organizational and environmental forces that drive CSR (e.g., sustainability, fair trade, globalization); stakeholder theory; the strategic context of CSR; and implementation of CSR into strategy and culture.

INSTITUTES AND CENTERS:

▦ *Sustainable Futures Institute*
The mission of the Sustainable Futures Institute is to enhance knowledge, develop technologies, and expand capabilities to achieve sustainability. The Sustainable Futures Institute focuses on the triple bottom line: industrial/economic, environmental, and societal sustainability (this focus is provided by the Sustainable Futures Model). The vision of Michigan Tech's Sustainable Futures Institute is to become internationally recognized for its teaching, research, and outreach contributions to the field of sustainable systems.

PROGRAMS:

▦ *Eco-design/Sustainable Development*
Eco-design/Sustainable Development is a three-day seminar series on eco-design and sustainability. Lecture topics include introduction to eco-design—product evaluation; product improvement; legislation and environmental communication; and a diversity roundtable discussion on culture, sustainable development, and the environment.

QUESTIONS TO CONSIDER:

Does any required course contain some element of Social Impact Management? **YES**

Is any required course entirely dedicated to social, environmental, or ethical issues? **NO**

Is there a Net Impact Chapter on campus? **NO**

SCHOOL DEMOGRAPHICS

Number of Full-Time Students	**26**
International Students	**16%**
Female Students	**36%**

Pre-MBA Employment:

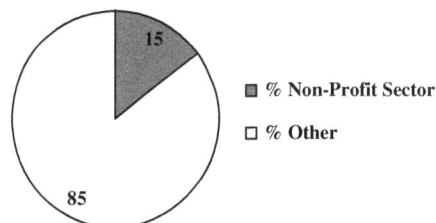

■ % Non-Profit Sector
□ % Other

15
85

2006/2007 School Year

THE CENTER FOR BUSINESS EDUCATION'S BOTTOM LINE ON MICHIGAN TECHNOLOGICAL UNIVERSITY:
Compared to other business schools in our survey, Michigan Technological University does a good job in relevant courses explicitly addressing how mainstream business improves the world. Michigan Technological University requires 2 core courses featuring relevant content.

A Closer Look at:
Monterey Institute of International Studies

Robert L. and Marilyn J. Fisher Graduate School of International Business / Monterey, CA
http://fisher.miis.edu/

THE ASPEN INSTITUTE
Center for Business Education

WHAT THE SCHOOL SAYS:

Fisher School students are exposed to corporate social impact issues through core business curriculum. Our students are provided with a unique exposure to emerging economies and sustainable development issues, and graduate with a facility to conduct business practicing the triple bottom line: sustainable economic development, social responsibility, and environmental stewardship.

A QUICK LOOK

NOTE: All information is self-reported data submitted to the Center for Business Education

COURSES*

Accounting (**3**)
Business & Government (**3**)
Economics (**4**)
Entrepreneurship (**4**)
Environmental (**5**)
Finance (**2**)
Information Technology (**1**)
International Management (**3**)
Marketing (**2**)
Organizational Behavior (**1**)
Operations Management (**1**)
Public/Nonprofit Mgt (**2**)
Strategy (**3**)

KEY CONCENTRATIONS

Corporate Social Responsibility

Globalization/Localization Management

KEY JOINT DEGREES

MBA & MA International Environmental Policy

MBA & MA International Trade Policy

ACTIVITIES*

Speakers/Seminars (**2**)
Orientation Activities (**1**)
Internship/Consulting (**1**)
Clubs & Programs (**3**)
Career Development (**1**)
Institutes/Centers (**3**)
Concentrations (**3**)
Joint Degrees (**4**)

* Figures in parentheses indicate the number of courses/activities that, in whole or in part, integrate social, environmental, or ethical perspectives

NOTABLE FEATURES

CORE COURSES:

▨ Business Development Project
Students admitted to the Master's International MBA program in conjunction with the US Peace Corps complete both a 27-month Peace Corps assignment as small business advisors and their MBA program. Students maintain contact with a Fisher School faculty advisor as they conduct research and gather information for a business development project related to their Peace Corps assignment. The project is then completed as a course upon return to the Fisher School during the final semester of study.

▨ International Organizational Behavior
An entire class lecture addresses issues of social impact management. Ethics and social responsibility issues are explored in various team-based assignments and in assigned text.

ELECTIVE COURSES:

▨ International Trade and Investment Simulation
Students take leadership roles in designing and justifying foreign investment projects to serve the US market. They negotiate with students role-playing government officials and satisfy their concerns regarding environmental and other local impacts of their investments. The challenges of managing outside the US are anticipated or addressed. Teams balance responsibilities to shareholders, workers, and the community.

▨ Environmental Issues in Business
This workshop will explore how business can benefit from reductions in energy and water use, waste minimization, reduced material and energy content in products, innovative business models and management tools, toxics substitution, packaging redesign, and other "green" business practices. Students learn to document progress with careful metrics: beginning baselines, appropriate benchmarks, clear indicators, and transparent reporting.

INSTITUTES AND CENTERS:

▨ Globalization and Localization of Business Exports Center (GLOBE Center)
The GLOBE Center at the Monterey Institute of International Studies provides education, consulting, and research in the rapidly expanding area of business globalization and localization. The center assists companies in adapting their products and strategies for a global marketplace. The GLOBE Center places an emphasis on programs on sustainable business and cultural adaptation.

▨ Development Project Management Institute (DPMI)
The DPMI is a professional training program designed to prepare those who aspire to engage in humanitarian aid or long-term development work in areas where extensive poverty is present. DPMI provides participants with the skills needed for effective professional practice in an environment that addresses both local and global responses to important development challenges. The DPMI program teaches practical skills, such as project design, project monitoring, strategic partnering, and the training of trainers.

QUESTIONS TO CONSIDER:

Does any required course contain some element of Social Impact Management? **YES**

Is any required course entirely dedicated to social, environmental, or ethical issues? **NO**

Is there a Net Impact Chapter on campus? **YES**

Monterey Institute of International Studies

THE ASPEN INSTITUTE
Center for Business Education

Robert L. and Marilyn J. Fisher Graduate School of International Business / Monterey, CA

ANNUAL EVENTS:

■ *GROW: Gaining Real Opportunities for Women*

GROW is a conference providing a forum for women to connect with other women who are making a difference in their communities and workplaces. Topics include working in international development, work/life balance, working in the nonprofit sector, influencing public policy, and entrepreneurship.

■ *Net Impact Conference: Greening Outside the Niche*

This conference explores the practical applications of sustainability, including topics such as green leadership, sustainable tourism, sustainable food chains, greening the home and office, and triple bottom line. Renewable energy credits are purchased to offset the energy consumption for the conference. Serving plates and utensils are made of recycled materials.

OTHER PROGRAMS:

■ *GLOBE Center Consulting Program*

Students have opportunities to work on consulting projects through the GLOBE Center for companies, adapting not only language but cultural issues, business systems, technology, and other issues related to the success of the project.

STUDENT CLUBS AND PROGRAMS:

■ *Peace Corps Club*

Peace Corps Club members hold social gatherings, take part in the annual Peace Corps week activities by speaking on campus or at local schools, hold fund-raising events to support PCMI (Peace Corps Monterey Institute) students serving abroad, and exhibit at the International Bazaar (campus event) to provide information on their countries of service.

■ *Net Impact*

The Net Impact club presents a speaker series and an annual conference and networks with the alumni chapter in San Francisco through workshops and volunteer opportunities.

SCHOOL DEMOGRAPHICS	
Number of Full-Time Students	92
International Students	36%
Female Students	60%
Pre-MBA Employment:	

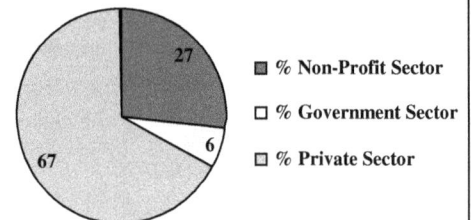

■ % Non-Profit Sector
□ % Government Sector
□ % Private Sector

27
6
67

2006/2007 School Year

THE CENTER FOR BUSINESS EDUCATION'S BOTTOM LINE ON MONTEREY INSTITUTE OF INTERNATIONAL STUDIES:
Compared to other business schools in our survey, Monterey Institute of International Studies offers an excellent number of courses featuring relevant content, and does a truly extraordinary job in those courses explicitly addressing how mainstream business improves the world. Monterey Institute of International Studies requires 7 core courses featuring relevant content.

A Closer Look at:
National University of Singapore (NUS)
NUS Business School / Singapore
http://www.bschool.nus.edu/

WHAT THE SCHOOL SAYS:

The NUS Business School offers the "Best of East and West" in business education and research. The NUS MBA is a modern, challenging, and stimulating program that focuses on modern business principles strongly contextualized to global and Asian business practices. We have made important strides in social and environmental issues and intend to continue our efforts.

A QUICK LOOK

NOTE: All information is self-reported data submitted to the Center for Business Education

COURSES*

Accounting (1)
Economics (1)
General Management (1)
Marketing (1)
Organizational Behavior (2)
Strategy (1)

KEY JOINT DEGREES

MBA & Healthcare Management

ACTIVITIES*

Speakers/Seminars (9)
Orientation Activities (1)
Internship/Consulting (2)
Student Competitions (1)
Clubs & Programs (3)
Career Development (2)
Institutes/Centers (2)
Joint Degrees (1)

* Figures in parentheses indicate the number of courses/activities that, in whole or in part, integrate social, environmental, or ethical perspectives

NOTABLE FEATURES

CORE COURSES:

Managerial Economics

Managerial Economics exposes students to a rigorous foundation in microeconomics, game theory, and industrial organization. It aims to develop students' capacity to analyze the economic environment in which business entities operate and understand how managerial decisions can vary under the different constraints that each economic environment places on a manager's pursuit of goals. It analyzes the functioning of markets and the economic behavior of firms and other economic agents.

Management and Organization

This course explores sociological and psychological perspectives on management. It also introduces students to basic aspects of planning and strategic decision making. Students will explore the implications of individual differences for effective management of organizations, such as attitudes and attitude change; the exercise of power and influence in organizations; and the role of values in the discharge of the social responsibilities of management.

ELECTIVE COURSES:

Global Marketing

Through theories and concepts, case analyses, problem sets, class debates, and project assignments, this course prepares students for marketing challenges on a global scale. The course addresses issues major environmental trends and consumer behavior differences are affecting global marketing.

Asia in the Global Economy

This course examines the impact of globalization and modernization on Asian economics. Models of economic development, international trade, foreign direct investment and global multilateral institutions are discussed in the context of their impact on Asia. Patterns of economic development and political and social change in different Asian countries are compared and studied.

INSTITUTES AND CENTERS:

Saw Centre for Financial Studies

The Saw Centre's purpose is to conduct quality research, educational activities, and training program s related to the financial services industry. It has defined its mission broadly and has conducted activities related to the nonprofit and non-governmental organization sectors.

Corporate Governance and Financial Reporting Centre

The Corporate Governance and Financial Reporting Centre aims to research, disseminate, and promote best practices in corporate governance and financial reporting. To achieve this aim, it conducts annual conferences and regular forums and seminars on the issues of corporate governance, corporate social responsibility, directors' responsibilities, corporate transparency and disclosure, and other related issues. The centre has focused on improving the governance and management capacities of nonprofit and non-government organizations through seminars and talks.

QUESTIONS TO CONSIDER:

Does any required course contain some element of Social Impact Management? **YES**

Is any required course entirely dedicated to social, environmental, or ethical issues? **NO**

Is there a Net Impact Chapter on campus? **NO**

All information in this profile is drawn and/or adapted from the self-reported data of the Center for Business Education's Beyond Grey Pinstripes 2007 MBA survey. The Center for Business Education is housed within the Business and Society Program at the Aspen Institute. For more info, visit www.AspenCBE.org.

National University of Singapore

NUS Business School / Singapore

ANNUAL EVENTS:

■ *Reforming Governance in the Nonprofit Sector: Beyond Rules and Regulations"*

The NUS Business School held its inaugural conference on reforming governance; the aim is to improve governance of nonprofit and non-government organizations to enable them to better achieve their mission and to deliver value-for-money services to their stakeholders. The conference brings together experienced directors, industry professionals and thought leaders, and members of the nonprofit sector to share their knowledge and experience in improving governance of nonprofit organizations.

■ *Social Entrepreneurship Forum*

The forum aims to improve awareness of social entrepreneurship among students through exposure to individuals and organizations playing important roles in solving society's problems. The focus is on applying business solutions to society's problems by introducing innovative approaches.

OTHER PROGRAMS:

■ *Asian Development Bank Internship Program*

The Business School participates in the Asian Development Bank Internship program, which provides students with the opportunity to research and work on a range of social and environmental problems around the world. The program aims to increase awareness of and interest in such issues and to give students analytical tools to understand and deal with social and environmental issues.

STUDENT CLUBS AND PROGRAMS:

■ *Corporate Ethics Focus Group*

This Club focuses on the themes of business ethics and sustainability. It emphasizes the importance of these aspects on firms' long-term strategy. This emphasis follows from the view that connecting ethics and sustainability with the bottom line is an effective way to approach need for shared value-creation, sustainable operations, and robust corporate governance in creating a lasting competitive advantage. The club holds regular events to raise awareness within and outside the school.

■ *Corporate Social Responsibility (CSR) Group*

The CSR Group aims to raise awareness, interest, and research of CSR within the student body. The club annually presents CSR Awareness Month, which includes a range of activities aimed at raising awareness of corporate responsibility and the importance of business ethics among students. Other events include a speaker series that features prominent representatives from firms and non-government organizations, a CSR Exhibition, an exhibit of CSR-themed books and multimedia resources in selected NUS libraries, and a series of film screenings related to the theme of business ethics.

SCHOOL DEMOGRAPHICS

Number of Full-Time Students	240
International Students	87%
Female Students	28%
Pre-MBA Employment:	

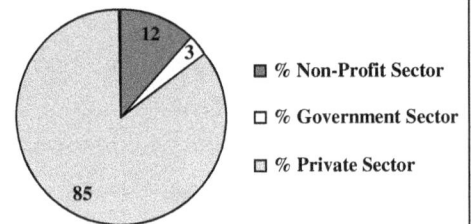

- ■ % Non-Profit Sector
- □ % Government Sector
- □ % Private Sector

12
3
85

2006/2007 School Year

THE CENTER FOR BUSINESS EDUCATION'S BOTTOM LINE ON NATIONAL UNIVERSITY OF SINGAPORE:
Compared to other business schools in our survey, National University of Singapore offers a good number of courses featuring relevant content, and requires 2 core courses featuring relevant content.

A Closer Look at:
New York University
Leonard N. Stern School of Business / New York, NY
http://www.stern.nyu.edu/

THE ASPEN INSTITUTE
Center for Business Education

WHAT THE SCHOOL SAYS:

At NYU Stern, our philosophy as a management education institution is to instill a sense of social responsibility into our MBA students, who will be required to make ethical business decisions, effectively lead people, and manage their company's relationship with the larger community.

A QUICK LOOK

NOTE: All information is self-reported data submitted to the Center for Business Education

COURSES*

Accounting (6)
Business Law (1)
CSR/Business Ethics (4)
Economics (4)
Entrepreneurship (2)
Finance (9)
General Management (14)
Marketing (14)
Organizational Behavior (2)
Strategy (3)

KEY CONCENTRATIONS

Global Business

KEY JOINT DEGREES

MBA & Public Policy

ACTIVITIES*

Speakers/Seminars (6)
Orientation Activities (2)
Internship/Consulting (1)
Student Competitions (1)
Clubs & Programs (6)
Career Development (1)
Institutes/Centers (3)
Concentrations (2)
Joint Degrees (2)

* Figures in parentheses indicate the number of courses/activities that, in whole or in part, integrate social, environmental, or ethical perspectives

NOTABLE FEATURES

CORE COURSES:
▨ Competitive Advantage from Operations
This course emphasizes that the primary purpose of any organized activity, including businesses, is to improve the quality of life (not just work/life balance) of its employees. The class is taught to address social, technological, regulatory, economic and political (STREP) factors in every session.

▨ Professional Responsibility: Markets, Ethics and Law
Faculty across multiple disciplines teach this course and also regularly write material for the textbook, *Professional Responsibility*. The book includes the most up-to-date case studies and issues, ranging from the impact of the Sarbanes-Oxley Act to the aggressive marketing tactics practiced by the pharmaceutical industry.

ELECTIVE COURSES:
▨ Social Venture Capital: Finance with a Double Bottom Line
This course examines financial instruments designed to produce not only financial returns but also social returns; these instruments are commonly known as "double bottom line" investments. Special purpose financial institutions called community development financial institutions have emerged that use a range of investments to achieve social goals; this course will examine the structures and social missions of these institutions.

▨ Managerial Ethics: Lessons from Literature and Film
This course examines seminal works of literature and film to explore the social and moral context of business and the businessperson. Students consider selected novels, short stories, and films in an effort to relate ethical issues portrayed in current news headlines to the literary and film portrayls of business.

INSTITUTES AND CENTERS:
▨ The Global Business Institute
The Global Business Institute works with faculty to provide incremental financial support to facilitate and publicize productive research, hosts visiting scholars on short-term and long-term residencies at Stern in order to promote interaction with faculty and students, and works with the administration in organizing linkages to academic institutions around the world supporting global exposure for both undergraduate and MBA students. The institute also organizes conferences, workshops, and symposia on global issues of interest and importance to the academic, business, and policymaking communities.

▨ The Berkley Center for Entrepreneurial Studies
The Berkley Center for Entrepreneurial Studies is dedicated to the exploration and encouragement of entrepreneurship, new venture creation, and innovation within the business school curriculum and through the support of entrepreneurship research. The center underwrites research grants for faculty members and doctoral students, conducts conferences for scholars and practitioners, engages in specialized executive education, and produces a variety of publications that contribute to understanding the entrepreneurial process and public policy and educational issues associated with encouraging new enterprise development.

QUESTIONS TO CONSIDER:

Does any required course contain some element of Social Impact Management? **YES**

Is any required course entirely dedicated to social, environmental, or ethical issues? **YES**

Is there a Net Impact Chapter on campus? **YES**

All information in this profile is drawn and/or adapted from the self-reported data of the Center for Business Education's Beyond Grey Pinstripes 2007 MBA survey. The Center for Business Education is housed within the Business and Society Program at the Aspen Institute. For more info, visit www.AspenCBE.org.

A Closer Look at:
New York University

Leonard N. Stern School of Business / New York, NY

ANNUAL EVENTS:

▣ *Conference of Social Entrepreneurs*

This conference convenes leaders dedicated to advancing the social entrepreneurship field through the education and acceleration of social entrepreneurs. Participants include thought leaders, investors, social entrepreneurs, educators, researchers, and policy makers who each contribute a unique perspective to this important conversation. The conference includes panel discussions, "fishbowls" to help understand diverse perspectives, living case studies, small group facilitated brainstorming, and keynote presentations.

▣ *Stern's Business Plan Competition*

NYU Stern's Business Plan Competition, open to the greater NYU community, is a year-long experiential program designed to unite the innovations developed throughout NYU's graduate schools with the business acumen of the Stern community. In the Social Entrepreneurship track, teams compete for the Stewart Satter Family Prize of $100,000 and $10,000 of in-kind support.

OTHER PROGRAMS:

▣ *Stern Consulting Corps*

The Stern Consulting Corps aims to create opportunities for MBA students to apply what they have learned in the classroom to the needs of the not-for-profits and the underrepresented minority community in New York City. To further enhance the students' consulting experience, the school has also developed a mentorship program with top-tier strategy consulting firms.

SCHOOL DEMOGRAPHICS	
Number of Full-Time Students	816
International Students	32%
Female Students	33%

2006/2007 School Year

▣ *The Office of Career Development*

The Office of Career Development employs several critical resources related to social impact in its career development initiatives. Specifically, its partnership with the Social Enterprise Association has resulted in the sponsorship of guest speakers to discuss career trends in social enterprise, as well as an annual career fair bringing for-profit CSR companies, educational and social ventures, socially responsible investing firms, and nonprofit organizations to campus to connect interested students with potential career opportunities.

STUDENT CLUBS AND PROGRAMS:

▣ *The Emerging Markets Association (EMA)*

The Emerging Markets Association is composed of a large cross-section of international and domestic students interested in and/or with experience in emerging markets. EMA's mission is to promote careers with an emerging markets focus, to foster the exchange of information and ideas about doing business in developing countries; to create forums for discussion about emerging economies; and to provide contact with emerging market professionals and academics. The club's flagship event is the annual Global Business Conference, which brings together business leaders, academics, students, and alumni to discuss pressing issues related to doing business across borders.

▣ *Stern Community Service*

The mission of Stern Community Service is to maximize the community service impact of Stern students by providing a range of philanthropic opportunities. This program promotes and coordinates projects for a variety of causes including, but not limited to, underprivileged youth and their schools, the homeless, New York City parks, leukemia awareness, and breast cancer awareness.

FACULTY PIONEER:

▣ *2007 – Rising Star Award, Jeffrey Robinson*

Professor Jeffrey Robinson is currently analyzing the role of entrepreneurship in the rebuilding of New Orleans. His work highlights how social entrepreneurs navigate social and institutional barriers to create social and economic value. As an advisor to NYU Stern's Berkley Center for Entrepreneurial Studies, Robinson supports numerous initiatives, most prominently the annual Business Plan Competition which includes a social venture as well as a traditional track. He recently completed his second edited conference volume on social entrepreneurship which includes empirical research and theory and makes a scholarly contribution to the field.

THE CENTER FOR BUSINESS EDUCATION'S BOTTOM LINE ON NEW YORK UNIVERSITY:

Compared to other business schools in our survey, New York University offers a truly extraordinary number of courses featuring relevant content, and does an excellent job in those courses explicitly addressing how mainstream business improves the world. New York University requires 7 core courses featuring relevant content.

A Closer Look at:
North Carolina State University
College of Management / Raleigh, NC
http://mgt.ncsu.edu/mba/

WHAT THE SCHOOL SAYS:

NC State University's MBA is a specialized degree emphasizing innovation and technology management. The program's focus on technology opens the door toward a wide range of social and environmental issues, especially in biotech-pharma management, entrepreneurship, innovation management, and supply chain management concentrations.

A QUICK LOOK

NOTE: All information is self-reported data submitted to the Center for Business Education

COURSES*

Economics (1)
Entrepreneurship (3)
Finance (2)
HR Management (1)
Information Technology (3)
International Management (1)
General Management (5)
Marketing (1)
Operations Management (2)
Strategy (1)

KEY CONCENTRATIONS

Innovation Management

Entrepreneurship & Technology Commercialization

KEY JOINT DEGREES

MBA & Masters of Microbial Biotechnology

ACTIVITIES*

Speakers/Seminars (4)
Internship/Consulting (1)
Clubs & Programs (1)
Career Development (1)
Institutes/Centers (2)
Concentrations (3)
Joint Degrees (2)

* Figures in parentheses indicate the number of courses/activities that, in whole or in part, integrate social, environmental, or ethical perspectives

NOTABLE FEATURES

CORE COURSES:

Managing People in the High Tech Environment

This course covers a variety of organizational issues that relate to social and environmental concerns. Special attention is paid to the consequences of health insurance being tied to employers and how the changes in employer benefits affects individuals and our society. The course covers the issue of "the commons" as it relates to managerial thinking and action about the use of natural and other common resources and addresses the role of the business manager as a steward of the common good.

Production and Operations Management

This course addresses waste reduction, "green production" and the use of reusable packaging material, the importance of ethical relationships with suppliers, job design, and quality management.

ELECTIVE COURSES:

Networking Infrastructure for E-Commerce

This course covers necessary privacy considerations and the ethical issues associated with information management. The goal of the course will be to provide the skills and knowledge necessary for today's professionals to assess and manage information security and customer privacy. A large part of the course is devoted to legal compliance and public policy.

High Technology Entrepreneurship

This course is an applied practicum in organizing new organizations to create value through a process of clarifying the latent potential of new science and technology to support a wide variety of product and service innovations. Students actively seek projects in which the source of innovation is the replacement of environmentally degrading industrial processes with economically and environmentally sound and sustainable technology.

INSTITUTES AND CENTERS:

Enterprise Risk Management (ERM) Initiative

The ERM Initiative provides leadership in the management of entity-wide risks for boards of directors, senior executives, and other stakeholders seeking to preserve and enhance entity value. The ERM Initiative is pioneering the development of this emergent discipline through outreach to business professionals, with its ongoing ERM Roundtable Series; research, advancing knowledge and understanding of ERM issues; and undergraduate and graduate business education for the next generation of business executives.

Supply Chain Resource Cooperative (SCRC)

The SCRC was established to help companies fill the void in qualified human resources. It focuses on serving the needs of member companies by providing applied research and knowledge creation to help them achieve supply chain excellence. The fusion of the SCRC with the academic experience in the NC State MBA program creates a unique pairing of industry professionals with Supply Chain Management faculty and students.

QUESTIONS TO CONSIDER:

Does any required course contain some element of Social Impact Management? **YES**

Is any required course entirely dedicated to social, environmental, or ethical issues? **NO**

Is there a Net Impact Chapter on campus? **YES**

North Carolina State University

College of Management / Raleigh, NC

ANNUAL EVENTS:

Cherokee Investments Internships and Full-Time Positions

Cherokee Investments is a private equity firm whose mission is to acquire environmentally impaired properties, remediate them, and return them to public use. Cherokee Investments' philosophy is to promote sustainable redevelopment. NC State MBA students serve in both internship roles and full-time positions upon graduation.

OTHER PROGRAMS:

NC Greenpower Presentation

NC Greenpower is an independent nonprofit approved by the North Carolina Utilities Commission whose purpose is to promote renewable energy in North Carolina. A speaker from the organization gave a presentation on establishing renewable energy sources in the state, getting green power onto the state power grid the organization's work toward these goals.

STUDENT CLUBS AND PROGRAMS:

Net Impact

The Net Impact chapter of NC State hosts and visits local companies that are making a positive impact on the community and/or are taking steps to be more environmentally friendly. Chapter members also network with the student chapters of Net Impact from local universities and with the professional Triangle Net Impact chapter.

SCHOOL DEMOGRAPHICS

Number of Full-Time Students	**71**
International Students	**32%**
Female Students	**32%**

Pre-MBA Employment:

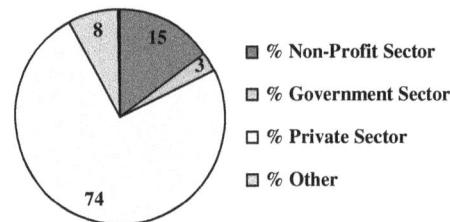

- ■ % Non-Profit Sector
- □ % Government Sector
- □ % Private Sector
- □ % Other

2006/2007 School Year

THE CENTER FOR BUSINESS EDUCATION'S BOTTOM LINE ON NORTH CAROLINA STATE UNIVERSITY:
Compared to other business schools in our survey, North Carolina State University offers an excellent number of courses featuring relevant content, and requires 6 core courses featuring relevant content.

A Closer Look at:
Oregon State University
College of Business / Corvallis, OR
http://www.bus.oregonstate.edu/

THE ASPEN INSTITUTE
Center for Business Education

WHAT THE SCHOOL SAYS:

The College of Business provides a distinctive educational and research program focused on sustainability so that students entering the business world understand that a sustainable business meets economic, social, and environmental needs without compromising the future of any of them. The program's mission is to accumulate and disseminate information on the relationship among business, the environment, and society.

A QUICK LOOK

NOTE: All information is self-reported data submitted to the Center for Business Education

COURSES*

Business & Government (1)
Entrepreneurship (1)
Operations Management (1)
Strategy (1)

ACTIVITIES*

Speakers/Seminars (2)
Student Competitions (1)
Institutes/Centers (1)

*Figures in parentheses indicate the number of courses/activities that, in whole or in part, integrate social, environmental, or ethical perspectives

NOTABLE FEATURES

CORE COURSES:

Legal Aspects of Managing Technology and E-Business
Topics relating to ethics and corporate social responsibility are covered in this course, for example, legal issues of operating and management of e-commerce firms—focus on managing human resources and corporate governance and social responsibility.

Integrated Business Project
This is a project class that requires students to complete a business plan as a means of directing the development of a business. The business plan helps focus a business idea, chart a course for strategic business development, and facilitate setting objectives and creating evaluative benchmarks for projects. The class emphasizes projects based on research discoveries from OSU that have commercialization applications. Many projects involve business opportunities related to sustainability.

INSTITUTES AND CENTERS:

Institute for Natural Resources
This institute works to provide Oregon leaders with ready access to current, science-based information and methods for better understanding resource management challenges and developing solutions. The institute expands OSU's leadership role in coordinating research, supporting policy analysis, and facilitating information-sharing and actions by partnering with natural resources agencies, other universities, private businesses, conservation groups, and various levels of government.

PROGRAMS:

College of Business Dean's Distinguished Lecture Series
Business leaders addresses students on topics ranging from ethics to social and environmental issues in business.

SCHOOL DEMOGRAPHICS

Number of Full-Time Students	45
International Students	32%
Female Students	44%

2006/2007 School Year

QUESTIONS TO CONSIDER:

Does any required course contain some element of Social Impact Management? **YES**

Is any required course entirely dedicated to social, environmental, or ethical issues? **NO**

Is there a Net Impact Chapter on campus? **NO**

THE CENTER FOR BUSINESS EDUCATION'S BOTTOM LINE ON OREGON STATE UNIVERSITY:
Compared to other business schools in our survey, Oregon State University does a good job in relevant courses explicitly addressing how mainstream business improves the world. Oregon State University requires 4 core courses featuring relevant content.

All information in this profile is drawn and/or adapted from the self-reported data of the Center for Business Education's Beyond Grey Pinstripes 2007 MBA survey. The Center for Business Education is housed within the Business and Society Program at the Aspen Institute. For more info, visit www.AspenCBE.org.

A Closer Look at:
Pepperdine University
George L. Graziadio School of Business and Management / Malibu, CA
http://bschool.pepperdine.edu/

THE ASPEN INSTITUTE
Center for Business Education

WHAT THE SCHOOL SAYS:
The mission of the George L. Graziadio School of Business and Management is to develop values-centered leaders for contemporary business practice through a commitment to an education that is entrepreneurial in spirit, ethical in focus, and global in orientation.

A QUICK LOOK

NOTE: All information is self-reported data submitted to the Center for Business Education

COURSES*

Accounting (2)
Business & Government (1)
Business Law (1)
Economics (3)
Entrepreneurship (1)
Finance (8)
Information Technology (3)
International Management (1)
Marketing (3)
Organizational Behavior (10)
Quantitative Methods (2)
Strategy (2)

KEY CONCENTRATIONS

International MBA

Dispute Resolution

KEY JOINT DEGREES

MBA & Masters in Public Policy

ACTIVITIES*

Speakers/Seminars (11)
Orientation Activities (4)
Internship/Consulting (1)
Student Competitions (2)
Clubs & Programs (3)
Institutes/Centers (1)
Concentrations (2)
Joint Degrees (2)

* Figures in parentheses indicate the number of courses/activities that, in whole or in part, integrate social, environmental, or ethical perspectives

NOTABLE FEATURES

CORE COURSES:
▪ *Legal, Political, Ethical and Regulatory Issues of Management*
In this course seeks to get students are encouraged to understand who they are and their responsibilities to themselves and the larger community. Environmental issues are used to raise fundamental ethical responsibilities, such as "What duty, if any, does business owe to its employees, community, and the environment?" These are fundamental issues that are discussed in a number of ways as legal principles are studied.

▪ *Quantitative Business Analysis*
In this course we assign case studies to which students apply quantitative business analysis techniques to solve problems with social and ethical aspects. The objective is to introduce students to real-world problems with conflicting goals and decision making objectives. Students work in small teams to prepare a quantitative analysis of the case problem, debate all of the issues and context for the firm's decision, and then prepare an insightful report presenting the decision options, implications and trade-offs, and a clear recommendation.

ELECTIVE COURSES:
▪ *Social Entrepreneurship*
This course explores social entrepreneur's role in positively impacting socially responsible organizations concerned with improving economic, educational, health care, and cultural institutions. Students complete a social entrepreneurship project—a consulting report in the form of business plans, marketing plans, organizational development recommendations, and financial reports.

▪ *Marketing New Ventures*
Recognizing that many managers today find themselves working in the context of start-ups or smaller businesses generally, this course will examine the unique marketing challenges present in such circumstances and the impact these challenges have on society. Various methods are used in this course to explore societal, environmental, and ethical issues, including the development of an entrepreneurial marketing plan (with a section on social responsibility) and identifying a mentor for each of the students.

INSTITUTES AND CENTERS:
▪ *Values-Centered Leadership Lab*
In 2006 a group of students created an interest group at the Graziadio School that explores social enterprise. A case competition, business plan competition and faculty/student research are conducted; all concern social, environmental, and ethical concerns.

QUESTIONS TO CONSIDER:

Does any required course contain some element of Social Impact Management? **YES**

Is any required course entirely dedicated to social, environmental, or ethical issues? **NO**

Is there a Net Impact Chapter on campus? **YES**

All information in this profile is drawn and/or adapted from the self-reported data of the Center for Business Education's Beyond Grey Pinstripes 2007 MBA survey. The Center for Business Education is housed within the Business and Society Program at the Aspen Institute. For more info, visit www.AspenCBE.org.

A Closer Look at:
Pepperdine University

George L. Graziadio School of Business and Management / Malibu, CA

ANNUAL EVENTS:

■ *Social Enterprise Case Competition*

The inaugural case competition was held in November. The competition focuses on cases related to social, environmental, or ethical issues. Students integrate knowledge and skills learned in the classroom in presenting a case analysis to a panel of judges.

■ *Magill Symposium*

The Magill Symposium brings together MBA students, faculty, and leaders from the business community for a day of sharing insights and ideas on contemporary business practice. The annual themes complement the Graziadio School's core mission of developing values-centered business leaders.

OTHER PROGRAMS:

■ *Malibu 5/10K Run for Charity*

The Malibu 5/10K Run is sponsored by the Graziadio School's Challenge for Charity interest group. The money raised is used to support Tri-Valley Special Olympics and Children's Lifesaving Foundation.

■ *Net Impact Service Corp and Board Fellows*

Members of the Graziadio School's Net Impact chapter have partnered with the Malibu Chamber of Commerce to engage in a series of activities to assist small businesses in the Malibu area.

STUDENT CLUBS AND PROGRAMS:

■ *Challenge for Charity*

The club sponsors a number of activities to raise funds for Special Olympics and Children's Lifesaving Foundation. They compete with other business schools on the West Coast. Club members also devote time to projects for these two organizations.

■ *Net Impact*

The Graziadio School chapter of Net Impact has more than 40 members. The club is currently engaged with the Malibu Chamber of Commerce assisting local business with issues related to responsiveness to California Coastal Commission regulations regarding environmental responsibility.

SCHOOL DEMOGRAPHICS

Number of Full-Time Students	**226**
International Students	**37%**
Female Students	**40%**

Pre-MBA Employment:

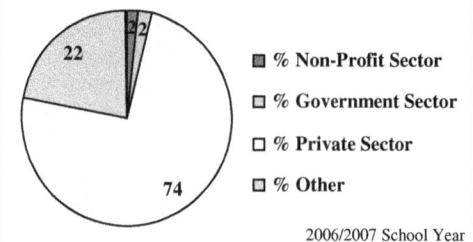

22, 2, 2, 74

- ■ % Non-Profit Sector
- □ % Government Sector
- □ % Private Sector
- □ % Other

2006/2007 School Year

THE CENTER FOR BUSINESS EDUCATION'S BOTTOM LINE ON PEPPERDINE UNIVERSITY:

Compared to other business schools in our survey, Pepperdine University offers an excellent number of courses featuring relevant content, and does a good job in those courses explicitly addressing how mainstream business improves the world. Pepperdine University requires 14 core courses featuring relevant content.

A Closer Look at:
Portland State University

School of Business Administration / Portland, OR
http://www.sba.pdx.edu/programs/graduate/

WHAT THE SCHOOL SAYS:

Unlike any other MBA program, Portland State University's MBA+ program places dual emphasis on the hard and soft skills of successful business management. It does so within the context of managing for innovation and sustainability. Portland State University's MBA+ program is dedicated to producing leaders who will invigorate tomorrow's business community with their innovative spirit and their commitment to social, economic, and environmental stewardship.

A QUICK LOOK

NOTE: All information is self-reported data submitted to the Center for Business Education

COURSES*

Accounting (1)
CSR/Business Ethics (1)
Economics (2)
Entrepreneurship (1)
Environmental (2)
Finance (1)
HR Management (1)
Information Technology (2)
General Management (2)
Marketing (3)
Strategy (5)

KEY CONCENTRATIONS

Sustainability

International Business

KEY JOINT DEGREES

**MBA & Masters in
   Environmental Management**

ACTIVITIES*

Speakers/Seminars (4)
Orientation Activities (2)
Internship/Consulting (1)
Clubs & Programs (1)
Career Development (1)
Institutes/Centers (2)
Concentrations (3)
Joint Degrees (1)

* Figures in parentheses indicate the number of courses/activities that, in whole or in part, integrate social, environmental, or ethical perspectives

NOTABLE FEATURES

CORE COURSES:

Ethics in Organizations
This course is designed to provide students with an understanding of how political, social, legal, regulatory, and environmental issues impact business organizations within a global context. Topics covered include business ethics, corporate social responsibility, managerial integrity, public policy process in relation to business, and economic, social, and environmental sustainability.

Managing Operations and the Value Chain
This course views business as living organizations of natural living systems and focuses on how business operations might look were they designed according to principles that guide the operation of living systems. This course contrasts the worldview underlying conventional operations with the worldview implicit in operations that conform to natural system principles.

ELECTIVE COURSES:

Measuring the Sustainability Performance of Global Corporations
This course helps students develop an understanding of how the measurement of a global company's environmental and social performance can contribute to business goals and strategies. Students examine how different global companies measure and report on their environmental and social performance, and how their different approaches link to their market strategies, business fundamentals, and management philosophies.

Consumer Packaged Goods Marketing
This class focuses on retail food, beverage, and CPG products marketed by vendors through retail consumer channels. Multicultural and ethnic trends are examined for impact on market opportunities and on workforce and management implications. Natural, organic, and sustainable products are examined in the context of a market opportunity and as a way to build healthy communities. The class also examines the role and responsibility of industry firms to help educate consumers about health, economic, and environmental impacts of the industry.

INSTITUTES AND CENTERS:

Center for Professional Integrity and Accountability
The Center for Professional Integrity and Accountability articulates and accentuates organizational management and the accounting profession's responsibility for acting in the public interest. The center develops international networks of scholars and professionals, sponsors various university and community workshops, and encourages student involvement in contributory programs.

Center for Sustainable Processes and Practices
The Center for Sustainable Processes and Practices' purpose is to foster multidisciplinary research that contributes to the development of sustainable solutions and strategies of relevance to public and private sector communities locally, regionally, and internationally.

QUESTIONS TO CONSIDER:

Does any required course contain some element of Social Impact Management? **YES**

Is any required course entirely dedicated to social, environmental, or ethical issues? **YES**

Is there a Net Impact Chapter on campus? **YES**

A Closer Look at:
Portland State University
School of Business Administration / Portland, OR

ANNUAL EVENTS:

■ *Social Sustainability Colloquium*

This speaker series is designed to cover a number of subtopics surrounding social Sustainability, such as international issues, policy applications, catalysts for social change, social sustainability and the family, measuring and methodology in social sustainability research, and community governance.

OTHER PROGRAMS:

■ *Career Services*

Speakers are invited to discuss social impact and environmental management topics and job search strategies. The Graduate Programs Office establishes students in mentor relationships with community members employed in social impact and/or environmental management, and MBA alumni also counsel and mentor current MBA students. Faculty members who conduct research in the area of sustainable development notify the Graduate Programs Office regarding internship and job opportunities in the community.

■ *Business Briefings Breakfast Series*

In the Business Briefings Breakfast Series, which occur monthly or bimonthly, panels of speakers from the business world discuss relevant and timely topics. Some topics have been related to social and environmental sustainability.

STUDENT CLUBS AND PROGRAMS:

■ *Net Impact*

Portland State University's School of Business Administration Net Impact chapter upholds the mission to improve the world by growing and strengthening a network of new leaders who are using the power of business to make a positive net social, environmental, and economic impact. The chapter also invites speakers to the Portland School of Business to discuss environmental and social sustainability.

SCHOOL DEMOGRAPHICS

Number of Full-Time Students	62
International Students	10%
Female Students	36%

Pre-MBA Employment:

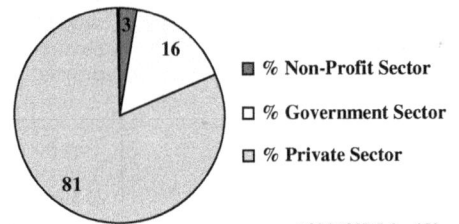

- ■ % Non-Profit Sector
- ☐ % Government Sector
- ☐ % Private Sector

(Pie chart values: 3, 16, 81)

2006/2007 School Year

THE CENTER FOR BUSINESS EDUCATION'S BOTTOM LINE ON PORTLAND STATE UNIVERSITY:
Compared to other business schools in our survey, Portland State University offers an excellent number of courses featuring relevant content, and does a truly extraordinary job in those courses explicitly addressing how mainstream business improves the world. Portland State University requires 8 core courses featuring relevant content.

A Closer Look at:
Presidio School of Management
San Francisco, CA
http://www.presidiomba.org/

THE ASPEN INSTITUTE
Center for Business Education

WHAT THE SCHOOL SAYS:
Presidio School of Management offers one of the first MBA programs in Sustainable Management, which integrates environmental, ethical, and socially responsible concerns into every course. Through the project-oriented curriculum and practical experience offered through the Presidio MBA program, students help a variety of organizations solve real-time challenges while they're learning how to think like sustainable managers. The program prepares professionals to lead organizations—private, public, or nonprofit—in ways that are responsible and successful.

A QUICK LOOK

NOTE: All information is self-reported data submitted to the Center for Business Education

COURSES*

Accounting (1)
Business & Government (1)
Business Law (1)
CSR/Business Ethics (1)
Economics (2)
Entrepreneurship (1)
Finance (1)
HR Management (1)
General Management (4)
Marketing (1)
Organizational Behavior (1)
Operations Management (1)
Strategy (1)

KEY CONCENTRATIONS

Sustainable Management

ACTIVITIES*

Speakers/Seminars (10)
Orientation Activities (3)
Internship/Consulting (1)
Student Competitions (1)
Clubs & Programs (5)
Career Development (2)
Concentrations (1)
Institutes/Centers (1)

* Figures in parentheses indicate the number of courses/activities that, in whole or in part, integrate social, environmental, or ethical perspectives

NOTABLE FEATURES

CORE COURSES:
- *Principles of Sustainable Management*

This course reviews the major frameworks of sustainability that provide the scientific foundations and economic principles of how sustainability can help managers achieve natural, competitive advantage.

- *Integrative Capstone Course*

Integrating the entire sustainable management business education, the Presdio MBA Integrative Capstone course provides the platform for students—either individually or in a team—to plan, start, and build an ethical, sustainable, and profitable venture for a new or existing business, nonprofit, or governmental organization. The course focuses on business strategy and strategic management, reviews the functional areas of business, and examines the principles, frameworks, and techniques central to understanding markets, competitive positioning, and launching new ventures.

INSTITUTES AND CENTERS:
- *LiveNeutral*

LiveNeutral, an enterprise of Presidio School of Management, enables individuals and organizations to offset their own emissions through direct participation in emerging markets for greenhouse gas emission reductions. Developed by students in a Presidio MBA course, LiveNeutral is now a self-sustaining non-profit committed to climate change action and education.

.

QUESTIONS TO CONSIDER:

Does any required course contain some element of Social Impact Management? **YES**

Is any required course entirely dedicated to social, environmental, or ethical issues? **YES**

Is there a Net Impact Chapter on campus? **YES**

A Closer Look at:
Presidio School of Management
San Francisco, CA

ANNUAL EVENTS:

- *Pragmatic Inquiry Workshop*

In this workshop, led by Presidio MBA Provost Dr. Ron Nahser, students are encouraged to explore the work they're called to do in the world and how it relates to their values of sustainability. This is the process that starts Presidio MBA students on the path to creating and developing their business plan. Pragmatic Inquiry provides the opportunity for students to uncover, define, articulate, and test their calling—the work they sense they need to do—engaging others and leading them toward their goals of furthering a more humane, sustainable world.

- *Faculty Panel*

Presidio MBA faculty representatives give an overview of their courses and how sustainability is integrated in each one. They also share their academic and professional backgrounds as well as their particular passions related to sustainability.

OTHER PROGRAMS:

- *Presidio Sustainable Business Partnership Program*

The Presidio Sustainable Business Partnership program provides an excellent opportunity for students to team up with companies and organizations and help them solve real-time business challenges. Working within the Presidio MBA course framework, student teams undertake an organization's project using both traditional business performance metrics such as dollar profitability and other important sustainability metrics such as social justice and environmental sustainability to deliver significant business value to organizations.

STUDENT CLUBS AND PROGRAMS:

- *Green Building Club*

The Presidio MBA Green Building Club is committed to promoting the ideals of green building and renewable energy systems. By bringing students together with leaders of green building and related communities, we aspire to advance the discussion about and facilitate the evolution of the way structures are designed, financed, built, and utilized.

- *International Sustainable Development Club*

The Presidio International Sustainable Development Club seeks to apply sustainability to the developing world and provide a collaborative network of students, faculty, and professional leaders to promote real action in eradicating poverty worldwide.

SCHOOL DEMOGRAPHICS	
Number of Full-Time Students	95
International Students	14%
Female Students	53%
Pre-MBA Employment:	

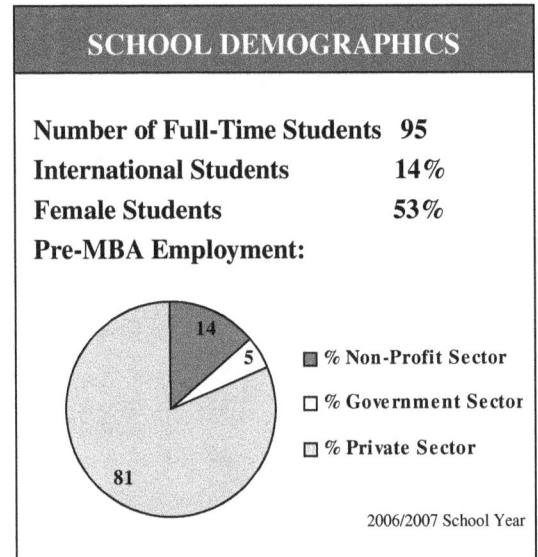

■ % Non-Profit Sector

□ % Government Sector

□ % Private Sector

2006/2007 School Year

THE CENTER FOR BUSINESS EDUCATION'S BOTTOM LINE ON PRESIDIO SCHOOL OF MANAGEMENT:
Compared to other business schools in our survey, Presidio School of Management offers a good number of courses featuring relevant content, and does a good job in those courses explicitly addressing how mainstream business improves the world. Presidio School of Management Institute requires 16 core courses featuring relevant content.

A Closer Look at:
Rhodes University

Rhodes Investec Business School / Grahamstown, South Africa

http://www.ribs.ru.ac.za/

WHAT THE SCHOOL SAYS:

The curriculum of the Rhodes MBA degree includes a number of components addressing the management of social and environmental issues, particularly within the African context. Furthermore, the curriculum is unique in that it is the only MBA in Africa to offer an environmental management elective stream.

A QUICK LOOK

NOTE: All information is self-reported data submitted to the Center for Business Education

COURSES*

CSR/Business Ethics (**1**)
Economics (**1**)
Environmental (**3**)

KEY CONCENTRATIONS

Environmental Management

ACTIVITIES*

Speakers/Seminars (**1**)
Orientation Activities (**1**)
Institutes/Centers (**2**)
Concentrations (**1**)

* Figures in parentheses indicate the number of courses/activities that, in whole or in part, integrate social, environmental, or ethical perspectives

NOTABLE FEATURES

CORE COURSES:

🔲 *Principles of Sustainability*

This module is dedicated to the understanding of the impacts and response of organizations to the principles of sustainable development. Topics include ethics, the triple bottom line, corporate sustainability reporting, climate change, and sustainable development in a changing world.

ELECTIVE COURSES:

🔲 *Environmental Law and Policy*

This module is aimed at providing MBA students with background on the history of environmental legislation in South Africa, as well as the ability to identify, locate, and interpret key national environmental legislation. This module forms a foundation for subsequent modules on environmental risk assessment and environmental management systems.

🔲 *Environmental Risk and Impact Assessment*

This course will introduce the idea that development does not occur in isolation but has impacts on the natural, physical, and social environment. Furthermore any negative impacts need to be predicted and mitigated and positive impacts maximized. For the purposes of the MBA program , this topic must be considered from various viewpoints, such as the potential developer, funding bodies, environmental practitioners, and the regulatory authority.

INSTITUTES AND CENTERS:

🔲 *Department of Environmental Science*

Department of Environmental Science research focuses on current environmental challenges within Southern Africa, and considers the interface between human populations and ecological systems. Of particular interest is the reliance on ecosystems for livelihood in rural areas.

🔲 *Institute for Social and Economic Research*

The Institute for Social and Economic Research provides planning and coordination for social research in the Eastern Cape and elsewhere in the republic, and trains research workers of all races.

🔲

QUESTIONS TO CONSIDER:

Does any required course contain some element of Social Impact Management? **YES**

Is any required course entirely dedicated to social, environmental, or ethical issues? **YES**

Is there a Net Impact Chapter on campus? **NO**

A Closer Look at:
Rhodes University

Rhodes Investec Business School / Grahamstown, South Africa

ANNUAL EVENTS:

■ *Industrial Tours*

The theoretical component of the Principles of Sustainability module is reinforced by industrial tours to obtain a firsthand understanding of the challenges, benefits, and tools associated with sustainable development and environmental management. The visits include one multinational organization and one SME so students are able to contrast the approaches of organizations with very different markets and resources (financial and human). Students are required to assess the overall performance of the companies with respect to meeting sustainable development goals by scoring each using the Johannesburg Stock Exchange's (JSE's) Socially Responsible Investment (SRI) Index.

SCHOOL DEMOGRAPHICS	
Number of Full-Time Students	**22**
Female Students	**35%**
	2006/2007 School Year

OTHER PROGRAMS:

■ *Industry and the Environment: An African Perspective*

This series of lectures provides South African MBA students with a perspective of the relationship between industrial development and environmental issues within the broader African context. The particular challenges associated with management of environmental issues within a developing country context are highlighted and case studies focus on the implementation and rewards of cleaner production in small- to medium-sized enterprises. Possible solutions to common problems are discussed.

THE CENTER FOR BUSINESS EDUCATION'S BOTTOM LINE ON RHODES UNIVERSITY:
Compared to other business schools in our survey, Rhodes University offers a good number of courses featuring relevant content, and does a good job in those courses explicitly addressing how mainstream business improves the world. Rhodes University requires 1 core course featuring relevant content.

A Closer Look at:
Rice University

Jesse H. Jones Graduate School of Management / Houston, TX
http://jonesgsm.rice.edu/

WHAT THE SCHOOL SAYS:

The Jesse H. Jones Graduate School of Management at Rice University believes that there is more to business education than learning about the bottom line. We place theories and strategies into a larger context—in the community, the nation, and the world. We encourage all of our students to become principled, responsible business leaders.

A QUICK LOOK

NOTE: All information is self-reported data submitted to the Center for Business Education

COURSES*

Accounting (**1**)
Business & Government (**2**)
CSR/Business Ethics (**2**)
Economics (**2**)
Entrepreneurship (**1**)
Finance (**1**)
Information Technology (**1**)
Marketing (**1**)
Organizational Behavior (**4**)
Operations Management (**1**)
Public/Nonprofit Mgt (**1**)
Strategy (**2**)

KEY JOINT DEGREES

**MBA & Civil and
 Environmental Engineering**

ACTIVITIES*

Speakers/Seminars (**7**)
Orientation Activities (**2**)
Internship/Consulting (**2**)
Student Competitions (**1**)
Clubs & Programs (**7**)
Institutes/Centers (**2**)
Joint Degrees (**2**)

* Figures in parentheses indicate the number of courses/activities that, in whole or in part, integrate social, environmental, or ethical perspectives

NOTABLE FEATURES

CORE COURSES:

Business Government Relations

This course examines the government's effect on the private sector through regulations and legislation. Students discuss the reaction of business to these restrictions and strategies for gaining political influence. Students also discuss companies' loss of control in other situations.

Business Ethics

In this course, students are exposed to the theory and practice of business ethics in biotechnology, law, finance, accounting, international business, marketing, strategy, leadership, and more. This course follows a preterm introductory ethics workshop, while all required courses and many electives also incorporate additional concepts of ethics and its practical business applications.

ELECTIVE COURSES:

Social Enterprise

This course addresses the role private enterprise and consumption should play in alleviating national and global social problems. Students consider production-side activities such as sourcing, corporate community affairs, philanthropy, "bottom of the pyramid," and cause-related marketing. On the consumption side, students analyze ethical consumption and the fair trade movement. Students also study relationships between firms and governmental and non-governmental organizations, and the role of each party in meeting social needs.

Corporate Crisis Management Strategies

In this course students identify corporate crises and formulate strategies to manage them. Assignments examine crises in areas such as financial performance, environmental management, adverse litigation or legislation, diversity or discrimination management, accidents, and criminal or ethical breaches.

INSTITUTES AND CENTERS:

Center for Biological and Environmental Nanotechnology (CBEN)

CBEN is a National Science Foundation funded Nanoscale Science and Engineering Center at Rice University. Aiming to transform nanoscience into a field with the impact of a modern-day polymer science, CBEN focuses on research at the interface between "dry" nanomaterials and aqueous media such as biology and the environment, developing the nanoscience workforce of the future, and transferring discoveries to industry. The center has also developed outreach programs to educate the nanoscience workforce.

Center for Technology in Teaching and Learning (CTTL)

CTTL addresses the ways in which information technology can expand and enrich education. It is currently researching a variety of areas, including participation of underrepresented groups in information technology. CTTL has explored gender differences in computer use, deployed electronic learning tools in Hispanic communities to bridge the digital divide, and researched the factors affecting Latino participation in the information technology economy.

QUESTIONS TO CONSIDER:

Does any required course contain some element of <u>*Social Impact Management*</u>*?* **YES**

Is any required course entirely dedicated to social, environmental or ethical issues? **YES**

Is there a <u>*Net Impact*</u> *Chapter on campus?* **YES**

Rice University

Jesse H. Jones Graduate School of Management / Houston, TX

ANNUAL EVENTS:

Rice Summer Business Institute: Money and Business 101

This annual summer program introduces underserved and economically disadvantaged schoolchildren to the fundamentals of business and the financial markets. In addition, these students learn how to make ethical business decisions and to inspire others to do the same. Jones School students from the Black and Hispanic MBA student associations assist student teams. Alumni receive invitations to other Jones School events and useful education and career planning information.

Annual Women in Leadership Conference

The National Association of Women MBAs presents the Annual Women in Leadership Conference. This conference helps women in MBA programs across the country develop as women and as leaders. The organization provides networking and mentoring opportunities and develops awareness in the Jones School and in the larger community.

OTHER PROGRAMS:

Action Learning Project

Each year, one or two not-for-profit organizations sponsor Action Learning Projects. Students form teams to assist organizations with real problems. This is a unique experiential learning opportunity for students to apply classroom knowledge to the real world.

Ethics Orientation Workshop

During orientation, students participate in an intensive business ethics seminar. This introductory workshop focuses primarily on a case reading regarding business ethics. Faculty continue to emphasize its importance in core courses and electives throughout the first and second years.

STUDENT CLUBS AND PROGRAMS:

Biotechnology and Healthcare Club

This club helps students explore careers in these rapidly growing business segments. The club helps foster interactions between MBA candidates and graduate students in the life sciences and local healthcare and life science companies.

National of Association of Women MBAs (NAWMBA) Jones School Chapter

This chapter of NAWMBA provides networking and mentoring opportunities, develops community awareness, and hosts events concerning work-related issues affecting women.

SCHOOL DEMOGRAPHICS	
Number of Full-Time Students	241
International Students	19%
Female Students	31%
Pre-MBA Employment:	

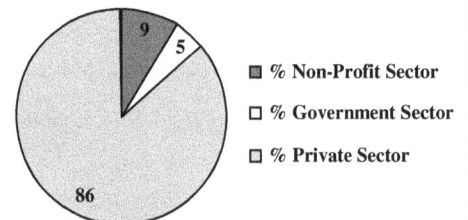

- % Non-Profit Sector
- % Government Sector
- % Private Sector

2006/2007 School Year

THE CENTER FOR BUSINESS EDUCATION'S BOTTOM LINE ON RICE UNIVERSITY:
Compared to other business schools in our survey, Rice University offers an excellent number of courses featuring relevant content, and does a good job in those courses explicitly addressing how mainstream business improves the world. Rice University requires 4 core courses featuring relevant content.

A Closer Look at:
RSM Erasmus University
Rotterdam, Netherlands
http://www.rsm.nl/portal/page/portal/RSM2/Programmes/MBA

THE ASPEN INSTITUTE
Center for Business Education

WHAT THE SCHOOL SAYS:

RSM Erasmus University develops an appreciation of social and environmental stewardship among its students throughout the MBA programs. The school sees stewardship and the awareness of individual responsibility as key in creating sustainable businesses that go beyond being environmentally or socially neutral to being agents for positive change.

A QUICK LOOK

NOTE: All information is self-reported data submitted to the Center for Business Education

COURSES*

Accounting (1)
Business & Government (2)
Business Law (1)
CSR/Business Ethics (7)
Entrepreneurship (1)
Finance (2)
HR Management (3)
International Management (1)
General Management (3)
Marketing (9)
Organizational Behavior (1)
Operations Management (2)
Quantitative Methods (1)
Strategy (6)

KEY CONCENTRATIONS

International Business

Business & Society Management

ACTIVITIES*

Speakers/Seminars (30)
Orientation Activities (5)
Internship/Consulting (2)
Student Competitions (2)
Clubs & Programs (4)
Career Development (1)
Institutes/Centers (8)
Concentrations (2)
Joint Degrees (1)

* Figures in parentheses indicate the number of courses/activities that, in whole or in part, integrate social, environmental, or ethical perspectives

NOTABLE FEATURES

CORE COURSES:

Marketing Management
In this course, social and ethical issues are examined in the areas of product strategy and design, branding, and pricing strategy. Students study a case that examines the impacts of poor corporate practices on sales and on marketing programs. Students also examine a case where a marketing strategy based on good social practices fails when the message does not match the corporate practices.

Operations Management
The Operations Management course includes environmental and social impact issues in the examination of process analysis, quality, reengineering, supply chain management, and lean operations. The concepts of waste reduction and process efficiency are considered in the context of clean technologies and new processes to reduce pollution and with the effiicient use of resources. The ethics of quality and reengineering are also explored.

ELECTIVE COURSES:

Creating Value from Values: Business and Sustainable Development
This course emphasizes the business aspects of improved environmental and social performance. The course examines the following topics: sustainable development at a global level; the role the private sector is currently being called upon to play in improving the quality of life of the world's citizens; how sustainability issues are affecting a number of critical sectors such as energy, agriculture, and tourism; and the role financial markets are playing in translating sustainable strategies into market value.

Companies in Ecologies
This master elective explores state-of-the-art ideas concerning corporate sustainability and systems thinking. Students maintain a "field journal" or complete an individual project that focuses on reducing their own ecological footprint; they also develop a strategic plan to help a company reduce its footprint.

INSTITUTES AND CENTERS:

The European Centre for Corporate Engagement (ECCE)
ECCE is a "lab" for sustainable finance that helps practitioners and scholars understand how businesses and financial markets can promote sustainable development by considering environmental, social and corporate governance issues.

Ethicon
Ethicon is the centre for ethics management at the Erasmus University of Rotterdam. Ethicon is an integrated academic knowledge centre in the field of integrity, corporate social responsibility, and sustainability for both companies and nonprofit organizations. It aims to be fully embedded in the corporate, scientific, and social world at a national and international level.

QUESTIONS TO CONSIDER:

Does any required course contain some element of Social Impact Management? **YES**

Is any required course entirely dedicated to social, environmental, or ethical issues? **NO**

Is there a Net Impact chapter on campus? **YES**

A Closer Look at:
RSM Erasmus University
Rotterdam, Netherlands

ANNUAL EVENTS:

▥ *RSM Day—The World in the Palm of Your Hands*

This learning and networking event is aimed at creating a platform for the examination of a wide range of issues (threats and opportunities) within the context of globalization, including sustainability, entrepreneurship, intercultural communication and technology.

▥ *ECCEllence Student Challenge*

The ECCEllence competition encourages students to solve case-based sustainability problems. Participants include several international universities known for their strong track records in the domain of sustainable finance.

▥ *Personal Leadership Development (PLD) Workshop*

During orientation, this simulation places students in groups that represent competitors operating within the fishing industry. The competitive nature of the game forces students to reflect on long-term industry survival as the exclusive goal of their firms not short-term profitability. The simulation provides a striking demonstration of how easy it is to ignore longer-term impacts in spite of the inevitable consequences for a firm and, more important, for the entire society and environment in which the industry operates.

OTHER PROGRAMS:

▥ *Consultancy Project to NGOs in Johannesburg, South Africa*

This is an optional one-week immersion trip to Johannesburg, South Africa that is comprised of guest lectures, company visits, and a short consulting project that students do in groups of five-to-six people. After the project leaders describe the contexts, constraints, and opportunities of the NGOs, students deliver their recommendations in the area of fundraising/financing or marketing/communication.

STUDENT CLUBS AND PROGRAMS:

▥ *Sustainability in Business Club*

The goal of this club is to help RSM students recognize the impact and importance of sustainability in business in improving long-term prospects and overall benefits, to both the company and to society. The Sustainability in Business Club also works closely with experts in other fields.

▥ *Finance Club*

The Finance Club significantly supplements the efforts of the Sustainability Club through its increasing focus on micro finance. The significant percentage of students in the program from emerging economies with substantial marginalized segments of their societies makes concerns for microfinance to "un-banked" segments of society of ever-increasing concern. Student interest in the area is motivated from a social transformation perspective and from the recognition of the sector as having increasing commercial importance.

SCHOOL DEMOGRAPHICS	
Number of Full-Time Students	216
International Students	96%
Female Students	26%
Pre-MBA Employment:	

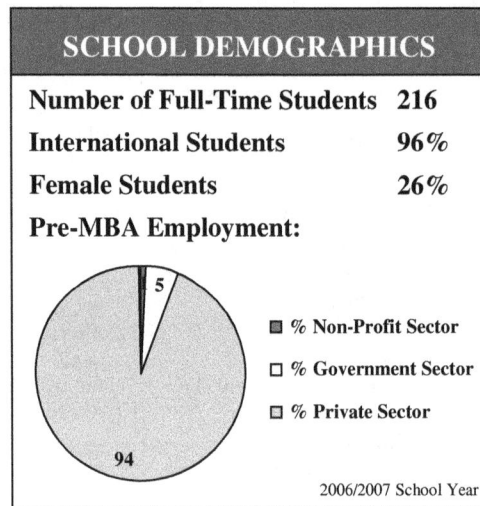

■ % Non-Profit Sector
□ % Government Sector
□ % Private Sector

2006/2007 School Year

THE CENTER FOR BUSINESS EDUCATION'S BOTTOM LINE ON RSM ERASMUS UNIVERSITY:

Compared to other business schools in our survey, RSM Erasmus University offers an excellent number of courses featuring relevant content, and does a good job in those courses explicitly addressing how mainstream business improves the world. RSM Erasmus University requires 9 core courses featuring relevant content.

A Closer Look at:
Saginaw Valley State University
College of Business and Management / University Center, MI
http://www.svsu.edu/cbm/

THE ASPEN INSTITUTE
Center for Business Education

WHAT THE SCHOOL SAYS:
All MBA students are required to take a core course in managing social and environmental issues in business. Since this topic is one of our goals, the goal is assessed according to assurance of learning dogma as regulated by The Association to Advance Collegiate Schools of Business **International (AACSB).**

A QUICK LOOK

NOTE: All information is self-reported data submitted to the Center for Business Education

COURSES*

CSR/Business Ethics **(1)**

ACTIVITIES*

Speakers/Seminars **(2)**

* Figures in parentheses indicate the number of courses/activities that, in whole or in part, integrate social, environmental, or ethical perspectives

NOTABLE FEATURES

CORE COURSES:
▦ *Social Responsibility and Ethics in Business*
The purpose of this course is to enable students to reason about the role of ethics in business administration. Specific course objectives include the following: to develop an enhanced ability to recognize the social, ethical, political, environmental, and technological dimensions of business activity; to be able to explain the impact of external environmental forces on business decision making and the impact of business on society; to be able to develop a management perspective in order to formulate, analyze, and defend decisions in ethical terms; and to be able to apply several different frameworks for moral reasoning to complex business issues.

ANNUAL EVENTS:
▦ *Executive Speaker Series*
Two executive speakers, both entrepreneurs, are brought to campus each year to discuss their companies' development, and to address the topics of social impact and environmental management as a part of developing their business.

SCHOOL DEMOGRAPHICS

Number of Full-Time Students	22
International Students	22%
Female Students	29%
Pre-MBA Employment:	

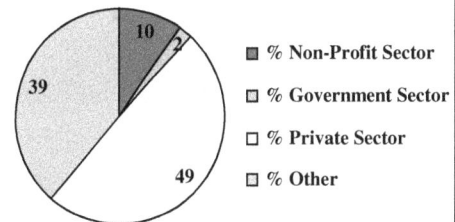

- 10 — ▪ % Non-Profit Sector
- 2 — ☐ % Government Sector
- 39 — ☐ % Private Sector
- 49 — ☐ % Other

2006/2007 School Year

QUESTIONS TO CONSIDER:

Does any required course contain some element of Social Impact Management? **YES**

Is any required course entirely dedicated to social, environmental, or ethical issues? **YES**

Is there a Net Impact Chapter on campus? **NO**

THE CENTER FOR BUSINESS EDUCATION'S BOTTOM LINE ON SAGINAW VALLEY STATE UNIVERSITY:
By participating in the Center for Business Education's Beyond Grey Pinstripes 2007 MBA survey, Saginaw Valley State University demonstrates great dedication to integrating environmental and social impact management issues into its teaching and research. Saginaw Valley State University requires 1 core course featuring relevant content.

All information in this profile is drawn and/or adapted from the self-reported data of the Center for Business Education's Beyond Grey Pinstripes 2007 MBA survey. The Center for Business Education is housed within the Business and Society Program at the Aspen Institute. For more info, visit www.AspenCBE.org.

A Closer Look at:
St. John's University
The Peter J. Tobin College of Business / Queens, NY
http://www.stjohns.edu/academics/graduate/tobin

WHAT THE SCHOOL SAYS:
The Tobin College has a long history of developing in our students an appreciation for social issues in the context of successful business careers. This goes to the core of our philosophy on business instruction: being successful carries with it inherent responsibilities to others and to society more broadly.

A QUICK LOOK

NOTE: All information is self-reported data submitted to the Center for Business Education

COURSES*

Accounting **(1)**
Business & Government **(1)**
General Management **(1)**

KEY CONCENTRATIONS

International Business

ACTIVITIES*

Speakers/Seminars **(1)**
Orientation Activities **(1)**
Internship/Consulting **(1)**
Concentrations **(2)**

* Figures in parentheses indicate the number of courses/activities that, in whole or in part, integrate social, environmental, or ethical perspectives

NOTABLE FEATURES

CORE COURSES:

Law, Ethics and Society
This course introduces the legal and ethical environment of business and covers legal principles essential for proper managerial decision making.

Organizational Behavior and Business Ethics
This course provides a study of the latest theoretical and empirical factors influencing human attitudinal, behavioral, and ethical responses in and around organizations. Topics include individual and organizational ethics, corporate social responsibility, intracultural diversities, intercultural/globalization issues, leadership, organizational culture, and decision making.

ELECTIVE COURSES:

Accounting Ethics and Professionalism
This course covers ethical reasoning, integrity, objectivity, independence, core values, and professional issues in accounting.

PROGRAMS:

Service Learning
A variety of servicelearning projects are offered to students through management courses at the college. These include provision of business consulting services to mental health and other nonprofit organizations.

SCHOOL DEMOGRAPHICS

Number of Full-Time Students	**230**
International Students	**35%**
Female Students	**39%**

Pre-MBA Employment:

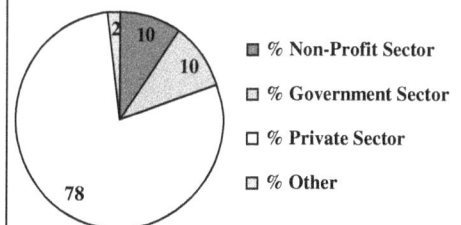

- ■ % Non-Profit Sector
- □ % Government Sector
- □ % Private Sector
- □ % Other

2006/2007 School Year

ANNUAL EVENTS:

Annual Conference on Business Ethics
St. John's cosponsors an annual international conference on business ethics. It offers a variety of speakers and perspectives on the importance of ethics in the workplace and social responsibility of leaders more generally. It annually attracts more than 100 individuals and organizations.

QUESTIONS TO CONSIDER:

Does any required course contain some element of Social Impact Management? **YES**

Is any required course entirely dedicated to social, environmental or ethical issues? **NO**

Is there a Net Impact Chapter on campus? **NO**

THE CENTER FOR BUSINESS EDUCATION'S BOTTOM LINE ON ST. JOHN'S UNIVERSITY:
By participating in the Center for Business Education's Beyond Grey Pinstripes 2007 MBA survey, St. John's University demonstrates great dedication to integrating environmental and social impact management issues into its teaching and research. St. John's University requires 2 core courses featuring relevant content.

A Closer Look at:
Saint Joseph's University

Erivan K. Haub School of Business/ Philadelphia, Pennsylvania
http://www.sju.edu.

WHAT THE SCHOOL SAYS:

The Haub School of Business (HBS) at Saint Joseph's University takes a two-pronged approach to preparing MBA students to manage social and environmental issues—focus on the student and focus on the faculty. These characteristics, along with a strong focus on business ethics, develop leaders with strong analytical skills, technical competence, and social responsibility.

A QUICK LOOK

NOTE: All information is self-reported data submitted to the Center for Business Education

COURSES*

Accounting (1)
CSR/Business Ethics (1)
General Management (4)
Organizational Behavior (1)

KEY CONCENTRATIONS

International Business
Public and Non-Profit Management

KEY JOINT DEGREES
MBA/DO

ACTIVITIES*

Speakers/Seminars (5)
Orientation Activities (2)
Student Competitions (1)
Clubs & Programs (1)
Career Development (1)
Institutes/Centers (1)
Concentrations (3)
Joint Degrees (1)

* Figures in parentheses indicate the number of courses/activities that, in whole or in part, integrate social, environmental, or ethical perspectives

NOTABLE FEATURES

CORE COURSES:

■ *Stakeholder Theory and Social Responsibility*
This course addresses corporate social responsibility through a stakeholder theory of business. The course will center on the question, "Which interests of which stakeholders impose obligations of business?" The internal and external stakeholders addressed include investors, employees, customers, and the natural environment, among others.

■ *Empowering Human Potential at Work*
This course focuses on an organization's most salient resource—its human capital. It investigates the foundation of and strategies for empowering organizational members to manage organizational transformation processes in a national and global environment. Empowering human potential requires an understanding of how to manage oneself, other individuals, and groups effectively, creatively, legally, and ethically in work organizations.

ELECTIVE COURSES:

■ *Managing Workforce Diversity*
This course is designed to help students become aware of the multiple dimensions of diversity, such as race, class, gender, physical ability, sexual orientation, age, and nationality. In addition, differences in function, perspective, and work style will be explored to examine their potential impact in the workplace.

■ *Managing the Nonprofit Organization*
This course builds on the MBA core curriculum and covers managing and improving nonprofit organizations in today's changing environment, with emphasis on the differences between nonprofit and business organizations.

INSTITUTES AND CENTERS:

■ *Pedro Arrupe Center for Business Ethics*
The Pedro Arrupe Center for Business Ethics is an intellectual resource for business ethics in both academic and business contexts. Its mission is to integrate ethics into every aspect of business education in practice and the Arrupe Center applies an interdisciplinary approach to capitalize on the diverse expertise of HSB faculty.

■ *Career Development Center*
Much of Saint Joseph's University's Career Development Center's programming effort addresses issues of social impact: cosponsorship (with Idealist.org) of an annual not-for-profit career fair to assist students interested in working with and for not-for-profit organizations in securing jobs and internships; The SJU CDC's "Road Trips to the Real World" series of employer site visits, which includes area organizations that serve the community; the "Our Year of Service" alumni panel affords students the opportunity to hear from alumni who completed a year of service (full-time volunteer work) after graduation; sponsorship of employer information sessions with nonprofit organizations, such as Philly Fellows.

QUESTIONS TO CONSIDER:

Does any required course contain some element of Social Impact Management? **YES**

Is any required course entirely dedicated to social, environmental, or ethical issues? **YES**

Is there a Net Impact Chapter on campus? **YES**

Saint Joseph's University
Erivan K. Haub School of Business/Philadelphia, PA

ANNUAL EVENTS:

▪ Faith-Justice Outreach Lectures

SJU's Pedro Arrupe Center for Business Ethics cosponsors seminars, lectures, and conferences that present rigorous analysis of ethical issues or promote social justice to our on- and off-campus communities. A prominent lecture series at Saint Joseph's University is the Faith-Justice Institute Outreach Lecture Series. The Arrupe Center partners with the Faith-Justice Institute to cosponsor most outreach lectures. Examples of the outreach lecture topics include, but are not limited to, globalization, poverty, sustainability, workers' rights, and leadership.

▪ Graduate Student Business Ethics Paper Competition

The Arrupe Center issues a call for papers each academic term to all Haub School graduate business students. This semiannual competition enables students to demonstrate proficiency in integrating issues of ethics and social responsibility with a business case or decision. Topics may be based on issues addressed in current or past courses or may be completely independent of any specific course. Papers should include a theoretical analysis, applying ethical principles to the facts of the business case or issue, and should provide a recommended course of action as ethically superior to other available alternatives. Winning authors receive small monetary awards.

STUDENT CLUBS AND PROGRAMS:

▪ Net Impact

Saint Joseph's Net Impact chapter is comprised of graduate business students who want to use the power of business to make a positive difference in society. SJU Net Impact aims to contribute to the educational community by bringing speakers to campus who have knowledge of topics like socially responsible investment, corporate social responsibility, nonprofit management, business ethics, economic development, and social entrepreneurship; to influence the Graduate Business curriculum; to help students find and secure career opportunities by providing programmatic resources and a strong network; and to represent Saint Joseph's at the Annual Net Impact Conference.

THE CENTER FOR BUSINESS EDUCATION'S BOTTOM LINE ON SAINT JOSEPH'S UNIVERSITY:
Compared to other business schools in our survey, Saint Joseph's University offers a good number of courses featuring relevant content, and does a good job in those courses explicitly addressing how mainstream business improves the world. Saint Joseph's University requires 7 core courses featuring relevant content.

A Closer Look at:
San Francisco State University
College of Business / San Francisco, CA
http://www.cob.sfsu.edu/

WHAT THE SCHOOL SAYS:

San Francisco State University's College of Business MBA program continues to build its capacity to help students learn how to innovate and exercise leadership in socially responsible and environmentally sustainable business practices. The College of Business' new emphasis in Sustainable Business was introduced in the spring of 2007.

A QUICK LOOK

NOTE: All information is self-reported data submitted to the Center for Business Education

COURSES*

Accounting (4)
CSR/Business Ethics (3)
Entrepreneurship (1)
Environmental (1)
Information Technology (3)
International Management (7)
General Management (3)
Marketing (4)
Operations Management (3)
Strategy (1)

KEY CONCENTRATIONS

Sustainable Business

ACTIVITIES*

Speakers/Seminars (2)
Clubs & Programs (1)
Career Development (1)
Concentrations (1)

* Figures in parentheses indicate the number of courses/activities that, in whole or in part, integrate social, environmental, or ethical perspectives

NOTABLE FEATURES

CORE COURSES:

▦ *The Political, Social and Legal Environment of Business*

Many of the most complex issues confronting business leaders concern social, political, and legal issues outside their formal business training. This is a course to develop the leadership skills necessary to understand and anticipate or respond to these complex emerging issues. Students learn about the historical evolution of the business-society relationship in the U.S., social responsibility, the ethical aspects of management, business-government relations, management of corporate environmental responsibilities, globalization, corporate governance, and more.

▦ *Strategic Marketing*

This course is designed to acquaint business students with concepts, principles, and practices in marketing strategy. The course objectives explicitly include developing students' understanding of ethical and social responsibility implications of marketing issues. Case studies focus on topics including sustainable and socially responsible positioning, fairness in pricing, truth in advertising and planned obsolescence, targeting of children and other vulnerable populations, and ethical issues in competitive intelligence gathering.

ELECTIVE COURSES:

▦ *Business Management and Environmental Leadership*

This seminar is for students interested in the impact of business organizations on the natural environment and the types of approaches businesses are taking and can take to effectively respond to environmental issues. Students completing this course will be better prepared to assist organizations in incorporating environmental considerations into their decision making.

▦ *Sustainability and Business Opportunity*

This course is designed as a seminar for students interested in business opportunities developing at the intersection between business and society's emerging needs. The focus of this seminar is business opportunities that address problems associated with global poverty. The primary objective is to provide practical knowledge and experience in developing proactive business strategies to address needs not met effectively by current business practices. Specific topics covered include sustainability, bottom of the pyramid, microfinance, and social enterprise.

QUESTIONS TO CONSIDER:

Does any required course contain some element of Social Impact Management? **YES**

Is any required course entirely dedicated to social, environmental, or ethical issues? **YES**

Is there a Net Impact Chapter on campus? **YES**

San Francisco State University
College of Business / San Francisco, CA

ANNUAL EVENTS:

Business Ethics Week
During Business Ethics Week, business students hear from over 50 business people and experts on the topic of business ethics during speeches and panel discussions. MBA faculty introduce ethics modules or invite speakers to discuss the topic of business ethics during this event.

OTHER PROGRAMS:

Career Skill Seminars
Career Skill Seminars are conducted once per month for MBAs. San Franciso State Univeresity has a commitment to include seminars relating to socially responsible businesses and to the government sector.

Net Impact Phone Conference Workshop
This workshop was conceived by Net Impact to provide MBA students with hands-on approaches they could use to assist their professors in introducing short modules relating to relevant social and environmental issues. This conference discusses how to design active learning classroom modules based on current events, news articles, NGO reports, etc.

STUDENT CLUBS AND PROGRAMS:

Net Impact Chapter
San Francisco State's chapter upholds Net Impact's mission "to improve the world by growing and strengthening a network of new leaders who are using the power of business to make a positive net social, environmental, and economic impact."

SCHOOL DEMOGRAPHICS	
Number of Full-Time Students	136
International Students	35%
Female Students	52%

Pre-MBA Employment:

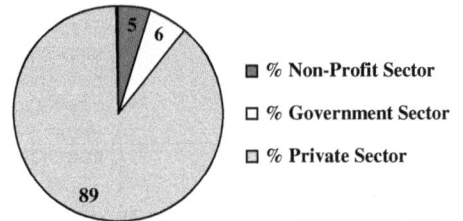

- ■ % Non-Profit Sector
- □ % Government Sector
- □ % Private Sector

2006/2007 School Year

THE CENTER FOR BUSINESS EDUCATION'S BOTTOM LINE ON SAN FRANCISCO STATE UNIVERSITY:
Compared to other business schools in our survey, San Francisco State University offers an excellent number of courses featuring relevant content, and does an excellent job in those courses explicitly addressing how mainstream business improves the world. San Francisco State University requires 13 core courses featuring relevant content.

A Closer Look at:
Seton Hall University

The Stillman School of Business / South Orange, NJ
http://www.shu.edu/academics/business/

THE ASPEN INSTITUTE
Center for Business Education

WHAT THE SCHOOL SAYS:
Seton Hall University's mission is articulated as developing servant leaders in a global society. Corporate Social Responsibility is considered "essential knowledge" in the MBA program at The Stillman School of Business.

A QUICK LOOK

NOTE: All information is self-reported data submitted to the Center for Business Education

COURSES*

Accounting (1)
CSR/Business Ethics (1)
HR Management (1)
International Management (1)
General Management (2)

KEY CONCENTRATIONS

International Business

KEY JOINT DEGREES

MBA & MS Diplomacy

ACTIVITIES*

Speakers/Seminars (2)
Orientation Activities (1)
Student Competitions (1)
Clubs & Programs (3)
Career Development (1)
Institutes/Centers (2)
Concentrations (3)
Joint Degrees (3)

* Figures in parentheses indicate the number of courses/activities that, in whole or in part, integrate social, environmental, or ethical perspectives

NOTABLE FEATURES

CORE COURSES:

Corporate Social Responsibility
The objective of this course is to provoke participants to think critically about ethical behavior in business. The relationship of business enterprise to its stakeholders is examined and questions about socially responsible and ethical conduct of the enterprise in relation to those stakeholders are raised, in the context of some of the most problematic issues facing managers today.

International Perspectives
This course is designed to introduce students to the world of international business, international trade, foreign direct investment, international law and organizations, and political economy. It approaches these subjects from the viewpoint of a generalist, offering information and insights from the broad perspectives of business, economics, finance, political and economic geography, risk management, marketing, ethics, and international law.

ELECTIVE COURSES:

Gender and Diversity Issues in Management
The objective of this course is to explore how contemporary attitudes toward diversity, i.e., gender, race, ethnicity, and other characteristics, influence work and business. Diversity based on gender, race, ethnicity, and national origin, as well as differences based on religion and sexual orientation are examined. Federal and state laws prohibiting discrimination are addressed. Students examine the social-economic-legal-political context of diversity, behaviors and perceptions associated with diversity, and personal and management strategies for addressing diversity.

Managerial Negotiating
This course introduces students to the art of negotiations. The goal is to explore both the theoretical and practical aspects of negotiations. In this seminar, students review the literature dealing with negotiating, engage in negotiations in a variety of settings, and study the negotiating process.

INSTITUTES AND CENTERS:

Center for Entrepreneurial Studies
The Center for Entrepreneurial Studies was created in 2003 to raise student awareness of self-employment as a career option. The Center fosters the collaboration of faculty, students, alumni and entrepreneurs to engage in activities and projects that advance hands-on entrepreneurial learning at the Stillman School. The Center is integral to the Stillman School's mandate to prepare students for careers in the 21st century by acknowledging the growing importance of entrepreneurship in the U.S. and global economy.

Institute for International Business
The Institute for International Business coordinates the core curriculum for both the undergraduate and MBA programs and sponsors international trips.

QUESTIONS TO CONSIDER:

Does any required course contain some element of Social Impact Management? **YES**

Is any required course entirely dedicated to social, environmental, or ethical issues? **YES**

Is there a Net Impact Chapter on campus? **NO**

All information in this profile is drawn and/or adapted from the self-reported data of the Center for Business Education's Beyond Grey Pinstripes 2007 MBA survey. The Center for Business Education is housed within the Business and Society Program at the Aspen Institute. For more info, visit www.AspenCBE.org.

A Closer Look at:
Seton Hall University
The Stillman School of Business / South Orange, NJ

ANNUAL EVENTS:

■ *Integrity and Professionalism Colloquia*

Two Integrity and Professionalism Colloquia are scheduled during each academic year.

■ *Orientation Meeting and Dinner*

MBA candidates are introduced to the MBA program in an orientation and dinner. The MBA program requirements, including the service project requirement of 20 hours, are addressed by a series of speakers. The goal of the MBA service project is to encourage graduates to engage in lifelong service, and articulates with the mission of Seton Hall University.

SCHOOL DEMOGRAPHICS	
Number of Full-Time Students	43
International Students	1%
Female Students	40%
Pre-MBA Employment:	

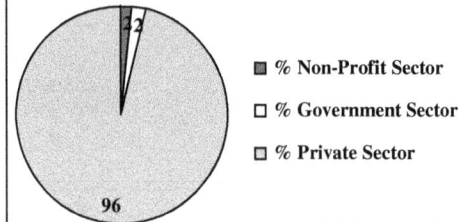

- ■ % Non-Profit Sector
- ☐ % Government Sector
- ☐ % Private Sector

2006/2007 School Year

THE CENTER FOR BUSINESS EDUCATION'S BOTTOM LINE ON SETON HALL UNIVERSITY:

Compared to other business schools in our survey, Seton Hall University offers a good number of courses featuring relevant content, and does a good job in those courses explicitly addressing how mainstream business improves the world. Seton Hall University requires 5 core courses featuring relevant content.

A Closer Look at:
Simmons College

Simmons School of Management / Boston, MA
http://www.simmons.edu/som/mba/

WHAT THE SCHOOL SAYS:

The Simmons School of Management prepares women for power and principled leadership. Our aspiration is to educate principled leaders who will build organizations that are successful by all traditional measures and respected for providing equitable workplaces, for adhering assiduously to ethical decision-making, and for aligning social responsibility and profitability in their business strategy.

A QUICK LOOK

NOTE: All information is self-reported data submitted to the Center for Business Education

COURSES*

Accounting (4)
Business Law (1)
CSR/Business Ethics (2)
Economics (2)
Entrepreneurship (4)
Finance (1)
HR Management (1)
Information Technology (1)
International Management (2)
General Management (2)
Marketing (2)
Organizational Behavior (6)
Operations Management (1)
Quantitative Methods (1)
Strategy (1)

KEY CONCENTRATIONS

Entrepreneurship

ACTIVITIES*

Speakers/Seminars (17)
Orientation Activities (1)
Clubs & Programs (4)
Career Development (1)
Institutes/Centers (1)
Concentrations (1)

* Figures in parentheses indicate the number of courses/activities that, in whole or in part, integrate social, environmental, or ethical perspectives

NOTABLE FEATURES

CORE COURSES:

Business, Government and the Global Economy

This course explores the relationship between business, society, and the global economy. Through country case studies it explores cross-national differences in norms of acceptable practice in business-government relations and the interaction of business and politics. It explores the role of multinational business as social change agents. It explores evidence of and possible explanations for changing patterns of income inequality within countries, between countries, and between workers and property owners.

Technology and Operations Management

This class provides a foundation for understanding the role of production and delivery capabilities in creating business value. Two case studies on technology management feature organizational initiatives that demonstrate the role IT can play in building the economy in the developing world. Discussions of supply chain management provide a platform to discuss the ethical issues involved with procurement, sourcing, and working with suppliers. The topics of assembly lines and job design are used to highlight employers' social responsibility to provide work that is meaningful and safe.

ELECTIVE COURSES:

Corporate Reporting and the Triple Bottom Line

This seminar examines the Triple Bottom Line (3BL) concept along with its many aspects and applications. At this stage of development, the 3BL idea is a collection of proposals designed to enhance the economic, environmental, and social reporting by organizations of all types. Discussions focus on an analysis and synthesis of these themes, the credibility of the proposals, and the applicability of the 3BL concept.

Global Diversity

This course is an intensive examination of multicultural competence. Students increase their cross-cultural awareness, knowledge, and skills to respond appropriately to the problems and opportunities of both domestic and international demographic changes and globalization. The course engages students in a redefinition of their professional identity to include civic responsibility for themselves and their profession, with a personal commitment to a deeper engagement with society.

INSTITUTES AND CENTERS:

Center for Gender in Organizations (CGO)

The CGO focuses its research and involvement at the level of work practice and deep cultural assumptions about work and how it gets accomplished. The CGO engages in consultations and action learning projects with organizations to translate CGO concepts into practical actions and convenes public events, seminars, and workshops to highlight new research and practice on gender and diversity in organizations.

QUESTIONS TO CONSIDER:

Does any required course contain some element of Social Impact Management? **YES**

Is any required course entirely dedicated to social, environmental or ethical issues? **YES**

Is there a Net Impact Chapter on campus? **YES**

A Closer Look at:
Simmons College
Simmons School of Management / Boston, MA

ANNUAL EVENTS:

Corporate Social Responsibility: Learning from Best Practices
This panel discussion features leaders who have found that social responsibility and success are not mutually exclusive concepts. Panelists share best practices and demonstrate how their organizations are incorporating social responsibility into their profit goals. The panel is jointly sponsored by Simmons Net Impact.

Simmons Women's Leadership Conference
The Simmons School of Management's annual Leadership Conference is the world's premier leadership event for women, consistently attracting world-class leaders from business, government, education, media, and the arts.

OTHER PROGRAMS:

The Career Services Office (CSO)
The CSO works hand in hand with the Center for Gender in Organizations, Simmons Net Impact, and the Office of the Dean, in building relationships with both nonprofit organizations and private sectorcompanies that participate in Simmons School of Management events focused on corporate social responsibility. The school funds student participation in industry and academic conferences related to principled leadership and environmental/social impact management.

Foundations of Business
This orientation course provides an introduction to the Simmons School of Management community and the MBA experience to our incoming students. Students are exposed to the importance of ethical, social, and environmental issues in management through the use of cases, simulations, guest speakers, scholarly articles, reflection questions, and examination of current events.

STUDENT CLUBS AND PROGRAMS:

Ethics Club
The mission of the Ethics Club is to serve as a learning resource to Simmons School of Management MBA students for a wide range of business ethics issues, including how ethical decisions impact business successes or failures. The assumption is that ethical issues are complex business dilemmas for which better decisions can be found through ongoing discussion. Areas of interest include sustainability, economic, social, and environmental concerns; corporate accountability; ethical decision making; socially responsible investing; and social enterprise.

Latina Club
The SOM Latina Club was established to learn about business opportunities in the workplace, develop management skills, learn how bilingualism and biculturalism can be used to advance careers, and network with other area Latino groups. The group sponsors several speakers who share their experiences about being Hispanic in today's workplace.

SCHOOL DEMOGRAPHICS	
Number of Full-Time Students	58
International Students	25%
Female Students	100%

Pre-MBA Employment:

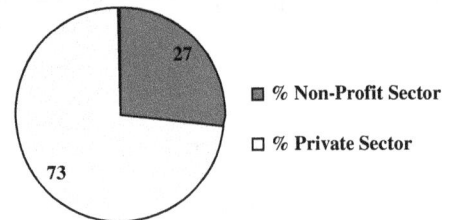

27

■ % Non-Profit Sector

□ % Private Sector

73

2006/2007 School Year

THE CENTER FOR BUSINESS EDUCATION'S BOTTOM LINE ON SIMMONS COLLEGE:
Compared to other business schools in our survey, Simmons College offers an excellent number of courses featuring relevant content, and does a good job in those courses explicitly addressing how mainstream business improves the world. Simmons College requires 15 core courses featuring relevant content.

A Closer Look at:
S. P. Jain Institute of Management and Research
Business School / Mumbai, India

http://www.spjimr.org/index.asp

THE ASPEN INSTITUTE
Center for Business Education

WHAT THE SCHOOL SAYS:

At the heart of our institute's approach is our mission to influence the practice here and now and to promote value-based growth. Our endeavor is to ensure that the experience with the institute is a significant value addition to an individual's career and indeed his or her entire life.

A QUICK LOOK

NOTE: All information is self-reported data submitted to the Center for Business Education

COURSES*

CSR/Business Ethics (1)

KEY JOINT DEGREES

MBA & Resource Mobilization Management

ACTIVITIES*

Speakers/Seminars (1)
Orientation Activities (2)
Internship/Consulting (1)
Student Competitions (1)
Clubs & Programs (2)
Institutes/Centers (1)
Joint Degrees (1)

* Figures in parentheses indicate the number of courses/activities that, in whole or in part, integrate social, environmental, or ethical perspectives

NOTABLE FEATURES

CORE COURSES:

DOCC Project

In DOCC, students work on a project in the social sector for six weeks. In the process, students learn to work in unstructured environments and under resource constraints. Students develop a understanding of how to make a difference.

ANNUAL EVENTS:

Social Impact Award Competition

The Social Impact Award Competition was instituted to recognize and appreciate the success stories in the social sector, which reflect the interdependencies of business practices and showcase their impact on society. Corporations and NGOsare invited to demonstrate their exemplary work with social impact.

Orientation Field Visits

Orientation Field Visits involve visits to live social projects, where students witness the challenges and tasks firsthand and interact with social workers to learn the power of volunteeism and the ability to manage with meager resources.

OTHER PROGRAMS:

Consulting Project

This project involves exploring and identifying livelihood opportunities for people of Ladakh, a region in the Himalayas that, due to heavy snow, is disconnected from the mainland for almost six months a year. The project sensitized faculty and students to the challenges involved and the need to contribute their best abilities to such sectors.

SCHOOL DEMOGRAPHICS

Number of Full-Time Students	**230**
Female Students	**30%**

Pre-MBA Employment:

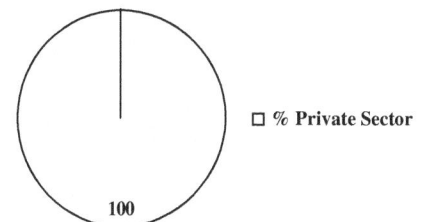

□ % Private Sector

100

2006/2007 School Year

STUDENT CLUBS AND PROGRAMS:

Ehsaas

Ehsaas is a student initiative that promotes the appreciation of the issues of differently abled children. Ehsaas also organizes a cultural event where experts share their perspectives on the subject with the institute's community.

LIFE

This club promotes environmental awareness and action in the campus and the city. The Club organized a competition and an exhibition of eco-friendly idols of Ganapati, a popular festival in India for schoolchildren (more than 300 participated), thus spreading the concern for environment among them.

QUESTIONS TO CONSIDER:

Does any required course contain some element of Social Impact Management? **YES**

Is any required course entirely dedicated to social, environmental, or ethical issues? **YES**

Is there a Net Impact Chapter on campus? **NO**

THE CENTER FOR BUSINESS EDUCATION'S BOTTOM LINE ON S. P. JAIN INSTITUTE OF MANAGEMENT AND RESEARCH:
By participating in the Center for Business Education's Beyond Grey Pinstripes 2007 MBA survey, S.P. Jain Institute demonstrates great dedication to integrating environmental and social impact management issues into its teaching and research. S.P. Jain Institute of Management and Research requires 1 core course featuring relevant content.

A Closer Look at:
Stanford University
Graduate School of Business / Stanford, CA

http://www.gsb.stanford.edu/

THE ASPEN INSTITUTE
Center for Business Education

WHAT THE SCHOOL SAYS:

Stanford Graduate School of Business (GSB) believes that organizational leadership is a noble and critical pursuit. MBA students are prepared to tackle social and environmental issues as corporate managers, nonprofit leaders, government officials, board members, and volunteers.

A QUICK LOOK

NOTE: All information is self-reported data submitted to the Center for Business Education

COURSES*

Accounting (8)
Business & Government (5)
Business Law (2)
CSR/Business Ethics (6)
Economics (11)
Entrepreneurship (3)
Environmental (1)
Finance (13)
HR Management (4)
Information Technology (4)
International Management (3)
General Management (5)
Marketing (5)
Organizational Behavior (24)
Operations Management (12)
Public/Nonprofit Mgt (1)
Strategy (14)

KEY CONCENTRATIONS

Nonprofit Management

Socially Responsible Business

KEY JOINT DEGREES

MBA & Environmental Sciences

MBA & Public Policy

ACTIVITIES*

Speakers/Seminars (67)
Orientation Activities (6)
Internship/Consulting (5)
Student Competitions (2)
Clubs & Programs (11)
Career Development (1)
Institutes/Centers (9)
Concentrations (5)
Joint Degrees (4)

* Figures in parentheses indicate the number of courses/activities that, in whole or in part, integrate social, environmental, or ethical perspectives

NOTABLE FEATURES

CORE COURSES:

Operations
This course explores topics ranging from environmental concerns to educational systems. Specific issues discussed are waste reduction, pollution prevention, and sustainability in the context of carpet fiber, paper, automobile, and semiconductor manufacturing plants and the costs/benefits of the New York City Public School System.

Managerial Economics
Through case analysis and discussion, this Managerial Economics course includes social impact and environmental management topics. Ethical discussions range from employee incentive programs to price discrimination and profit maximization. Environmental focus includes the importance of including analysis of environmental externalities in the economic analysis of managerial decisions.

ELECTIVE COURSES:

Strategic Leadership of Nonprofits
This course is focused on the leadership and management of nonprofits and examines the challenge of formulating, evaluating, and implementing an organization's mission and strategy. The course highlights the mechanisms underlying the relationship between a robust strategy and economic prosperity. It also illustrates the psychological and emotional power of a clear and compelling mission.

International Development
This course examines global poverty from a business-school point of view, i.e., starting from the proposition that nations are poor because their markets and firms aren't working as they should. The issues examined range from doing business in an emerging economy to what policies could reduce global poverty. Topics include Angola's troubles, AIDS and foreign aid, microcredit, corruption and transparency, education in developing nations: what works?, social entrepreneurship, Jamaica's music industry, and entrepreneurship in China.

INSTITUTES AND CENTERS:

Center for Social Innovation
Stanford GSB created the Center for Social Innovation to invest its resources in a society confronted by profound needs and complex problems. The center reaches thousands of individuals and organizations each year through executive education, conferences, lectures, and pro bono nonprofit consulting.

Global Supply Chain Management Forum
The Stanford Global Supply Chain Management Forum is a leading research institute in partnership with the School of Engineering, which advances the theory and practice of excellence in global supply chain management. The Responsible and Sustainable Supply Chains conference in 2006 brought together corporate and nonprofit leaders, policy makers, and academics to share best practices for creating sustainable supply chains that can improve business performance.

QUESTIONS TO CONSIDER:

Does any required course contain some element of Social Impact Management? **YES**

Is any required course entirely dedicated to social, environmental, or ethical issues? **YES**

Is there a Net Impact Chapter on campus? **YES**

A Closer Look at:
Stanford University
Graduate School of Business / Stanford, CA

ANNUAL EVENTS:

■ *Service Learning Consulting Program*

The Service Learning Consulting Program exposes students to social and environmental innovations around the world by working alongside globally recognized social entrepreneurs. The program has three primary objectives: (1)To highlight the relevance of business skills in solving social and environmental problems (2)To contribute through on-the-ground service activities and follow-up projects (3)To build students' active involvement in and commitment to service throughout their lives. Four-week trips have included Brazil, New Orleans, and Kenya/Uganda.

■ *Conradin von Gugelberg Memorial Lecture on the Environment*

The von Gugelberg Fund promotes an environmental ethic among GSB students and alumni, particularly by annually hosting a major environmental leader to highlight the important role business can play in protecting the environment. Events include a group discussion, workshop, lecture, and reception.

■ *BASES Social E-Challenge*

Furthering its vision of creating the next generation of entrepreneurs, BASES (Business Association of Stanford Entrepreneurial Students) a club comprised of Stanford undergrads, grad students, and business students launched Stanford's fourth annual Social E-Challenge. The Social E-Challenge is a business plan competition for socially conscious for-profit and nonprofit startups.

OTHER PROGRAMS:

■ *Stanford Management Internship Fund (SMIF)*

The SMIF encourages students to pursue summer job opportunities and professional careers in the nonprofit and public sectors, provide high-quality management skills to those sectors, and enrich the Stanford GSB community's understanding of management issues in the nonprofit and public sectors. The GSB funds SMIF internships to approximate students' median summer salary.

STUDENT CLUBS AND PROGRAMS:

■ *Health Care Club*

The Health Care Club brings students with any level of interest or experience in health care together with alumni, industry experts, and thought leaders who share common interests. It is an interdisciplinary club with membership from the business school, medical school, law school, biosciences program, and other medically related programs. Members have access to career and networking opportunities, speakers, the Stanford Health Care Symposium, and site visits to area biotech, medical device, and health care firms.

SCHOOL DEMOGRAPHICS	
Number of Full-Time Students	757
International Students	32%
Female Students	31%
Pre-MBA Employment:	

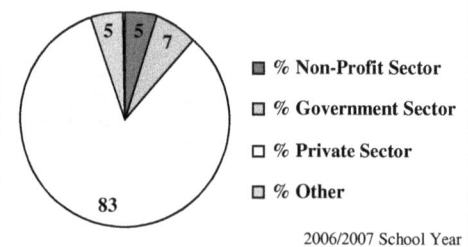

Pie chart values: 5, 5, 7, 83

■ % Non-Profit Sector
□ % Government Sector
□ % Private Sector
□ % Other

2006/2007 School Year

■ *Stanford fACT!*

Stanford fACT! (Future Alumni Consulting Team) is a group designed to enable current students to work on meaningful pro bono ACT consulting projects with Stanford Graduate School of Business alumni. fACT! is ideal for students who want to work with organizations on a project basis, rather than committing to longer-term relationships.

FACULTY PIONEER:

■ *2005 – Rising Star Award, Erica Plambeck*

Professor Plambeck's teachings and research reflect commitment to critical environmental issues. She has researched the diverse implications of the emerging regulation of electronics waste and her core operations course introduces students to topics ranging from waste reduction and pollution prevention in semiconductor manufacturing to the ethics of "management by stress" in assembly line optimization. In her Environmental Entrepreneurship elective course she encourages students to envision private solutions to environmental concerns. Dr. Plambeck represents the business school on the Stanford University Provost's Committee on the Environment.

THE CENTER FOR BUSINESS EDUCATION'S BOTTOM LINE ON STANFORD UNIVERSITY:
Compared to other business schools in our survey, Stanford University offers a truly extraordinary number of courses featuring relevant content, and does a truly extraordinary job in those courses explicitly addressing how mainstream business improves the world. Stanford University requires 23 core courses featuring relevant content.

A Closer Look at:
Thunderbird School of Global Management
Glendale, AZ
http://www.thunderbird.edu/

WHAT THE SCHOOL SAYS:

Thunderbird's commitment to preparing MBA students to manage social and environmental issues begins with our mission statement : "We educate global leaders who create sustainable prosperity worldwide." Through our educational programs, we train talented business managers who also understand the social and environmental impact of their decisions.

A QUICK LOOK

NOTE: All information is self-reported data submitted to the Center for Business Education

COURSES*

Accounting (1)
Business & Government (2)
CSR/Business Ethics (2)
Entrepreneurship (1)
HR Management (1)
International Management (5)
Marketing (2)
Organizational Behavior (1)
Operations Management (1)
Strategy (1)

KEY CONCENTRATIONS

International Development

ACTIVITIES*

Speakers/Seminars (4)
Orientation Activities (1)
Internship/Consulting (1)
Student Competitions (1)
Clubs & Programs (3)
Career Development (1)
Institutes/Centers (2)
Concentrations (1)

* Figures in parentheses indicate the number of courses/activities that, in whole or in part, integrate social, environmental, or ethical perspectives

NOTABLE FEATURES

CORE COURSES:

Global Enterprise
Global Enterprise is an introduction to the issues of developing and launching new business initiatives. A core module of the course is dedicated to addressing governance, social, and environmental issues facing entrepreneurs. Sessions are dedicated to personal and professional ethics, corruption, corporate governance, codes of conduct, social enterprise, and base of the pyramid business strategy.

Operations Management
This course examines processes that deliver value to customers in the form of products and services. Global operations present special challenges because of complexities associated with customer preferences, government regulations, cultural factors, workplace safety, community concerns, and environmental responsibility. The course explicitly highlights five operating priorities, one of which is social responsibility, and emphasizes that operations must be designed not only for customers but also for other stakeholders.

ELECTIVE COURSES:

Conflict Management and Social Change
This course notes that economic development and social change can offer business opportunities for global managers, but the development process can lead to social, cultural, ecological, and political conflicts. This course explores the roots of such conflicts and methods of conflict management, such as negotiations, stakeholder engagement, and multicultural communications.

Sustainable Business Development
This course covers issues of sustainable business strategy, ecotourism, economics and the environment, international environmental policy, global climate change, ecosystem markets, community engagement, energy management, and base of the pyramid business opportunities.

INSTITUTES AND CENTERS:

Lincoln Center for Ethics in Global Management
The Lincoln Center for Ethics in Global Management promotes ethics, sustainability, and social and environmental awareness among Thunderbird's students and corporate partners through instruction, consultation, executive education, and online resources. The center acts as a foundation that supports student-led initiatives in the areas of corporate social responsibility and sustainability.

Thunderbird for Good
Thunderbird for Good, the school's office for social responsibility, leverages the school's expertise to help non-profits and social entrepreneurs achieve their missions. The office sponsors in-class projects that bring students together with real clients to address their current business challenges and gives students hands-on experience in responsible business, both in and out of the classroom.

QUESTIONS TO CONSIDER:

Does any required course contain some element of Social Impact Management? **YES**

Is any required course entirely dedicated to social, environmental, or ethical issues? **NO**

Is there a Net Impact Chapter on campus? **YES**

All information in this profile is drawn and/or adapted from the self-reported data of the Center for Business Education's Beyond Grey Pinstripes 2007 MBA survey. The Center for Business Education is housed within the Business and Society Program at the Aspen Institute. For more info, visit www.AspenCBE.org.

Thunderbird School of Global Management
Glendale, AZ

ANNUAL EVENTS:

Global Citizenship Events
A core pillar of the Thunderbird educational experience is an introduction to global citizenship, which occurs through a variety of extracurricular events. Events include Ethics Day and the Charles Olin Norton Lecture Series, where feature speakers discuss issues of sustainability.

Thunderbird Sustainable Innovation Challenge
The Thunderbird Sustainable Innovation Challenge, cosponsored by Net Impact, tests MBA teams from around the world to address real corporate issues in ways that simultaneously create business and societal value.

OTHER PROGRAMS:

The Thunderbird Oath of Honor
An important part of Thunderbird's Foundations Week during orientation is The Thunderbird Oath of Honor, which is a pledge by Thunderbirds to act as responsible professional managers upon graduation. The oath serves as a professional commitment to respect the dignity of all peoples, oppose corruption and exploitation, and to strive toward creating sustainable prosperity. Students take this promise with them when they leave campus to guide their decision making throughout their careers.

Career Management Center (CMC)
The CMC has a dedicated professional with full time focus on international development and NGO/non profits business development, employer relationships, and student advising. The CMC also sponsors training on the social sector, develops and maintains an online guide for students with social impact goals, hosts thought leaders/speakers, funds Corporate Social Responsibility company visits, and annually visits Washington, D.C., to build awareness and lobby for school/student relationships with more than 50 government, development, and social sector organizations.

STUDENT CLUBS AND PROGRAMS:

Net Impact
The Thunderbird Net Impact chapter leads several initiatives on campus, including the school's climate change strategy for reducing our carbon footprint.

International Development Association
The International Development Association participates in the Thunderbird Sustainable Innovation Summit.

SCHOOL DEMOGRAPHICS	
Number of Full-Time Students	600
International Students	45%
Female Students	25%
	2006/2007 School Year

THE CENTER FOR BUSINESS EDUCATION'S BOTTOM LINE ON THUNDERBIRD:
Compared to other business schools in our survey, Thunderbird offers a good number of courses featuring relevant content, and does a good job in those courses explicitly addressing how mainstream business improves the world. Thunderbird requires 9 core courses featuring relevant content.

A Closer Look at:
Tulane University

A. B. Freeman School of Business / New Orleans, LA
http://www.freeman.tulane.edu/academicprogs/mba/

WHAT THE SCHOOL SAYS:
The Freeman School focuses on the individual's relationships in the global context. Through courses and exposure the MBA student experiences business, the environment, and social issues on three continents. By exploring the relationships inherent in a community interdependent on the business world, we develop managers capable of making informed decisions on the global stage.

A QUICK LOOK

NOTE: All information is self-reported data submitted to the Center for Business Education

COURSES*

Business Law (1)
Entrepreneurship (1)
Environmental (2)
Finance (4)
International Management (1)
Marketing (1)
Organizational Behavior (2)

KEY CONCENTRATIONS

**Public and Nonprofit
  Management**

KEY JOINT DEGREES

MBA & Public Health

ACTIVITIES*

Speakers/Seminars (10)
Orientation Activities (2)
Internship/Consulting (4)
Student Competitions (4)
Clubs & Programs (3)
Career Development (2)
Institutes/Centers (2)
Concentrations (1)
Joint Degrees (2)

* Figures in parentheses indicate the number of courses/activities that, in whole or in part, integrate social, environmental, or ethical perspectives

NOTABLE FEATURES

CORE COURSES:
▣ *Global Leadership II*
Global Leadership II focuses on Latin America. The course examines the differences in the business environment across nations from a social, cultural, and political perspective as well as the effect of business environments. The course features a required five-day excursion to Mexico.

ELECTIVE COURSES:
▣ *Environmental Management and Sustainable Development*
This course provides an overview of environmental management with an emphasis on business strategies in our globalizing marketplace. The course begins with a survey of major environmental issues and a discussion of sustainable development. The course then addresses corporate strategies at the broad perspective and at the level of specific elements such as risk, pollution, waste, design, and public affairs. Student teams prepare a business plan presentation for a sustainable enterprise.

▣ *Community Service Consulting*
This course provides students an introduction to a career in consulting with emphasis placed upon consulting to not-for-profit organizations. A field project is required; teammates provide consulting to a real organization. The course includes speakers who address the following class topics: the difference between for-profit and not-for-profit consulting, management of not-for-profit organizations, and careers in not-for-profit consulting.

INSTITUTES AND CENTERS:
▣ *The Levy/Rosenblum Center for Entrepreneurship*
The Levy/Rosenblum Center for Entrepreneurship is actively involved in various programs that reach out to family businesses, small businesses, nonprofit organizations, and community organizations. The center administers the following social entrepreneurship programs: TABA Community Service Program, Social Entrepreneur of the Year Award, Individual Development Account Collaborative of Louisiana, Volunteer Income Tax Assistance, Tulane Business Plan Competition, Social Entrepreneurship Track, and Social Entrepreneurship internships.

▣ *Burkenroad Center for Ethics and Leadership in Management*
The goal of the Burkenroad Center is to increase the understanding of and promote through research and education the ethical decision making of business leaders. The center also fosters open forums among students, faculty, executives, and community leaders on the moral obligations of business professionals.

QUESTIONS TO CONSIDER:

Does any required course contain some element of Social Impact Management? **YES**

Is any required course entirely dedicated to social, environmental, or ethical issues? **NO**

Is there a Net Impact Chapter on campus? **YES**

A Closer Look at:
Tulane University
A. B. Freeman School of Business / New Orleans, LA

ANNUAL EVENTS:

■ *Tulane Business Forum*

The Tulane Business Forum is a conference that currently focuses on rebuilding New Orleans and funding businesses in the recovery mode. Recent topics included the goals of the Recovery Commission, accelerating business to meet demand, and the restoration of local historical sites.

■ *Game Simulation*

An introductory case/simulation during orientation focuses on economic impact in the global community. Students are challenged to examine the impacts associated with business expansion opportunities, labor cost, transportation, and the community impacts associated with imbalanced political and social outcomes.

OTHER PROGRAMS:

■ *Freeman Consulting Group*

The Freeman Consulting Group coordinates community consulting projects. There is special focus on the public and nonprofit sector. Students who contribute a minimum of 20 hours to the consulting group are recognized at graduation by the alumni association with a special recognition program.

STUDENT CLUBS AND PROGRAMS:

■ *Tulane Chapter of Net Impact*

Tulane's chapter of Net Impact upholds the organization's goals of raising awareness of social and environmental issues affecting business and offering networking opportunities for alternative career choices.

■ *Black MBA Association*

Tulane's chapter of the National Black MBA Association hosts local monthly meetings. The association conducts business-awareness sessions at local colleges and supports community initiatives.

FACULTY PIONEER:

■ *2001 – Academic Leadership Award, Arthur P. Brief*

Arthur Brief has been a consistent voice for humane and ethical organizational management and work design throughout his distinguished faculty career. He has exercised academic leadership not only through his own extensive and highly regarded publishing record but also in his active and wide-ranging editorial roles, promoting quality scholarship in his field.

SCHOOL DEMOGRAPHICS	
Number of Full-Time Students	141
International Students	31%
Female Students	29%

Pre-MBA Employment:

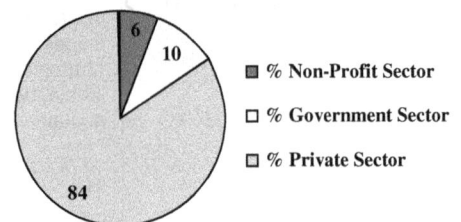

- ■ % Non-Profit Sector
- □ % Government Sector
- □ % Private Sector

2006/2007 School Year

THE CENTER FOR BUSINESS EDUCATION'S BOTTOM LINE ON TULANE UNIVERSITY:
Compared to other business schools in our survey, Tulane University offers a good number of courses featuring relevant content, and does a good job in those courses explicitly addressing how mainstream business improves the world. Tulane University requires 1 core course featuring relevant content.

A Closer Look at:
Universidad de Los Andes
School of Management / Bogota, Colombia
http://ingles.uniandes.edu.co/ECO/MBA.php

WHAT THE SCHOOL SAYS:

The preparation of MBA students to manage social and environmental issues is integrated in the Universidad de Los Andes School of Management's mission, which is to "educate socially responsible people that embrace an international perspective and that are capable of creating, understanding and furthering the advancement of organizations."

A QUICK LOOK

NOTE: All information is self-reported data submitted to the Center for Business Education

COURSES*

CSR/Business Ethics (1)
Marketing (2)
Operations Management (1)

KEY JOINT DEGREES

MBA & Public Administration

MBA & Engineering and Environmental Management

ACTIVITIES*

Speakers/Seminars (13)
Orientation Activities (1)
Internship/Consulting (2)
Student Competitions (1)
Career Development (1)
Institutes/Centers (2)
Joint Degrees (2)

* Figures in parentheses indicate the number of courses/activities that, in whole or in part, integrate social, environmental, or ethical perspectives

NOTABLE FEATURES

CORE COURSES:

Public Responsibilities of Management
This course discusses the context of public interest from a business and citizenship perspective. Society and business interact permanently and influence continuous improvement and changes. The course addresses the following main topics: ethics and individual responsibility, social responsibility of business, social responsibility of universities, and responsibility of public institutions.

Operations Management
This course provides an introduction of cleaner production strategy as a way to reduce environmental impacts and costs of production and logistic processes.

ELECTIVE COURSES:

Social Marketing
This course introduces management tools for NGOs to strengthen their fund-raising and institutional positioning. The course also discusses experiences and cases of collaboration of the private sector and NGOs as a strategy of CSR.

Marketing Strategies for Low Income Families
The purpose of this course is to present and discuss the importance of low income consumer markets in Latin America (challenges and opportunities), recent data developed through market researches about profile and consumer behavior, and marketing strategies aiming to reach and stimulate growth in this enormous consumer market.

INSTITUTES AND CENTERS:

Program on Social Initiatives IESO
IESO seeks to understand and change our surroundings through concrete proposals for action with social and business leaders, students, teachers, and volunteers. IESO aims at supporting the economic viability of social initiatives and the proper social impact of lucrative ones. IESO conducts research that seeks to understand concrete cases of initiatives that have social goals, provides teachings that explore these experiences in the classroom, and provides service to individuals and organizations that are dedicated to improving the life conditions of different populations in our society.

Center for Strategy and Competitiveness
The Center for Strategy and Competitiveness is focused on research and consultancy on issues related to free trade agreements, clusters, business strategy, environmental management strategies, and assistance programs to SMEs in the Colombian and Latin American context.

QUESTIONS TO CONSIDER:

Does any required course contain some element of Social Impact Management? **YES**

Is any required course entirely dedicated to social, environmental, or ethical issues? **YES**

Is there a Net Impact Chapter on campus? **NO**

All information in this profile is drawn and/or adapted from the self-reported data of the Center for Business Education's Beyond Grey Pinstripes 2007 MBA survey. The Center for Business Education is housed within the Business and Society Program at the Aspen Institute. For more info, visit www.AspenCBE.org.

A Closer Look at:
Universidad de Los Andes
School of Management / Bogota, Colombia

ANNUAL EVENTS:

■ *Social Responsibility in Small to Medium- Sized Enterprises (SMEs)*

This workshop is organized by the School of Management in alliance with the Global Compact program of the United Nations, the Chamber of Commerce of Bogota, Colsubsidio (a provider of social services), and CEMEX (a cement company). The aim of the workshop is to promote the development of socially responsible practices in SMEs. Over the course of three days, representatives of SMEs are trained in best practices and prepare their own action plan. Afterwards, the facilitators of the workshops accompany the SMEs in the implementation of their action plans.

SCHOOL DEMOGRAPHICS	
Number of Full-Time Students	60
International Students	14%
Female Students	45%
	2006/2007 School Year

■ *Beyond Duty: Projects with a Social Impact*

This is a competition that aims at the promotion of social consciousness and competencies among all students of Los Andes University. It's designed to encourage the participation of students in multidisciplinary projects that lead toward social changes though the identification, design, and development of practical, appropriate alternatives to social problems.

OTHER PROGRAMS:

■ *National Environmental Forum*

Los Andes School of Management is a leading member of the National Environmental Forum, an alliance of seven Colombian NGOs and universities. Seminars address environmental issues and recently have included topics such as environmental politics in Colombia, water supply and management, and biodiversity conservation strategies.

■ *CSR in Bogota*

This consulting project focuses on the participation of the private sector in the social development of Bogota. The project is carried out together with the municipality of Bogota and the main industrial branch organisation.

THE CENTER FOR BUSINESS EDUCATION'S BOTTOM LINE ON UNIVERSIDAD DE LOS ANDES:
Compared to other business schools in our survey, Universidad de Los Andes does a good job in relevant courses explicitly addressing how mainstream business improves the world. Universidad de Los Andes requires 2 core courses featuring relevant content.

A Closer Look at:
University of Alaska Anchorage
College of Business and Public Policy / Anchorage, AK
http://www.scob.alaska.edu/default.asp

THE ASPEN INSTITUTE
Center for Business Education

WHAT THE SCHOOL SAYS:
The MBA degree in the College of Business and Public Policy program at the University of Alaska Anchorage is comprised of four components, many of which specifically address social and environmental issues inherent in mainstream business. Available Public Health Administration courses emphasize environmental protection, health education, and environmental quality engineering.

A QUICK LOOK

NOTE: All information is self-reported data submitted to the Center for Business Education

COURSES*

Organizational Behavior (1)

ACTIVITIES*

Speakers/Seminars (2)
Concentrations (1)

* Figures in parentheses indicate the number of courses/activities that, in whole or in part, integrate social, environmental, or ethical perspectives

NOTABLE FEATURES

ELECTIVE COURSES:

Creating Successful Organizations
The principal goals of this course are to survey our academic and practitioner knowledge about organizations, their structures, and processes; to understand the tools and practices available to successfully intervene in the development and change of organizations; and to undertake a project to create organizational development tools and implementing those tools.

PROGRAMS:

Doing Business in and with China
This conference explored "areas of opportunity" for business ventures and investment within and between Alaska and China and addressed the methods, procedures, requirements, and considerations of market entry and international marketing management.

QUESTIONS TO CONSIDER:

Does any required course contain some element of Social Impact Management? **NO**

Is any required course entirely dedicated to social, environmental, or ethical issues? **NO**

Is there a Net Impact Chapter on campus? **NO**

SCHOOL DEMOGRAPHICS	
Number of Full-Time Students	50
International Students	20%
Female Students	58%
2006/2007 School Year	

THE CENTER FOR BUSINESS EDUCATION'S BOTTOM LINE ON UNIVERSITY OF ALASKA ANCHORAGE:
By participating in the Center for Business Education's Beyond Grey Pinstripes 2007 MBA survey, University of Alaska Anchorage demonstrates great dedication to integrating environmental and social impact management issues into its teaching and research.

All information in this profile is drawn and/or adapted from the self-reported data of the Center for Business Education's Beyond Grey Pinstripes 2007 MBA survey. The Center for Business Education is housed within the Business and Society Program at the Aspen Institute. For more info, visit www.AspenCBE.org.

A Closer Look at:
University of Alberta
School of Business / Edmonton, Canada
http://mba.bus.ualberta.ca/

THE ASPEN INSTITUTE
Center for Business Education

WHAT THE SCHOOL SAYS:

As future leaders of both the public and private sector, Alberta MBA graduates have the opportunity to bring social and environmental issues into the forefront of mainstream business. The Alberta MBA program is designed to ensure that students develop a high degree of awareness of social and ethical concepts and issues and the ability to recognize and deal with the core issues.

A QUICK LOOK

NOTE: All information is self-reported data submitted to the Center for Business Education

COURSES*

Business Law (1)
CSR/Business Ethics (2)
Entrepreneurship (1)
Environmental (3)
Information Technology (1)
International Management (1)
Marketing (1)
Organizational Behavior (3)
Strategy (2)

KEY CONCENTRATIONS

Natural Resources and Energy
International Business

KEY JOINT DEGREES

MBA & Forestry
MBA & Agriculture

ACTIVITIES*

Speakers/Seminars (10)
Orientation Activities (1)
Internship/Consulting (3)
Student Competitions (1)
Clubs & Programs (1)
Career Development (1)
Institutes/Centers (3)
Concentrations (4)
Joint Degrees (2)

* Figures in parentheses indicate the number of courses/activities that, in whole or in part, integrate social, environmental, or ethical perspectives

NOTABLE FEATURES

CORE COURSES:

- *Natural Resource and Energy Capstone*

This course provides an opportunity to develop a better and deeper understanding of international aspects of energy/resource markets, particularly Canada-U.S. issues. The course is structured around a visit to Houston hosted by the Centre for Energy Economics of the Bureau of Economic Geology of the University of Texas at Austin.

- *Environmental Economics*

This course is intended to introduce students to the theory of environmental economics and to examine its role in management and policymaking. The first half of the course is devoted to the development of a model of pollution, the evaluation of policy in this context, and to the setting of optimal environmental policies. The second half of the course is devoted to applications. Particular policies and practices implemented in North America will be examined.

ELECTIVE COURSES:

- *Internet Strategy for Small Business*

The focus of this course pertains to developing an understanding of how small- to medium-sized businesses and not-for-profit organizations may utilize the Internet as part of their business strategy. In the initial part of the course students will familiarize themselves with the Internet as it relates to e-business and e-philanthropy. In the second part, students will prepare advisory reports for a business or a not-for-profit organization that has expressed interest in developing or refining its Internet strategy.

- *Managing International Business*

This course aims to develop skills in analyzing international business situations, generating alternative courses of action, and developing recommendations for firms and individual managers. Students develop a richer understanding of how different economic, sociopolitical, cultural, and regulatory environments affect management practice and increase the complexity of managing multinational businesses.

INSTITUTES AND CENTERS:

- *Centre for Applied Business Research in Energy and the Environment (CABREE)*

CABREE is dedicated to providing applied economic analysis to inform public policy debates on issues of vital importance to Alberta and Canada as a whole. CABREE's research efforts focus on energy markets, electricity restructuring and climate change issues.

- *Canadian Centre for Social Entrepreneurship (CCRE)*

CCRE's mission is to build a collective understanding of the scope of social entrepreneurship and to encourage entrepreneurial thinking and approaches in matters of interest between and within the voluntary, private and public sectors.

QUESTIONS TO CONSIDER:

Does any required course contain some element of Social Impact Management? **YES**

Is any required course entirely dedicated to social, environmental, or ethical issues? **NO**

Is there a Net Impact Chapter on campus? **YES**

All information in this profile is drawn and/or adapted from the self-reported data of the Center for Business Education's Beyond Grey Pinstripes 2007 MBA survey. The Center for Business Education is housed within the Business and Society Program at the Aspen Institute. For more info, visit www.AspenCBE.org.

A Closer Look at:
University of Alberta
School of Business / Edmonton, Canada

THE ASPEN INSTITUTE
Center for Business Education

ANNUAL EVENTS:

Orientation Ethics Primer
During new student orientation, students are presented with an ethics primer. The primer is in a discussion format and covers both professional ethics and academic integrity. In addition to the specific ethics primer during orientation, students also take part in a leadership course, where ethical awareness is one of the eight key learning goals.

EPCOR Lecture Series
The EPCOR Lecture Series is dedicated to environmental issues. Recent topics have included discussion on sustainable fossil fuels and future water supplies.

OTHER PROGRAMS:

MBA Games Case Competition
Teams from MBA programs across Canada compete in the MBA Games, hosted by the University of Alberta. The academic portion of this competition features a strategic case that has an international social development focus.

Kendall Foundation / Parks Canada Partnership
The Kendall Foundation provides funding to the Centre for Applied Business Research in Energy and the Environment for an initiative between the University of Alberta and Parks Canada. This initiative is designed to bring business practice improvements to Parks Canada operations and provide challenging opportunities for MBA students.

STUDENT CLUBS AND PROGRAMS:

Net Impact, University of Alberta Chapter
Net Impact's University of Alberta chapter organizes speaker events, community volunteer opportunities, and supports a group of students attending the annual Net Impact conference.

SCHOOL DEMOGRAPHICS

Number of Full-Time Students	88
International Students	33%
Female Students	40%

Pre-MBA Employment:

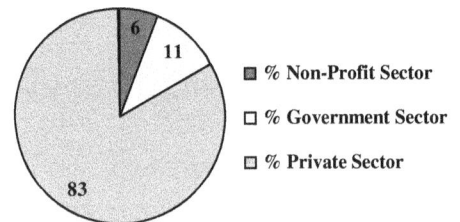

- 6
- 11
- 83
- % Non-Profit Sector
- % Government Sector
- % Private Sector

2006/2007 School Year

THE CENTER FOR BUSINESS EDUCATION'S BOTTOM LINE ON UNIVERSITY OF ALBERTA:
Compared to other business schools in our survey, University of Alberta offers a good number of courses featuring relevant content, and does a good job in those courses explicitly addressing how mainstream business improves the world. University of Alberta requires 7 core courses featuring relevant content.

The University of Arizona

Eller College of Management / Tucson, AZ
http://www.eller.arizona.edu/

WHAT THE SCHOOL SAYS:

At Eller, we believe that our students and alumni have not only a responsibility to master academic concepts but also to develop a commitment to community involvement. We are a business school that offers a program in social entrepreneurship and we coordinate activities throughout the year to put our students in situations to develop their social responsibility.

A QUICK LOOK

NOTE: All information is self-reported data submitted to the Center for Business Education

COURSES*

Information Technology (1)
General Management (1)
Organizational Behavior (1)
Public/Nonprofit Mgt (2)

KEY CONCENTRATIONS

Human Resources Management

KEY JOINT DEGREES

MBA & Natural Resource Studies

ACTIVITIES*

Speakers/Seminars (1)
Orientation Activities (1)
Internship/Consulting (1)
Student Competitions (1)
Clubs & Programs (1)
Career Development (1)
Concentrations (1)
Joint Degrees (3)

* Figures in parentheses indicate the number of courses/activities that, in whole or in part, integrate social, environmental, or ethical perspectives

NOTABLE FEATURES

ELECTIVE COURSES:

▪ *Social and Ethical Issues/Internet*

This course aims to provide a broad survey of the individual, organizational, and cultural impacts of computers and to stimulate reflection upon the social and ethical issues provoked by current and projected uses of computers. Some topics include an in-depth look at computers as they relate to workplaces, communities, public policy, legal issues, education, privacy, and moral values.

▪ *Social Entrepreneurship*

In this course, students focus their business and entrepreneurial skills on social and/or environmental problem solving. Through a series of readings, class discussions, guest speakers, and assignments, they become aware of a number of contemporary social problems. Students review case studies of social entrepreneurship and get the opportunity to apply their skills to a social or environmental problem of their choice.

QUESTIONS TO CONSIDER:

Does any required course contain some element of Social Impact Management? **NO**

Is any required course entirely dedicated to social, environmental or ethical issues? **NO**

Is there a Net Impact Chapter on campus? **YES**

A Closer Look at:
The University of Arizona
Eller College of Management / Tucson, AZ

ANNUAL EVENTS:

■ *Distinguished Speakers Series*
The Eller College of Management presents distinguished executives in positions of CEO, president, or vice president of national or global organizations who address contemporary topics in business and offer practical advice for professional success. Many of these topics cover social impact in the areas of ethics, leadership, and corporate social responsibility.

■ *Orientation Activities*
During orientation, students participate in a "Day of Giving" and volunteer at local agencies in order to learn the importance of corporate citizenship and community involvement. Students also compete in a case competition, not only working to collectively solve a business problem but also strategizing how their decisions will affect the community.

OTHER PROGRAMS:

■ *Consulting Program: MBA Field Projects*
Students are given the opportunity to apply what they have learned in the classroom to real-world business challenges and problems. Business sponsors engage student teams to address an actual problem over the course of the semester. Each engagement, or field project, involves rigorous research and analysis, culminating in a final written report with actionable recommendations. Participating business sponsors range from Fortune 100 companies to start-ups to nonprofit organizations.

STUDENT CLUBS AND PROGRAMS:

■ *Net Impact*
Net Impact provides an opportunity for MBA students to participate with leaders focused on changing the world through business. This is accomplished by providing MBA students the chance to participate in conference calls with industry leaders, to conduct campus initiatives, and to attend the national conference with other MBA students and professionals.

SCHOOL DEMOGRAPHICS	
Number of Full-Time Students	119
International Students	42%
Female Students	33%

Pre-MBA Employment:

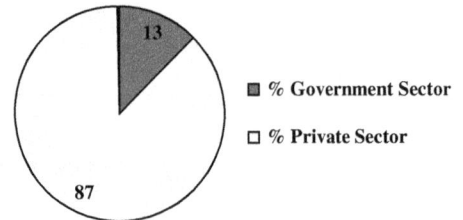

■ % Government Sector
□ % Private Sector

2006/2007 School Year

THE CENTER FOR BUSINESS EDUCATION'S BOTTOM LINE ON THE UNIVERSITY OF ARIZONA:
Compared to other business schools in our survey, The University of Arizona offers a good number of courses featuring relevant content, and does a good job in those courses explicitly addressing how mainstream business improves the world.

A Closer Look at:
The University of Auckland
Business School / Auckland, New Zealand
http://www.business.auckland.ac.nz/

WHAT THE SCHOOL SAYS:
As a leading institution, the Business School takes seriously its responsibilities as the critic and conscience of society. This is especially true given New Zealand's size and its reliance on its "clean green" image. Going beyond the theoretical and into the practical, over the years the MBA program and its students have worked with a wide range of projects for not-for-profit organizations as a way of contributing to society.

A QUICK LOOK

NOTE: All information is self-reported data submitted to the Center for Business Education

COURSES*

Organizational Behavior (1)

ACTIVITIES*

Speakers/Seminars (4)
Institutes/Centers (2)

* Figures in parentheses indicate the number of courses/activities that, in whole or in part, integrate social, environmental, or ethical perspectives

NOTABLE FEATURES

CORE COURSES:
* *Leadership and Ethics*
This course examines the nature, need for, and impacts of creativity, responsibility, and probity in enterprise leadership and related communications. Other topics include alternative leadership styles, self-knowledge, and the dynamics of leadership as a vital process.

INSTITUTES AND CENTERS:
* *Mira Szászy Research Centre*
The Mira Szászy Research Centre is dedicated to enhancing the quality of life for Mäori, Pacific Island, and other indigenous peoples, their communities, small-medium enterprises, and nations.

* *Excelerator: New Zealand Leadership Institute*
Some of the overarching goals of Excelerator are to grow and develop leadership in New Zealand across the sectors of business, education, community, charity, government, sport, and the creative arts in order to effect positive change and outstanding performance; and to create a nexus between academic theory, research, and practice to transform the understanding and practice of leadership in New Zealand.

ANNUAL EVENTS:
* *The Dean's Distinguished Speaker Series*
The Dean's Distinguished Speaker Speaker Series presents topical issues to the wider business community.
Amongst the topics presented are New Zealand trade policy: Doha suspended;
taking the New Zealand economy global; and the role an entrepreneurial university
plays in economic development.

SCHOOL DEMOGRAPHICS

Number of Full-Time Students   2

2006/2007 School Year

OTHER PROGRAMS:
* *Earth in the Balance Sheet*
The University of Auckland Business School hosted climate change campaigner and former U.S. Vice President Al Gore on campus during a brief visit to New Zealand. His presentation at the university, "Earth in the Balance Sheet," examined the impact of climate change on business and investment.

QUESTIONS TO CONSIDER:

Does any required course contain some element of Social Impact Management? **YES**

Is any required course entirely dedicated to social, environmental, or ethical issues? **NO**

Is there a Net Impact Chapter on campus? **NO**

THE CENTER FOR BUSINESS EDUCATION'S BOTTOM LINE ON THE UNIVERSITY OF AUCKLAND:
By participating in the Center for Business Education's Beyond Grey Pinstripes 2007 MBA survey, The University of Auckland demonstrates great dedication to integrating environmental and social impact management issues into its teaching and research. The University of Auckland requires 1 core course featuring relevant content.

University of Bath

School of Management / Bath, United Kingdom

http://www.bath.ac.uk/management/

WHAT THE SCHOOL SAYS:

The ethos of the Bath MBA is to look beyond business processes and techniques to emphasize the importance of self-awareness, intuition, cross-cultural sensitivity, and entrepreneurship skills as well as having a socially responsible and ethical approach to business and management.

A QUICK LOOK

NOTE: All information is self-reported data submitted to the Center for Business Education

COURSES*

Accounting (1)
Entrepreneurship (1)
HR Management (1)
Information Technology (1)
General Management (2)
Organizational Behavior (1)
Operations Management (3)
Strategy (1)

ACTIVITIES*

Speakers/Seminars (17)
Orientation Activities (3)
Clubs & Programs (1)
Career Development (1)
Institutes/Centers (3)

* Figures in parentheses indicate the number of courses/activities that, in whole or in part, integrate social, environmental, or ethical perspectives

NOTABLE FEATURES

CORE COURSES:

Managing Operational Processes

This module provides exposure to a range of practical tools and frameworks and aims to develop a critical understanding of the strategic challenge of reconciling operational resources with customer and other stakeholder requirements, including influence by regulatory and pressure groups. The course discusses the idea of sustainable value incorporating public and private sectors and notions of the triple bottom line.

The Claverton Entrepreneurship Program

Claverton Enterprises is an investment company that invites proposals from MBA teams selecting a promising idea and developing a detailed business plan for the venture's creation. In deciding whether to invest in a new business venture, there is a specific requirement to "Be legal, ethical, and environmentally sound". In addition to being profitable, projects should make a positive contribution to the well-being of society, whether locally, nationally, or transnationally.

ELECTIVE COURSES:

Managing Innovation in Supply Networks

This module focuses on the key strategic and conceptual issues that affect the supply process, especially the need to manage within multiorganisational networks. Discussions include new structures for strategic supply; network theory, leanness and agility; virtual organizations; innovation and the management of technology in supply chains; development in relationship management: advanced concepts in collaboration management; environmentally sound supply management; and corporate social responsibility.

Strategic Supply: Concepts and Implementation

This module focuses on the contextual and theoretical setting for the study of strategic supply management and the competitive environments and networks within which it must be managed. It is designed to enable the student to understand where supply fits within the business decision making model. The module focuses on why firms choose to subcontract activities and to purchase goods and services and, having done so, what drives their decision-making.

INSTITUTES AND CENTERS:

Centre for Action Research in Professional Practice (CARPP)

CARPP's interest and concern is with approaches to action research that integrate action and reflection, so that the knowledge gained in the inquiry is directly relevant to the issues being studied. Action Research involves the formation of new "communicative spaces" in which significant issues can be explored, undertaking a series of "experiments in action," each of which gather new data for reflection and then refocusing action and (often) the focus and the domain of action.

Centre for Business Organizations and Society (CBOS)

CBOS is concerned with the relationship between corporations and the societies within which they operate, the ethical position of modern corporations in different societal contexts, and the study of corporate social responsibility as a strategic phenomenon. CBOS undertakes research that informs decision makers in government, companies, and finance houses of the changing nature of business responsibilities and the merits of social responsiveness.

QUESTIONS TO CONSIDER:

Does any required course contain some element of Social Impact Management? **YES**

Is any required course entirely dedicated to social, environmental, or ethical issues? **NO**

Is there a Net Impact Chapter on campus? **NO**

A Closer Look at:
University of Bath
School of Management / Bath, United Kingdom

ANNUAL EVENTS:

■ *Orientation Workshop*

At this workshop, students are encouraged to build connections between the macro-level of social and environmental sustainability debates and the micro-level of their own professional development through a range of activities. These include connecting economic, social, and environmental debates to professional development. Students consider what economic, social, political, and ecological factors influence professional development in contemporary work settings.

OTHER PROGRAMS:

■ *Economic Regulators and Sustainable Development—Promoting Good Governance*

This seminar focused on two key themes: first, the need to codify key principles of good regulatory governance, as well as implement the "polluter pays" and the precautionary principles; second, to reform the institutional arrangements of government such that it can speak with one voice.

STUDENT CLUBS AND PROGRAMS:

■ *OneWorld*

OneWorld is a student campaigning group concerned with human rights, the environment, inequality, and injustice.

SCHOOL DEMOGRAPHICS	
Number of Full-Time Students	**30**
International Students	**34%**
Female Students	**66%**

Pre-MBA Employment:

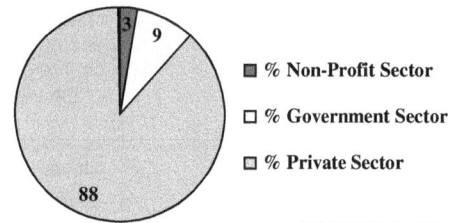

- ■ % Non-Profit Sector
- □ % Government Sector
- □ % Private Sector

2006/2007 School Year

THE CENTER FOR BUSINESS EDUCATION'S BOTTOM LINE ON UNIVERSITY OF BATH:
Compared to other business schools in our survey, University of Bath offers a good number of courses featuring relevant content, and requires 8 core courses featuring relevant content.

A Closer Look at:
University of British Columbia
Sauder School of Business / Vancouver, Canada
http://www.sauder.ubc.ca/

WHAT THE SCHOOL SAYS:

Central to the University of British Columbia MBA is an innovative, award-winning Integrated Core program that weaves together seven key business disciplines into one foundation course. During the Integrated Core, students are first exposed to important social, environmental, and ethical issues that they will face throughout the MBA program and their careers.

A QUICK LOOK

NOTE: All information is self-reported data submitted to the Center for Business Education

COURSES*

Business & Government (1)
Business Law (1)
CSR/Business Ethics (4)
Economics (2)
Environmental (1)
HR Management (3)
Information Technology (1)
International Management (3)
General Management (3)
Marketing (4)
Organizational Behavior (2)
Strategy (4)

KEY CONCENTRATIONS

Sustainability and Business

KEY JOINT DEGREES

MBA & Asia Pacific Policy Studies

ACTIVITIES*

Speakers/Seminars (11)
Orientation Activities (2)
Internship/Consulting (4)
Student Competitions (2)
Clubs & Programs (1)
Career Development (1)
Institutes/Centers (4)
Concentrations (2)
Joint Degrees (1)

* Figures in parentheses indicate the number of courses/activities that, in whole or in part, integrate social, environmental, or ethical perspectives

NOTABLE FEATURES

CORE COURSES:

▣ *Integrated Core—Critical Issue Session on* The Corporation
This class discussion revolves around *The Corporation*, a book that provides an interesting and controversial perspective on organizations' pursuit of profit and power.

▣ *Integrated Core— Ethics*
This course is designed to give students skills and tools for use in everyday ethical decision-making. Rather than providing black-and-white answers to common ethical problems, this course recognizes that a great deal depends on context. Two main topics include special challenges involved in stakeholder interaction in a business area that is central to the Canadian economy—natural resource extraction, and emerging ethical dilemmas involved in the commercialization and use of medical technologies.

ELECTIVE COURSES:

▣ *Corporate Governance*
This course examines the foundations and constituent elements of the modern corporation with a view to understanding the concept of corporate governance. In addition to considering applicable theory and rules, the course takes a detailed look at some of the more controversial recent corporate governance failures and the fallout for all parties involved with corporations, whether as employees, managers, directors, shareholders, or advisors.

▣ *Corporate Social Responsibility*
This course is designed to engage students in a discussion of corporate social responsibility through a series of interactive learning activities. Students discuss and debate the definition and importance of CSR to a company's strategy and examine situations in which companies have and have not done a very good job at demonstrating good CSR practices. The class depends highly on student participation; student interests will drive the topics and situations that are considered and discussed.

INSTITUTES AND CENTERS:

▣ *Institute for Resources, the Environment and Sustainability (IRES) at UBC*
IRES at UBC is both an interdisciplinary research institute and a major interdisciplinary graduate education program. It is the mission of IRES to work to foster sustainable futures through integrated research and learning about the linkages among human and natural systems, to support decision making for local to global scales.

▣ *UBC Centre for Interactive Research on Sustainability (CIRS)*
CIRS has been designed as a globally unique state-of-the-art living laboratory, in which researchers and building industry partners can research and assess current and future sustainable building systems and technologies. CIRS will offer advanced visualization, simulation, and community engagement technologies and processes that will support research with citizens in exploring sustainable lifestyles.

QUESTIONS TO CONSIDER:

Does any required course contain some element of Social Impact Management? **YES**

Is any required course entirely dedicated to social, environmental, or ethical issues? **YES**

Is there a Net Impact Chapter on campus? **YES**

University of British Columbia
Sauder School of Business / Vancouver, Canada

THE ASPEN INSTITUTE
Center for Business Education

ANNUAL EVENTS:

Entrepreneurship 101

Entrepreneurship 101 is a program designed to assist low-income residents of Vancouver's downtown east side (the poorest postal code area in Canada) by providing them assistance with formulating and developing business plans in support of their entrepreneurial ideas. Faculty, staff, and MBA students volunteer their time to organize lectures, teaching sessions, and group work to assist one of the most impoverished communities in Canada.

The Corporate Environmental and Social Responsibility Conference (CESR) and Business Plan Competition

The CESR conference is an annual event that features a business case competition and workshops to educate students on social and environmental issues faced by Canadian companies. In the case competition, teams of students are challenged with green marketing cases provided by local companies and compete to solve sustainability issues.

OTHER PROGRAMS:

Business Career Centre

The Business Career Centre facilitates several programs, events, and conferences that address social impact and environmental management. The Centre supports the annual Leadership and Social Change Career Fair and Conference, which aims to educate students on career alternatives and connect them with not-for-profit organizations. The centre facilitates scholarship funding for students who intern with nonprofit organizations.

SCHOOL DEMOGRAPHICS	
Number of Full-Time Students	208
International Students	64%
Female Students	35%
	2006/2007 School Year

Social Entrepreneurship (SE) 101: Africa

Through lectures, study sessions, and group work, a team of Sauder faculty members and students helped Kiberan youth develop business plans for their innovative and socially conscious ideas, that had the greatest potential to make a positive impact on the local community (food retailing, Internet communications, and establishment of a kerosene depot). The team is currently working with youth organizations, and Canadian and Kenyan government agencies and businesses, to make SE 101 into a self-sustaining educational program.

STUDENT CLUBS AND PROGRAMS:

Net Impact Club, Sauder School of Business at UBC

UBC has an active Net Impact chapter that focuses on a wide variety of social and environmental initiatives. Through events, discussions, competitions, and job placements, members are exposed to a variety of experiences and educational opportunities that are complementary to academic course work.

THE CENTER FOR BUSINESS EDUCATION'S BOTTOM LINE ON UNIVERSITY OF BRITISH COLUMBIA:
Compared to other business schools in our survey, University of British Columbia offers an excellent number of courses featuring relevant content, and does a good job in those courses explicitly addressing how mainstream business improves the world. University of British Columbia requires 10 core courses featuring relevant content.

A Closer Look at:
University of Calgary

Haskayne School of Business / Calgary, Canada
http://www.haskayne.ucalgary.ca/

THE ASPEN INSTITUTE
Center for Business Education

WHAT THE SCHOOL SAYS:

The Haskayne School of Business at the University of Calgary is closely linked to the globally oriented resource-based industries headquartered in western Canada, namely energy, mining, forestry, and tourism. Consequently, the Haskayne School has played a pioneering role in integrating the management of environmental and social issues into the MBA curriculum.

A QUICK LOOK

NOTE: All information is self-reported data submitted to the Center for Business Education

COURSES*

Accounting (1)
Business & Government (1)
Business Law (1)
CSR/Business Ethics (4)
Entrepreneurship (1)
Environmental (4)
Finance (1)
HR Management (3)
Information Technology (1)
General Management (4)
Marketing (1)
Public/Nonprofit Mgt (1)
Strategy (3)

KEY CONCENTRATIONS

**Global Energy Management
& Sustainable Development**

KEY JOINT DEGREES

MBA & Master of Social Work

ACTIVITIES*

Speakers/Seminars (19)
Orientation Activities (3)
Internship/Consulting (2)
Student Competitions (2)
Clubs & Programs (4)
Career Development (2)
Institutes/Centers (4)
Concentrations (1)
Joint Degrees (2)

* Figures in parentheses indicate the number of courses/activities that, in whole or in part, integrate social, environmental, or ethical perspectives

NOTABLE FEATURES

CORE COURSES:

🔲 *Global Environment of Canadian Business*
Sections of this course include business and government relations, business ethics, and the legal environment for business. Topics include social impacts of regulation, public/private partnerships, social impact of key economic concepts, fair competition, corporate reputation, impacts of product development, and employee rights. Overall, this course develops the knowledge and ability to analyze and deal with complexities of the business environment.

🔲 *Management of Information Systems*
This course emphasizes the technologies in IS and management of IT/IS. Topics discussed in this class include ethical aspects of privacy in data management systems, impact on workers and consumers of embedded "monitoring" technologies, and the impact of electricity usage by massive IT-based companies. Overall, students will be able to understand the potential impact of current and emerging information technologies on business environments, societal interests, and organizational strategy.

ELECTIVE COURSES:

🔲 *International Tourism*
This course explores international tourism as a social/cultural phenomenon, economic force, business activity, and agent of change. We examine trends and underlying forces, emphasizing current issues of global significance. Students assess and forecast social, cultural, economic, and environmental consequences.

🔲 *Strategies for Sustainable Development*
The purpose of this course is to provide the strategic context for making business decisions with respect to sustainable development issues. It takes the perspective of a broad range of stakeholders and how environmental and social issues affect business performance and public policy. The course allows students to investigate management issues from a "big picture" perspective.

INSTITUTES AND CENTERS:

🔲 *International Institute for Resource Industries and Sustainability Studies (IRIS)*
IRIS researches state-of-the-art innovative management practices and their impacts on societal issues, both environmental and social, and the role that those practices may play in moving industry toward a more sustainable posture. The mission of IRIS is to create and disseminate leading-edge sustainability research through publications, teaching, and various forms of outreach to industry and community audiences.

🔲 *World Tourism Education and Research Centre (WTERC)*
WTERC's mission is to create a greater understanding of tourism and its role in global economic, social, and cultural development; to improve the effectiveness of those responsible for managing the human, physical, and financial resources of tourism regions; and to enhance, through tourism, greater international understanding and goodwill in an environmentally responsible manner.

QUESTIONS TO CONSIDER:

Does any required course contain some element of Social Impact Management? **YES**

Is any required course entirely dedicated to social, environmental, or ethical issues? **YES**

Is there a Net Impact Chapter on campus? **NO**

University of Calgary
Haskayne School of Business / Calgary, Canada

THE ASPEN INSTITUTE
Center for Business Education

ANNUAL EVENTS:

Haskayne Case Competition
This multi-round case competition among Haskayne MBA students is the culmination of the course "Personal Skills and Business Acumen." The cases cover a wide variety of topics, including social impact and environmental management issues. The course is designed to improve each student's managerial skill set and improve business acumen. A wide variety of activities lead up to the case competition, including guest speakers, case analysis, career skills and personal development workshops, and information literacy seminars.

MBA Consulting Alliance (MBACA)
Run by the Haskayne MBA students, the MBACA provides consulting services in a variety of specialized areas including environmental management, nonprofit management, and energy. Each year, MBACA provides consulting services at no cost to a not-for-profit organization that needs assistance with a project.

Career Development Workshop—Building Businesss Relationships and Networks
Janice McDougall, president of the board of the Pembina Institute was a presenter in 2005--2006 at the Career Development Workshop and mentored students in 2006--2007. By sharing her personal experience she introduced natural systems principles and discussed how students can adapt natural systems thinking to the design of job search and relationship-building tactics for business success.

OTHER PROGRAMS:

MBA Mentorship Program
The Haskayne MBA Mentorship program provides important community connections for students. Senior business leaders from a diverse range of industries with an economic and operational impact locally, regionally, and internationally provide professional development opportunities for full-time MBA students. Mentors are encouraged to get students involved in socially responsible activities for the community and discuss the importance of social responsibility to the business community and the community as a whole.

IRIS Seminar Series
The International Institute for Resource Industries and Sustainability Studies (IRIS) offers a regular seminar series featuring global leaders and the latest research on sustainability.

STUDENT CLUBS AND PROGRAMS:

Canadian Futures Eco-Tourism Club
The club's mission is to improve Canadian society through academic inquiry and action-based research into Canadian environmental cases. Objectives are to gain experience across disciplines, collaborate with like-minded students, address real-life issues; and improve our environment.

Advancing Canadian Entrepreneurship (ACE)
ACE is a national not-for-profit organization dedicated to improving the communities it serves through educating students, stakeholders, and citizens through four basic principles: market economics, entrepreneurship, personal financial success skills, and business ethics. The Haskayne chapter runs a number of entrepreneurial conferences, a microbusiness selling t-shirts, and an online textbook-swapping program. It also runs several community programs.

SCHOOL DEMOGRAPHICS	
Number of Full-Time Students	63
International Students	34%
Female Students	37%
Pre-MBA Employment:	

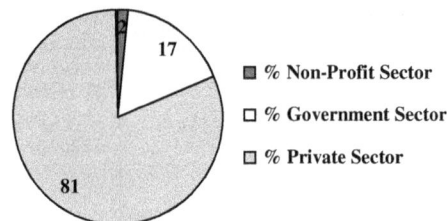

- % Non-Profit Sector
- % Government Sector
- % Private Sector

2006/2007 School Year

THE CENTER FOR BUSINESS EDUCATION'S BOTTOM LINE ON UNIVERSITY OF CALGARY:
Compared to other business schools in our survey, University of Calgary offers an excellent number of courses featuring relevant content, and does an excellent job in those courses explicitly addressing how mainstream business improves the world. University of Calgary requires 6 core courses featuring relevant content.

A Closer Look at:
University of California, Berkeley

Walter A. Haas School of Business / Berkeley, CA

http://www.haas.berkeley.edu/

THE ASPEN INSTITUTE
Center for Business Education

WHAT THE SCHOOL SAYS:

Corporate responsibility permeates the Haas School of Business. Since its founding in 1898, Berkeley's business school has been a central force in social thought leadership and in challenging students to think beyond traditional paradigms of business, society, and the environment by educating MBA students to make the most of the economic opportunities available to them and instilling in the students the values to share what they create.

A QUICK LOOK

NOTE: All information is self-reported data submitted to the Center for Business Education

COURSES*

Business & Government (5)
Business Law (2)
CSR/Business Ethics (6)
Economics (5)
Entrepreneurship (11)
Environmental (1)
Finance (5)
International Management (10)
General Management (5)
Marketing (6)
Organizational Behavior (5)
Operations Management (4)
Public/Nonprofit Mgt (6)
Quantitative Methods (1)
Strategy (1)

KEY CONCENTRATIONS

Corporate Social Responsibility

Nonprofit & Public Management

KEY JOINT DEGREES

MBA & MA International and Area Studies

MBA & Health Management

ACTIVITIES*

Speakers/Seminars (20)
Orientation Activities (5)
Internship/Consulting (5)
Student Competitions (5)
Clubs & Programs (9)
Career Development (1)
Institutes/Centers (6)
Concentrations (6)
Joint Degrees (2)

* Figures in parentheses indicate the number of courses/activities that, in whole or in part, integrate social, environmental, or ethical perspectives

NOTABLE FEATURES

CORE COURSES:

Ethics and Responsibility in Business

This course strengthens students' ability to anticipate, analyze, and appropriately respond to some of the critical ethical and social challenges that confront managers in a global economy. Instruction is based primarily on the case method, supplemented by both topical and philosophical articles and essays.

Data and Decisions

Data and Decisions is an introductory course in data analysis and the application of statistical techniques to management problems. The objective is to enable students to become critical consumers of statistical analyses. This course focuses on uncovering central tendencies and patterns in data with regard to making business decisions, as well as common pitfalls and abuses in their interpretation as it may relate to areas such as health care and ethical issues.

ELECTIVE COURSES:

Strategic Corporate Social Responsibility and Projects

This course exposes students to the complex field of corporate social responsibility as a business strategy. In the classroom component of this course, students will learn the theories, frameworks, and cases of CSR. The class also includes live consulting projects with real companies, in which students will help their clients develop CSR investments with a corporate strategy focus aligned with business objectives and core competencies. It is expected that the company will be implementing the students' recommendations, which will be backed with solid data.

Social Sector Solutions

The purpose of this course is to provide students with practical, hands-on experience in nonprofit organizations and management consulting and to help nonprofit clients succeed in entrepreneurial ventures. Social Sector Solutions is a partnership between the Haas School of Business, the Center for Nonprofit and Public Leadership, a leading consulting firm, and select nonprofit clients.

INSTITUTES AND CENTERS:

Center for Nonprofit and Public Leadership

The Center for Nonprofit and Public Leadership prepares leaders with the practical business skills to found, lead, manage, and govern nonprofit and public organizations for the public good. The center provides MBA students an opportunity to augment the core business curriculum with specialized course work, practical application, and career opportunities in public and nonprofit management and aims to prepare the Haas student body with the skills and knowledge to serve in community and public life.

Center for Responsible Business

The Center for Responsible Business educates its stakeholders on the roles and responsibilities of business in society through research, teaching, experiential learning, and outreach; integrates the discipline of CSR into the general management core; acts as a catalyst in creating a new generation of business leaders who are committed to and knowledgeable about CSR; and serves as an educational center that bridges research, theory, and practice of CSR.

QUESTIONS TO CONSIDER:

Does any required course contain some element of Social Impact Management? **YES**

Is any required course entirely dedicated to social, environmental, or ethical issues? **YES**

Is there a Net Impact Chapter on campus? **YES**

A Closer Look at:
University of California, Berkeley
Walter A. Haas School of Business / Berkeley, CA

THE ASPEN INSTITUTE
Center for Business Education

ANNUAL EVENTS:

▦ *Peterson Lecture Series on Corporate Responsibility*

The Peterson Lecture Series on Corporate Responsibility brings thoughtful and diverse leaders to Haas to address topics related to business ethics, corporate responsibility, the environment, and social entrepreneurship. Hosted by the Center for Responsible Business at the Haas School, the series creates a unique opportunity for provocative dialogue about the evolving role of business in society with engaging, high-profile speakers.

▦ *Global Social Venture Competition (GSVC)*

Organized by the Haas School of Business at UC Berkeley, the Global Social Venture Competition (GSVC) is the largest and oldest student-led business plan competition providing mentorship, exposure, and financial awards to emerging social ventures from around the world. The GSVC's mission is to catalyze the creation of social ventures, educate future leaders, and build awareness around social enterprise. The competition supports the creation of real businesses that bring about positive social change in a sustainable manner and is held each year at UC Berkeley in partnership with Columbia Business School, London Business School, Indian School of Business, and Yale School of Management.

▦ *Education Leadership Case Competition*

The Haas Education Club's Education Leadership Case Competition will be the nation's first case competition for MBAs focusing on the challenges of education leadership. The goal is to give talented graduate students the opportunity to apply their skills to the challenges faced by leaders of education reform.

OTHER PROGRAMS:

▦ *Haas for Students*

The Haas for Students student-led program supports first-year MBA students who take internships in the nonprofit and public sectors. These grants allow students to put their Haas MBA to use for organizations that are doing important work in communities around the world but cannot offer a private sector MBA salary. Throughout the year, students build awareness through fundraisers, special events, and donation drives. Eligible students apply for the grant in the spring to receive their grant for their summer internships.

STUDENT CLUBS AND PROGRAMS:

▦ *Berkeley Energy and Resources Collaborative (BERC)*

The mission of BERC is to connect and educate leaders in the rapidly evolving field of energy and resources. Through speakers, workshops, career recruiting events, and the Berkeley Energy Symposium, BERC works to create cross-disciplinary dialogue on the Berkeley campus on topics such as renewable energy, climate change, and energy markets. BERC also partners with industry, government, and major research institutions to sponsor student projects in energy innovation and commercialization.

▦ *Global Initiatives at Haas (GIH) Club*

GIH is a student club at the Haas School of Business at UC Berkeley focused on international development. GIH members have a deep interest in international development issues, including sustainable development, public health, and microfinance. The activities of GIH aim to connect the Haas community with leading practitioners, researchers, and specialists in the field to understand current practices and explore future career opportunities.

FACULTY PIONEER:

▦ *2005 – Institutional Leadership Award, Kellie A. McElhaney*

Dr. McElhaney is an agent of change. She developed the Center for Responsible Business at the Haas School of Business. This Center is helping to place corporate responsibility squarely as one of the core competencies and competitive advantages of the Haas School. She influences students and practitioners alike. Her pioneering teaching methods which combine theory, best practices, case studies, and high-profile strategic CSR projects, win high acclaim from students.

SCHOOL DEMOGRAPHICS

Number of Full-Time Students	**487**
International Students	**41%**
Female Students	**27%**

Pre-MBA Employment:

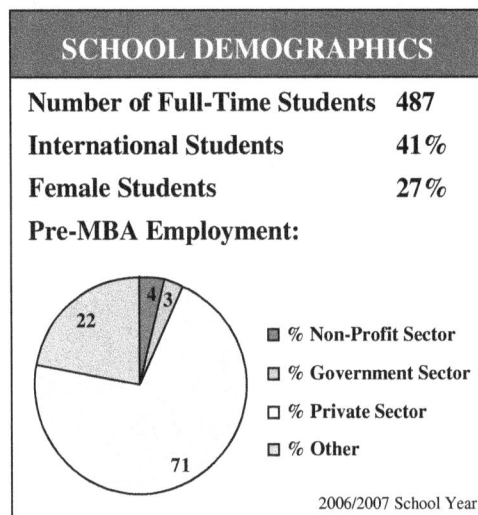

Pie chart values: 4, 3, 22, 71

- ▣ % Non-Profit Sector
- ☐ % Government Sector
- ☐ % Private Sector
- ☐ % Other

2006/2007 School Year

THE CENTER FOR BUSINESS EDUCATION'S BOTTOM LINE ON UNIVERSITY OF CALIFORNIA, BERKELEY:

Compared to other business schools in our survey, University of California, Berkeley offers a truly extraordinary number of courses featuring relevant content, and does a truly extraordinary job in those courses explicitly addressing how mainstream business improves the world. University of California, Berkeley requires 7 core courses featuring relevant content.

A Closer Look at:
University of California, Davis
Graduate School of Management / Davis, CA
http://www.gsm.ucdavis.edu/

THE ASPEN INSTITUTE
Center for Business Education

WHAT THE SCHOOL SAYS:

Giving back to the community—creating positive social change, both locally and globally—is woven into the culture of the UC Davis Graduate School of Management. The school's curriculum and activities are fostering a new generation of business leaders who are dedicated to community involvement, social responsibility, and making a difference.

A QUICK LOOK

NOTE: All information is self-reported data submitted to the Center for Business Education

COURSES*

Accounting (6)
Business & Government (1)
Business Law (1)
CSR/Business Ethics (1)
Entrepreneurship (1)
Finance (5)
Information Technology (2)
International Management (1)
General Management (3)
Marketing (3)
Organizational Behavior (3)
Operations Management (1)
Public/Nonprofit Mgt (1)
Quantitative Methods (1)

KEY CONCENTRATIONS

Corporate Social Responsibility

Nonprofit Management

KEY JOINT DEGREES

MBA & MS in Environmental Policy Analysis

MBA & MA Education

ACTIVITIES*

Speakers/Seminars (6)
Orientation Activities (5)
Internship/Consulting (4)
Student Competitions (1)
Clubs & Programs (6)
Career Development (2)
Institutes/Centers (5)
Concentrations (3)
Joint Degrees (6)

* Figures in parentheses indicate the number of courses/activities that, in whole or in part, integrate social, environmental, or ethical perspectives

NOTABLE FEATURES

CORE COURSES:

Financial Accounting
This course will introduce a variety of financial reporting topics. Social responsibility is emphasized as students are exposed to ethical dilemmas that they may encounter in the business world. Managerial incentives and opportunities for financial disclosure management (e.g., earnings management) are discussed and the corresponding need for integrity and accountability in reporting systems.

The Individual and Group Dynamics
This course examines justice and ethics at work in several case studies and within discussions of performance appraisal and compensation. Topics discussed include gender and racial diversity, stereotypes, and bias in promotion and hiring. The course examines leadership and its roles in developing a diverse and ethical culture at work.

ELECTIVE COURSES:

Seminar on Sustainable and Responsible Business
This seminar-style course examines the challenge of meeting the needs and interests of all stakeholders in a way that balances social, environmental, and economic resources and impacts. The goal is to investigate avenues for using market strategies to build a path toward global sustainability. Through a combination of case studies, lectures, movies, guest speakers, and a capstone research project, students will explore methods and rationale for simultaneously managing social, natural, and economic capital.

Pricing
This course focuses on pricing laws and ethics. In particular, it discusses price-fixing and its effects on consumers, competitors, and innovation. The course addresses the issues of the morality of setting prices to extract all of consumer surplus and alternative approaches to pricing, like fair pricing, and their implications.

INSTITUTES AND CENTERS:

Center for Investor Welfare and Corporate Responsibility
The center serves to infuse science into investment management and corporate practice. To do so, the center promotes research, teaching, and service that emphasizes the rigorous application of scientific principles to investment management and corporate practices.

Institute for Transportation Studies (ITS)
The primary program components of the ITS are research, education, and outreach. ITS partners with academic and research centers on- and off-campus, and with industry, government, and NGOsaround the world. Institute researchers are known for their expertise in travel behavior and transport systems modeling, environmental vehicle technologies, and climate change, air quality, and other environmental impacts of transportation.

QUESTIONS TO CONSIDER:

Does any required course contain some element of Social Impact Management? **YES**

Is any required course entirely dedicated to social, environmental, or ethical issues? **NO**

Is there a Net Impact Chapter on campus? **YES**

All information in this profile is drawn and/or adapted from the self-reported data of the Center for Business Education's Beyond Grey Pinstripes 2007 MBA survey. The Center for Business Education is housed within the Business and Society Program at the Aspen Institute. For more info, visit www.AspenCBE.org.

A Closer Look at:
University of California, Davis
Graduate School of Management / Davis, CA

THE ASPEN INSTITUTE
Center for Business Education

ANNUAL EVENTS:

Dean's Distinguished Speaker Series
The Graduate School of Management hosts high-level executives and business leaders from many socially responsible companies or with socially responsible track records to campus for special speaking engagements. These speakers share their experiences— their ups, downs, struggles, and successes. Students participate in question-and-answer sessions and one-on-one conversations.

Net Impact Teambuilding Trip
The UC Davis chapter of Net Impact hosts a weekend trip to Yosemite National Park. Students stay at Evergreen Lodge, a social enterprise that employs at-risk youths to help build job skills and instill the belief that supportive employment can help young people build momentum in their lives and realize their fullest potential. It is a way for incoming students to learn about social impact themes in a stunning environment.

OTHER PROGRAMS:

Net Impact Day on the Job
Net Impact Day on the Job is an opportunity for current MBA students to visit socially and environmentally responsible businesses.

Green Bag Speaker Series
The Green Bag Speaker Series brings speakers to campus approximately once per month to share their ideas on social and environmental issues.

Energy Efficiency Internships
These paid internships provide students the opportunity to work with innovative energy-efficient technologies, including managing projects like the implementation of pilot programs to test the effectiveness of new energy-efficient office lighting systems.

STUDENT CLUBS AND PROGRAMS:

International Business Club (IBC)
The mission of the IBC is to promote cross-cultural understanding and provide an outlet for those wanting to develop their international business and development knowledge. A key component of the club is the International Study Practicum; topics often include international trade, socioeconomic development, and/or environmental responsibility. Some countries previously visited: Brazil, China, Malaysia, and Mexico.

Community Consulting Group (CCG)
The CCG is an organization of MBA students who provide pro bono consulting services to nonprofits and other organizations with community-oriented projects. The CCG brings together the diverse professional and academic experiences of MBA candidates and professors to provide consulting services tailored to client-specific needs.

SCHOOL DEMOGRAPHICS	
Number of Full-Time Students	107
International Students	19%
Female Students	38%

2006/2007 School Year

THE CENTER FOR BUSINESS EDUCATION'S BOTTOM LINE ON UNIVERSITY OF CALIFORNIA, DAVIS:
Compared to other business schools in our survey, University of California, Davis offers an excellent number of courses featuring relevant content, and does an excellent job in those courses explicitly addressing how mainstream business improves the world. University of California, Davis requires 5 core courses featuring relevant content.

168

University of California, Los Angeles
UCLA Anderson School of Management / Los Angeles, CA
http://www.anderson.ucla.edu/

THE ASPEN INSTITUTE
Center for Business Education

WHAT THE SCHOOL SAYS:

The UCLA Anderson MBA program focuses on giving MBA students the traditional skills needed to be successful regardless of their choice of career. Students can choose several electives on social and environmental topics. The school is based around a strong core of traditional disciplines, with major flexibility for students to pursue their own interests.

A QUICK LOOK

NOTE: All information is self-reported data submitted to the Center for Business Education

COURSES*

Economics (1)
Entrepreneurship (1)
General Management (5)

KEY CONCENTRATIONS

Leaders in Sustainability

KEY JOINT DEGREES

MBA & Public Policy

MBA & Master of Urban Planning

ACTIVITIES*

Speakers/Seminars (7)
Orientation Activities (3)
Internship/Consulting (2)
Student Competitions (1)
Clubs & Programs (3)
Career Development (1)
Institutes/Centers (3)
Concentrations (1)
Joint Degrees (2)

* Figures in parentheses indicate the number of courses/activities that, in whole or in part, integrate social, environmental, or ethical perspectives

NOTABLE FEATURES

ELECTIVE COURSES:

▦ *Special Topics in Management: Social Entrepreneurship*
This course explores opportunities and challenges of using entrepreneurial and managerial abilities to help solve some of society's most intractable social problems.

▦ *Business and the Environment*
This course discusses the environmental issues facing business and society at large, including global warming, air and water pollution, soil contamination, etc. It also examines current and future legislation, both in the United States and elsewhere in the world related to each of these issues.

INSTITUTES AND CENTERS:

▦ *The Center for International Business Education and Research (CIBER)*
CIBER is part of a network of 30 CIBER university centers created by the United States Omnibus Trade and Competitiveness Act of 1988 with the goal of improving the competitiveness of US industry through the internationalization of management education. CIBER achieves its program goal through teaching and curriculum development, faculty development and research support, and outreach to the UCLA community. CIBER has funded research on environmental management and social issues in business, including sponsoring students to work with and visit an ecotourism company in Peru and microfinance companies in India.

▦ *The Institute of the Environment (IoE)*
The IoE is an innovative and vibrant intellectual community focused on the environment. Members and constituents represent every area of specialty that touches the environment, encompassing a broad array of academic disciplines, research interests, policy concerns, and outreach avenues. The mission of the IoE is to generate knowledge and provide solutions for regional and global environmental problems and to educate the next generation of professional leadership committed to the health of our planet.

QUESTIONS TO CONSIDER:

Does any required course contain some element of Social Impact Management? **NO**

Is any required course entirely dedicated to social, environmental, or ethical issues? **NO**

Is there a Net Impact Chapter on campus? **YES**

All information in this profile is drawn and/or adapted from the self-reported data of the Center for Business Education's Beyond Grey Pinstripes 2007 MBA survey. The Center for Business Education is housed within the Business and Society Program at the Aspen Institute. For more info, visit www.AspenCBE.org.

A Closer Look at:
University of California, Los Angeles
UCLA Anderson School of Management / Los Angeles, CA

ANNUAL EVENTS:

■ *Global Development Series*

The Global Development Series aims to help students learn about current topics, theories, and applications of business and management in international development and creates opportunities for them to network with leading practitioners and like-minded individuals.

■ *Anderson Net Impact Nonprofit Consulting Challenge*

The Anderson Net Impact Nonprofit Consulting Challenge is one of the hallmarks of UCLA Anderson's commitment to raising awareness about the value of the public service and nonprofit sectors. By bringing together nonprofit organizations with teams of MBA students, the organizations benefit from strategic solutions for their most pressing business problems. The event is structured as a multiweek consultation between teams of Anderson students and nonprofit organizations, culminating in a one-day final event.

OTHER PROGRAMS:

■ *JA in a day*

The Net Impact Club, in partnership with Deloitte Consulting, participates in teaching Junior Achievement curriculum in area schools. This activity helps to develop needed critical thinking skills and exposure to the ideas of business within local urban school districts.

■ *J&J Programs Teaching Associate*

UCLA Anderson conducts two executive education programs through a partnership with Johnson and Johnson. These programs bring executives from Head Start and HRSA Healthcare organizations to the UCLA campus for a two-week intensive program. Several full-time MBA students complete their summer internship as teaching associates by assisting faculty in teaching curriculum and serving as consultants for participants as they develop a management-improvement project.

STUDENT CLUBS AND PROGRAMS:

■ *Affinity Clubs*

UCLA Anderson supports a range of student clubs dedicated to supporting all types of diversity within the student community and the larger business world.

■ *Anderson Net Impact Chapter*

The Anderson Net Impact Club is a chapter of the national Net Impact organization which strives to improve the world by growing and strengthening a network of leaders who use the power of business to make a positive net social, environmental, and economic impact.

SCHOOL DEMOGRAPHICS

Number of Full-Time Students	683
International Students	24%
Female Students	33%

Pre-MBA Employment:

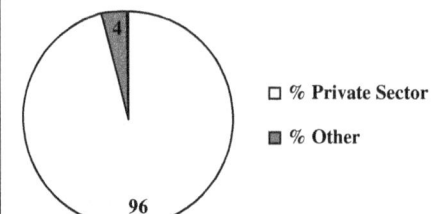

4
96

□ % Private Sector
■ % Other

2006/2007 School Year

THE CENTER FOR BUSINESS EDUCATION'S BOTTOM LINE ON UNIVERSITY OF CALIFORNIA, LOS ANGELES:
Compared to other business schools in our survey, University of California, Los Angeles offers a good number of courses featuring relevant content, and does a good job in those courses explicitly addressing how mainstream business improves the world.

A Closer Look at:
University of California, San Diego
Rady School of Management / La Jolla, CA
http://management.ucsd.edu/

WHAT THE SCHOOL SAYS:

The Rady School MBA is a program focused on innovation with deep resources in science, technology and other transformative industries. UC San Diego has established a campus-wide sustainability initiative.

<table>
<tr><td>

A QUICK LOOK

NOTE: All information is self-reported data submitted to the Center for Business Education

COURSES*

General Management (1)

ACTIVITIES*

Speakers/Seminars (14)
Clubs & Programs (1)
Institutes/Centers (1)

* Figures in parentheses indicate the number of courses/activities that, in whole or in part, integrate social, environmental, or ethical perspectives

</td></tr>
</table>

NOTABLE FEATURES

CORE COURSES:
  Negotiations
This course reviews the ethical issues surrounding difficult negotiations.

INSTITUTES AND CENTERS:
  Beyster Institute
The Beyster Institute identifies the needs of growth entrepreneurs and networks them with the resources they need to prosper. It provides training, consulting, education, and policy advocacy that enables owners and managers to expand their companies. This stimulates economic growth in local communities and international regions and is an effective social and economic strategy to get more capital into the hands of many.

ANNUAL EVENTS:
  Net Impact Speaker Series
The Net Impact club hosts global leaders in social and environmental sustainability.

SCHOOL DEMOGRAPHICS

Number of Full-Time Students	115
International Students	34%
Female Students	33%

Pre-MBA Employment:

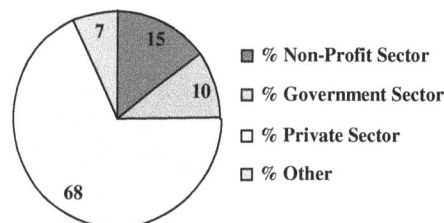

- % Non-Profit Sector (7)
- % Government Sector (15)
- % Private Sector (68)
- % Other (10)

2006/2007 School Year

OTHER PROGRAMS:
  Middle East and North Africa Businesswomen's Summit
This summit in Abu Dhabi, United Arab Emirates, was managed by the Beyster Institute at the Rady School and sponsored by the U.S. Department of State. It provided an opportunity for participants from the Middle East and North Africa to expand their networks, discuss real-world experiences, and build management and leadership skills as they take entrepreneurship in the region to a new level. The hope is that the summit will stimulate economic reform and opportunity as the women expand businesses, enter into international trade and form dynamic joint ventures.

  CA Clean Technology Summit 2007
The CA Clean Tech Summit 2007 was a two-day event creating an unprecedented opportunity for students, industry leaders, investors, entrepreneurs, government officials, and university innovators to discuss critical topics in clean technology at an affordable entrance price. Premier California universities (MBA, Science and Engineering programs) are joining forces to stimulate growth in clean technology, primarily focused on the following segments: energy, transportation, and materials science.

STUDENT CLUBS AND PROGRAMS:
  Net Impact
The Net Impact chapter at UC San Diego upholds Net Impact's mission to improve the world by growing and strengthening a network of new leaders who are using the power of business to make a positive net social, environmental, and economic impact.

QUESTIONS TO CONSIDER:

Does any required course contain some element of Social Impact Management? **YES**

Is any required course entirely dedicated to social, environmental, or ethical issues? **NO**

Is there a Net Impact Chapter on campus? **YES**

THE CENTER FOR BUSINESS EDUCATION'S BOTTOM LINE ON UNIVERSITY OF CALIFORNIA, SAN DIEGO:
By participating in the Center for Business Education's Beyond Grey Pinstripes 2007 MBA survey, University of California, San Diego demonstrates great dedication to integrating environmental and social impact management issues into its teaching and research. University of California, San Diego requires 1 core course featuring relevant content.

A Closer Look at:
University of Cape Town
Graduate School of Business / Cape Town, South Africa
http://www.gsb.uct.ac.za/gsbwebb/home.asp

THE ASPEN INSTITUTE
Center for Business Education

WHAT THE SCHOOL SAYS:

Students are encouraged to pursue environmental and social impact studies as part of their dissertation requirement, which forms a substantial component of the MBA program . Outside of the program , students are involved with local nonprofit and non-governmental organizations.

A QUICK LOOK

NOTE: All information is self-reported data submitted to the Center for Business Education

COURSES*

Business & Government (1)
Entrepreneurship (2)
Marketing (1)

KEY CONCENTRATIONS

Emerging Enterprise Consulting

Social Marketing

ACTIVITIES*

Speakers/Seminars (4)
Orientation Activities (1)
Internship/Consulting (1)
Student Competitions (2)
Institutes/Centers (4)
Concentrations (6)

* Figures in parentheses indicate the number of courses/activities that, in whole or in part, integrate social, environmental, or ethical perspectives

NOTABLE FEATURES

CORE COURSES:

▦ *Business, Government and Society*

This course forms the foundation of the MBA program . The objectives of the course include familiarity with global and national regimes for business laws and understanding of risk management and corporate governance; Understanding of business ethics; understanding of sustainable development, corporate social responsibility, and socially responsible investment; and understanding why companies in South Africa have adopted "Corporate Citizenship" strategies to deal with "Triple Bottom Line" issues such as broad-based black economic empowerment, governance and transparency, HIV/AIDS, corruption, globalization, climate change, and human rights.

ELECTIVE COURSES:

▦ *Emerging Enterprises in a Developing Economy*

The focus of this course is to facilitate the survival and growth of existing small businesses that are owned and managed by historically disadvantaged South Africans. The entire course is designed around the SEE (Supporting Emerging Enterprises) Model, which is a three-stage model intended to guide teams as they approach, decipher, and ultimately create value for the entrepreneurial enterprise. Teams are assigned to two emerging enterprise clients. The teams meet regularly with each client and, employing the SEE Model, move through an evolving series of steps that culminate in a set of value-creating deliverables for the client and a final consulting report.

▦ *Social Marketing*

This course focuses on applying the behavioral model to social marketing and nonprofit marketing cases, such as in the HIV/AIDS care provider and environmental sustainability (recycling) contexts and additional insights about how firms can respond successfully to marketplace diversity and find appropriate models that deliver sustainable profits.

INSTITUTES AND CENTERS:

▦ *Management Program in Infrastructure Reform and Regulation (MIR)*

The MIR strives to be a leading centre of excellence and expertise for Africa and other emerging and developing economies. MIR aims to enhance understanding and build capacity to manage reform and regulation of infrastructure sectors in support of sustainable development. MIR's main focus is in the electricity and water sectors but growth is expected in gas, transport, and potentially in telecommunications. MIR works on three fronts, providing executive and professional short courses; research related to the frontiers of infrastructure reform and regulation in Africa; and professional support and policy advocacy.

▦ *The Southern African-United States Centre for Leadership and Public Values*

The centre, in partnership with Duke University, seeks to do the following in South Africa and the United States: Enhance the capacity of highly promising emerging leaders to contribute to the empowerment of their communities and the transformation of their countries; Strengthen civil society with particular regard to mutual learning and collaborative initiatives between independent sector leaders; make a substantive contribution to the public discussion and understanding of the role of ethics and values in public life; and develop and strengthen community philanthropy and social investment.

QUESTIONS TO CONSIDER:

Does any required course contain some element of Social Impact Management? **YES**

Is any required course entirely dedicated to social, environmental, or ethical issues? **NO**

Is there a Net Impact Chapter on campus? **NO**

A Closer Look at:
University of Cape Town
Graduate School of Business / Cape Town, South Africa

THE ASPEN INSTITUTE
Center for Business Education

ANNUAL EVENTS:

Distinguished Speakers Program

The Distinguished Speakers Program is a monthly program designed for GSB students, alumni, and the business community. High-profile individuals from the private, public, and nonprofit sectors are invited to speak on a variety of topics. Examples of topics with social and environmental impact include international authority on good corporate governance, the challenges facing the state with respect to service delivery, and environmental topics concerning the state of the planet.

PWC Business Forum

The PWC Business Forum is a monthly forum presented by the UCT GSB for our students, alumni, and business community. High-profile individuals from the private, public, and nonprofit sectors are invited to speak on a variety of topics. While these vary, examples of issues of social impact include good corporate governance and an accelerated and shared growth initiative to achieve higher economic growth and socioeconomic inclusion.

OTHER PROGRAMS:

Small Business Week

Small Business Week underscores the government's drive in encouraging and supporting small and medium enterprises (SMEs) as a means to address the problem of unemployment in South Africa. The UCT MBA students volunteer their time to assist SMEs in creating business plans and to transfer their newly acquired business knowledge and skills where appropriate.

SCHOOL DEMOGRAPHICS	
Number of Full-Time Students	63
International Students	29%
Female Students	33%
Pre-MBA Employment:	

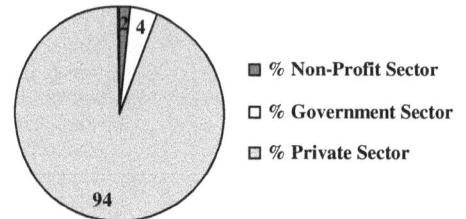

- ■ % Non-Profit Sector
- □ % Government Sector
- □ % Private Sector

2006/2007 School Year

THE CENTER FOR BUSINESS EDUCATION'S BOTTOM LINE ON UNIVERSITY OF CAPE TOWN:

Compared to other business schools in our survey, University of Cape Town does a good job in relevant courses explicitly addressing how mainstream business improves the world. University of Cape Town requires 1 core course featuring relevant content.

University of Colorado at Boulder

Leeds School of Business / Boulder, CO

http://leeds.colorado.edu/

WHAT THE SCHOOL SAYS:

At the Leeds School of Business, we seek to address social and environmental challenges by creating innovative, market-driven solutions. With a focus on mastering business fundamentals, integrating a spirit of innovation, and building strong networks, our students are uniquely prepared to create positive social, environmental, and financial results.

A QUICK LOOK

NOTE: All information is self-reported data submitted to the Center for Business Education

COURSES*

Accounting (2)
CSR/Business Ethics (1)
Entrepreneurship (6)
Environmental (3)
Finance (6)
Information Technology (3)
General Management (5)
Marketing (5)
Organizational Behavior (1)
Quantitative Methods (1)
Strategy (2)

KEY CONCENTRATIONS

Sustainable Venturing

KEY JOINT DEGREES

MBA & MS in Environmental Studies

ACTIVITIES*

Speakers/Seminars (4)
Orientation Activities (9)
Internship/Consulting (3)
Student Competitions (3)
Clubs & Programs (2)
Career Development (1)
Institutes/Centers (1)
Concentrations (1)
Joint Degrees (2)

* Figures in parentheses indicate the number of courses/activities that, in whole or in part, integrate social, environmental, or ethical perspectives

NOTABLE FEATURES

CORE COURSES:

Corporate Strategy

This course focuses on identifying and creating a competitive advantage within a company. Due to an international emphasis, stakeholders are more broadly considered in the decisions of the companies. Stakeholders discussed include those such as society, community, employees, and the environment. Specific cases studied in this course deal with issues of ethics, labor, and globalization.

Business Ethics and Corporate Responsibility

This course includes study and application of business ethics as well as compliance, corporate responsibility, and corporate governance. It addresses these critical business concerns at the individual, managerial, and executive/corporate level. This course has an emphasis on ethical decision making, critical evaluation of current ethical issues in business, and the responsibility of business to various stakeholders.

ELECTIVE COURSES:

Assessing Sustainable Energy Technologies

This course focuses on the technological and cost "fundamentals" of emerging energy technologies, including solar, wind, biomass, oceanic, geothermal, hydropower, fuel cell (hydrogen), nuclear, and other more exotic energy sources. A premise of the course is that a sustainable energy technology must both be technically feasible and economically viable.

Applied Financial Management

This case-based course focuses on financial planning, managing working capital, short-and long-term financing, capital budgeting, valuation, and capital structure policies. Topics include the role of corporate governance as well as the charitable role corporations should play; the personal financial incentives of managers to merge, and labor considerations in financial decision making.

INSTITUTES AND CENTERS:

Robert H. and Beverly A. Deming Center for Entrepreneurship

The Deming Center provides a unique opportunity for students to sample entrepreneurial thinking and pursue their entrepreneurial dreams.

QUESTIONS TO CONSIDER:

Does any required course contain some element of Social Impact Management? **YES**

Is any required course entirely dedicated to social, environmental, or ethical issues? **YES**

Is there a Net Impact Chapter on campus? **YES**

A Closer Look at:
University of Colorado at Boulder
Leeds School of Business / Boulder, CO

ANNUAL EVENTS:

Net Impact Case Competition
Since 2002, Leeds has hosted the national Net Impact Case Competition, a collaborative competition that brings together MBAs from different schools to work together in teams to address a business sustainability or social responsibility issue.

Entrepreneurship Retreat
This is an annual orientation event to introduce first-year MBAs to entrepreneurship and sustainable business practices by meeting and interacting through projects, roundtable discussions, and creative sessions with entrepreneurs, innovators, venture capitalists, faculty, and second year MBAs.

OTHER PROGRAMS:

Climate Change Strategies (CCS)
CCS is an interdisciplinary research and education initiative of the Leeds School of Business, a world-leading center for climate change research. Recognizing that the business community must be part of the solution to our most pressing global problem, climate change, CCS provides education and training programs with a business perspective.

TEAM-Transforming Energy and Markets
TEAM is the Energy Initiative's business outreach arm that assists businesses in a wide range of industry sectors. Its mission is to facilitate collaborations between researchers and the private sector to streamline the path to market for clean energy innovation. TEAM partners with industry leaders looking for ingenious ways to save money or capture new markets. TEAM offers access to cutting-edge research and a wide network of industry, university, and government energy experts.

STUDENT CLUBS AND PROGRAMS:

Graduate Entrepreneurs Association (GEA)
GEA enhances the graduate entrepreneurship experience by providing opportunities that prepare, inform, and excite MBA students with an interest in entrepreneurial endeavors. The GEA allows MBA students to meet and exchange ideas with each other, to interact with entrepreneurs and learn from their experiences, and to provide resources, insights, and an environment that encourages entrepreneurship.

Student Environmental Action Coalition (SEAC)
SEAC is a grassroots, student-run national network of progressive organizations and individuals whose aim is to uproot environmental injustices through action and education. SEAC empowers students to fight for environmental and social justice in schools and communities. It builds networks, teaches skills, educates about issues, and puts ideas into practice with campaigns through conferences, email, a magazine, training, caucuses, and campaign packets.

SCHOOL DEMOGRAPHICS

Number of Full-Time Students	**104**
International Students	**15%**
Female Students	**34%**

Pre-MBA Employment:

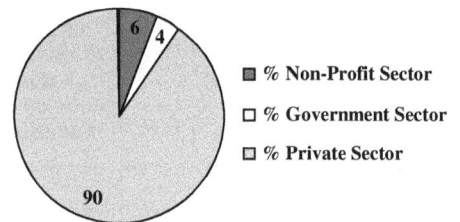

- ■ % Non-Profit Sector
- ☐ % Government Sector
- ☐ % Private Sector

2006/2007 School Year

THE CENTER FOR BUSINESS EDUCATION'S BOTTOM LINE ON UNIVERSITY OF COLORADO AT BOULDER:
Compared to other business schools in our survey, University of Colorado at Boulder offers an excellent number of courses featuring relevant content, and does an excellent job in courses explicitly addressing how mainstream business improves the world. University of Colorado at Boulder requires 9 core courses featuring relevant content.

A Closer Look at:
University of Denver
Daniels College of Business / Denver, CO
http://www.daniels.du.edu/

WHAT THE SCHOOL SAYS:
Core values are at the heart of our curriculum. Ethics and corporate social responsibility are taught, modeled and experienced throughout Daniels' programs. At Daniels, ethics and values are a total immersion activity. Here, academic excellence and a commitment to values-based leadership come together to change the way business students think about the world—and the way the world thinks about business.

A QUICK LOOK

NOTE: All information is self-reported data submitted to the Center for Business Education

COURSES*

Business Law (**6**)
CSR/Business Ethics (**4**)
Entrepreneurship (**1**)
General Management (**4**)
Marketing (**1**)
Organizational Behavior (**1**)
Strategy (**1**)

KEY CONCENTRATIONS

Values-Based Leadership

Not-for-Profit Management

KEY JOINT DEGREES

IMBA & Master of Arts in Global Finance, Trade, and Economic Integration

ACTIVITIES*

Speakers/Seminars (**2**)
Orientation Activities (**1**)
Internship/Consulting (**2**)
Student Competitions (**1**)
Clubs & Programs (**3**)
Career Development (**1**)
Institutes/Centers (**1**)
Concentrations (**2**)
Joint Degrees (**4**)

* Figures in parentheses indicate the number of courses/activities that, in whole or in part, integrate social, environmental, or ethical perspectives

NOTABLE FEATURES

CORE COURSES:

Global Business Imperative
This course focuses on overview issues such as globalization combined with operations issues, which include global marketing, global management, and global finance. A strong focus on cross-cultural issues and perspective from the developing world is built into the course. A major theme of the course has focused on doing business in South Africa. Issues of dual responsibility to both the host country constituents and to the corporation are emphasized.

Values-Based Leadership
This course explores workplace issues in terms of legal, public policy, and ethical dimensions. Students learn to prepare for a world where legal compliance, political pressures, and ethical choices are shifting from reactive processes to proactive and strategic approaches.

ELECTIVE COURSES:

Marketing Communication
This course uses cases to stimulate student awareness, involvement, and critical thinking about business and society and ethical issues within the marketing discipline. The cases dealing with these issues focus on the trade-offs between short-term profit and long-term effects. Students are asked to evaluate the alternatives facing organizations and to critically evaluate the solutions they recommend, understanding that such decisions would have short- and long-term impacts on the businesses, employees, specific segments of the population, the general well-being of society, and—in one case—the economic growth of a developing country.

Ethics and Compliance Post-WorldCom
This seminar course explores how proper ethics and corporate compliance are critical to public corporations, and their officers and directors in the post-WorldCom world. Drawing on the failures of ethics and compliance at companies like Enron, WorldCom, Tyco, and Adelphia, this seminar examines the current regulatory environment for public companies; the "nuts and bolts" of implementing and managing a corporate compliance program; the best practices in corporate ethics, compliance and governance; developing and fostering an ethical corporate culture; and assessing and managing risk in a corporate environment.

INSTITUTES AND CENTERS:

Carl M. Williams Institute for Ethics and Values
This institute advances the interdisciplinary study of ethics and values through broad-based philosophical inquiry, rational deliberation, and practical application. Created to advance the capacity for ethical decision making in personal, institutional, and community contexts, the institute provides leadership in the development of values and the practice of ethics for our global society.

QUESTIONS TO CONSIDER:

Does any required course contain some element of Social Impact Management? **YES**

Is any required course entirely dedicated to social, environmental, or ethical issues? **YES**

Is there a Net Impact Chapter on campus? **YES**

A Closer Look at:
University of Denver
Daniels College of Business / Denver, CO

ANNUAL EVENTS:

Bridges to the Future
Bridges to the Future was created to build a framework of programs that stimulate civic dialogue and discussion among Colorado communities. Programming includes lectures, panel discussions, and classes. All are free and open to the public. The 2006–07 University of Denver Bridges to the Future program was dedicated to "The Pursuit of Peace"—a concept that has both enticed and eluded global society.

Race and Case
The college's premier event is the Race and Case competition, a business ethics case competition at Daniels followed by a ski race in Vail, Colorado. Teams present four distinctive viewpoints (community, management, Employees, and shareholders) and convey an in-depth understanding of the case, key issues, possible impacts, and future government regulations. They provide a strategic decision analysis, present a clear resolution, and demonstrate both a proactive management process and creative presentation.

SCHOOL DEMOGRAPHICS	
Number of Full-Time Students	248
International Students	31%
Female Students	37%

2006/2007 School Year

OTHER PROGRAMS:

Service Corps
Net Impact's Service Corps program provides an opportunity for members to use their business skills to help their community. Volunteers engage in short-term, part-time consulting projects related to finance, marketing, new program development, business planning, fundraising, and strategic planning at various nonprofit organizations.

Extreme Experience
Daniels coordinates its internships through the award-winning, internationally recognized Suitts Center for Career Services. Suitts Center personnel work closely with Daniels student group leaders, including key leaders in the school's Net Impact chapter. Suitts and Net Impact collaborate to attract and develop relationships with employers who practice social, economic, and ecological accountability.

STUDENT CLUBS AND PROGRAMS:

Graduates Involved in Volunteer Efforts (GIVE)
GIVE promotes and coordinates volunteer and community service opportunities. These events include varied activities with service organizations such as Family Homestead and March of Dimes, as well as environmentally themed activities such as roadside clean-ups, trail clearing, and park landscaping.

Net Impact
The Net Impact Daniels chapter is the largest network of business students and alumni dedicated to integrating social responsibility into the business community and the Daniels experience. Its mission is to make community commitment and enlightened practice a reality by raising awareness of and promoting socially responsible business practices. Throughout the year, Net Impact hosts a variety of speakers and discussion panels, follows through on initiatives such as the recycling program at Daniels, participates in the Net Impact national conference, and competes in a case competition.

FACULTY PIONEER:

2001 – Institutional Leadership Award, R. Bruce Hutton
Dr. Bruce Hutton is a Professor of Marketing in the Daniels College of Business of the University of Denver and has served as Dean of the college. While serving as Dean, Professor Hutton started a newly focused interdisciplinary MBA program with major emphasis on issues of values and social responsibility, including environmental ethics and sustainable development. He has received numerous local, regional, and national honors for his contributions to business education, applied market research, and community service.

THE CENTER FOR BUSINESS EDUCATION'S BOTTOM LINE ON UNIVERSITY OF DENVER:
Compared to other business schools in our survey, University of Denver offers a good number of courses featuring relevant content, and does an excellent job in those courses explicitly addressing how mainstream business improves the world. University of Denver requires 6 core courses featuring relevant content.

University of Florida
Warrington College of Business Administration / Gainesville, FL
http://www.cba.ufl.edu/

WHAT THE SCHOOL SAYS:
The University of Florida MBA program offers students leadership and ethics classes as part of their elective MBA curriculum. Additionally, students are provided ample opportunities to gain knowledge about social and environmental issues through the Poe Ethics Fellows.

A QUICK LOOK

NOTE: All information is self-reported data submitted to the Center for Business Education

COURSES*

CSR/Business Ethics (1)
Entrepreneurship (1)

ACTIVITIES*

Clubs & Programs (1)
Institutes/Centers (1)

* Figures in parentheses indicate the number of courses/activities that, in whole or in part, integrate social, environmental, or ethical perspectives

NOTABLE FEATURES

ELECTIVE COURSES:

Business Ethics and Social Responsibility
This course examines the ethical issues managers face in business organizations. It explores ethical and moral problems in business and uses a variety of materials, including both classic and popular literature, to analyze and evaluate the manager's options and decisions. Subjects include ethical theories, the origins of moral and legal duties, whistle-blowing, bribery, drug testing, workplace safety, environmental responsibility, privacy, secrecy and disclosure, bluffing, lying, cheating, and stealing.

Social Entrepreneurship
The purpose of this course is to provide students with an introduction to the major opportunities and challenges facing social entrepreneurs and their ventures. Students have an opportunity to meet with several social entrepreneurs, learn about specific social issues, and volunteer at local nonprofit organizations and community agencies.

INSTITUTES AND CENTERS:

Public Utility Research Center
The Public Utility Research Center provides international training and strategic research in public utility regulation, market rules, and infrastructure management in the energy, telecommunications, and water industries. Its outreach activities support the expanded deployment and efficient delivery of telecommunications, energy and water/wastewater services, including the achievement of environmental objectives.

STUDENT CLUBS AND PROGRAMS:

Poe Ethics Fellows
The Poe Ethics Fellows are MBA students who meet regularly to discuss current issues in business and managerial ethics. Books, articles, and speakers stimulate discussion and provoke critical thinking about business ethics. Poe Fellows have represented the program at business ethics conferences nationally and hosted important speakers and guests in the Warrington College.

SCHOOL DEMOGRAPHICS

Number of Full-Time Students	154
International Students	21%
Female Students	21%

Pre-MBA Employment:

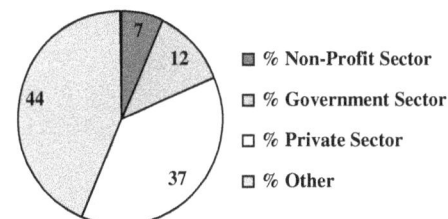

Pie chart values: 7, 12, 44, 37

- ■ % Non-Profit Sector
- □ % Government Sector
- □ % Private Sector
- □ % Other

2006/2007 School Year

QUESTIONS TO CONSIDER:

Does any required course contain some element of Social Impact Management? **NO**

Is any required course entirely dedicated to social, environmental, or ethical issues? **NO**

Is there a Net Impact Chapter on campus? **YES**

THE CENTER FOR BUSINESS EDUCATION'S BOTTOM LINE ON UNIVERSITY OF FLORIDA:
Compared to other business schools in our survey, University of Florida does a good job in relevant courses explicitly addressing how mainstream business improves the world.

A Closer Look at:
University of Geneva

THE ASPEN INSTITUTE
Center for Business Education

HEC (Hautes Etudes Commerciales) Geneva / Geneva, Switzerland
http://hec-executive.ch/iomba/

WHAT THE SCHOOL SAYS:

Welcome to the University of Geneva's International Organizations MBA (IOMBA). We have developed this unique program to address a major unfilled need: training professionals to pursue careers in the increasingly interconnected fields of international governmental and nongovernmental organizations and companies that work with these institutions.

A QUICK LOOK

NOTE: All information is self-reported data submitted to the Center for Business Education

COURSES*

Business & Government (1)
Business Law (1)
CSR/Business Ethics (1)
Economics (13)
Entrepreneurship (2)
Environmental (2)
General Management (4)
Marketing (1)
Organizational Behavior (1)
Public/Nonprofit Mgt (2)

KEY CONCENTRATIONS

International Organizations MBA (IOMBA)

KEY JOINT DEGREES

IOMBA & Master of Public Policy

IOMBA & Master in International Studies

ACTIVITIES*

Speakers/Seminars (8)
Orientation Activities (2)
Internship/Consulting (1)
Student Competitions (1)
Clubs & Programs (1)
Career Development (1)
Concentrations (1)
Joint Degrees (3)

* Figures in parentheses indicate the number of courses/activities that, in whole or in part, integrate social, environmental, or ethical perspectives

NOTABLE FEATURES

CORE COURSES:

Global Political Economy
This course seeks to identify the impact of globalization on firms and governments and the choices they face and make in responding to the challenge of a globalizing political economy.

Social Entrepreneurship Parts I and II
This course takes a strategic perspective on social change. It asks how emerging leaders, social entrepreneurs, social "intrapreneurs," and high-impact philanthropists can stimulate systemic change through local interventions and collaboration. Part II focuses on social entrepreneurship in health care using a case study method that integrates a presentation by a world-recognized social entrepreneur, members of the venture capital community in the United States and Europe, and leaders in the health care industry. The course will end with a business plan competition.

ELECTIVE COURSES:

Water Conflict, Security and Cooperation
This seminar will examine some of the contemporary and conceptual issues relating to disputes over transboundary water resources, such as hydropolitics, hydro-political complex theory, processes of securitization and de-securitization, hydro-hegemony, and patterns of conflict and cooperation. Considering the many international dimensions of water, the discussions will also incorporate policy, economic, environmental, and legal perspectives.

Democracy, Development and Decline in Sub-Saharan Africa
This course will explore a series of transitions—from war to peace, from one party to multi-party democracies, and from state to private sector-driven economies—that have taken place in countries as diverse as Angola, South Africa, Mozambique, and Uganda. We will discuss the theoretical literature on civil society, institutions, culture, and globalization in order to explain why the transitions occurred and what impact they have had on political alliances, economic development, and civic participation within African countries.

QUESTIONS TO CONSIDER:

Does any required course contain some element of Social Impact Management? **YES**

Is any required course entirely dedicated to social, environmental, or ethical issues? **YES**

Is there a Net Impact Chapter on campus? **YES**

University of Geneva

HEC (Hautes Etudes Commerciales) Geneva / Geneva, Switzerland

THE ASPEN INSTITUTE
Center for Business Education

ANNUAL EVENTS:

▪ *UN International Organizations, and NGOs Presentations*

During orientation week, members of different United Nations organizations, international organizations, and representatives of NGOs make presentations to the new students to introduce them to the many different organizations in Geneva working on various humanitarian, social, and development issues.

▪ *The Global Social Venture Competition*

The IOMBA program hosted an initial in-house round of the "The Global Social Venture Competition". As of 2008, the IOMBA program will be hosting a regional semifinals round on campus.

SCHOOL DEMOGRAPHICS	
Number of Full-Time Students	**36**
International Students	**92%**
Female Students	**55%**
2006/2007 School Year	

OTHER PROGRAMS:

▪ *The IOMBA Internship/Consultancy Project*

The IOMBA Internship/Consultancy Project consists of three months of full-time employment with an IO, NGO, or a social enterprise. The IOMBA internship provides opportunities for valuable work experience, enables students to explore career options, and provides a unique opportunity for developing a professional network.

▪ *IOMBA Career Services*

The IOMBA Career Services organizes a series of seminars that allow students to interact with visiting professionals from international organizations in Geneva and beyond that focus on the social and environmental impact of management.

STUDENT CLUBS AND PROGRAMS:

▪ *Net Impact Geneva*

The Geneva IOMBA chapter of Net Impact is committed to utilizing its unique positioning among international organizations and NGOs in Geneva to bring together the business leaders and the thought leaders who are interested in making a positive and meaningful impact on the society through their ideas and actions.

THE CENTER FOR BUSINESS EDUCATION'S BOTTOM LINE ON UNIVERSITY OF GENEVA:
Compared to other business schools in our survey, University of Geneva offers an excellent number of courses featuring relevant content, and does an excellent job in those courses explicitly addressing how mainstream business improves the world. University of Geneva requires 12 core courses featuring relevant content.

University of Jyväskylä

School of Business and Economics / Jyväskylä, Finland
http://www.jyu.fi/economics/

THE ASPEN INSTITUTE
Center for Business Education

WHAT THE SCHOOL SAYS:

The School of Business and Economics at the University of Jyväskylä creates and disseminates expertise based on scientific research for management, entrepreneurship, and economic decision making needs, maintaining strong links to the surrounding community by actively promoting our latest research results and professional expertise. Environmental and/or social issues are an important part integrated in the strategic focus areas of the School of Business and Economics.

A QUICK LOOK

NOTE: All information is self-reported data submitted to the Center for Business Education

COURSES*

Accounting (1)
Economics (4)
Entrepreneurship (5)
Environmental (9)
General Management (6)
Marketing (1)

KEY CONCENTRATIONS

Corporate Environmental Management

KEY JOINT DEGREES

MBA & Masters in Renewable Energy

ACTIVITIES*

Speakers/Seminars (4)
Orientation Activities (2)
Internship/Consulting (2)
Clubs & Programs (4)
Career Development (1)
Institutes/Centers (1)
Concentrations (1)
Joint Degrees (1)

*Figures in parentheses indicate the number of courses/activities that, in whole or in part, integrate social, environmental, or ethical perspectives

NOTABLE FEATURES

CORE COURSES:

Environmental Management in Networks

The goal of this course is to familiarize students with the benefits of collaboration among companies in the area of environmental management. In addition, the course is meant to increase the understanding of competition and cooperation as a basis for environmental management in networks. Students are introduced to network thinking and network theories, industrial ecology, and strategies for establishing eco-industrial relationships.

Material Flow Management

This course is designed to explore the principles of material flow analysis and the different types of material flow models: life cycle assessment, eco-balance, MIPS (Material Input per Service Unit), etc. Students are introduced to management applications of material flow analysis and to eco design.

ELECTIVE COURSES:

Environmental Economics

This course introduces theoretical and empirical issues of environmental economics. The key topics are the relations of production and environment and the analysis of the pollution effects of production.

Corporate Environmental Management

Specific goals of this course are to create a coherent picture of corporate environmental management research in Finland in relation to international research and to build a common methodological understanding for this novel field of research. Supervising professors conduct presentations on current research topics and methods in corporate environmental management.

INSTITUTES AND CENTERS:

Expert Services Research Unit

The activities of the Expert Services Research Unit are strongly linked to the development of the region and to local challenges in the areas of economics, entrepreneurship, and policy-making. The Expert Services Research Unit has been established in order to bridge academic research and applied science, which is being achieved through numerous regional development projects. The Expert Services Research Unit has extensive experience in regional development and policy, entrepreneurship and the SME sector, evaluation studies and impact analysis.

QUESTIONS TO CONSIDER:

Does any required course contain some element of Social Impact Management? **YES**

Is any required course entirely dedicated to social, environmental, or ethical issues? **NO**

Is there a Net Impact Chapter on campus? **NO**

A Closer Look at:
University of Jyväskylä
School of Business and Economics / Jyväskylä, Finland

THE ASPEN INSTITUTE
Center for Business Education

ANNUAL EVENTS:

Annual Summer Research Seminar of the School of Business and Economics

This seminar provides students and researchers at the School of Business and Economics the opportunity to present their work and to have it published. The seminar is open to all disciplines and topics related to social impact and environmental management are often raised by the presenting researchers.

Summer Internship Program

The School of Business and Economics offers summer internships for students, particularly in the public sector. Internships have included positions at the Environmental Protection Agency of Central Finland. Funding for summer internships is provided by the School of Business and Economics.

OTHER PROGRAMS:

Student Consulting Projects

Students of the Corporate Environmental Management master's degree program annually offer their consulting services to local companies, NGOs, and the public sector. The School of Business and Economics mediates the consulting to ensure quality and suitability of the services.

STUDENT CLUBS AND PROGRAMS:

Finnish Business and Society/Corporate Social Responsibility Network

The purpose of this network of companies, public sector, consumers, and academia is to promote corporate social responsibility by conducting activities such as publishing a monthly magazine and organizing seminars.

Porssi Student Club of the School of Business and Economics

Porssi focuses on student activities. It is actively involved in social and environmental activities and conducts annual fundraisers.

SCHOOL DEMOGRAPHICS	
Number of Full-Time Students	350
International Students	5%
Female Students	60%
2006/2007 School Year	

THE CENTER FOR BUSINESS EDUCATION'S BOTTOM LINE ON UNIVERSITY OF JYVÄSKYLÄ:
Compared to other business schools in our survey, University of Jyväskylä offers an excellent number of courses featuring relevant content, and does an excellent job in those courses explicitly addressing how mainstream business improves the world. University of Jyväskylä requires 13 core courses featuring relevant content.

The University of Michigan

Stephen M. Ross School of Business / Ann Arbor, MI

http://www.bus.umich.edu/

THE ASPEN INSTITUTE
Center for Business Education

WHAT THE SCHOOL SAYS:

At the University of Michigan's Stephen M. Ross School of Business, social and environmental responsibility is a cornerstone of broad-based management education. A Ross MBA prepares students to address fundamental issues of social responsibility and environmentally sustainable business whether they work in the public, private, or nonprofit sectors—or all three.

A QUICK LOOK

NOTE: All information is self-reported data submitted to the Center for Business Education

COURSES*

Accounting (2)
Business Law (7)
Economics (8)
Entrepreneurship (1)
Finance (2)
Information Technology (1)
General Management (17)
Marketing (3)
Operations Management (2)
Strategy (12)

KEY JOINT DEGREES

MBA/MS Natural Resources and Environment

MBA/MPP Public Policy

MBA/MS Health Services

ACTIVITIES*

Speakers/Seminars (10)
Internship/Consulting (6)
Student Competitions (1)
Clubs & Programs (10)
Career Development (5)
Institutes/Centers (10)
Joint Degrees (24)

* Figures in parentheses indicate the number of courses/activities that, in whole or in part, integrate social, environmental, or ethical perspectives

NOTABLE FEATURES

CORE COURSES:

▦ *Applied Microeconomics*

This course provides students with the foundations of microeconomic analysis. The primary objective is to develop the abilities of students to apply fundamental microeconomic concepts to a wide range of managerial decisions, and public policy issues. Foundation topics include the nature of the firm, its costs and supply behavior; consumer behavior and market demand; and market power and price-setting behavior.

▦ *Human Behavior and Organization*

This course emphasizes bringing people together to create and deliver value and identifying opportunities in this complex, sometimes chaotic everyday life, mobilizing resources around opportunities, and organizing to deliver on opportunities. This is a course about the transition from being competent to being wise in the world of work. Success will depend on the ability to generate energy and commitment among people—within and outside the organization.

ELECTIVE COURSES:

▦ *Non-Market Strategy*

This course examines influences on business that arise from public policies, government regulation, non-governmental organizations, and media, which have come to be called the "non-market environment." A simulation game designed for the course considers the setting of national fuel economy standards; students will play the roles of auto company executives, members of Congress, and members of environmental NGOs.

▦ *Finance and the Sustainable Enterprise*

This course explores the financial valuation aspects unique to sustainability issues confronted by businesses. The assumptions and institutions necessary to ensure the success of any modern firm in maximizing shareholder value without adversely affecting broader economic and societal values will be critically assessed. More importantly, existing economic and financial frameworks will be modified to evaluate the effects of emerging regulatory and strategic environmental issues on the value of projects and firms.

INSTITUTES AND CENTERS:

▦ *Erb Institute for Global Sustainable Enterprise*

The Erb Institute at the University of Michigan fosters global sustainable enterprise through interdisciplinary research and education initiatives, including the acclaimed MBA/MS program. Utilizing a collaborative approach, the Erb Institute helps business, government, and civil society organizations to achieve meaningful progress toward sustainability.

▦ *Center for International Business Education*

The Center for International Business Education at Michigan is one of 31 centers located around the United States and is based at the Stephen M. Ross School of Business. It serves as an umbrella organization for innovative programs that prepare students, faculty, and business-community leaders for competing in a globally interdependent world.

QUESTIONS TO CONSIDER:

Does any required course contain some element of Social Impact Management? **YES**

Is any required course entirely dedicated to social, environmental, or ethical issues? **YES**

Is there a Net Impact Chapter on campus? **YES**

All information in this profile is drawn and/or adapted from the self-reported data of the Center for Business Education's Beyond Grey Pinstripes 2007 MBA survey. The Center for Business Education is housed within the Business and Society Program at the Aspen Institute. For more info, visit www.AspenCBE.org.

The University of Michigan

Stephen M. Ross School of Business / Ann Arbor, MI

THE ASPEN INSTITUTE
Center for Business Education

ANNUAL EVENTS:

Erb Institute Speaker Series

The Erb Institute Speaker Series showcases a wide range of practitioners from the corporate, consulting, nonprofit, and government sectors whose work is primarily concerned with making business more environmentally and socially sustainable. The Erb Institute also connects MBA students to myriad alumni and external partners working in the areas of sustainable business, CSR, and nonprofit management. The institute regularly convenes alumni panels and holds an internship/career forum for its students each year.

Nonprofit and Public Management Speaker Series

This speaker series includes leaders from the nonprofit, public, and private sectors whose work is primarily concerned with making the role of nonprofit organizations more effective and prominent.

Domestic Corps

This program provides challenging, high-level, paid consulting summer internships in a nonprofit organization. The program offers a variety of projects, including business development, entrepreneurship, strategic planning, marketing, and fund development, in diverse communities across the U.S.

OTHER PROGRAMS:

WDI Global Impact Internship Program

The WDI (William Davidson Institute) Global Impact Internship Program supports partnerships between University of Michigan graduate students and non-profits, businesses, and other organizations in emerging market economies. Each year, WDI sponsors numerous internships for MBA students with interests in Base of the Pyramid and Social Enterprise initiatives in developing countries.

SCHOOL DEMOGRAPHICS	
Number of Full-Time Students	825
International Students	35%
Female Students	32%

2006/2007 School Year

Ross Habitat for Humanity Builders

Ross Habitat for Humanity Builders focuses on building houses for low income residents. The club provides a number of hands-on opportunities along with providing a lively auction to raise funds for building supplies.

STUDENT CLUBS AND PROGRAMS:

Emerging Markets Club

The Emerging Markets Club focuses on issues emanating from the rapid growth in developing world economies and on the unique challenges facing companies and people doing business in these countries.

Net Impact

At Ross, Net Impact's primary focus is to cultivate MBAs who wish to leverage their influence for the benefit of society, the economy, and the environment. This goal is accomplished by equipping members with tools and resources that enable them to add sustainable value in private and public enterprises.

FACULTY PIONEER:

2005 – Lifetime Achievement Award, C. K. Prahalad

For nearly 30 years Professor Prahalad has produced cutting-edge scholarship on corporate strategy and multinational corporations. Long before it was in vogue to do so, Prahalad was thinking broadly and creatively about the role of the multinational corporation and its impacts on society and the environment. With Stuart Hart, Prahalad wrote the path-breaking 2002 article, "The Fortune at the Bottom of the Pyramid," which provided the first articulation of how business could profitably serve the needs of the four billion poor in the developing world. Not only is his work prompting companies to rethink their global strategies, it is changing global development policy at international institutions like the U.S. State Department, United Nations, and World Economic Forum.

2003 – Lifetime Achievement Award, Thomas N. Gladwin

Thomas Gladwin is the recipient of 26 foundation and academic awards for research on ecologically and socially sustainable commerce, including major awards from the National Science Foundation and the Energy Foundation. Gladwin is the author of over 130 articles, cases, and chapters, and eight books on international and environmental management.

2003 – Rising Star Award, Andrew J. Hoffman

Professor Hoffman's research deals with the nature and dynamics of change within institutional and cultural systems. He applies that research toward understanding the cultural and managerial implications of environmental protection and sustainability for industry.

THE CENTER FOR BUSINESS EDUCATION'S BOTTOM LINE ON THE UNIVERSITY OF MICHIGAN:
Compared to other business schools in our survey, The University of Michigan offers a truly extraordinary number of courses featuring relevant content, and does a truly extraordinary job in those courses explicitly addressing how mainstream business improves the world. The University of Michigan requires 4 core courses featuring relevant content.

A Closer Look at:
University of Navarra

IESE Business School / Barcelona, Spain

http://www.iese.edu/en/home.asp

WHAT THE SCHOOL SAYS:

Since its founding, IESE has always treated ethics and social responsibility as essential to the training of future business leaders. The hallmark of the IESE experience is the school's dedication to the individual development of each and every participant in our programs. Central to our aim is that students leave the school with a sense of corporate and personal responsibility.

A QUICK LOOK

NOTE: All information is self-reported data submitted to the Center for Business Education

COURSES*

Accounting (1)
Economics (3)
HR Management (4)
International Management (1)
General Management (5)
Marketing (1)
Organizational Behavior (1)
Strategy (2)

ACTIVITIES*

Speakers/Seminars (9)
Orientation Activities (1)
Internship/Consulting (3)
Student Competitions (1)
Clubs & Programs (4)
Career Development (1)
Institutes/Centers (7)

* Figures in parentheses indicate the number of courses/activities that, in whole or in part, integrate social, environmental, or ethical perspectives

NOTABLE FEATURES

CORE COURSES:

Global Economics
This course has a particular focus on how the free market affects the distribution of wealth within and between countries, and especially how societies with a high level of poverty can become richer by embracing trade, in turn increasing the consumer base and middle class and alleviating poverty. The cases of emerging economies such as China, Africa, and India are considered.

Marketing Management
Through cases on general marketing management, the aim of this course is to develop an understanding of the basic elements of marketing strategy. A particular focus is given to the effect society has on marketing and vice versa. Ethical issues are dealt with, particularly in regard to assessing where to establish boundaries in advertising. Environmental issues are also key when considering market selection and distribution network options.

ELECTIVE COURSES:

Social Entrepreneurship: Creating Economic and Social Value
The main objectives of this course are to map a wide variety of entrepreneurial and innovative initiatives; to introduce the concepts, practices, opportunities, and challenges of social entrepreneurship; to illustrate how established corporations can collaborate with social entrepreneurs; and to engage students in a joint learning process as they develop a better understanding of this emerging field.

Strategy Introduction
The objective of this course is to study the relationship between strategy and organization, to recognize various types of organization, and to gain practice in processes of change, management ,and government. Throughout the course students are encouraged to consider strategic issues from many viewpoints, always looking at the effect a particular decision or restructure might have on all those involved.

INSTITUTES AND CENTERS:

Center for Enterprise in Latin America (CELA)
The CELA is designed to research the economic reality of Latin American countries and favor the exchange of academic information and experiences with companies in the area. The center's main lines of research are zones, social-political legal and fiscal aspects, management and general management, financial control, personnel management and human behavior, marketing and operations management, and business ethics. Much of the research centers on ethics and public administration, the use of microfinance facilities, and the role of business in Latin American society.

Center for Business in Society (CBS)
The following are some of the goals of the CBS: Develop well-founded concepts and arguments as a basis for human quality in business and a beneficial impact of business activity on society and the environment, devise management models that make it easier to grasp the complexity and the systemic nature of companies' relationships with society and the environment, and encourage the application of criteria of social responsibility and sustainable development in every aspect of business.

QUESTIONS TO CONSIDER:

Does any required course contain some element of Social Impact Management? **YES**

Is any required course entirely dedicated to social, environmental, or ethical issues? **NO**

Is there a Net Impact Chapter on campus? **YES**

A Closer Look at:
University of Navarra

IESE Business School / Barcelona, Spain

ANNUAL EVENTS:

■ *Doing Good Doing Well (DGDW)*

DGDW is the leading student conference on responsible business in Europe. The event brings together 300 students, professors, and professionals from all over the world to engage in two days of discussion and challenge on IESE's Barcelona campus. DGDW is a world-class event with over 25 speakers and panelists who inspire people with compelling stories about successful initiatives in responsible business.

■ *IESE-Ronald Berger International MBA Case Competition*

The IESE-Ronald Berger International MBA Case Competition focuses on the relationship between business decisions and social impact. Teams from different schools compete and debate the best solution to a pre-selected case in terms of profitability and sustainability. The objective of the event is to develop both the analytical abilities of the participating students in a competitive environment and their communication skills in written and oral forms.

SCHOOL DEMOGRAPHICS	
Number of Full-Time Students	445
International Students	78%
Female Students	24%
	2006/2007 School Year

OTHER PROGRAMS:

■ *International Finance Corporation (IFC) Internships*

The IFC, a member of the World Bank Group, promotes its mission to reduce poverty and improve the lives of people in developing countries by financing private sector projects, assisting companies in the developing world, mobilizing financing in the international financial markets, and providing technical assistance to businesses and governments' privatization efforts. The World Bank has been recruiting on campus for at least 10 years and hires IESE students for summer internships.

■ *International Symposium on Ethics, Business and Society*

This biannual symposium aims to explore the problems of current management theories and practices and the prospects for improving them. At the same time, new proposals for a more comprehensive integration of ethics into management are welcome.

STUDENT CLUBS AND PROGRAMS:

■ *Club Solidario*

Club Solidario consists of a team of IESE students who share the common purpose of promoting social and economic justice and access to resources by supporting projects in Barcelona, the rest of Spain, and worldwide. The club serves as an organizational base for dealing with these concerns and holds events in the hope of encouraging and inspiring related activities on and off campus. The club aims to socially engage IESE students and staff in purposeful, sustainable activities, for example, by organising charitable and fund-raising events.

■ *Responsible Business Club*

The purpose of this club is to provide a means by which students can learn how businesses gain more through responsible practices and to help IESE students nurture responsible behavior in their studies and to later apply this to their career. The club organizes conferences, speaker series, events, and internships with the twofold intention of raising social and environmental awareness within a business school context and actively involving IESE students in projects with a social premise.

THE CENTER FOR BUSINESS EDUCATION'S BOTTOM LINE ON UNIVERSITY OF NAVARRA:
Compared to other business schools in our survey, University of Navarra offers a good number of courses featuring relevant content, and does a good job in those courses explicitly addressing how mainstream business improves the world. University of Navarra requires 8 core courses featuring relevant content.

A Closer Look at:
The University of New Mexico
The Robert O. Anderson School of Management / Albuquerque, NM
http://www.mgt.unm.edu/

WHAT THE SCHOOL SAYS:
The Robert O. Anderson Graduate School of Management at the University of New Mexico is committed to preparing students for ethical and responsible management. Training in ethical decision making mirrors corporate models for ethical education and culture, with students participating in dedicated ethics curriculum plus a wide range of academic activities that reinforce that curriculum.

A QUICK LOOK

NOTE: All information is self-reported data submitted to the Center for Business Education

COURSES*

Accounting (4)
Business & Government (3)
Business Law (1)
CSR/Business Ethics (2)
Economics (1)
Entrepreneurship (3)
Environmental (1)
Finance (2)
HR Management (4)
International Management (1)
Marketing (3)
Organizational Behavior (1)
Operations Management (2)
Strategy (1)

KEY CONCENTRATIONS

Policy and Planning

ACTIVITIES*

Speakers/Seminars (5)
Clubs & Programs (2)
Career Development (1)
Institutes/Centers (1)
Concentrations (1)

* Figures in parentheses indicate the number of courses/activities that, in whole or in part, integrate social, environmental, or ethical perspectives

NOTABLE FEATURES

CORE COURSES:
Organizational Behavior and Diversity
This course emphasizes the application of knowledge, the relationship of theory and practice, and the dynamic and uncertain environment within which organizations interact, and the moral dilemmas that people in organizations encounter. Topics include the relationship of behaviors and attitudes, perception and stereotyping, culture and the global marketplace, group behavior, power and politics in organizations, conflict management and negotiations, and the impact of diversity on the organization's culture.

Technology Commercialization and the Global Environment
This course covers the fundamentals of technology commercialization and international management and the relationships between the two. It incorporates issues such as operating in economically disadvantaged areas and emerging markets, facility-siting decisions, impacts of capital flows across borders, social impacts of property rights, social impacts of regulation, corruption, human capital and workforce relations, and international efforts to improve social and environmental conditions.

ELECTIVE COURSES:
International Marketing Management
This course focuses on the international marketing environment and the development of an international marketing plan. Various case studies emphasize a number of social issues facing international marketing strategies, for example McDonald's and obesity, marketing to the bottom of the pyramid, and marketing to developing nations.

Employment Law
The social and ethical impetuses for the passage of antidiscrimination laws and other employment laws are discussed in detail in this course, as well as why the laws continue today. This course discusses the fact that discrimination of all types still exist and the effect such discrimination has on society and business. Concepts are addressed through discussion, case studies, problem solving, presentations, reaction papers, and lectures.

INSTITUTES AND CENTERS:
New Mexico Ethics Alliance
The New Mexico Ethics Alliance is a nonprofit community-governed organization partnering with the Anderson School to provide ethics education and training to organizations throughout New Mexico.

QUESTIONS TO CONSIDER:

Does any required course contain some element of Social Impact Management? **YES**

Is any required course entirely dedicated to social, environmental, or ethical issues? **YES**

Is there a Net Impact Chapter on campus? **YES**

All information in this profile is drawn and/or adapted from the self-reported data of the Center for Business Education's Beyond Grey Pinstripes 2007 MBA survey. The Center for Business Education is housed within the Business and Society Program at the Aspen Institute. For more info, visit www.AspenCBE.org.

The University of New Mexico

The Robert O. Anderson School of Management / Albuquerque, NM

THE ASPEN INSTITUTE
Center for Business Education

ANNUAL EVENTS:

■ *Annual Executive Lecture Series*

During this lecture Series, business leaders address students, faculty, and staff on topics ranging from corporate governance to the challenges associated with ethical behavior and social responsibility. The event is followed by a networking dinner.

OTHER PROGRAMS:

■ *Career Services*

Career Services makes a special effort to send job postings to students with an expressed interest in environmental management, community relations, nonprofit management, and economic development.

SCHOOL DEMOGRAPHICS	
Number of Full-Time Students	140
International Students	10%
Female Students	50%
	2006/2007 School Year

■ *An Evening with New Mexico's Corporate Socially Responsible Community*

Three student clubs—Net Impact, Beta Alpha Psi, and Anderson Graduate Business Students—hosted an evening with business leaders whose presentations centered around social responsibility programs, sustainability and renewable energy, and economic development strategies for low-income entrepreneurs. One hour was then devoted to networking. The event included students, faculty, and staff.

STUDENT CLUBS AND PROGRAMS:

■ *Beta Alpha Psi*

Beta Alpha Psi is the student honors society for accounting, finance, and Management and Information Systems students. It provides information to students about scholarships, internships, and other events related to career and business development. The local chapter has cohosted events on sustainability, renewable energy, and social responsibility. It also organizes community service activities every semester, including tax assistance, financial literacy, and support for local nonprofit organizations.

■ *Net Impact*

Net Impact's Anderson chapter sends members to annual conferences and hosts local events, all themed around sustainability and social responsibility. Supported by both staff and students, Net Impact at Anderson is a growing student organization/club with many sources of information and contacts.

THE CENTER FOR BUSINESS EDUCATION'S BOTTOM LINE ON THE UNIVERSITY OF NEW MEXICO:
Compared to other business schools in our survey, The University of New Mexico offers an excellent number of courses featuring relevant content, and does a good job in those courses explicitly addressing how mainstream business improves the world. The University of New Mexico requires 9 core courses featuring relevant content.

A Closer Look at:

The University of North Carolina at Chapel Hill

THE ASPEN INSTITUTE
Center for Business Education

Kenan-Flagler Business School / Chapel Hill, NC

http://www.kenan-flagler.unc.edu/

WHAT THE SCHOOL SAYS:

UNC Kenan-Flagler was among the first business schools to offer a comprehensive educational, research and outreach program in sustainable enterprise. Through classes, workshops, and enrichment activities, UNC Kenan-Flagler equips MBA students with the skills and tools necessary to identify opportunities that create competitive advantage in the context of sustainability.

A QUICK LOOK

NOTE: All information is self-reported data submitted to the Center for Business Education

COURSES*

Accounting (2)
CSR/Business Ethics (3)
Economics (1)
Entrepreneurship (3)
Environmental (1)
Finance (2)
HR Management (1)
International Management (6)
General Management (2)
Marketing (1)
Organizational Behavior (2)
Operations Management (4)
Public/Nonprofit Mgt (1)
Strategy (9)

KEY CONCENTRATIONS

Sustainable Enterprise

Global Supply Chain Management

KEY JOINT DEGREES

MBA & Masters of Public Health

MBA & Master of Regional Planning (MRP)

ACTIVITIES*

Speakers/Seminars (9)
Orientation Activities (2)
Internship/Consulting (1)
Student Competitions (2)
Clubs & Programs (5)
Career Development (7)
Institutes/Centers (4)
Concentrations (4)
Joint Degrees (4)

* Figures in parentheses indicate the number of courses/activities that, in whole or in part, integrate social, environmental, or ethical perspectives

NOTABLE FEATURES

CORE COURSES:

Ethical Aspects of Management

This course provides an introduction to the ethical issues involved in business management. It examines the ethical aspects of managerial decision making by means of cases and background readings. The class addresses issues such as international/cultural issues, diversity issues, fraud and deception, health care access, sexual harassment, privacy, and social responsibility.

Sustainable Enterprise

This course examines the origins, evolution, and current schools of thought regarding sustainable development. Study and discussion of sustainability as a theory of industrial development and accompanying models of commerce provide a context for understanding current models of business and its effects on other systems. The course also focuses on strategy, leadership, and innovation as applied to the sustainable enterprise.

ELECTIVE COURSES:

Entrepreneurship and Minority Economic Development

This course is designed to promote entrepreneurship as a strategy for accelerating upward mobility and wealth accumulation among minority communities, strengthening the capacity and sustainability of local community development organizations, and enhancing the overall economic competitiveness of places, especially economically distressed urban and rural communities.

International Business-NGO Partnering

Over the past 10 years, activists and corporations have created more than two dozen specialized nonprofit organizations to improve compliance of multinational corporations' suppliers with corporate codes of conduct. Through readings, case studies, and class discussion, students learn how the new "compliance industry" is taking shape, examine questions of scale, impact, and sustainability, and gain insights into the application of business management principles to global nonprofits.

INSTITUTES AND CENTERS:

The UNC Kenan-Flagler Center for Sustainable Enterprise (CSE)

The CSE examines how global social and environmental issues are redefining the competitive landscape of business. Its education, research, and outreach initiatives help students and executives learn how to position their organizations for maximum competitive advantage through "triple bottom line" business practices.

Urban Investment Strategies Center (UISC)

The UISC promotes entrepreneurial and market-based solutions to poverty alleviation, job creation, and community development in America's economically distressed communities. UISC builds partnerships between universities, urban communities, and the private sector to spark urban revitalization and reinvestment. Its programs strengthen the inner-city workforce, grow inner-city businesses, help promising minority- and women-owned businesses access capital, and bring an entrepreneurial attitude to charitable organizations.

QUESTIONS TO CONSIDER:

Does any required course contain some element of Social Impact Management? **YES**

Is any required course entirely dedicated to social, environmental, or ethical issues? **YES**

Is there a Net Impact Chapter on campus? **YES**

A Closer Look at:
The University of North Carolina at Chapel Hill
Kenan-Flagler Business School / Chapel Hill, NC

ANNUAL EVENTS:

■ *Annual Weatherspoon Lecture Series*

The Weatherspoon Lecture, held annually at UNC Kenan-Flagler, provides lectures by outstanding visiting scholars and world leaders from the fields of politics, education, business, and government. The Weatherspoon Lecture highlights current issues such as globalization, public policy, macroeconomics, and geopolitics—all relevant to social impact management and global business leadership.

■ *Sustainable Venture Capital Investment Competition (SVCIC)*

SVCIC is a national MBA competition that gives students from top business schools a real-world venture capitalist experience and awareness of double and triple bottom line evaluation techniques. The SVCIC experience exposes students to a variety of activities that must be integrated into a cohesive investment strategy to be pitched to real venture capitalists.

OTHER PROGRAMS:

■ *Center for Sustainable Enterprise (CSE) Consulting Group*

CSE Consulting Group offers world-class sustainability consulting during the summer, using MBA interns handpicked from among the school's most promising first-year students in the Sustainable Enterprise program. CSE consulting services include social/environmental impact assessment, sustainability benchmarking, sustainability reporting, development of a business case for sustainability, and sustainable enterprise business planning.

■ *Annual "Careers in Sustainability" Forum*

This daylong event gives students information about different career paths, functions, and industries in the field of sustainable enterprise. It is organized and hosted by the UNC Kenan-Flagler Net Impact Club. Over 100 students come from as far away as Massachusetts to hear panelists speak about possible career paths in sustainable business.

SCHOOL DEMOGRAPHICS	
Number of Full-Time Students	566
International Students	28%
Female Students	27%
	2006/2007 School Year

STUDENT CLUBS AND PROGRAMS:

■ *"The House that Kenan-Flagler Built"*

UNC Kenan-Flagler values its positive relationship with the greater community and, for this reason, it has partnered with Habitat for Humanity to build a home for a local family each year. MBA students plan and manage fund-raising events to sponsor the house, raising over $30,000 each year. A committee of students, staff, and faculty manages all aspects of coordinating volunteer management and fundraising.

■ *Alliance of Minority Business Students (AMBS)*

The AMBS seeks to meet the needs of minority students, advance diversity throughout the UNC Kenan-Flagler community and promote scholarship, leadership, and community service among its members. The AMBS is instrumental in promoting workplace diversity, a fundamental issue for social impact management.

FACULTY PIONEER:

■ *1999 – James Johnson, Jr.*

Professor James Johnson, Jr., director of the Urban Investment Strategies Center, which focuses on revitalizing urban areas, has research interest in the areas of community and economic development, the effects of demographic changes on the U.S. workplace, interethnic minority conflict in advanced industrial societies, urban poverty and public policy in urban America, and workforce diversity issues. He has published more than 100 scholarly research articles and three research monographs and has co-edited four theme issues of scholarly journals on these and related topics.

THE CENTER FOR BUSINESS EDUCATION'S BOTTOM LINE ON THE UNIVERSITY OF NORTH CAROLINA AT CHAPEL HILL:
Compared to other business schools in our survey, The University of North Carolina at Chapel Hill offers an excellent number of courses featuring relevant content, and does a truly extraordinary job in those courses explicitly addressing how mainstream business improves the world. The University of North Carolina at Chapel Hill requires 7 core courses featuring relevant content.

A Closer Look at:
University of Notre Dame
Mendoza College of Business / Notre Dame, IN
http://www.nd.edu/~cba

WHAT THE SCHOOL SAYS:

Discussion of social, ethical, and environmental issues pervades the MBA program at the University of Notre Dame. Examination of these issues begins at orientation, is integrated into the core curriculum, supported by many electives, is and is interwoven in meaningful ongoing activities.

A QUICK LOOK

NOTE: All information is self-reported data submitted to the Center for Business Education

COURSES*

Accounting (4)
Business Law (1)
CSR/Business Ethics (11)
Economics (1)
Finance (11)
General Management (36)
Marketing (8)

KEY CONCENTRATIONS

Management Development

KEY JOINT DEGREES

MBA & Engineering

ACTIVITIES*

Speakers/Seminars (22)
Orientation Activities (4)
Internship/Consulting (3)
Student Competitions (1)
Clubs & Programs (7)
Career Development (4)
Institutes/Centers (5)
Concentrations (7)
Joint Degrees (3)

* Figures in parentheses indicate the number of courses/activities that, in whole or in part, integrate social, environmental, or ethical perspectives

NOTABLE FEATURES

CORE COURSES:
Microeconomic Analysis
This course explores ways to think creatively about how business is done. It demonstrates that business does not happen in a vacuum but is both affected by and affects society and the environment. Every year, one class is dedicated to the discussion of ethics in microeconomics and has been guided by an ethics professor.

Conceptual Foundations of Business Ethics
This course explores the ethical dimension in the study and practice of business, applies the major normative ethical theories to business situations, discusses the relevance of stakeholders to business decisions, and seeks to improve the skills of moral reasoning and ethical decision making. Students are encouraged to examine and articulate their own values, develop the ability to think clearly about complex ethical situations, and to report conclusions in oral and written form.

ELECTIVE COURSES:
Corporate Citizenship and Sustainability
This course familiarizes students with concepts of corporate citizenship and sustainability. Students examine the interface among corporate, social, environmental, and ethical responsibilities, which leads to an understanding of the relevance of multiple stakeholders in business decisions. Invited executives share how their companies pursue socially responsible policies; a Notre Dame engineering professor presents research about energy issues.

Ten Years Hence
The annual Ten Years Hence course brings leading experts on environmental and social impact implications of special topics to present and meet with MBA students each spring semester. The course explores ideas, issues, and trends likely to affect business and society over the next decade.

INSTITUTES AND CENTERS:
Institute for Ethical Business Worldwide
This institute was created with the vision to advocate ethical business conduct in a global setting. The institute sponsors the Berges Lecture Series in Business Ethics every fall (six speakers), a research conference every November, and the Hesburgh Award/Cahill Lecture annually in the spring.

Gigot Center for Entrepreneurial Studies
Recognizing the unique role entrepreneurialism plays in our global community in terms of poverty alleviation and economic empowerment, the Gigot Center for Entrepreneurial Studies created the Social Entrepreneurship Program to foster and support life-giving entrepreneurial initiatives with disadvantaged communities throughout the world.

QUESTIONS TO CONSIDER:

Does any required course contain some element of Social Impact Management? **YES**

Is any required course entirely dedicated to social, environmental, or ethical issues? **YES**

Is there a Net Impact Chapter on campus? **YES**

All information in this profile is drawn and/or adapted from the self-reported data of the Center for Business Education's Beyond Grey Pinstripes 2007 MBA survey. The Center for Business Education is housed within the Business and Society Program at the Aspen Institute. For more info, visit www.AspenCBE.org.

A Closer Look at:
University of Notre Dame
Mendoza College of Business / Notre Dame, IN

ANNUAL EVENTS:

■ *John A. Berges Lecture Series in Business Ethics*

The Berges Lecture Series has been presented each fall and is primarily attended by MBA and undergraduate students. The series features senior executives speaking on the ethical dimensions of business. Speakers are models of leadership with integrity and good works. Opportunity for discussion is incorporated. The series features a debate on a current issue in business by interdisciplinary Notre Dame faculty.

■ *USAID T.I.E.S. (Training, Internships, Exchanges and Scholarships) MBA Exchange Entrepreneur Internship*

This program teaches an entrepreneurship curriculum to visiting faculty from the Universidad de Guadalajara (UG), Mexico. When they return to Guadalajara, the UG faculty work with Notre Dame and UG MBA students to help local agricultural workers use their experience and talents to start ventures that might replace income lost due to the consolidation of production in Mexico. Notre Dame MBAs visit Guadalajara and work with UG students each summer. The program is an opportunity for MBAs to put their skills into action by working as consultants and to experience a new culture and business environment.

■ *Social Venture Competition*

Members of the Notre Dame community submit and present business proposals that identify and pursue innovative solutions to systemic social problems. It includes business ideas related to innovative public/private partnerships as well as for-profit business models focused on social missions. It also accepts submissions related to creative ideas for spurring more socially oriented entrepreneurial activity within the private sector for greater social/environmental impact.

OTHER PROGRAMS:

■ *Community Partners Orientation*

Community Partners is a cornerstone of the MBA orientation. All incoming students participate in this two-day professional development and community engagement event, presented through Career Development. Student teams meet with local nonprofit and corporate leaders to examine strengths and to identify areas of collaboration and opportunities for new partnerships. Students learn from business leaders who integrate stewardship into professional life and witness collaboration between nonprofits and businesses as vital to the success of both.

STUDENT CLUBS AND PROGRAMS:

■ *Marketing Club*

In addition to hosting speakers and other initiatives, including the 2007 Marketing Symposium, the MBA Marketing Club is assisting Notre Dame Vision, an annual series of residential conferences for high school youth and practitioners held at Notre Dame, dedicated to the issue of vocation. The project team has undertaken several focus group interviews with Notre Dame Vision stakeholders (administration, mentors, and attendees) to determine the best way for Notre Dame Vision to increase enrollment while maintaining its focus and mission.

SCHOOL DEMOGRAPHICS	
Number of Full-Time Students	381
International Students	24%
Female Students	23%
Pre-MBA Employment:	

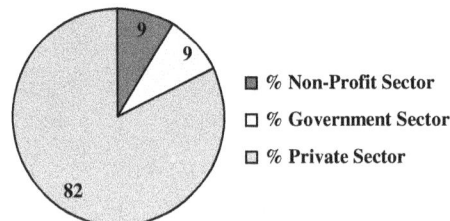

- ■ % Non-Profit Sector
- □ % Government Sector
- □ % Private Sector

Pie chart values: 9, 9, 82

2006/2007 School Year

THE CENTER FOR BUSINESS EDUCATION'S BOTTOM LINE ON UNIVERSITY OF NOTRE DAME:
Compared to other business schools in our survey, University of Notre Dame offers a truly extraordinary number of courses featuring relevant content, and does an excellent job in those courses explicitly addressing how mainstream business improves the world. University of Notre Dame requires 16 core courses featuring relevant content.

A Closer Look at:
The University of Nottingham

Nottingham University Business School / Nottingham, United Kingdom

http://www.nottingham.ac.uk/business/

WHAT THE SCHOOL SAYS:

Nottingham University Business School is a leading centre for management education in one of the most prominent and popular universities in the United Kingdom. Throughout its history, the Business School has been actively involved in research in the areas of social, environmental, and ethical impact. The school has developed specialist postgraduate CSR education and training, including an MBA in CSR, the first MBA of its kind in Britain.

A QUICK LOOK

NOTE: All information is self-reported data submitted to the Center for Business Education

COURSES*

Accounting (1)
Business Law (1)
CSR/Business Ethics (4)
Economics (2)
Entrepreneurship (1)
Finance (1)
HR Management (1)
Information Technology (1)
International Management (1)
General Management (5)
Marketing (2)
Organizational Behavior (2)
Operations Management (1)
Strategy (2)

KEY CONCENTRATIONS

Corporate Social Responsibility

ACTIVITIES*

Speakers/Seminars (7)
Orientation Activities (1)
Internship/Consulting (2)
Student Competitions (1)
Clubs & Programs (1)
Career Development (1)
Institutes/Centers (7)
Concentrations (1)

* Figures in parentheses indicate the number of courses/activities that, in whole or in part, integrate social, environmental, or ethical perspectives

NOTABLE FEATURES

CORE COURSES:

Managerial Economics and Business Policy

This module provides students with critical understanding of key concepts and models for the economic analysis of business activity in order to generate insight into the operation of the market economy. Social impacts are explicitly addressed when considering the nature of the firm and its objectives. The course also discusses the nature of externalities, the causes of market failure, and the implications for government intervention and voluntary engagement in social and environmental programs by firms.

Management Information Systems

This course examines the current issues and debates relating to managing information systems in a modern business and includes IT/ IS strategy, information management, systems development and implementation, the management of IT-leveraged change, and e-business. It considers social, environmental, and ethical issues from different stakeholder perspectives, using practical experiences and case studies from both the public and private sectors.

ELECTIVE COURSES:

Social Entrepreneurship

This module provides students with an introduction to the phenomena of social enterprise and social entrepreneurship. Social enterprise has moved to the forefront of the political and economic landscape in the UK, and the number of firms engaging in social entrepreneurship is growing rapidly each year. Students develop new social or environmental initiatives as part of the course work.

Corporate Finance

This module examines the major financial decisions made in large organizations and the performance measurement systems that support them. The idea that companies should operate in the interests of shareholders is examined and its consequences explored. The stakeholder perspective and possible conflicts between stakeholders are also examined.

INSTITUTES AND CENTERS:

International Centre for Corporate Social Responsibility (ICCSR)

Nottingham University Business School's ICCSR has established an international reputation for its teaching programs and for the quality of its academic research. The ICCSR engages in mainstream teaching and research under the following broad headings: understanding CSR, the scope and limits of CSR, CSR in context, measuring and reporting CSR, CSR skills, knowledge, and education, and CSR—creating value and evaluating outcomes.

Centre for Environmental Management

The Centre for Environmental Management undertakes research and training at the interface of people and the environment. Its work explores ways of identifying the choices we face in developing and implementing strategies for a sustainable future.

QUESTIONS TO CONSIDER:

Does any required course contain some element of Social Impact Management? **YES**

Is any required course entirely dedicated to social, environmental, or ethical issues? **NO**

Is there a Net Impact Chapter on campus? **YES**

A Closer Look at:
The University of Nottingham

Nottingham University Business School / Nottingham, United Kingdom

ANNUAL EVENTS:

Doing the Business

The Business School's International Centre for Corporate Social Responsibility (ICCSR) hosts a series of films about social and ethical issues in business. This event is in conjunction with Nottingham's independent Broadway Cinema and accompanied by an introduction from either ICCSR staff or a guest speaker.

Orientation CSR Workshop

This is a series of workshops designed to integrate CSR learning into the core curriculum of the first semester. Annual workshops includean introduction to CSR, Boots (a U.K. mass-retailer) support assessment workshop, a CSR skills/employment workshop, CSR in management theory and practice, and an internship workshop.

OTHER PROGRAMS:

CSR Employment Workshop

The CSR skills/employment workshop forms part of the MBA in CSR workshop series. A panel of CSR practitioners from the corporate, consultancy, and not-for-profit sectors share their views on CSR skills and employment opportunities, followed by questions and answers.

Boots Social Accountability Assessments

MBA students take part in Boots Social Accountability Assessments, an opportunity to provide students with practical experience in social assessment. Students gain invaluable experience while providing Boots with a spare pair of hands, and in some cases useful language skills and other competencies to facilitate Boots supplier assessments in the UK, Ireland, France, and Germany.

STUDENT CLUBS AND PROGRAMS:

Net Impact

Nottingham MBA students uphold Net Impact's mission to improve the world by growing and strengthening a network of new leaders who are using the power of business to make a positive net social, environmental, and economic impact.

FACULTY PIONEER:

2005 – European Award, Jeremy Moon

Professor Moon's corporate social responsibility research spans 20 years. His research interests focus on theories of CSR, CSR and public policy, and CSR in business education. Under his direction the International Centre for Corporate Social Responsibility has become one of the foremost centres for research, teaching, and dialogue on CSR in Europe.

SCHOOL DEMOGRAPHICS

Number of Full-Time Students	53
International Students	78%
Female Students	38%

Pre-MBA Employment:

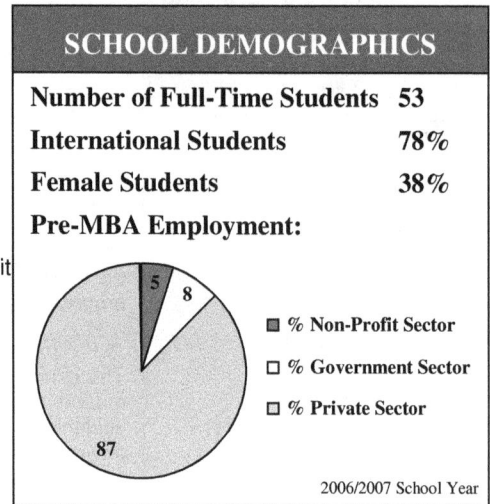

- ■ % Non-Profit Sector
- □ % Government Sector
- □ % Private Sector

2006/2007 School Year

THE CENTER FOR BUSINESS EDUCATION'S BOTTOM LINE ON THE UNIVERSITY OF NOTTINGHAM:
Compared to other business schools in our survey, The University of Nottingham offers an excellent number of courses featuring relevant content, and does a good job in those courses explicitly addressing how mainstream business improves the world. The University of Nottingham requires 8 core courses featuring relevant content.

A Closer Look at:
University of Oxford

Saïd Business School / Oxford, United Kingdom
http://www.sbs.ox.ac.uk/mba/

THE ASPEN INSTITUTE
Center for Business Education

WHAT THE SCHOOL SAYS:

At Saïd Business School, we encourage the leaders of tomorrow to see the stewardship of social and environmental assets as an integral part of their own and their organization's future success. We understand that managers today want more than financial success and career status. They want to have a positive impact on the world. By offering them a flexible MBA program that integrates social and environmental issues, we help to meet this need.

A QUICK LOOK

NOTE: All information is self-reported data submitted to the Center for Business Education

COURSES*

Accounting (1)
Business & Government (2)
Environmental (2)
Marketing (3)
Organizational Behavior (1)
Operations Management (1)
Public/Nonprofit Mgt (6)
Strategy (1)

KEY CONCENTRATIONS

Social Entrepreneurship

ACTIVITIES*

Speakers/Seminars (17)
Orientation Activities (2)
Student Competitions (2)
Clubs & Programs (2)
Career Development (1)
Institutes/Centers (3)
Concentrations (1)

Figures in parentheses indicate the number of courses/activities that, in whole or in part, integrate social, environmental, or ethical perspectives

NOTABLE FEATURES

CORE COURSES:

Capstone- Preparing for a Lifetime of Leadership Challenges
This course takes place over several full days and is business focused with the first topical focus on energy and climate change. It combines a provocative leadership conference approach, similar to those that will be faced during a management career, with a fast results delivery project.

International Business and Global Governance
The principal aim of this course is to provide students with tools needed to formulate strategies for global expansion. Students evaluate the drivers of strategic global expansion, assess the challenges facing managers creating global strategy, and explore the opportunities and challenges of global expansion with a focus on emerging markets. Topics include the 'bottom of the pyramid', the future evolution of the global economy, and strategic reasons that firms seek to improve their social, environmental, or human rights record through CSR initiatives.

ELECTIVE COURSES:

Social Innovation
Topics covered in this class include the dimensions of innovation, social enterprise models, the intersection between technology and social innovation, the legitimacy and governance of social innovation, and social accounting.

Risk Management of New and Emerging Technologies
This course examines the social and environmental controversies associated with new and emerging technologies and with issues identified through scientific research. Topics covered include biotechnology and climate change and past controversies such as asbestos and ozone depletion. The course provides a grounding in the main social science perspectives on these issues drawing on sociology, political science, and risk management.

INSTITUTES AND CENTERS:

Skoll Centre for Social Entrepreneurship
The Skoll Centre is a leading international hub in social entrepreneurship and is distinctive for building the academic legitimacy of social entrepreneurship studies, delivering a world-class management education to social entrepreneurs, and creating an environment in which social entrepreneurs and their supporters can determine practical agendas for strengthening the movement.

The James Martin Institute for Science and Civilization
The James Martin Institute has a core competency in "futures and practices." "Futures" employ tools such as scenario development and understanding of complex adaptive systems to identify possible future states of the world at many levels. "Practices" focus on entrenched ways of doing things through investigation of social, economic, political, cultural, and institutional aspects of science and technology.

QUESTIONS TO CONSIDER:

Does any required course contain some element of Social Impact Management? **YES**

Is any required course entirely dedicated to social, environmental, or ethical issues? **NO**

Is there a Net Impact Chapter on campus? **NO**

University of Oxford
Saïd Business School / Oxford, United Kingdom

ANNUAL EVENTS:

■ *Skoll World Forum on Social Entrepreneurship*

The Skoll World Forum on Social Entrepreneurship is an annual event attracting a stellar cast of speakers (social entrepreneurs, academics, financiers, thought leaders, and policy makers). The Skoll World Forum also hosts the University Network for Social Entrepreneurship meeting developed in partnership with Ashoka. The meeting offers MBAs opportunities to engage with leading academic institutions concerned with environmental and social innovation.

■ *Health Accelerator Program*

The Skoll Centre for Social Entrepreneurship runs a program for dynamic individuals who want to learn more about how socially entrepreneurial approaches can drive innovation and better health outcomes.

OTHER PROGRAMS:

■ *Career Opportunities*

The Skoll Centre for Social Entrepreneurship takes an active interest in developing the careers of MBA students eager to work in the field of social entrepreneurship. Skoll scholars specifically attend individual monthly academic progress meetings with a focus on future career options. With the centre's assistance, scholars are expected to take the lead in organizing various networking events, including the Skoll World Forum and also liaising with other social entrepreneurship networks. Contacts gained enable students to access both the expertise and financing essential to further their own future social entrepreneurship projects.

SCHOOL DEMOGRAPHICS	
Number of Full-Time Students	214
International Students	92%
Female Students	23%
	2006/2007 School Year

STUDENT CLUBS AND PROGRAMS:

■ *Oxford Business Network for Social Entrepreneurship (OBN SE)*

The OBN SE is one of the largest and most active student groups at the Saïd Business School and is focused on exploring and building the field of social entrepreneurship. The OBN SE works hard to maintain a high profile for social entrepreneurship within the school, encouraging its study in entrepreneurial and consulting projects that students can undertake as part of their MBA. Activities also include social events to recruit future MBAs and planning and organizing other relevant guest speakers and networking events.

■ *James Martin Institute MBA Association*

Through this institute, students become affiliated in a "common room style" membership, which provides social and tutorial get - togethers and a modest networking budget. Students champion the activities of the institute among their classmates and can help shape projects in their courses by leveraging the institute's wider portfolio of research.

THE CENTER FOR BUSINESS EDUCATION'S BOTTOM LINE ON UNIVERSITY OF OXFORD:
Compared to other business schools in our survey, University of Oxford offers a good number of courses featuring relevant content, and does an excellent job in those courses explicitly addressing how mainstream business improves the world. University of Oxford requires 4 core courses featuring relevant content.

A Closer Look at:
University of Pittsburgh

The Joseph M. Katz Graduate School of Business / Pittsburgh, PA

http://www.katz.pitt.edu/

THE ASPEN INSTITUTE
Center for Business Education

WHAT THE SCHOOL SAYS:

The Katz School has a long history of dedicated teaching and research in business ethics, corporate social performance, and business-government relations. Katz has been among the leaders in graduate education in this area, producing many leading scholars in the field.

A QUICK LOOK

NOTE: All information is self-reported data submitted to the Center for Business Education

COURSES*

Accounting (1)
Finance (1)
Information Technology (1)
Marketing (1)
Organizational Behavior (1)
Quantitative Methods (2)
Strategy (1)

ACTIVITIES*

Speakers/Seminars (2)
Orientation Activities (1)
Student Competitions (1)
Career Development (1)
Institutes/Centers (1)

* Figures in parentheses indicate the number of courses/activities that, in whole or in part, integrate social, environmental, or ethical perspectives

NOTABLE FEATURES

CORE COURSES:

▣ *Decision Technologies in Manufacturing and Operations Management*

This course utilizes a case study that involves making plant location/relocation decisions purely based on some optimization models versus building social implications of closing plants and how we should build that "indirect" cost to society into the decision models. Similar issues are also discussed in personnel scheduling situations.

▣ *Financial Management*

In this course, ethics and social impact issues are integrated into discussions of typical finance topics including issues dealing with separation of ownership and control, incentives, reporting, and maximizing behavior of various agents. Particular topics raise focused discussion on where agency costs and asymmetric information are involved and on insider trading.

INSTITUTES AND CENTERS:

▣ *David Berg Center for Ethics and Leadership*

The David Berg Center for Ethics and Leadership works with all programs in the Katz School to develop ethics and leadership attributes in its students. The Katz School sponsors the MBA ethics case competition, the one-of-a-kind undergraduate certificate program in leadership and ethics, the Pittsburgh Business Ethics awards program, and faculty and student research.

QUESTIONS TO CONSIDER:

Does any required course contain some element of Social Impact Management? **YES**

Is any required course entirely dedicated to social, environmental, or ethical issues? **NO**

Is there a Net Impact Chapter on campus? **NO**

University of Pittsburgh

The Joseph M. Katz Graduate School of Business / Pittsburgh, PA

ANNUAL EVENTS:

■ *Distinguished Speaker Series in Leadership and Ethics*
Each year, various executives come to campus to speak about important topics related to issues surrounding ethics and social issues.

■ *Orientation Ethics Workshop*
This workshop provides models of ethical decision making and incorporates a number of important business ethics cases. The workshop provides the basic conceptual frameworks utilized by students in their required courses.

■ *Katz MBA Ethics Case Competition*
All full-time MBA students participate in a two-day ethics case competition. Students work together in teams to evaluate and present their analysis of a business ethics case to a group of faculty and corporate judges. Finalist teams prepare and present a second case to judges. All students discuss their cases and presentations with judges. The competition is accompanied by a keynote speech.

OTHER PROGRAMS:

■ *Giving to the Community*
Each year, MBA students provide charitable acts of service to the local, regional, and world community. Among the recipients of their service are American Red Cross, Habitat for Humanity, Greater Pittsburgh Food Bank, Pittsburgh Cares, Make-a-Wish, tsunami victims, Humane Society, and Treasures for Children.

FACULTY PIONEER:

■ *2007 – Academic Impact Award, Carrie Leana*
Professor Carrie Leana does groundbreaking research on people at work and the conditions inside and outside organizations that can positively affect employees and employers. Her research is aimed at improving the experience of work and enhancing its consequences for business and society as a whole. A premise underlying Leana's teaching is that MBA education must both reflect prevailing business practices and, more importantly, reflect upon them. She has developed unique and "hands-on" project courses to this end.

SCHOOL DEMOGRAPHICS	
Number of Full-Time Students	265
International Students	49%
Female Students	37%
Pre-MBA Employment:	

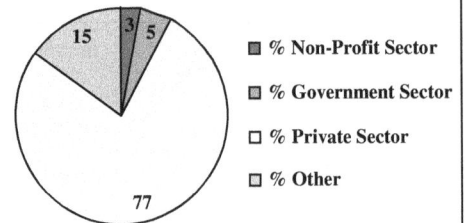

Pie chart values: 15, 3, 5, 77

■ % Non-Profit Sector
■ % Government Sector
□ % Private Sector
□ % Other

2006/2007 School Year

THE CENTER FOR BUSINESS EDUCATION'S BOTTOM LINE ON UNIVERSITY OF PITTSBURGH:
Compared to other business schools in our survey, University of Pittsburgh offers a good number of courses featuring relevant content, and does a good job in those courses explicitly addressing how mainstream business improves the world. University of Pittsburgh requires 8 core courses featuring relevant content.

A Closer Look at:
University of San Diego
School of Business Administration / San Diego, CA
http://www.sandiego.edu/business/programs/graduate/mba/

WHAT THE SCHOOL SAYS:
The Master of Business Administration program develops socially responsible leaders and provides them with the analytical tools to make thoughtful business decisions. Graduates emerge with a mastery of analytical techniques and an understanding of how to apply business theory to solve real-world problems for their companies and society.

A QUICK LOOK

NOTE: All information is self-reported data submitted to the Center for Business Education

COURSES*

Accounting (1)
CSR/Business Ethics (3)
Economics (1)
Finance (3)
International Management (5)
General Management (4)
Marketing (3)
Strategy (2)

KEY CONCENTRATIONS

International Business

KEY JOINT DEGREES

MBA & MS Nursing

ACTIVITIES*

Speakers/Seminars (1)
Orientation Activities (1)
Clubs & Programs (1)
Institutes/Centers (6)
Concentrations (1)
Joint Degrees (3)

* Figures in parentheses indicate the number of courses/activities that, in whole or in part, integrate social, environmental, or ethical perspectives

NOTABLE FEATURES

CORE COURSES:

Legal and Social Environment of Business
This course examines the complex array of political, legal, historical, and ethical concerns in the business world today by analyzing the principles of social responsibility, ethics, diversity, law, and stakeholder theory as they apply to organizations, domestically and abroad. Particular attention is given to cultivating moral reasoning skills. Fundamentally, students evaluate how businesses operate, and more significantly, how they should operate.

Peace through Commerce
This course focuses on the ways in which businesses contribute to the peace and prosperity of the global community through commerce and wealth creation. It examines how business and political environments affect the strategies and competitive advantage of domestic and international firms. Students will study the political and business environment of BRIC (Brazil, Russia, India, and China) countries and learn to develop win-win business strategies both for business success and raising the living standards of emerging economies.

ELECTIVE COURSES:

Financial Management for New Ventures
This course is an examination of issues in managing the financial functions involved in both start-up and rapid-growth opportunities. It identifies potential sources of financing such as venture capital, investment banking, commercial banking, and private investors. Students develop a business plan to demonstrate socially responsible entrepreneurship—enhancing the positive contribution of a company to society while minimizing negative impacts on people and the environment.

Marketing for International Managers
This course introduces students to the opportunities and problems facing marketing managers in the global marketplace. It provides an up-to-date overview of international marketing and institutions involved in the process. Topics include global environment, product development, promotion strategies, and pricing and distribution for worldwide markets. Overall, the course focuses on practical decision making within a socially responsible and ethical framework.

INSTITUTES AND CENTERS:

Joan B. Kroc Institute for Peace and Justice
Through education, research, and peacemaking activities, the institute offers programs that advance scholarship and practice in conflict resolution and human rights.

Center for Community Service Learning
The Center for Community Service Learning engages USD students, faculty, staff, and alumni to learn in partnership with the community, and make lifelong commitments to promote social change and justice. Programs include course-based service-learning, student run cocurricular service, America Reads/Counts work-study tutoring, and a campuswide Social Issues committee, which sponsors an annual conference and speakers and special events.

QUESTIONS TO CONSIDER:

Does any required course contain some element of Social Impact Management? **YES**

Is any required course entirely dedicated to social, environmental, or ethical issues? **YES**

Is there a Net Impact Chapter on campus? **YES**

A Closer Look at:
University of San Diego
School of Business Administration / San Diego, CA

ANNUAL EVENTS:

▪ *Thanksgiving House Project*

The Thanksgiving House Project focuses on improving the quality of life of deserving citizens of a developing San Diego community by renovating their houses. This mission is accomplished by USD graduate students enrolled in the Project Management course. The house renovation project provides students with the opportunity to learn and apply the tools and techniques of project management while doing community service. The Project Management course is offered every fall semester and the renovation work is completed the week before Thanksgiving.

STUDENT CLUBS AND PROGRAMS:

▪ *USD Net Impact Chapter*

USD's chapter of Net Impact upholds the organization's goals of raising awareness of social and environmental issues affecting business and offering networking opportunities for alternative career choices.

SCHOOL DEMOGRAPHICS

Number of Full-Time Students	**69**
International Students	**40%**
Female Students	**45%**

Pre-MBA Employment:

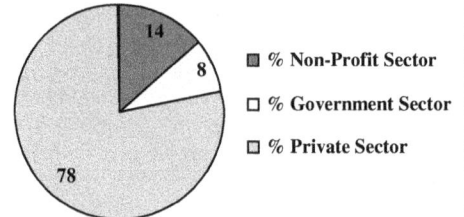

- ▪ % Non-Profit Sector
- ☐ % Government Sector
- ☐ % Private Sector

14
8
78

2006/2007 School Year

THE CENTER FOR BUSINESS EDUCATION'S BOTTOM LINE ON UNIVERSITY OF SAN DIEGO:
Compared to other business schools in our survey, University of San Diego offers an excellent number of courses featuring relevant content, and does an excellent job in those courses explicitly addressing how mainstream business improves the world. University of San Diego requires 9 core courses featuring relevant content.

University of San Francisco
School of Business and Management / San Francisco, CA
http://www.usfca.edu/sobam/mba/mba.html

THE ASPEN INSTITUTE
Center for Business Education

WHAT THE SCHOOL SAYS:
USF offers a dual degree in Environmental Management and the Master of Business Administration. Most professors of regular MBA courses have integrated social and environmental issues into their courses.

A QUICK LOOK

NOTE: All information is self-reported data submitted to the Center for Business Education

COURSES*

CSR/Business Ethics (**2**)
Entrepreneurship (**1**)

KEY JOINT DEGREES

MBA & Environmental Management

ACTIVITIES*

Speakers/Seminars (**10**)
Internship/Consulting (**1**)
Student Competitions (**1**)
Clubs & Programs (**1**)
Career Development (**1**)
Institutes/Centers (**1**)
Joint Degrees (**1**)

* Figures in parentheses indicate the number of courses/activities that, in whole or in part, integrate social, environmental, or ethical perspectives

NOTABLE FEATURES

CORE COURSES:
▪ *Managerial Environment: Ethical, Public Policy and Global Issues*
This course focuses upon the social, legal, and ethical factors in the external environment that impose boundaries upon managerial practices and strategies. Topics include frameworks for ethical analysis, legal and regulatory standards, and the historical context in which present social, legal, and ethical norms have developed. Specific issues may involve: criminal liability for managerial misconduct, overseas bribery and other cross-cultural and international problems, employment discrimination, corporate governance, and intellectual property.

ELECTIVE COURSES:
▪ *Sustainable Business*
This course will use theory, case studies, readings and projects to give students practical insights into the issues managers must consider in deciding the extent to which they should incorporate sustainable business principles into company strategy. Lectures are often from a guest speaker who will discuss an important issue of relevance to the course.

▪ *Social Entrepreneurship*
This course explores social entrepreneurship by translating the business planning framework of start-ups and early business ventures seeking wealth creation into objective applications for the common social good.

INSTITUTES AND CENTERS:
▪ *The Leo T. McCarthy Center for Public Service and the Common Good*
The Leo T. McCarthy Center for Public Service and the Common Good seeks to inspire and equip students for lives and careers of ethical public service and serving others. The center is dedicated to sponsoring academic programs, public events, service learning opportunities, conferences, and faculty and student research that encourage civic engagement and ethical public leadership. The center will embody the mission of USF, which is "to educate leaders who will fashion a more humane and just world."

QUESTIONS TO CONSIDER:

Does any required course contain some element of Social Impact Management? **YES**

Is any required course entirely dedicated to social, environmental, or ethical issues? **YES**

Is there a Net Impact Chapter on campus? **YES**

All information in this profile is drawn and/or adapted from the self-reported data of the Center for Business Education's Beyond Grey Pinstripes 2007 MBA survey. The Center for Business Education is housed within the Business and Society Program at the Aspen Institute. For more info, visit www.AspenCBE.org.

University of San Francisco
School of Business and Management / San Francisco, CA

THE ASPEN INSTITUTE
Center for Business Education

ANNUAL EVENTS:

▦ Net Impact Board Fellows Program
The Net Impact Board Fellows program places USF MBA students as fellows on local nonprofit boards of directors for a six-month to one-year term. During the school year, Fellows would work closely with board members and executive directors, serve on board committees, attend board meetings, and participate in special events and projects.

▦ USF International Business Plan Competition
USF International Business Plan Competition is internationally recognized as a world-class educator of socially responsible entrepreneurial leaders who will develop new products and services that will improve the lives of people around the world.

OTHER PROGRAMS:

▦ Days on the Job
As part of its ongoing effort to promote socially responsible and sustainable business practices among future business leaders, the USF Net Impact chapter hosted its first "Days on the Job" networking and informational event. Nearly 80 graduate business students participated and met with senior executives from eight host companies. Net Impact also conducts field trips to sustainable businesses.

▦ A Panel Discussion: CSR & Sustainable Business Practices
Members of Net Impact's Bay Area Professional chapters joined USF MBA students in learning about corporate social responsibility and sustainable business practices from a distinguished panel of seven expert speakers.

STUDENT CLUBS AND PROGRAMS:

▦ Net Impact
The Net Impact Club at USF is the largest and most active club on campus. The club has sponsored workshops, organized field trips to sustainable businesses, and hosted its first "Days on the Job" networking/informational event.

SCHOOL DEMOGRAPHICS	
Number of Full-Time Students	290
International Students	31%
Female Students	48%
Pre-MBA Employment:	

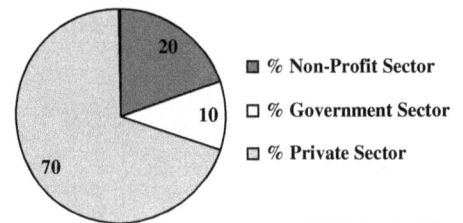

Pie chart values: 20, 10, 70
- ■ % Non-Profit Sector
- □ % Government Sector
- □ % Private Sector

2006/2007 School Year

THE CENTER FOR BUSINESS EDUCATION'S BOTTOM LINE ON UNIVERSITY OF SAN FRANCISCO:
Compared to other business schools in our survey, University of San Francisco does a good job in relevant courses explicitly addressing how mainstream business improves the world. University of San Francisco requires 1 core course featuring relevant content.

A Closer Look at:
University of South Carolina
Moore School of Business / Columbia, SC
http://mooreschool.sc.edu/moore/mba_programs/

WHAT THE SCHOOL SAYS:
The Moore School of Business' International MBA (IMBA) is a comprehensive master's program with a global focus. Our two most important goals are the creation of knowledge and the education of future business leaders. The Moore School wants to ensure that these future leaders have a solid footing in the vital areas of environmental sustainability, resource management, and corporate social responsibility.

A QUICK LOOK

NOTE: All information is self-reported data submitted to the Center for Business Education

COURSES*

Accounting (2)
Business & Government (1)
Economics (1)
Entrepreneurship (1)
Finance (2)
International Management (9)
Marketing (1)
Organizational Behavior (4)

ACTIVITIES*

Speakers/Seminars (10)
Orientation Activities (1)
Student Competitions (2)
Clubs & Programs (3)

* Figures in parentheses indicate the number of courses/activities that, in whole or in part, integrate social, environmental, or ethical perspectives

NOTABLE FEATURES

CORE COURSES:

Globalization and Corporate Responsibility
This course examines different perspectives on the future course of the global economy. The students focus particularly on the interaction between globalization and corporate social responsibility and look at the role that social values and identities are playing in shaping the future course of globalization, as well as the role that globalization is playing in shaping new social expectations of corporate responsibility. Also discussed are the challenges of managing social responsibility under conditions of rapid change in the global environment.

Global Marketing Management
This course explores international social, economic, political, regulatory, and cultural environments and how they interface with industry and competitive structures. Students analyze how managers can develop and implement effective strategies that achieve economic, social, and community objectives. Case studies with social and environmental issues help students understand the management of these processes.

ELECTIVE COURSES:

Economics of Growth and Development
Issues discussed in this course include the major modern problem of the effect of economic growth on the environment in developing nations, how population growth affects the economy and how it may have detrimental effects on the ecology, and gender and other social issues that affect the rate of population growth.

International Business and Sustainable Development
This course provides an introduction to international and national environmental and social management issues that affect a company's operations and management practices. Students are shown the correlation between environmental management systems, including ISO 14001, European Eco-Management, and Auditing Scheme and a company's ability to manage, measure, and improve the environmental and business aspects of its operations.

QUESTIONS TO CONSIDER:

Does any required course contain some element of Social Impact Management? **YES**

Is any required course entirely dedicated to social, environmental, or ethical issues? **NO**

Is there a Net Impact Chapter on campus? **YES**

University of South Carolina

Moore School of Business / Columbia, SC

THE ASPEN INSTITUTE
Center for Business Education

ANNUAL EVENTS:

■ *Wachovia Executive Lecture Series*

The Wachovia Executive Lecture Series, sponsored by Wachovia Bank, brings renowned executives from around the country and around the world to share their wisdom and business experience with students, faculty, and friends of the Moore School. Many lectures revolve around social issues such as emerging market investments, community initiatives both nationally and abroad, health care, and corporate governance.

OTHER PROGRAMS:

■ *Robin Emery Memorial Business Scholarship*

The Robin Emery Memorial Business Scholarship is open to all IMBA students engaged in an internship in economic development who maintain good academic standing. Eligible students compete for the award by completing a 500-word essay. The scholarship was created to assist IMBA students who want to pursue internships with NGOs.

SCHOOL DEMOGRAPHICS	
Number of Full-Time Students	202
International Students	16%
Female Students	26%
	2006/2007 School Year

STUDENT CLUBS AND PROGRAMS:

■ *The Moore School of Business Chapter of Net Impact*

The Moore School of Business chapter of Net Impact works to improve job-placement mechanisms and professional networks for students interested in using their business skills for positive social, environmental, and economic impact; increase awareness and strengthen the quality of education at USC; and provide immediate opportunities for practical experiences to IMBA students using business for positive social, environmental, and economic impacts.

■ *Moore School National Association of Women MBAs*

The Moore School National Association of Women MBAs group is an organization dedicated to addressing women's issues in the workplace and helping members to prepare for a career in the dynamic work environment. The group's past activities include a women's panel and reception, guest speakers, networking events, and social activities.

THE CENTER FOR BUSINESS EDUCATION'S BOTTOM LINE ON UNIVERSITY OF SOUTH CAROLINA:
Compared to other business schools in our survey, University of South Carolina offers an excellent number of courses featuring relevant content, and does an excellent job in those courses explicitly addressing how mainstream business improves the world. University of South Carolina requires 7 core courses featuring relevant content.

A Closer Look at:
University of South Florida St. Petersburg
College of Business / St. Petersburg, FL
http://www.stpt.usf.edu/cob/graduate_studies/mba_program.htm

THE ASPEN INSTITUTE
Center for Business Education

WHAT THE SCHOOL SAYS:

Our progress toward an MBA program that uniquely prepares students for managing and leading in the complex corporate world today has been extraordinarily rapid and rewarding. Stakeholder considerations, understanding the triple bottom line, and corporate social responsibility form the foundation of the MBA program as a whole.

A QUICK LOOK

NOTE: All information is self-reported data submitted to the Center for Business Education

COURSES*

Accounting (5)
Business & Government (2)
CSR/Business Ethics (1)
Finance (2)
International Management (1)
General Management (5)
Marketing (1)
Organizational Behavior (1)

KEY CONCENTRATIONS

Corporate Social Responsibility

International Business

ACTIVITIES*

Speakers/Seminars (7)
Orientation Activities (1)
Internship/Consulting (1)
Career Development (1)
Institutes/Centers (1)
Concentrations (5)

* Figures in parentheses indicate the number of courses/activities that, in whole or in part, integrate social, environmental, or ethical perspectives

NOTABLE FEATURES

CORE COURSES:

Regulatory and Reporting Environments of Business
This course provides exposure to the regulatory and reporting environments that affect contemporary businesses and an overview of current board and governance matters. The course includes an overview of securities regulation, including the Sarbanes-Oxley Act, with an emphasis on corporate reporting issues, transparency, corporate governance analyses, and training for boards of directors. The interaction of the business model within various spheres of economic, social, cultural, environmental, political, and legal influence will be considered and developed throughout the course.

Creating Community Leaders and Partners
Student groups conduct a strategic in-depth stakeholder analysis of an organization in the community resulting in short-term and long-term plans for achieving the organization's vision. The focus for large, profit-driven organizations might be how they could form stronger alliances with the community. Smaller for-profits may be interested in improving their business practices. Not-for-profit organizations might need assistance with identifying target donors for fundraising, planning a charity event, or forging new relationships with the community as a whole.

ELECTIVE COURSES:

Ethics in Marketing
This course focuses on the impact of the marketing system, broadly construed, on a variety of external stakeholders. As expected, the ethical component of organizational decision making is central to the establishment of long-term relationships with a variety of constituencies, including the firm's customers.

Partnership Taxation: Advanced Issues
This course is a study of advanced income tax problems involving partnerships, including organization, operation, distributions, liquidations, basis, family partnerships, and sales and exchanges. A study of limited liability companies is an integral part of this course. Ethical issues in tax reporting are also discussed.

INSTITUTES AND CENTERS:

Program for Social Responsibility and Corporate Reporting (SRCR)
The SRCR program has provided multidisciplinary study and outreach in areas of interest to the business and academic communities following the corporate scandals and frauds that touched so many in our society early in this decade. Built on a foundation of emphasizing ethical behavior, transparency, corporate social responsibility, and effective corporate governance, the program encourages scholarly research and study by faculty, students, and the community across all business disciplines. The program has organized several guest lectures and presentations on SRCR topics.

QUESTIONS TO CONSIDER:

Does any required course contain some element of Social Impact Management? **YES**

Is any required course entirely dedicated to social, environmental, or ethical issues? **YES**

Is there a Net Impact Chapter on campus? **NO**

University of South Florida St. Petersburg

College of Business / St. Petersburg, FL

ANNUAL EVENTS:

■ *Orientation Speaker*

Orientation for incoming MBA students includes an in-depth introduction to the College of Business's strategic focus on CSR and the Program of Distinction in Social Responsibility and Corporate Reporting. The program director discusses the triple bottom line and the CSR track and also explains the specifics of SRCR activities.

■ *Prosperity Campaign*

This program is a cooperative venture between the Internal Revenue Service and MBA students in the College of Business. Students receive appropriate training and become IRS Certified Volunteers. They are required to prepare tax filings for residents of the low-income African-American community of Midtown for a minimum of 30 hours from January 11 to April 15.

SCHOOL DEMOGRAPHICS	
Number of Full-Time Students	77
International Students	4%
Female Students	63%
Pre-MBA Employment:	

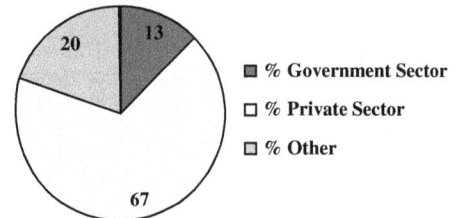

■ % Government Sector
□ % Private Sector
□ % Other

2006/2007 School Year

THE CENTER FOR BUSINESS EDUCATION'S BOTTOM LINE ON UNIVERSITY OF SOUTH FLORIDA ST. PETERSBURG:
Compared to other business schools in our survey, University of South Florida St. Petersburg offers a good number of courses featuring relevant content, and does a good job in those courses explicitly addressing how mainstream business improves the world. University of South Florida St. Petersburg requires 6 core courses featuring relevant content.

A Closer Look at:
University of Stellenbosch
Business School / Bellville, South Africa

http://www.usb.sun.ac.za/usb/index.asp

THE ASPEN INSTITUTE
Center for Business Education

WHAT THE SCHOOL SAYS:

Stellenbosch Business School follows an integrated approach in preparing MBA students for the complexities of the social and environmental realities of global business. Students are exposed to systems thinking to create comfort with a worldview of interrelatedness, continuous change, complexity, and contradiction.

A QUICK LOOK

NOTE: All information is self-reported data submitted to the Center for Business Education

COURSES*

Accounting (1)
Business & Government (1)
CSR/Business Ethics (2)
Finance (2)
HR Management (2)
General Management (3)
Organizational Behavior (1)

KEY CONCENTRATIONS

International Management

ACTIVITIES*

Speakers/Seminars (8)
Orientation Activities (2)
Clubs & Programs (1)
Career Development (1)
Institutes/Centers (4)
Concentrations (1)

* Figures in parentheses indicate the number of courses/activities that, in whole or in part, integrate social, environmental, or ethical perspectives

NOTABLE FEATURES

CORE COURSES:

▣ Business Ethics and Corporate Governance
The aim of this module is to introduce students to the concepts of business ethics and corporate governance, and to illustrate— through theoretical and practical examples—why these concepts are critical to business success in the 21st century. The following are some of the topics addressed: conceptual overview of corporate governance, business ethics/organisational integrity and sustainability; business drivers for organizational integrity (governance, ethical investment, reputation, sustainable development); sustainability; and triple bottom line reporting.

▣ Financial Evaluation
This course demonstrates analyses of companies to help determine value. In discussing the quality of management, the issues of corporate governance and ethics are addressed, citing cases where ethics gone awry leads to weak performance of companies or their eventual demise.

ELECTIVE COURSES:

▣ Sustainable Enterprise: Opportunities at the Base of the Pyramid
This course provides an overview of the current challenges posed to business by globalization; poverty and the growing gap between rich and poor, and global warming and environmental degradation. The course focuses on turning these challenges into opportunities for entrepreneurship at the base of the income pyramid (BOP, where about four billion people are to be found). The course deals in depth with cocreating value with customers at the lower end of the market and engaging with those previously regarded as fringe stakeholders.

▣ Environmental Finance
This elective incorporates aspects of risk management, corporate finance, investment analysis, climate mitigation and pollution costs, and renewable energy and energy efficiency practices. It aims to empower professionals to incorporate the impact of environmental finance into their decision making and includes understanding the economic justification and impact of sustainable development, understanding which environmental drivers have an effect on business, and understanding what opportunities exist to do well while doing good.

INSTITUTES AND CENTERS:

▣ Centre for Leadership Studies
The Centre for Leadership Studies is regarded as a prominent player in leadership development of students. The centre develops knowledge and expertise regarding leadership and presents state-of-the-art leadership development program s. The centre's uniquely South African Leadership Behavior Inventory is a research tool that enables candidates to hone in on those personal leadership dimensions that require further development.

▣ Centre for Development Policy and Partnership
This centre aims to develop high-level development strategy and policy research in support of Pan African organizations. It is part of an African and international network of development research institutions. Some focus areas are strategies against poverty in African countries, partnerships between government, private sector, NPOs, and civil society; and advancement of foreign investment. The centre supports research of these issues through reports, articles, workshops and conferences, international research partnerships, and training of post-graduate students and executives.

QUESTIONS TO CONSIDER:

Does any required course contain some element of Social Impact Management? **YES**

Is any required course entirely dedicated to social, environmental, or ethical issues? **YES**

Is there a Net Impact Chapter on campus? **NO**

University of Stellenbosch

Business School / Bellville, South Africa

ANNUAL EVENTS:

▣ Leader's Angle Speaker Series

From their first day on campus, new MBA students are exposed to the university's well-known Leader's Angle Speaker Series. High-level speakers from the private, NPO, and public sectors are invited to take part in this monthly event. Recently the focus has been on social and environmental topics, such as "Business Ethics and Governance in Africa," "Corporate Social Responsibility: Towards a New Paradigm?" "Corporate Social Responsibility: Obligation or Opportunity?" "Lucid Business: Forging Strength from Diversity."

OTHER PROGRAMS:

▣ Key Elements of Success – Leadership, Management and Governance Strategies for Nonprofit and NGO's

This three-day certificate program focused on the key elements of leadership and management required for the successful operation of nonprofit or nongovernmental organizations. It was aimed at leaders and managers in the NGO/NPO sector to address the challenges of governance, sustainability, organisational effectiveness, and leadership. The workshop offered an opportunity to obtain high-level international input on managing and leading NGOs and NPOs.

▣ Base of the Pyramid Learning Laboratory

Prominent foreign academics were among the 50 participants in the first Base of the Income Pyramid Learning Laboratory in South Africa which took place at the University of Stellenbosch Business School. The purpose of the two-day event was to debate and promote sustainable development by making markets and organizations work for the poor in Southern Africa.

STUDENT CLUBS AND PROGRAMS:

▣ USB MBA Alumni Association

The Business School has a strong MBA Alumni Association with branches/chapters all over the country, in Africa, and abroad. Through the activities of this association, funds are raised for MBA scholarships and other community projects that reflect social and environmental stewardship. Among these good causes for which money is raised is an adult literacy project and a management program for NPOs. The NPO program is offered at a hugely discounted fee and MBA alumni teach in the program for free and act as mentors for participants.

SCHOOL DEMOGRAPHICS	
Number of Full-Time Students	64
International Students	43%
Female Students	21%
Pre-MBA Employment:	

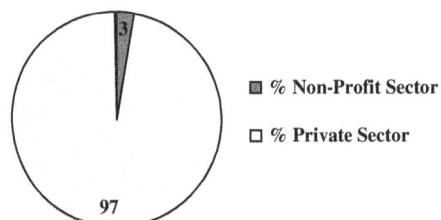

■ % Non-Profit Sector
□ % Private Sector

3
97

2006/2007 School Year

THE CENTER FOR BUSINESS EDUCATION'S BOTTOM LINE ON UNIVERSITY OF STELLENBOSCH:
Compared to other business schools in our survey, University of Stellenbosch offers a good number of courses featuring relevant content, and does a good job in those courses explicitly addressing how mainstream business improves the world. University of Stellenbosch requires 7 core courses featuring relevant content.

A Closer Look at:
The University of Texas at Dallas
School of Management / Richardson, TX

http://som.utdallas.edu/

THE ASPEN INSTITUTE
Center for Business Education

WHAT THE SCHOOL SAYS:

The mission statement for The University of Texas at Dallas declares that we will transform ideas into actions that directly benefit the personal, economic, social, and cultural lives of the citizens of Texas. With transforming ideas into actions in mind, our full-time Cohort MBA program focuses on developing leaders for a global economy—leaders who are ready to apply their knowledge of business to address economic and social issues.

A QUICK LOOK

NOTE: All information is self-reported data submitted to the Center for Business Education

COURSES*

Accounting (1)
International Management (1)
Marketing (1)

KEY CONCENTRATIONS

Strategic Management

International Management

ACTIVITIES*

Speakers/Seminars (1)
Orientation Activities (1)
Student Competitions (4)
Clubs & Programs (1)
Institutes/Centers (2)
Concentrations (2)

* Figures in parentheses indicate the number of courses/activities that, in whole or in part, integrate social, environmental, or ethical perspectives

---

NOTABLE FEATURES

CORE COURSES:

■ *Global Business*

This course examines global business and covers the roles of public policy makers toward the business community, economic freedoms, ethics in international business, fighting against corruption in global markets, corporate governance within a global context, and international business negotiations and fair play.

ELECTIVE COURSES:

■ *Corporate Governance and Accounting*

This course examines the relationships and responsibilities among the board of directors, senior officers, external auditors, internal auditors, various board committees, financial analysts, regulators, and institutional investors. Emphasis is on issues relating to the history and recent developments in corporate governance. Topics include risk management, corporate ethics, landmark legislation such as Sarbanes-Oxley, role of institutional investors, corporate social responsibility, internal investigations for fraud, and incentives and compensation issues.

■ *Advertising and Promotion Strategy*

This course discusses the increasing role of advertising and promotions in the formulation of public policy and their impact on businesses, consumers, and the social environment at large. Topics include the effects of public service announcements, deceptive advertising, Americanization of global consumption values, ethics in advertising, advertising's affect on societal materialism, the appropriateness of advertising to children and senior citizens, and the invasive and pervasive nature of advertising.

INSTITUTES AND CENTERS:

■ *Institute for Excellence in Corporate Governance (IECG)*

The focus of the IECG is on enhancing the abilities of corporate directors, senior management, and institutional investors to effectively and ethically protect and promote the interests of organizational stakeholders. The IECG provides timely, multi-disciplinary, research-driven programs dedicated to the issues permeating corporate governance systems. The IECG produces research, provides seminars, and hosts executives in residence to enhance the ethical protection of the interests of organizational stakeholders.

■ *Institute for Innovation and Entrepreneurship*

The institute provides a focal point and serves as a catalyst for programs and activities encouraging creativity and innovation across the university, engaging and supporting each of the schools in a collaborative effort to advance and pursue innovation and entrepreneurial activity in the artistic, social, scientific, and commercial arenas. The institute's programs are designed to engage and educate faculty and students about innovation and entrepreneurship, foster collaboration, support new academic and research initiatives, and extend our reach beyond the boundaries of the university.

QUESTIONS TO CONSIDER:

Does any required course contain some element of Social Impact Management? **YES**

Is any required course entirely dedicated to social, environmental, or ethical issues? **NO**

Is there a Net Impact Chapter on campus? **NO**

A Closer Look at:
The University of Texas at Dallas
School of Management / Richardson, TX

THE ASPEN INSTITUTE
Center for Business Education

ANNUAL EVENTS:

▩ *Contemporary Business Issues in Strategy and Policy*

A professional seminar class is offered on contemporary business issues in strategy and policy. This includes cases where corporate policies and irresponsible decision making may have adversely impacted the environment and the community.

▩ *LEAD Orientation Camp*

Students are required to participate in a two week pre-term program on leadership enhancement and academic development. This includes, among other development sessions, a speaker session on ethics and corporate responsibility, as well as the importance of social responsibility and personal accountability in decision making for managers and business leaders.

STUDENT CLUBS AND PROGRAMS:

▩ *Community Outreach*

Students organize and participate in a minimum of two to three community outreach activities each semester contributing to the social and environmental well-being of the community.

SCHOOL DEMOGRAPHICS

Number of Full-Time Students	**75**
International Students	**50%**
Female Students	**28%**

Pre-MBA Employment:

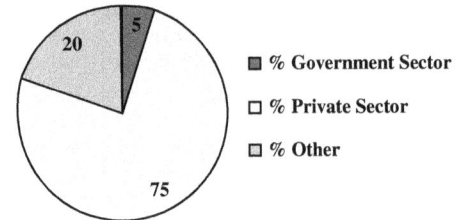

- ▣ % Government Sector
- ☐ % Private Sector
- ☐ % Other

2006/2007 School Year

THE CENTER FOR BUSINESS EDUCATION'S BOTTOM LINE ON THE UNIVERSITY OF TEXAS AT DALLAS:
Compared to other business schools in our survey, the University of Texas at Dallas does a good job in relevant courses explicitly addressing how mainstream business improves the world. The University of Texas at Dallas requires 1 core course featuring relevant content.

A Closer Look at:
The University of Vermont
School of Business Administration / Burlington, VT
http://www.bsad.uvm.edu/_Comm/MBA/

THE ASPEN INSTITUTE
Center for Business Education

WHAT THE SCHOOL SAYS:

The MBA program at the University of Vermont serves the needs of early and mid-career working professionals. The MBA curriculum is designed to provide an integrated understanding of the core functional areas of business and a strong appreciation for the relationship between business, society, and the environment. The focus is on developing individuals who are prepared to initiate and lead change in complex settings.

A QUICK LOOK

NOTE: All information is self-reported data submitted to the Center for Business Education

COURSES*

Accounting (2)
Environmental (1)
International Management (1)
General Management (5)

ACTIVITIES*

Speakers/Seminars (3)
Internship/Consulting (1)
Career Development (1)
Institutes/Centers (3)

* Figures in parentheses indicate the number of courses/activities that, in whole or in part, integrate social, environmental, or ethical perspectives

NOTABLE FEATURES

CORE COURSES:

◾ *Fundamentals of the Legal Environment of Business*

The objective of this course is to analyze the evolution of national and international regulation of business and the broader political, legal, social, and cultural forces affecting business.

ELECTIVE COURSES:

◾ *Business and the Environment*

The goal of this course is to critically examine the complex interactions between business and the environment using ecological economics and a dynamic systems perspective. Using the best available data drawn from case studies, corporate and nonprofit Internet sites, corporate environmental reports and peer-reviewed scientific literature, students examine in depth the ways in which business, society, and the physical environment have coevolved in the global ecological-economic system.

◾ *Sustainable Business: Practices of People, Profits and Principles*

This course offers the opportunity to learn and apply new principles of designing, organizing, and managing based on sustainability. It supports hands-on learning, helping participants to integrate theory and practice. The course has four major components: sustainable venturing and marketing—introduction and application; fostering a values-led internal culture through sustainable leadership; corporate environmental reporting communicating progress toward sustainability, and research application.

INSTITUTES AND CENTERS:

◾ *Gund Institute for Ecological Economics*

The Gund Institute develops, tests, and implements innovative methods and models that reflect the need to integrate the social, built, natural, and human capital components of our world. The focus is to shift the world's economies away from their present emphasis on infinite economic growth and toward a focus on sustainable human well-being.

◾ *Vermont Family Business Initiative*

The goal of this initiative is to give Vermont businesses the tools and support they need to compete in both the local and global arenas. It is supported by members and contributing partners who strive to work through the issues of leadership, communication, and complex legal and financial challenges to business transition and succession. Through a series of forums that provide interactive learning, the free exchange of ideas, and the opportunity to share challenges and solutions to business issues, this initiative is committed to assisting both family businesses and closely held businesses as they evolve and strive to grow to their full potential.

QUESTIONS TO CONSIDER:

Does any required course contain some element of Social Impact Management? **YES**

Is any required course entirely dedicated to social, environmental, or ethical issues? **NO**

Is there a Net Impact Chapter on campus? **NO**

All information in this profile is drawn and/or adapted from the self-reported data of the Center for Business Education's Beyond Grey Pinstripes 2007 MBA survey. The Center for Business Education is housed within the Business and Society Program at the Aspen Institute. For more info. visit www.AspenCBE.org.

The University of Vermont

School of Business Administration / Burlington, VT

THE ASPEN INSTITUTE
Center for Business Education

ANNUAL EVENTS:

■ *Annual Career Panel*

Every year the School of Business coordinates and facilitates a career forum on a specific career field. During this event, successful UVM alumni share their knowledge and experience on a variety of panels throughout the day. This event helps students gain more awareness about the nature of the career field and the opportunity to network with highly respected professionals. Issues pertaining to social impact/environmental sustainability have been discussed by panelists with expertise in this area.

OTHER PROGRAMS:

■ *Community Development*

An affiliation with Vermont Businesses for Social Responsibility and the Vermont Sustainable Jobs Fund provides opportunities for students to observe and assist more than 400 small- and mid-size companies committed to working proactively to improve the fit between profitability, employment continuity, and environmental responsibility.

SCHOOL DEMOGRAPHICS	
Number of Full-Time Students	20
International Students	20%
Female Students	60%

2006/2007 School Year

THE CENTER FOR BUSINESS EDUCATION'S BOTTOM LINE ON THE UNIVERSITY OF VERMONT:
Compared to other business schools in our survey, the University of Vermont offers a good number of courses featuring relevant content, and does a good job in those courses explicitly addressing how mainstream business improves the world. The University of Vermont requires 1 core course featuring relevant content.

A Closer Look at:
University of Virginia
Darden Graduate School of Business Administration / Charlottesville, VA
http://www.darden.virginia.edu/html/default.aspx

THE ASPEN INSTITUTE
Center for Business Education

WHAT THE SCHOOL SAYS:
At The Darden School, ethics is a core discipline of business, on par with finance, marketing, and operations. Ethics, seen as creating value for stakeholders in a moral environment, is core to Darden's mission of improving society by developing leaders in the world of practical affairs.

A QUICK LOOK

NOTE: All information is self-reported data submitted to the Center for Business Education

COURSES*

Accounting (2)
CSR/Business Ethics (6)
Economics (2)
Entrepreneurship (8)
International Management (2)
General Management (2)
Organizational Behavior (3)
Strategy (1)

KEY JOINT DEGREES

MBA & MA In East Asian Studies

ACTIVITIES*

Speakers/Seminars (13)
Orientation Activities (1)
Internship/Consulting (1)
Student Competitions (1)
Clubs & Programs (7)
Career Development (1)
Institutes/Centers (4)
Joint Degrees (2)

*Figures in parentheses indicate the number of courses/activities that, in whole or in part, integrate social, environmental, or ethical perspectives

NOTABLE FEATURES

CORE COURSES:
Business Ethics
The purpose of this course is to enable students to reason about the role of ethics in business administration in a complex, dynamic, global environment. Throughout the course, students will be encouraged to think deeply about the nature of business, the responsibilities of management, and how business and ethics can be put together. Discussions will focus on developing a framework for analyzing the issues in moral terms and then making a decision and developing a set of reasons for why the decision was justified.

Leading Organizations
This course helps students cultivate mind-sets and use tools to influence behavior in organizations. Students will master several foundational skills, including how to take a global-leadership point of view, identify critical business challenges, understand the drivers of those challenges, act to turn those challenges into opportunities, and adopt a global mind-set no matter what the organization or where it operates.

ELECTIVE COURSES:
Management of International Business
This course explores the relationships among domestic and foreign firms in economic development, particularly in emerging economies. This course gives students theories and frameworks for understanding the nature of economic development and growth and the effects of private firms' trade and investment activities on local economies.

Social Responsibility and Entrepreneurship
This course explores the multiple ways that an individual, company, or corporation can participate in ventures that impact social and/or environmental issues while simultaneously focusing on financial goals. Through direct dialogue and interaction with guests, students will query, discuss, and argue answers to questions.

INSTITUTES AND CENTERS:
Olsson Center for Applied Ethics
The Olsson Center for Applied Ethics is an international leader in the field of business ethics and serves as a critical resource for executives, scholars, students, and Darden alumni who are faced with the challenges of integrating ethical thinking into business decision making. The center enhances the intellectual life of the University of Virginia by contributing to a university-wide conversation about the role of ethics in modern society.

The Batten Institute
The Batten Institute invests in applied research and outreach programs to achieve thought leadership and academic preeminence. Its four major areas of field research are corporate innovation to achieve internally generated revenue growth; sustainable business practices; economic development in emerging regions through entrepreneurship; and the growth of new industries, with a focus on life sciences.

QUESTIONS TO CONSIDER:

Does any required course contain some element of Social Impact Management? **YES**

Is any required course entirely dedicated to social, environmental, or ethical issues? **YES**

Is there a Net Impact Chapter on campus? **YES**

A Closer Look at:
University of Virginia

Darden Graduate School of Business Administration / Charlottesville, VA

ANNUAL EVENTS:

Darden Conference on Emerging Markets

This conference is focused on high-quality research and on issues relevant to managers, investors, and policy makers in emerging markets and features speakers from major universities, government and business.

Latin American Student Association's (LASA) Annual Conference

The LASA Conference helps enhance the understanding, not only of Latin America as a very different business environment and also of the intricacies of pursuing investment opportunities in the region.

Walter Shipley Case Competition

This case competition is designed as an exercise to raise awareness about the social impact of management among first-year MBA students and to provide an opportunity for these students to compete for scholarship money. Student teams are given a case illustrating a challenging situation with social and ethical dilemmas faced by managers in the course of meeting their organization's overall objectives.

SCHOOL DEMOGRAPHICS	
Number of Full-Time Students	639
International Students	25%
Female Students	22%

2006/2007 School Year

OTHER PROGRAMS:

Outreach at Darden

Outreach is Darden's umbrella community service organization that facilitates opportunities where Darden students, partners, and faculty can serve as positive agents of change in the Darden and Charlottesville communities, ranging from one-time to weekly opportunities.

STUDENT CLUBS AND PROGRAMS:

Latin American Student Organization (LASA)

LASA is a student-run organization that gathers not only Latin American students at Darden but also students and faculty with any kind of interest in the region. LASA strives to be a resource for its members—especially for first years— in terms of both academic and career development support, and also to enhance Darden's international perspective and contribute to the diversity of its student body by organizing events that showcase the mosaic of different cultures within Latin America.

Darden African Business Organization

The Darden African Business Organization's mission is to contribute to the learning environment, diversity, and global leadership initiative at Darden in addition to providing students and faculty an opportunity to learn more about African businesses, economies, cultures, and politics.

FACULTY PIONEER:

2001 – Lifetime Achievement Award, R. Edward Freeman

Professor Freeman is an American economist and is particularly known for his work on stakeholder theory and on business ethics. Freeman has written or edited 10 books on business ethics, environmental management, and strategic management. He has also authored more than 40 Darden case studies. Freeman serves on the advisory board of the University of Virginia Institute for Practical Ethics.

THE CENTER FOR BUSINESS EDUCATION'S BOTTOM LINE ON UNIVERSITY OF VIRGINIA:
Compared to other business schools in our survey, University of Virginia offers an excellent number of courses featuring relevant content, and does an excellent job in those courses explicitly addressing how mainstream business improves the world. University of Virginia requires 4 core courses featuring relevant content.

A Closer Look at:
University of Western Ontario
Richard Ivey School of Business / London, Canada
http://www.ivey.uwo.ca/

WHAT THE SCHOOL SAYS:

The Ivey Business School's mission is to develop business leaders who think globally, act strategically, and contribute to the societies within which they operate. At Ivey, our approach to addressing the issue of corporate social responsibility is to diffuse it throughout the organization. There could be no higher level of commitment to making a substantial contribution to society on the part of the students, faculty, and staff at Ivey.

A QUICK LOOK

NOTE: All information is self-reported data submitted to the Center for Business Education

COURSES*

Accounting (1)
CSR/Business Ethics (1)
Economics (1)
Entrepreneurship (2)
Finance (2)
HR Management (1)
Information Technology (1)
International Management (4)
General Management (1)
Marketing (7)
Organizational Behavior (3)
Operations Management (3)
Strategy (5)

KEY CONCENTRATIONS

Health Care

ACTIVITIES*

Speakers/Seminars (17)
Orientation Activities (2)
Internship/Consulting (5)
Student Competitions (1)
Clubs & Programs (3)
Institutes/Centers (5)
Concentrations (1)

* Figures in parentheses indicate the number of courses/activities that, in whole or in part, integrate social, environmental, or ethical perspectives

NOTABLE FEATURES

CORE COURSES:

Leading a Culturally Diverse Workforce

This course focuses on the development of knowledge and skills needed to manage effectively in diverse cultural/virtual environments and/or to work effectively with people from other cultures. Issues explored include cross-cultural management, the pervasive and hidden influence of culture on management behavior, dividual values and cross-cultural competencies, and the impact on personal behavior of living and working in another culture.

Managing the Relationship between Individuals, Corporations and Societies

This course sensitizes students about the role of individuals in the corporation and the role of corporations in society. It is intended to give students a better understanding of why it is important for individuals and their corporations to attend to societal issues and how to incorporate these issues into all strategic decisions. Students are exposed to societal issues such as climate change, nutrition and consumption, and the state of the oceans; firsthand experience by working directly with a local not-for-profit agency; and *The Corporation*: the award-winning documentary film.

ELECTIVE COURSES:

Managing for Sustainable Development

In this course, students develop tools to characterize the drivers of current social and environmental issues; integrate financial, social, and environmental performance within a general business model; review and critique the strategies adopted by firms on sustainable development based on decision-oriented frameworks; and formulate effective approaches to make progress toward improving the triple bottom line.

Technology, Economy and Society

This course focuses on understanding the economic and societal forces that shift in subtle ways with advances in technology and to examine the unintended consequences that technology invariably has on societies, economies, and the world of business.

INSTITUTES AND CENTERS:

United Nations' Global Compact

Ivey is the first Canadian business school to join with other academic stakeholders committed to implementing the United Nations' Global Compact's principles and to using the compact as a forum for advancing responsible corporate citizenship. Participants are asked to embrace, support, and enact, within their sphere of influence, a set of core values in the areas of human rights, labor standards, the environment, and anticorruption.

Research Centre- Building Sustainable Value

This centre provides practitioners and students with the knowledge, tools, and capabilities to manage both private and public interests effectively through organizational actions. It researches organizational issues that simultaneously build private and public value across the enterprise and educate students and practitioners in the corporate, non-profit, and government sectors to understand the intersection of the private and public sectors.

QUESTIONS TO CONSIDER:

Does any required course contain some element of Social Impact Management? **YES**

Is any required course entirely dedicated to social, environmental, or ethical issues? **NO**

Is there a Net Impact Chapter on campus? **NO**

University of Western Ontario

Richard Ivey School of Business / London, Canada

ANNUAL EVENTS:

Ivey Ring Pledge and Ceremony

With a symbolic ring and a solemn pledge, Ivey graduates and alumni commit themselves to upholding the highest principles in business ethics: "To act honourably and ethically in all my dealings in the belief and knowledge that doing so will lead to a greater good...endeavour to act with moral clarity, grace, and nobility."

Partnership with CARE Canada

Ivey professors formed a partnership with CARE Canada to write case studies and set up a framework for working with Kenyan MBA students on market-based development projects in rural Kenya.

OTHER PROGRAMS:

Community Consulting Projects

Students are matched with community-based organizations for pro bono consulting projects and carry out activities such as analysis of current marketing and fund-raising strategies, evaluation of effectiveness of these strategies, and development of updated marketing and fund-raising plans.

SCHOOL DEMOGRAPHICS	
Number of Full-Time Students	463
International Students	52%
Female Students	25%
	2006/2007 School Year

STUDENT CLUBS AND PROGRAMS:

Ivey Connects

This club focuses on building stronger ties between the community and Ivey students. It seeks to enhance the educational experience of business students in the area of social responsibility and to advance the social and environmental health of not-for profit agencies; develop a strong sense of business ethics and community involvement; and encourage students to think about sustainable development, corporate social responsibility, and community involvement from a business perspective.

Sustainable Development Club

This club hosts guest speakers and networks with other clubs across North America through the Net Impact organization.

THE CENTER FOR BUSINESS EDUCATION'S BOTTOM LINE ON UNIVERSITY OF WESTERN ONTARIO:
Compared to other business schools in our survey, University of Western Ontario offers an excellent number of courses featuring relevant content, and does an excellent job in those courses explicitly addressing how mainstream business improves the world. University of Western Ontario requires 13 core courses featuring relevant content.

A Closer Look at:
University of Wisconsin–Madison
School of Business / Madison, WI
http://www.bus.wisc.edu/

WHAT THE SCHOOL SAYS:

The School of Business at the University of Wisconsin–Madison continues to excel in the social and environmental responsibility area. We take seriously our charge of preparing students to be future leaders. If we are to be successful in this endeavor, we believe that students must understand how environmental and social responsibility is integral to the long-term success of a business.

A QUICK LOOK

NOTE: All information is self-reported data submitted to the Center for Business Education

COURSES*

Accounting (3)
Business & Government (2)
CSR/Business Ethics (2)
Economics (1)
Environmental (2)
Finance (1)
HR Management (2)
General Management (3)
Marketing (3)
Organizational Behavior (1)
Operations Management (3)
Strategy (3)

KEY CONCENTRATIONS

Arts Administration

KEY JOINT DEGREES

MBA & Masters in Land and Resources

ACTIVITIES*

Speakers/Seminars (27)
Internship/Consulting (6)
Student Competitions (2)
Clubs & Programs (3)
Career Development (4)
Institutes/Centers (5)
Concentrations (1)
Joint Degrees (2)

* Figures in parentheses indicate the number of courses/activities that, in whole or in part, integrate social, environmental, or ethical perspectives

NOTABLE FEATURES

CORE COURSES:

▦ *Advanced Financial Reporting*
Coverage of social and ethical issues is pervasive within this course, through lectures, case analyses, and open in-class discussions. Specific topics addressed include the stewardship responsibilities of elected officials with respect to public resources; ethical issues pertaining to the reporting of asset balances in mergers and acquisitions; the social costs of money laundering, fraud, and downsizings; and social and ethical issues in the international business environment.

▦ *Ethics, Values and Sustainability*
This course will introduce students to the interconnectedness of ethics and sustainability. The area of corporate social responsibility is examined as a relatively new area of corporate decision-making. The class hears from senior business managers who have successfully integrated sustainability considerations into their business model.

ELECTIVE COURSES:

▦ *Fundamentals of Supply Chain Management*
This course discusses how ethics, the environment, and sustainability are emerging issues in supply chain management. The growth of outsourcing requires companies to be vigilant about the labor and environmental practices of suppliers in low-cost countries. The entire supply chain plays a role, from procuring raw materials, product design, distribution/transportation, and facility management as examples. These issues are being increasingly recognized not only as good for the environment but good for business in terms of long-term cost reduction and marketing.

▦ *Systems Thinking and Sustainable Businesses*
This course is for students interested in the concept of sustainability and how it applies to businesses. This class integrates students in the environmental studies program and other graduate studies to dialogue on the relevance of sustainability in a focused and constructive way. Students gain insights into how sustainable development can be a part of most decisions that are made, whether at the individual lifestyle level or at the organizational level.

INSTITUTES AND CENTERS:

▦ *Bolz Center for Arts Administration*
Bolz Center is an active voice in defining and developing the nonprofit arts and culture industry—through hosting and participating in national leadership roundtables, publishing dynamic analysis in print and online, and advising project initiatives of national significance. The field of arts administration places special emphasis on nonprofit or public organizations.

▦ *Strategic Management in the Life & Engineering Sciences (SMILES)*
The SMILES MBA program produces the founders, leaders, and advisors of organizations seeking to bring new technologies to market in ways that improve the quality of life for the world's peoples. Students who complete the SMILES program will leave with a well-established network of contacts in all the stakeholder groups essential to the success of high-growth science-based ventures.

QUESTIONS TO CONSIDER:

Does any required course contain some element of Social Impact Management? **YES**

Is any required course entirely dedicated to social, environmental, or ethical issues? **YES**

Is there a Net Impact Chapter on campus? **YES**

University of Wisconsin–Madison
School of Business / Madison, WI

ANNUAL EVENTS:

John J. Oros MBA Speaker Series
The John J. Oros MBA Speaker Series provides students the opportunity to interact with and learn from successful business leaders in a variety of fields. Speakers often incorporate social impact and ethical topics into the discussions.

Ethics and Professionalism Spring Symposium
The purpose of this program is to engage students and professionals in a discussion of the ethical challenges they are likely to encounter in their careers and to discuss strategies for further developing their ethical foundations in order to respond to these ethical challenges.

OTHER PROGRAMS:

Net Impact Employer Panel and Résumé Book
The Net Impact Employer Panel is composed of an alumni panel and topics focus on social responsibility. The Net Impact Résumé Book was created by Career Services and is an online resource that includes companies that have been identified as being socially responsible. The Résumé Book is used by current MBA students in their job searches.

MBA in Arts Administration Service Learning and Work Experience
All students in the MBA in Arts Administration work as project assistants during the academic year with campus or local cultural organizations or initiatives. Students also work with major national organizations through summer internships.

STUDENT CLUBS AND PROGRAMS:

Net Impact, UN–Madison Chapter
The Net Impact UW–Madison chapter invites speakers to campus, serves nonuniversity groups interested in sustainability outside the university, and serves as a conduit for students to become interested in sustainability while they work through the MBA program.

SCHOOL DEMOGRAPHICS	
Number of Full-Time Students	231
International Students	18%
Female Students	29%
	2006/2007 School Year

THE CENTER FOR BUSINESS EDUCATION'S BOTTOM LINE ON UNIVERSITY OF WISCONSIN-MADISON:
Compared to other business schools in our survey, University of Wisconsin-Madison offers an excellent number of courses featuring relevant content, and does a truly extraordinary job in those courses explicitly addressing how mainstream business improves the world. University of Wisconsin–Madison requires 10 core courses featuring relevant content.

A Closer Look at:
Utah State University
College of Business / Logan, UT
http://www.usu.edu/cob/

WHAT THE SCHOOL SAYS:
In addition to our speaker series and course components that address social and environmental stewardship, we have added several elements to our MBA program to more fully prepare our graduates to lead in the 21st century.

A QUICK LOOK

NOTE: All information is self-reported data submitted to the Center for Business Education

COURSES*

CSR/Business Ethics (2)

ACTIVITIES*

Speakers/Seminars (1)

* Figures in parentheses indicate the number of courses/activities that, in whole or in part, integrate social, environmental, or ethical perspectives

NOTABLE FEATURES

CORE COURSES:

▣ *Ethics for the Business Professional*

This class has two primary objectives: self-reflection and application. Students will consider several methods of moral reasoning (utilitarianism, deontology, and virtue theory). These three approaches are the backbone of the class. Students will look at some contemporary issues in business ethics as a way of applying these moral theories to concrete situations.

▣ *Special Topics in Management and Human Resources: Business Social Responsibility*

This class is designed to identify the key issues of corporate social responsibility and to provide a structural framework to understand them. It highlights the scope and the strategic importance of CSR in light of the internet, globalization, mass media, communication-driven environment and radical changes in the means of consumption. Finally, a list of issues that define corporate social responsibility in practice by organizational, economic, and societal stakeholders groups will be explored, discussed, and represented.

SCHOOL DEMOGRAPHICS

Number of Full-Time Students	**72**
International Students	**6%**
Female Students	**12%**

Pre-MBA Employment:

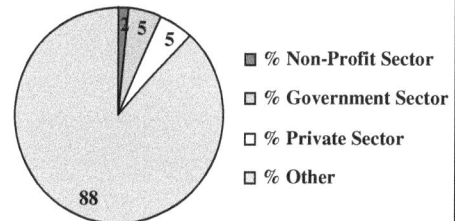

- ■ % Non-Profit Sector
- □ % Government Sector
- □ % Private Sector
- □ % Other

2006/2007 School Year

QUESTIONS TO CONSIDER:

Does any required course contain some element of Social Impact Management? **YES**

Is any required course entirely dedicated to social, environmental, or ethical issues? **YES**

Is there a Net Impact Chapter on campus? **NO**

THE CENTER FOR BUSINESS EDUCATION'S BOTTOM LINE ON UTAH STATE UNIVERSITY:
By participating in the Center for Business Education's Beyond Grey Pinstripes 2007 MBA survey, Utah State University demonstrates great dedication to integrating environmental and social impact management issues into their teaching and research. Utah State University requires 2 core courses featuring relevant content.

All information in this profile is drawn and/or adapted from the self-reported data of the Center for Business Education's Beyond Grey Pinstripes 2007 MBA survey. The Center for Business Education is housed within the Business and Society Program at the Aspen Institute. For more info, visit www.AspenCBE.org.

A Closer Look at:
Vanderbilt University
Owen Graduate School of Management / Nashville, TN
http://www.owen.vanderbilt.edu/

WHAT THE SCHOOL SAYS:

The Owen Graduate School of Management has made significant strides in implementing and infusing social and environmental stewardship across the entire school. Overall, social and environmental stewardship are topics that are discussed in the halls on a daily basis, the central point of multiple events each quarter, and the driving reason behind many activities.

A QUICK LOOK

NOTE: All information is self-reported data submitted to the Center for Business Education

COURSES*

Accounting (1)
CSR/Business Ethics (4)
Economics (1)
Entrepreneurship (1)
Environmental (1)
Finance (2)
HR Management (3)
International Management (1)
General Management (3)
Organizational Behavior (1)
Operations Management (3)
Strategy (4)

KEY CONCENTRATIONS

Environmental Management Studies

International Studies

ACTIVITIES*

Speakers/Seminars (31)
Orientation Activities (4)
Internship/Consulting (1)
Student Competitions (2)
Clubs & Programs (10)
Career Development (1)
Institutes/Centers (2)
Concentrations (3)
Joint Degrees (2)

Figures in parentheses indicate the number of courses/activities that, in whole or in part, integrate social, environmental, or ethical perspectives

NOTABLE FEATURES

CORE COURSES:

Business in the World Economy

This course integrates the economic, business, and social impacts throughout the discussion of core macro concepts. Part of the course requirement includes a research project on a country that encourages students to consider legal, political, and social issues when preparing their analysis.

Leadership in Practice: Corporate Social Responsibility in the Global Economy

This course will provide an overview of the cutting-edge topic of corporate social responsibility that corporate leaders are currently grappling. What makes it difficult to teach—and to absorb—is that there are few answers and too many questions! But that also makes it interesting and controversial.

ELECTIVE COURSES:

Bottom of the Pyramid

This class discusses the "Bottom of the Pyramid" concept which focuses on the majority of the world's population on less than $2 per day. In the past, governments, NGO's, and donor agencies have attempted, though unsuccessfully, to service this market. However, as technologies have advanced, primarily through telecommunications, these markets now show signs of hosting creative entrepreneurs and value-driven consumers. As future business leaders, students need to understand the dynamics and consumer behavior of this emerging frontier.

Private Environmental Law and Voluntary Overcompliance

This course examines the legal, economic, and social incentives that influence the environmental behavior of firms. Managers in private sector firms that engage in M&A activity, investment banking, commercial lending, and manufacturing all confront environmental compliance and remediation costs. This course will examine cutting-edge environmental business and legal issues by focusing on how firms identify, shift, disclose, and manage those risks.

INSTITUTES AND CENTERS:

Vanderbilt Center for Environmental Management Studies (VCEMS)

VCEMS promotes and develops alliances among industry, government, and academia to study the relationship of environmental policy to business management and operations. Center activities are interdisciplinary and focus on environmental business, management, and technology. Center funding is used to support curriculum development, student scholarships, faculty research projects, executive seminars, leadership summits, and Center marketing and administration.

Cal Turner Program in Moral Leadership for the Professions

The Cal Turner Program for Moral Leadership in the Professions is a university-wide program dedicated to the discussion and promotion of moral values relevant to the professional schools and the practice of the professions. It seeks to foster an environment conducive to faculty research and teaching in areas associated with moral leadership and develop students' abilities to provide moral leadership within their chosen profession and within the broader community.

QUESTIONS TO CONSIDER:

Does any required course contain some element of Social Impact Management? **YES**

Is any required course entirely dedicated to social, environmental, or ethical issues? **YES**

Is there a Net Impact Chapter on campus? **YES**

A Closer Look at:
Vanderbilt University
Owen Graduate School of Management / Nashville, TN

ANNUAL EVENTS:

■ *Strategy Projects*

All first year-students are required to complete a strategy project. Many of the projects include social and environmental stewardship. The focus of the projects range from green building development to marketing and fund-raising strategies for nonprofits.

■ *CSR Class*

During orientation, incoming students participate in a one-day CSR class taught by faculty. The class focuses on social and environmental responsibility and how present-day leaders strategically manage.

SCHOOL DEMOGRAPHICS	
Number of Full-Time Students	357
International Students	18%
Female Students	19%
2006/2007 School Year	

OTHER PROGRAMS:

■ *The Project Pyramid Case Competition*

The PPCC establishes a collaborative forum between students and businesses where viable ideas for the bottom of the pyramid are brought to life. The objective of the PPCC is to create products and services that improve the lives of the poor by being culturally adaptive, environmentally sustainable, and economically profitable.

STUDENT CLUBS AND PROGRAMS:

■ *100% Owen*

The 100% Owen club seeks to enrich the Owen experience for students, faculty, and staff through the promotion and organization of community service activities and fund-raising opportunities in the Nashville community.

■ *Global Business Association (GBA)*

One purpose of the GBA is to serve as a forum for cultural exchange. The current vision is to provide tangible value to the Owen experience through initiatives aimed at increasing globally focused academic and career opportunities. In the past year, the GBA has held fundraisers for global human aid initiatives.

THE CENTER FOR BUSINESS EDUCATION'S BOTTOM LINE ON VANDERBILT UNIVERSITY:
Compared to other business schools in our survey, Vanderbilt University offers an excellent number of courses featuring relevant content, and does a good job in those courses explicitly addressing how mainstream business improves the world. Vanderbilt University requires 6 core courses featuring relevant content.

A Closer Look at:
Wake Forest University

Babcock Graduate School of Management / Winston-Salem, NC
http://www.mba.wfu.edu

WHAT THE SCHOOL SAYS:

The Babcock Graduate School of Management remains true to Wake Forest University's tradition: to provide an education based on the values expressed in the university's motto, "Pro Humanitate" (education for the benefit of humanity). The school strives to be a leader by offering an outstanding educational experience in the context of recognized societal values.

A QUICK LOOK

NOTE: All information is self-reported data submitted to the Center for Business Education

COURSES*

Accounting (2)
Business Law (1)
CSR/Business Ethics (1)
Economics (3)
Entrepreneurship (5)
Finance (4)
Information Technology (5)
International Management (4)
General Management (6)
Marketing (8)
Organizational Behavior (1)
Operations Management (5)
Strategy (2)

ACTIVITIES*

Speakers/Seminars (6)
Orientation Activities (5)
Internship/Consulting (3)
Student Competitions (3)
Clubs & Programs (6)
Career Development (1)
Institutes/Centers (5)

* Figures in parentheses indicate the number of courses/activities that, in whole or in part, integrate social, environmental, or ethical perspectives

NOTABLE FEATURES

CORE COURSES:

■ *Managerial Economics*

Recurrent themes in this microeconomics course include efficient resource allocation and value-maximizing marginal decisions under asymmetric information. Significant time is devoted to discussing the principal-agent problem, executive incentives, moral hazard, governance mechanisms, executive pay, managing the regulatory licensing process, the market for pollution allowances and anticompetitive business practices.

■ *Management Consulting Practicum*

This course allows MBA students to deal directly with organizations and their managers. During the practicum, student teams act as project consultants to a local, regional or national business or nonprofit organization. Typical projects include planning a fund-raising and marketing campaign, creating a business plan for a developing firm, developing a restructuring study, and implementing an activity-based costing system.

ELECTIVE COURSES:

■ *Creativity and Feasibility*

With the launch of any new venture, there are numerous social and environmental impact issues to consider. Often, the new product or service is developed to meet a social or environmental need. This class addresses social and/or environmental impact issues associated with the beginning of a new venture.

■ *Marketing Strategy and Planning*

This is a decision-oriented course concerned with solutions to problems of product, price, promotion, and distribution channels. During the discussion of positioning, the class addresses the various social and environmental factors that influence the positioning of a company or brand. The class discusses how some of these factors can be proactive and positive and some can be unintentional and negative.

INSTITUTES AND CENTERS:

■ *Future Focus 2020*

Future Focus 2020 is a think tank dedicated to engaging urban America in futurist thinking. This organization focuses on the significant social, political, economic, technological, and environmental trends and events that will have the greatest impact on urban communities by the year 2020.

■ *Flow Institute for International Studies*

Babcock's Flow Institute for International Studies affords students the opportunity to develop their understanding of other countries' economies, businesses, and cultures through international summer study programs, speakers, and seminars. Tour destinations include Japan, China/Hong Kong, Central Europe, Latin America, and India. In sessions preceding the trips, students learn about the cultures of the countries, study the countries' primary economic, business, social, and environmental issues, and practice language skills.

QUESTIONS TO CONSIDER:

Does any required course contain some element of Social Impact Management? **YES**

Is any required course entirely dedicated to social, environmental, or ethical issues? **YES**

Is there a Net Impact Chapter on campus? **YES**

All information in this profile is drawn and/or adapted from the self-reported data of the Center for Business Education's Beyond Grey Pinstripes 2007 MBA survey. The Center for Business Education is housed within the Business and Society Program at the Aspen Institute. For more info, visit www.AspenCBE.org.

A Closer Look at:
Wake Forest University

Babcock Graduate School of Management / Winston-Salem, NC

ANNUAL EVENTS:

◼ *Babcock Leadership Series*

Throughout the school year, noted leaders from business and government address the Babcock community (and typically the public) through the Babcock Leadership Series. Lectures focus on current issues affecting business and contain themes that address social, leadership, or environmental issues.

◼ *Summer Entrepreneurial Internships*

The Angell Center for Entrepreneurship helps students obtain funding from institutes and foundations for entrepreneurial internships in the traditional and social (nonprofit) domains.

◼ *Wake Forest MBA Marketing Summit*

At the Wake Forest MBA Marketing Summit, teams of MBA students from the U.S. and abroad are presented with a company's marketing challenge and given 36 hours to formulate recommendations. Due to the nature of marketing, social issues are always addressed and some cases even encompass ethical and environmental issues.

OTHER PROGRAMS:

◼ *Biotechnology: Innovation, Funding and Ethics*

This event offers students, faculty, researchers, medical professionals, and the public the opportunity to discuss and debate critical issues of biotechnology and bioethics. Discussed issues include commercializing research, including funding and financing; challenges of technology transfer; legal and regulatory barriers; intellectual property; and new business models.

◼ *Babcock International Consulting Program*

This student-founded and -managed socially responsible business consulting program is dedicated to helping small businesses in developing countries create and implement better business practices. This year, at least seven faculty members and 30 students participated in the planning and implementation of a consulting project in Nicaragua, which involved small business development and the presentation of business seminars to rising entrepreneurs in and around the capital city of Managua.

STUDENT CLUBS AND PROGRAMS:

◼ *Babcock Women in Business (BWIB)*

BWIB is resource for female students, faculty, and staff at Babcock. BWIB helps its members build a network with other successful, empowered women by sponsoring various speakers, events, and community outreach activities.

◼ *Finance Club*

Throughout the fall of 2006, the Finance Club worked on a project that culminated in a presentation to the Forsyth County Department of Social Services on the topic of personal budgeting. After the main presentation, Babcock volunteers worked with groups of four to five participants to begin constructing personal budgets. This was the latest event in a continuing partnership between the Finance Club and the Forsyth County Department of Social Services to provide financial literacy training.

SCHOOL DEMOGRAPHICS

Number of Full-Time Students	177
International Students	18%
Female Students	26%

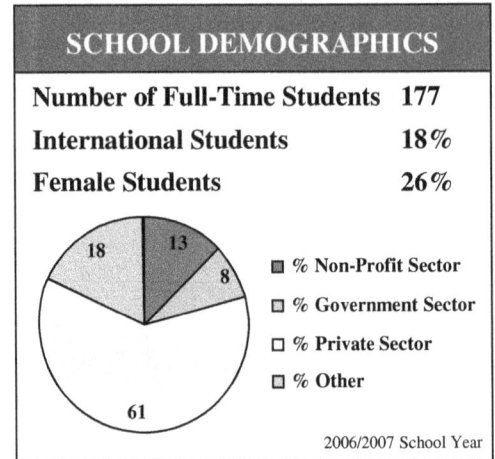

- ◼ % Non-Profit Sector
- ☐ % Government Sector
- ☐ % Private Sector
- ☐ % Other

2006/2007 School Year

THE CENTER FOR BUSINESS EDUCATION'S BOTTOM LINE ON WAKE FOREST UNIVERSITY:
Compared to other business schools in our survey, Wake Forest University offers a truly extraordinary number of courses featuring relevant content, and does an excellent job in those courses explicitly addressing how mainstream business improves the world. Wake Forest University requires 11 core courses featuring relevant content.

A Closer Look at:
Washington State University
College of Business and Economics / Vancouver, WA
http://www.business.wsu.edu/Graduate/Pages/index.aspx

WHAT THE SCHOOL SAYS:

Washington State University–Vancouver's MBA program is built around a stakeholder focus and its implications for competitive advantage and long-term organizational performance. A core concept of the program is that if we want managers who are capable of acting with integrity and understanding the broader system in which they work, then we must teach them to be mindfully aware of their belief systems, conscious of consequences, and capable of thinking broadly about the impact of their actions and decisions.

A QUICK LOOK

NOTE: All information is self-reported data submitted to the Center for Business Education

COURSES*

CSR/Business Ethics (1)
Finance (1)
Information Technology (1)
Marketing (1)
Organizational Behavior (1)
Operations Management (1)
Strategy (3)

KEY JOINT DEGREES

MBA & Masters in Public Administration

ACTIVITIES*

Speakers/Seminars (3)
Joint Degrees (1)

* Figures in parentheses indicate the number of courses/activities that, in whole or in part, integrate social, environmental, or ethical perspectives

NOTABLE FEATURES

CORE COURSES:

▣ *Business Ethics and Public Stakeholders*
This course introduces an explicit normative perspective into the understanding of firm-stakeholder relationships. Students examine the management of a firm's stakeholder relationships (shareholders, employees, customers, suppliers, publics) through developing and applying a formal decision making process to address ethical issues and conflicts among firms and stakeholders.

▣ *Strategy Formulation and Organizational Design*
This course addresses the topics of strategy formulation and implementation. Students learn to analyze a firm's competitive advantage, develop strategic recommendations to enhance competitive advantage, and formulate a comprehensive plan for implementing strategic recommendations that incorporate multiple organizational components such as the formal organization and culture. In developing strategic recommendations, students are asked to explicitly consider and address the ethical implications of these recommendations for multiple stakeholders.

ANNUAL EVENTS:

▣ *Speakers*
Leading business figures address topics such as the integration of corporate social responsibility into business strategy and social entrepreneurship.

SCHOOL DEMOGRAPHICS

Number of Full-Time Students	15
International Students	2%
Female Students	39%

Pre-MBA Employment:

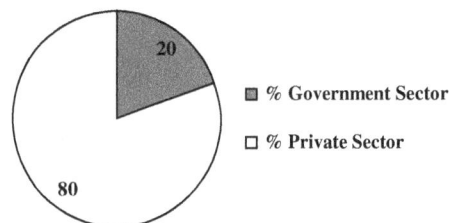

- ▣ % Government Sector
- ☐ % Private Sector

20
80

2006/2007 School Year

QUESTIONS TO CONSIDER:

Does any required course contain some element of Social Impact Management? **YES**

Is any required course entirely dedicated to social, environmental, or ethical issues? **YES**

Is there a Net Impact Chapter on campus? **NO**

THE CENTER FOR BUSINESS EDUCATION'S BOTTOM LINE ON WASHINGTON STATE UNIVERSITY:
Compared to other business schools in our survey, Washington State University offers a good number of courses featuring relevant content, and does a good job in those courses explicitly addressing how mainstream business improves the world. Washington State University requires 9 core courses featuring relevant content.

A Closer Look at:
Washington University in St. Louis
Olin School of Business / St. Louis, MO
http://www.olin.wustl.edu/

WHAT THE SCHOOL SAYS:
We believe that all MBA students should be prepared to lead and manage in a variety of environments, in a wide range of industries, and on a global playing field. Whether they pursue a career in the for-profit, not-for-profit, or governmental sector, there are certain bedrock principles, skills, and personal attributes that must be developed. We encourage, promote, and develop creative thinking, innovation, and risk-taking.

A QUICK LOOK

NOTE: All information is self-reported data submitted to the Center for Business Education

COURSES*

CSR/Business Ethics (1)
General Management (3)
Organizational Behavior (1)
Public/Nonprofit Mgt (1)

KEY CONCENTRATIONS

Organizational Leadership

KEY JOINT DEGREES

MBA & MS in Social Work

ACTIVITIES*

Speakers/Seminars (10)
Orientation Activities (1)
Internship/Consulting (1)
Student Competitions (1)
Clubs & Programs (2)
Career Development (3)
Institutes/Centers (2)
Concentrations (1)
Joint Degrees (1)

* Figures in parentheses indicate the number of courses/activities that, in whole or in part, integrate social, environmental, or ethical perspectives

NOTABLE FEATURES

CORE COURSES:

▦ *Organizational Behavior and Design: Leadership in Teams and Organizations*
This course introduces the conceptual tools and basic skills and frameworks needed for managing people in organizations. The course focuses on the basic problems that confront every manager: motivating and influencing individuals and teams, negotiating sound agreements, managing conflicts, and exercising leadership in work teams and varied organizational settings. It also considers the impact of power and influence on decision-making, ethics in organizations, and the practical problems of implementing large-scale organizational change.

ELECTIVE COURSES:

▦ *Management and Corporate Responsibility*
This course explores real situations in which the objectives of the corporation's various constituencies—shareholders, employees, and communities—are in conflict. It also focuses on situations in which societal concerns, environmental and health, for example, may be at odds with the immediate interests of important stakeholders. Through vigorous case discussions, dialogues with industry leaders, and role-play simulations, students wrestle with these often ambiguous dilemmas, gain insights into the conflicts, and develop their own approaches and decision making frameworks for resolving these situations and those they will face during their careers.

▦ *Social Entrepreneurship*
This course is about using entrepreneurial skills to craft innovative solutions to lead and fund efforts to resolve social needs. Entrepreneurs are particularly good at recognizing opportunities, exploring innovative approaches, mobilizing resources, managing risks, and building viable enterprises. These skills are just as valuable and essential in the "independent" social sector as they are in the private business sector.

INSTITUTES AND CENTERS:

▦ *Gephardt Institute for Public Service at Washington University*
The central mission of the Gephardt Institute is to focus attention on public service, its value, its importance, and its interest. In settings as diverse as large international organizations, small local governments, and non-profits of every description, there is a need for enthusiastic volunteers as well as for dedicated career employees. Through workshops, lectures, and occasional conferences, the Gephardt Institute intends to provide information about both public service and significant public issues. Most generally, the Gephardt Institute plans to provide services and programs intended to promote informed civic engagement, political participation, and public service.

▦ *Center for the Study of Ethics and Human Values*
The Center for the Study of Ethics and Human Values is a collaborative, interdisciplinary initiative with active participation from faculty, students, and practitioners in all major disciplines and professions. The center's mission is to advance knowledge of human values through scholarship and an understanding of the practical application of values in human affairs. The center fosters research, education, and community involvement in the study and greater appreciation of ethics and human values.

QUESTIONS TO CONSIDER:

Does any required course contain some element of Social Impact Management? **YES**

Is any required course entirely dedicated to social, environmental, or ethical issues? **NO**

Is there a Net Impact Chapter on campus? **YES**

Washington University in St. Louis
Olin School of Business / St. Louis, MO

THE ASPEN INSTITUTE
Center for Business Education

ANNUAL EVENTS:

■ *Social Entrepreneurship and Innovation Competition*

The purpose of the competition is to stimulate activity that leads to multiple innovative approaches to the area's social problems. Participants are eligible for a maximum of $65,000 in funding and will receive feedback from a panel of social investors and judges who are experts in social entrepreneurship and innovation. Both existing and new not-for-profit organizations are invited to participate. Washington University is working with YouthBridge and community partners to offer numerous workshops and public events to assist participants in their plan development.

OTHER PROGRAMS:

■ *Weston Career Center*

The Weston Career Center hosts a series of events throughout the year for first year MBA students including career exploration panels, 321 Action days, and career navigator activities. In each of these instances there are alumni and business professionals from the market of nonprofit organizations actively involved and engaged with students.

■ *Net Impact–Speaker Series*

Notable speakers and leaders in the areas of corporate social responsibility and sustainability speak to students.

STUDENT CLUBS AND PROGRAMS:

■ *Olin Net Impact Clubt*

Whether for-profit or not-for-profit, there is leading-edge work being done to find new ways to build sustainable businesses that outperform their peers and establish a long-term competitive advantage. The Olin Net Impact Club strives to explore these businesses and the challenging concepts of sustainable business and corporate social responsibility.

■ *Olin Cares*

Olin Cares works to provide Olin MBA students with opportunities to serve the greater St. Louis community.

SCHOOL DEMOGRAPHICS	
Number of Full-Time Students	262
International Students	34%
Female Students	21%
2006/2007 School Year	

THE CENTER FOR BUSINESS EDUCATION'S BOTTOM LINE ON WASHINGTON UNIVERSITY IN ST. LOUIS:
Compared to other business schools in our survey, Washington University in St. Louis offers a good number of courses featuring relevant content, and does a good job in those courses explicitly addressing how mainstream business improves the world. Washington University in St. Louis requires 1 core course featuring relevant content.

A Closer Look at:
Western Washington University
College of Business and Economics / Bellingham, WA
http://www.cbe.wwu.edu/

THE ASPEN INSTITUTE
Center for Business Education

WHAT THE SCHOOL SAYS:

Western Washington University's MBA program applies core values of the College of Business and Economics, including integrity, a free exchange of ideas, and independent thought. In turn, the college applies university values described in its mission statement and strategic plan of community service, civic engagement, social responsibility, effective citizenship, embrace of diversity, and sustainability.

A QUICK LOOK

NOTE: All information is self-reported data submitted to the Center for Business Education

COURSES*

General Management (5)

ACTIVITIES*

Speakers/Seminars (2)
Internship/Consulting (1)
Clubs & Programs (1)

* Figures in parentheses indicate the number of courses/activities that, in whole or in part, integrate social, environmental, or ethical perspectives

NOTABLE FEATURES

CORE COURSES:

▦ *Managerial Foundations*
Topics discussed in this course include the social and political environment of business, ecological context of business, ethical theory, ethical decision making, stakeholder management, enterprise strategy, accounting for environmental issues, and economics in the broader environment.

▦ *Internal and External Forces*
Topics in this course include globalization and its impact on society and public policy, accounting for environmental impact, diversity in organizations, and ethical issues.

ELECTIVE COURSES:

▦ *Ethics in Business Decisions*
This course is devoted to ethical theory and decision making in organizations.

▦ *Influence, Power and Politics in Organizations*
This course includes discussions of ethical and leadership issues related to influence in organizations.

ANNUAL EVENTS:

▦ *Strategic Management Executive Speaker Series*
As part of their presentations on strategic management at their firms, executives almost always discuss the social impact of their firms and environmental issues when appropriate during this speaker series.

▦ *Ethics and Social Responsibility Executive Speaker Series*
The topics discussed in this speaker series cover the social and environmental impact of organizations.

STUDENT CLUBS AND PROGRAMS:

▦ *MBA Association*
The MBA Association regularly participates in community-oriented volunteer work.

SCHOOL DEMOGRAPHICS

Number of Full-Time Students	35
International Students	10%
Female Students	53%

Pre-MBA Employment:

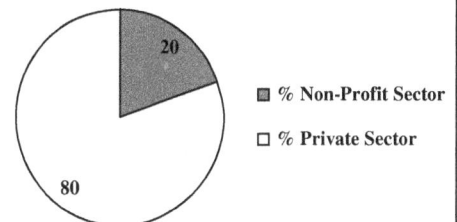

- ▦ % Non-Profit Sector
- ☐ % Private Sector

2006/2007 School Year

QUESTIONS TO CONSIDER:

Does any required course contain some element of Social Impact Management? **YES**

Is any required course entirely dedicated to social, environmental, or ethical issues? **NO**

Is there a Net Impact Chapter on campus? **NO**

THE CENTER FOR BUSINESS EDUCATION'S BOTTOM LINE ON WESTERN WASHINGTON UNIVERSITY:
Compared to other business schools in our survey, Western Washington University offers a good number of courses featuring relevant content, and requires 3 core courses featuring relevant content.

A Closer Look at:
Wilfrid Laurier University
School of Business and Economics / Waterloo, Canada
http://www.wlu.ca/sbe

WHAT THE SCHOOL SAYS:
We attempt to integrate in all of our courses, matters that are crucial to the social and environmental milieu.

A QUICK LOOK

NOTE: All information is self-reported data submitted to the Center for Business Education

COURSES*

Accounting (1)
CSR/Business Ethics (1)
Entrepreneurship (1)
Finance (1)
Marketing (4)
Organizational Behavior (5)
Operations Management (1)
Strategy (4)

ACTIVITIES*

Speakers/Seminars (1)
Orientation Activities (1)
Clubs & Programs (1)
Institutes/Centers (1)

* Figures in parentheses indicate the number of courses/activities that, in whole or in part, integrate social, environmental, or ethical perspectives

NOTABLE FEATURES

CORE COURSES:
▥ *Organizational Behavior*
This class focuses on understanding the importance of corporate social responsibility, with a three hour class devoted to the subject.

▥ *Applied Business Research*
The Applied Business Research course is a team project with a client organization. Approximately 20 percent of clients are not-for-profit organizations in need of management consulting from the MBA team. Additionally, all students enrolled in the course complete a "not-for-profit practicum" involving community service on behalf of a not-for-profit organization.

ELECTIVE COURSES:
▥ *Managing the Family Enterprise*
This course focuses on the work/life balance in family firms, influence of business on the family and society.

▥ *Strategy for a Sustainable World*
Through a combination of cases, readings, lectures, videos, and live projects, class sessions engage students in discussions aimed at developing strategy models and applying new strategy tools that incorporate principles of environmental management and social performance including the identification of sustainable business opportunities.

INSTITUTES AND CENTERS:
▥ *CMA Centre for Responsible Organizations*
The mission of the centre is to foster responsible organizations by establishing the School of Business and Economics at Wilfrid Laurier University as a preeminent research centre contributing to knowledge development and organizational capacity-building in this field. The centre will develop and disseminate knowledge to our stakeholders on the roles and responsibilities of organizations in society and act as a catalyst in creating a new generation of managers who are committed to, and knowledgeable about, societal responsibility.

QUESTIONS TO CONSIDER:

Does any required course contain some element of Social Impact Management? **YES**

Is any required course entirely dedicated to social, environmental, or ethical issues? **YES**

Is there a Net Impact Chapter on campus? **NO**

Wilfrid Laurier University

School of Business and Economics / Waterloo, Canada

THE ASPEN INSTITUTE
Center for Business Education

ANNUAL EVENTS:

■ *Orientation Ethics Workshop*
During this session on ethics and corporate social responsibility, students are presented with a number of "universal moral/ethical standards and principles," which form the basis for discussing a variety of social and ethical issues facing business such as monitoring employee emails, marketing products of questionable ethics (e.g., an internet-based business based on infidelity), and dealing with diversity in the workplace.

STUDENT CLUBS AND PROGRAMS:

■ *MBA Association*
This student club has a "community involvement" component that promotes and tracks the involvement of the students in the community.

SCHOOL DEMOGRAPHICS

Number of Full-Time Students	**159**
International Students	**5%**
Female Students	**30%**

Pre-MBA Employment:

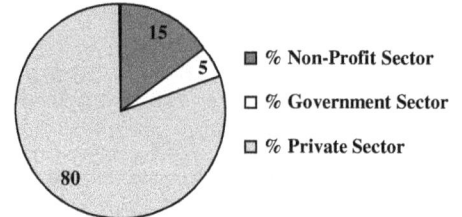

- 15
- 5
- 80

■ % Non-Profit Sector
□ % Government Sector
□ % Private Sector

2006/2007 School Year

THE CENTER FOR BUSINESS EDUCATION'S BOTTOM LINE ON WILFRID LAURIER UNIVERSITY:
Compared to other business schools in our survey, Wilfrid Laurier University offers a good number of courses featuring relevant content, and does a good job in those courses explicitly addressing how mainstream business improves the world. Wilfrid Laurier University requires 5 core courses featuring relevant content.

A Closer Look at:
Willamette University

Atkinson Graduate School of Management / Salem, OR
http://www.willamette.edu/agsm/

THE ASPEN INSTITUTE
Center for Business Education

WHAT THE SCHOOL SAYS:

Willamette's Atkinson Graduate School of Management was established to identify and convey principles shared by successful public, private, and nonprofit enterprises. Students emerge as leaders in their organizations and communities, positively impacting the social and natural environment in which they live and work.

A QUICK LOOK

NOTE: All information is self-reported data submitted to the Center for Business Education

COURSES*

Accounting (4)
CSR/Business Ethics (1)
Economics (1)
Entrepreneurship (1)
Finance (6)
HR Management (3)
Information Technology (3)
International Management (4)
General Management (3)
Marketing (3)
Organizational Behavior (2)
Public/Nonprofit Mgt (5)
Quantitative Methods (1)
Strategy (2)

KEY CONCENTRATIONS

Public Management

International Management

KEY JOINT DEGREES

MBA & Dispute Resolution

ACTIVITIES*

Speakers/Seminars (13)
Orientation Activities (3)
Internship/Consulting (2)
Student Competitions (5)
Clubs & Programs (4)
Career Development (3)
Institutes/Centers (1)
Concentrations (3)
Joint Degrees (3)

* Figures in parentheses indicate the number of courses/activities that, in whole or in part, integrate social, environmental, or ethical perspectives

NOTABLE FEATURES

CORE COURSES:

Managing Exchange

This course focuses on exchange relationships between organizations and their environments. It emphasizes marketing in the private sector but also exposes students to implications for the public sector, the not-for-profit, and the international arenas. It discusses how ethical practices contribute to the marketing relationship to create and retain customers and considers marketing concepts used in issue- or cause-related marketing.

Foundation of Quantitative Analysis

This course develops mathematical and statistical frameworks to assess situations, solve problems, and assess an organization's own practices. It helps students understand the ethical issues surrounding the interpretation and analysis of statistics and the use of statistics to ensure conformity with standards of fairness and ethics. Topics include using mathematical tools to maximize profits, minimize costs, and determine socially responsible options.

ELECTIVE COURSES:

Recent Trends in Corporate Finance—Private Equity

This course examines social venture capitalism. A project includes a trip to Dubai, United Arab Emirates, where students immerse themselves in a dramatically changing market fueled by private investment. The course explores how private equity leads to innovation and value creation for new entrepreneurs. Students are encouraged to evaluate the ethics of venture capitalism and its implications on domestic and international markets.

Nonprofit Management

This course examines the formation, financing, leadership, and management of nonprofit organizations. Topics include board governance, human resources, volunteer management, budgeting, information systems, fundraising, operations, strategic planning, regulatory environment, and the competitive environment. Students complete a team field project designed to assist a nonprofit organization in improving its effectiveness.

INSTITUTES AND CENTERS:

Public Policy Research Center (PPRC)

The PPRC supports and fosters public policy analysis and discussion at Willamette University and in the community. It creates research opportunities for students and faculty that also serve the needs of the policy community in Oregon and the Pacific Northwest, provides student research assistantships on campus, and helps place students in public policy related internships outside the university.

QUESTIONS TO CONSIDER:

Does any required course contain some element of Social Impact Management? **YES**

Is any required course entirely dedicated to social, environmental, or ethical issues? **YES**

Is there a Net Impact Chapter on campus? **NO**

A Closer Look at:
Willamette University
Atkinson Graduate School of Management / Salem, OR

THE ASPEN INSTITUTE
Center for Business Education

ANNUAL EVENTS:

Sustainability Retreat
Students, staff, faculty, administrators, and trustees come together to learn about institutional sustainability assessment procedures and goals and develop an action plan. They assess present curriculum, research, and operations in order to effectively plan, budget, and initiate new programs and policies for incorporating the 4 Es (equity, environment, economics, and education) into the fabric of Willamette University.

Private, Public and Community Enterprise Project (PACE)
Through the PACE project, every first-year student experiences real management challenges in entrepreneurship, consulting, community partnerships, and teamwork. PACE teams apply what they learn in class, research, and consultations with seasoned entrepreneurs and professionals to complete a consulting project that contributes value to their nonprofit client.

SCHOOL DEMOGRAPHICS	
Number of Full-Time Students	112
International Students	10%
Female Students	45%
	2006/2007 School Year

OTHER PROGRAMS:

PACE Team Competition
At the end of each academic year, PACE teams make formal presentations to the PACE Advisory Board and compete on the basis of the value their service-learning consulting project added to their partner nonprofit organization. PACE teams also present their plans for a sustainable, viable business and compete for the best business plan.

Internship Information Session
The Career Services Office hosts an annual on-campus Internship Information Session for social and environmental impact internship programs. This program is in addition to its hosting of general internship information sessions for business, government, and nonprofit organizations.

STUDENT CLUBS AND PROGRAMS:

Atkinson Management Today (AMT)
AMT is an online business journal written and produced by Willamette MBA students. AMT staff research top management techniques, trends, studies, and tips from the experts to bring practicing managers news they can use about a variety of important business topics. Articles include "Use of Government-Sponsored Boards to Further Business Interests"; "Creating Business and Social Value"; and "Young, Old Find Workplace Balance."

Business Women's Forum (BWF)
The BWF presents a women's perspective of business issues. BWF provides a series of interactive events designed to cover issues of interest to all future managers. Everyone in the Atkinson community, both male and female, is welcome to attend. BWF strives to make the events a place where businesspeople can network, listen to unique perspectives, and share their vision for tomorrow in a positive and engaging environment.

THE CENTER FOR BUSINESS EDUCATION'S BOTTOM LINE ON WILLAMETTE UNIVERSITY:
Compared to other business schools in our survey, Willamette University offers an excellent number of courses featuring relevant content, and does a good job in those courses explicitly addressing how mainstream business improves the world. Willamette University requires 11 core courses featuring relevant content.

A Closer Look at:
Yale University
School of Management / New Haven, CT
http://mba.yale.edu/

WHAT THE SCHOOL SAYS:

The mission of the Yale School of Management is to educate leaders for business and society. In 2006 the school launched a new integrated MBA curriculum to create a learning experience more focused on the complex problems facing contemporary organizations. Central to this new curriculum model is Yale SOM's long-established engagement with social and environmental issues.

A QUICK LOOK

NOTE: All information is self-reported data submitted to the Center for Business Education

COURSES*

Accounting (4)
Business & Government (3)
Business Law (5)
CSR/Business Ethics (2)
Economics (6)
Entrepreneurship (1)
Environmental (5)
Finance (7)
HR Management (3)
Information Technology (1)
International Management (10)
General Management (7)
Marketing (4)
Organizational Behavior (7)
Operations Management (2)
Public/Nonprofit Mgt (10)
Quantitative Methods (1)
Strategy (7)

KEY CONCENTRATIONS

Nonprofit Management

KEY JOINT DEGREES

MBA & Environmental Mgt

MBA & International Relations

ACTIVITIES*

Speakers/Seminars (7)
Orientation Activities (1)
Internship/Consulting (3)
Student Competitions (4)
Clubs & Programs (10)
Career Development (2)
Institutes/Centers (5)
Concentrations (2)
Joint Degrees (3)

* Figures in parentheses indicate the number of courses/activities that, in whole or in part, integrate social, environmental, or ethical perspectives

NOTABLE FEATURES

CORE COURSES:

▪ *The Competitor*
This course explicitly recognizes that relevant players in the environment include government and nonprofit organizations as well as corporations and that these players act both cooperatively and competitively. Thus an important premise of this course is that the environment within which organizations compete is multilayered, encompassing not only the market but political, cultural, and legal dimensions.

▪ *State and Society*
The State and Society course focuses on several objectives, one of which includes providing students with insight into the motives driving a diverse array of non-market constituencies that include elected and unelected public officials, leaders of NGOs, interest-group advocates, representatives of multinational organizations, and organized (and sometimes unorganized) movements that arise in a society.

ELECTIVE COURSES:

▪ *Investing in Renewable Energy in Emerging Markets*
This course discusses a range of renewable energies. Lectures cover the industry dynamics behind each type of renewable power. Emphasis is on private investing in wind, geothermal, hydro, and solar power and teams of students bid in a simulated wind-concession bidding process. The course continues with a detailed overview of emerging countries having effective policies and programs in attracting renewable power investment.

▪ *Services Marketing: Strategies for Non-profits and For-profits*
This course explores the role that marketing plays in creating and delivering services in both for-profit and nonprofit settings. The course explores concepts, frameworks, and models designed to facilitate analysis of different types of services, to compare and contrast nonprofit and for-profit environments. Areas of application include museums, health care, franchising, telecommunications, and nature sanctuaries.

INSTITUTES AND CENTERS:

▪ *The Millstein Center for Corporate Governance and Performance*
The Millstein Center sponsors multidisciplinary research and discussions to explore how corporate governance can better enable the corporation to be competitive in its markets and to enhance society. The center facilitates the interaction of scholars with policy makers and business leaders, and looks globally for models of governance that combine return to shareholders and social benefit.

▪ *Center for Business and Environment at Yale*
The Center for Business and Environment at Yale unites the Yale School of Management and the Yale School of Forestry and Environmental Studies in addressing environment issues in the business context and the need for better management in response to society's environmental challenges. The Center is the focal point for research, teaching, and outreach at the business-environment interface across the Yale campus.

QUESTIONS TO CONSIDER:

Does any required course contain some element of Social Impact Management? **YES**

Is any required course entirely dedicated to social, environmental, or ethical issues? **NO**

Is there a Net Impact Chapter on campus? **YES**

A Closer Look at:
Yale University
School of Management / New Haven, CT

ANNUAL EVENTS:

Program On NonProfit Organizations (PONPO) Seminar Series
The PONPO seminars are a series of presentations and discussions on international and indigenous non-governmental organizations (NGO's). Their main objective continues to be to map current research in the field. Presentations include both Yale and guest participants, scholars, and practitioners.

Yale SOM Net Impact Case Competition
Yale SOM Net Impact Club hosts a first-year case competition. The case involves a business with a social focus. The event acts to introduce double bottom-line concepts to the entire community in a fun way. Finalists compete before judges who are consultants from leading consulting firms.

The Future of Philanthropy
This is a full day of stimulating and informative discussion designed to unite leaders with future leaders along the continuum of positive societal impact. It is a unique opportunity to learn from business and society leaders as they share their insights with students. The conference explores the innovation and changing landscape of philanthropy.

OTHER PROGRAMS:

Global Social Enterprise
Students provide pro bono consulting services to internationally focused non-profit, public, and private sector organizations with the goal of making a positive social impact. Through these relationships, students encounter enriching learning opportunities that allow them to apply their business and management skills toward the support of an international social purpose.

The Internship Fund
The Yale School of Management established the Internship Fund in 1979, the first program of its kind among business schools, to provide financial support to students who wish to pursue employment as summer associates in the nonprofit and public sectors. Each year, the Internship Fund raises approximately $140,000 to provide financial support to students seeking summer internships in the public or not-for-profit sectors.

STUDENT CLUBS AND PROGRAMS:

Economic Development
The Economic Development group promotes the study and practice of management with regard to issues of economic security, justice, and prosperity both within the U.S. and internationally. It organizes events on topics such as education and workforce development, community space development, environmental and economic balancing, and others. It is supported by a broad base of active alumni who have professional and leadership interests in these and other topics.

SOM Outreach
SOM Outreach provides business and management advice to New Haven-area organizations that are unable to afford comparable services elsewhere.

SCHOOL DEMOGRAPHICS	
Number of Full-Time Students	420
International Students	21%
Female Students	34%
Pre-MBA Employment:	

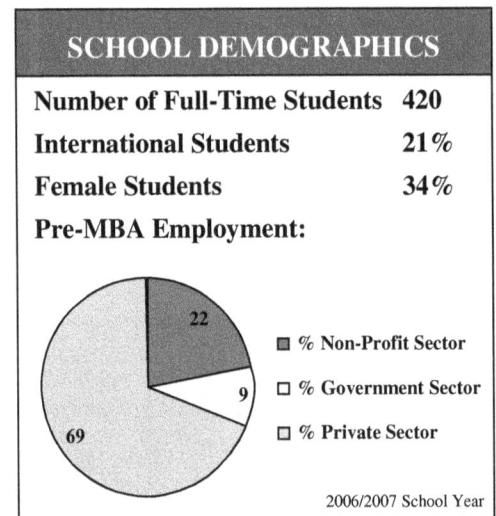

- ■ % Non-Profit Sector
- □ % Government Sector
- □ % Private Sector

22
9
69

2006/2007 School Year

THE CENTER FOR BUSINESS EDUCATION'S BOTTOM LINE ON YALE UNIVERSITY:
Compared to other business schools in our survey, Yale University offers a truly extraordinary number of courses featuring relevant content, and does a truly extraordinary job in those courses explicitly addressing how mainstream business improves the world. Yale University requires 28 core courses featuring relevant content.

A Closer Look at:
York University

Schulich School of Business / Toronto, Canada

http://www.schulich.yorku.ca

WHAT THE SCHOOL SAYS:

Global, innovative, and diverse, the Schulich School of Business at York University prepares its students to meet the needs of social and environmental stewardship in a rapidly changing world. Schulich remains at the forefront of integrating social and environmental impact issues into management education and exposing business students to the social and environmental challenges that are a growing component of business strategy in the 21st century.

A QUICK LOOK

NOTE: All information is self-reported data submitted to the Center for Business Education

COURSES*

Accounting (**10**)
Business & Government (**2**)
Business Law (**8**)
CSR/Business Ethics (**5**)
Economics (**8**)
Entrepreneurship (**2**)
Finance (**10**)
Information Technology (**1**)
International Management (**12**)
General Management (**15**)
Marketing (**14**)
Organizational Behavior (**8**)
Operations Management (**3**)
Public/Nonprofit Mgt (**13**)
Strategy (**5**)

KEY CONCENTRATIONS

Business and Sustainability

Health Industry Management

KEY JOINT DEGREES

MBA & Business and the Environment

MBA & Democratic Administration

ACTIVITIES*

Speakers/Seminars (**13**)
Orientation Activities (**3**)
Internship/Consulting (**4**)
Student Competitions (**3**)
Clubs & Programs (**5**)
Career Development (**2**)
Institutes/Centers (**5**)
Concentrations (**7**)
Joint Degrees (**4**)

* Figures in parentheses indicate the number of courses/activities that, in whole or in part, integrate social, environmental, or ethical perspectives

NOTABLE FEATURES

CORE COURSES:

International Business Seminars

Corporate social responsibility, ethics, and stakeholder engagement are major topics of discussion for these seminars. The seminars augment core courses and provide students with an opportunity to dialogue with executives and other international business experts about corporate socially responsible aspects of international business, and other practical components of operating a business on an international scale.

Strategy Field Study

Core issues of this study are sustainable value creation, the environmental impact of management decisions, stakeholder engagement, and the ethical and social impact of management preferences affecting an organization's success. Students work in groups to prepare a strategy study on a federal, provincial or municipal government, agency or program, or a Nonprofit agency that receives government subsidies.

ELECTIVE COURSES:

Environmental Economics for Business

This course focuses on the relationship between the economy and the environment. Environmental economics is the study of the allocation of the natural environment. Some topics to be addressed in this course include property rights and externalities, clean energy decision-making, and international environmental agreements.

Labor Relations

This course examines union-management relations and collective bargaining. Students work with case studies and simulation exercises in the classroom to learn both theory and practice with regard to conflict resolution and negotiations. Some topics covered in the course include union development, management as a bargaining organization, and contract administration and the grievance procedure.

INSTITUTES AND CENTERS:

Maytree Foundation

The York University-Maytree Foundation has been developed for executive directors and managers of settlement, employment, and neighborhood agencies working with immigrants and refugees to build their capacity and leadership skills. Program instructors are drawn from all corners of the academic and nonprofit world and include university faculty, experienced sector practitioners, consultants, and issue-specific experts.

Transparency International Canada Inc.

Transparency International Canada Inc. (TI-Canada) is a voluntary not-for-profit organization affiliated with more than 70 other national chapters around the world. TI-Canada's purpose is to inform the business community, the government, and the general public of the effects of corruption in the international marketplace, and to provide support and resources for public and private sector initiatives to prevent corrupt business practices.

QUESTIONS TO CONSIDER:

Does any required course contain some element of Social Impact Management? **YES**

Is any required course entirely dedicated to social, environmental, or ethical issues? **NO**

Is there a Net Impact Chapter on campus? **YES**

ANNUAL EVENTS:

The TATA Lecture Series: A Frontline Perspective on the Indian IT Revolution

The TATA Lecture Series aims to introduce leading thinkers and activists in the information and communications technology revolution to leaders in Canadian industry, government, and academia. Each year the TATA lecture series presents a distinguished speaker, notable for his or her contribution to extend the benefits of technology to all humanity.

The Social Adversity Challenge

The Social Adversity Challenge is an orientation event developed by the Community Social Planning Council of Toronto and is being used as part of the business skills training program for Schulich MBA students. The game simulates a few months in the life of society's most disadvantaged members and is a unique experiential training tool that allows MBA students to develop multiple-perspective thinking on a broad range of business issues such as community stakeholder relations and corporate social responsibility.

Schulich Sustainability Case Competition

Every January, Schulich Net Impact hosts a Sustainability Case Competition. Students are challenged to formulate sustainable and profitable solutions to a company's business issue. The top team will win the right to represent Schulich at the leading business and sustainability competition in the world.

SCHOOL DEMOGRAPHICS	
Number of Full-Time Students	655
International Students	50%
Female Students	37%

2006/2007 School Year

OTHER PROGRAMS:

Sustainability Networking Reception

Students connect with Canada's leading companies, non-profits, and government departments committed to sustainability that are recruiting the country's brightest and best-trained MBA students who offer a sustainability mindset.

STUDENT CLUBS AND PROGRAMS:

Nonprofit Management Association (NMA)

The NMA is open to any student interested in learning more about management and careers in the nonprofit sector, which includes areas as diverse as health care, education, environment, culture, community services, and international development. The NMA's mission is to enrich the experience of nonprofits and other students through professional, career development, and social activities.

Women in Leadership

The Women in Leadership Club is a non-exclusionary club open to all students, faculty and staff that recognizes women's contributions to business while seeking to create a space in which members can develop the skills and contacts needed to help them achieve their personal and career goals.

THE CENTER FOR BUSINESS EDUCATION'S BOTTOM LINE ON YORK UNIVERSITY:
Compared to other business schools in our survey, York University offers a truly extraordinary number of courses featuring relevant content, and does an excellent job in those courses explicitly addressing how mainstream business improves the world. York University requires 29 core courses featuring relevant content.

Appendix Topics

1) Faculty Pioneers – Comprehensive list of all Faculty Pioneers since the inception of the Awards in 1999

2) MBA Concentrations – Comprehensive list of self-reported environmental and social impact management related concentrations

3) Joint MBA Degrees – Comprehensive list of self-reported environmental and social impact management related joint MBA degrees

4) Participating Schools in the United States (listed geographically)
- Great Lakes Region
- Northeast/Mid-Atlantic
- Pacific Northwest and Alaska
- Southeast
- Southwest
- West Central

5) Participating Schools Around the World (listed geographically)
- Africa
- Americas
- Europe
- Asia and Pacific

Faculty Pioneers: 1999–2007

The Aspen Institute Center for Business Education's Alternative Guide to Global MBA Education

The commitment of business school faculty is critical in ensuring that social and environmental issues become more fully infused in business education and therefore business practice. The Center presents Faculty Pioneer Awards to exceptional faculty who are leaders in integrating social and environmental issues into their research and teaching both on as well as off campus. The following is a listing of all Faculty Pioneer Award Winners since the inception of the Awards in 1999 (for more information, please visit www.facultypioneers.org).

2007 Faculty Pioneer Award Winners

- **Academic Impact Award - Carrie Leana, Professor of Business Administration**
  University of Pittsburgh, Katz Graduate School of Business

- **External Impact Award - David Cooperrider, Professor of Organizational Behavior**
  Case Western Reserve, Weatherhead School of Management

- **External Impact Award - Warner Woodworth, Professor of Organizational Leadership & Strategy**
  Brigham Young University, Marriott School of Management

- **Institutional Impact Award - Daniel Diermeier, Professor of Managerial Economics and Decision Science (MEDS)**
  Northwestern University, Kellogg School of Management

- **Lifetime Achievement Award - Kirk Hanson, Professor of Organizations and Society**
  Santa Clara University, Markkula Center for Applied Ethics

- **Rising Star Award - Jeffrey Robinson, Professor of Management**
  New York University, NYU Stern School of Business

2006 Faculty Pioneer Award Winners

- **Academic Leadership Award - Pietra Rivoli, Professor of Finance**
  Georgetown University, Robert Emmett McDonough School of Business

- **European Award - Nigel Roome, Professor of Corporate Social Responsibility**
  Free University of Brussels, Solvay Business School

- **External Impact Award - Lawrence Pratt, Professor of Competitiveness and Sustainable Development**
  INCAE

- **Institutional Leadership Award - Byong-hun Ahn, Professor of Economics**
  Korea Advanced Institute of Science and Technology, KAIST Graduate School of Management

Faculty Pioneers: 1999–2007

The Aspen Institute Center for Business Education's Alternative Guide to Global MBA Education

- ▪ Lifetime Achievement Award - Max Bazerman, Professor of Business Administration
  Harvard University, Harvard Business School

- ▪ Rising Star Award - Ray Fisman, Professor of Finance and Economics
  Columbia University, Columbia Business School

2005 Faculty Pioneer Award Winners

- ▪ Academic Leadership Award - Richard M. Locke, Professor of Entrepreneurship & Political Science
  Massachusetts Institute of Technology, Sloan School of Management

- ▪ European Award - Jeremy Moon, Professor of Corporate Social Responsibility
  The University of Nottingham, Nottingham University Business School

- ▪ European Award - Craig Smith, Professor of Marketing and Business Ethics
  London Business School

- ▪ External Impact Award - Sandra Waddock, Professor of Management
  Boston College, Carroll School of Management

- ▪ Institutional Leadership Award - Luis Felipe Machado do Nascimento, Professor of Socio-Environmental Management
  Federal University of Rio Grande do Sul, School of Management

- ▪ Institutional Leadership Award - Kellie A. McElhaney, Professor of Corporate Responsibility
  University of California, Berkeley, Walter A. Haas School of Business

- ▪ Lifetime Achievement Award - C. K. Prahalad, Professor of Corporate Strategy
  The University of Michigan, Stephen M. Ross School of Business

- ▪ Rising Star Award - Erica Plambeck, Professor of Operations, Information, and Technology
  Stanford University, Graduate School of Business

2003 Faculty Pioneer Award Winners

- ▪ Academic Leadership Award - Timothy L. Fort, Professor of Business Ethics
  The George Washington University, School of Business

- ▪ Academic Leadership Award - Alyson C. Warhurst, Professor of Corporate Strategy and International Development

243

Faculty Pioneers: 1999–2007

The Aspen Institute Center for Business Education's Alternative Guide to Global MBA Education

Warwick University, Warwick Business School

- **External Impact Award - Chi Anyansi-Archibong, Professor of Business Administration**
North Carolina A&T State University, School of Business and Economics

- **External Impact Award - S. Prakash Sethi, Professor of Management**
Baruch Colleg—The City University of New York, The Zicklin School of Business

- **Institutional Leadership Award - James E. Austin, Professor of Business Administration**
Harvard University, Harvard Business School

- **Lifetime Achievement Award - Thomas N. Gladwin, Professor of Sustainable Enterprise, Corporate Strategy and International Business**
University of Michigan, Stephen M. Ross School of Business

- **Rising Star Award - Andrew J. Hoffman, Professor of Sustainable Enterprise**
University of Michigan, Stephen M. Ross School of Business

2001 Faculty Pioneer Award Winners

- **Academic Leadership Award - Arthur P. Brief, Professor of Business**
Tulane University, A. B. Freeman School of Business

- **External Impact Award - Marilyn L. Taylor, Professor of Finance, Information Management and Strategy**
University of Missouri-Kansas City, Bloch School of Business and Public Administration

- **Institutional Leadership Award - R. Bruce Hutton, Professor of Marketing**
University of Denver, Daniels College of Business

- **Lifetime Achievement Award - R. Edward Freeman, Professor of Business Administration**
University of Virginia, Darden Graduate School of Business Administration

- **Rising Star Award - Andrew King, Professor of Strategy**
Dartmouth College, Tuck School of Business

1999 Faculty Pioneer Award Winners

- **Lifetime Achievement Award - John Ehrenfeld, Retired Professor of Technology, Business and Environment**
Massachusetts Institute of Technology, Sloan School of Management

Faculty Pioneers: 1999–2007

The Aspen Institute Center for Business Education's Alternative Guide to Global MBA Education

- **Stuart Hart, Professor of Management**
  Cornell University, Samuel Curtis Johnson Graduate School of Management

- **James Johnson, Jr., Professor of Entrepreneurship**
  The University of North Carolina at Chapel Hill, Kenan-Flagler Business School

- **Lester B. Lave, Professor of Economics and Finance**
  Carnegie Mellon University, Tepper School of Business

MBA Concentrations

The Aspen Institute Center for Business Education's Alternative Guide to Global MBA Education

Asian Institute of Management
Development Management
Entrepreneurship for Social and Development Entrepreneurs
Management

AUDENCIA Nantes
Business Development

Bainbridge Graduate Institute
Industry Concentrations

Bentley College
Concentration in Business Ethics

Boston College
Business Ethics/Corporate Social Responsibility

Boston University
Public and Nonprofit Management

Brandeis University
Sustainable Development
Health Care Policy and Management
Child, Youth, Family Policy and Management
Social Policy and Management

Carnegie Mellon University
Global Enterprise Management Track (GEM)
Entrepreneurship in Organizations
Management of Innovation and Product Design
Biotechnology

Case Western Reserve University
International Management
Health Care Management
Non-profit Management
Organizational and Human Resource Development

Columbia University
Social Enterprise
Entrepreneurship
Real Estate
International Business

Concordia University
Corporate Governance
Global Business
Fraud Examination

Curtin University of Technology
Human Services

Dalhousie University
Environmental Management
International Business
Public Policy

Duke University
Social Entrepreneurship
Health Sector Management
Leadership and Ethics

Duquesne University
Environmental Management
Business Ethics

Emory University
Sustainability
International Business
Non-profit Management

Fundacao Getulio Vargas, Rio de Janeiro
Public Administration

HEC School of Management - Paris
Mission and Action Project (MAP)

IE Business School
Social Entrepreneurship

IESA (Instituto de Estudios Sup. De Administracion)
Entrepreneurship
Marketing
Organizations
Finance

Illinois Institute of Technology
Sustainable Enterprise

Iowa State University
Minor in Sustainable Agriculture

Lamar University
Experiential Business and Entrepreneurship

Loyola University Chicago
Business Ethics
Risk Management

Massachusetts Institute of Technology
Sustainability

McGill University
Management for Development (International Business)

Monterey Institute of International Studies
Corporate Social Responsibility
Globalization/Localization Management
Specialization in International Environmental Management

New York University
Entrepreneurship and Innovation
Global Business

North Carolina State University
Innovation Management
Entrepreneurship and Technology Commercialization
Supply Chain Management

Pepperdine University
International Master of Business Administration
Dispute Resolution

Portland State University
Sustainability
International Business

Presidio School of Management
Sustainable Management

Rhodes University
Environmental Management

Saint Joseph's University
International Business
Public and Non-Profit Management

San Francisco State University
Sustainability

Seton Hall University
International Business & Finance

Simmons College
Entrepreneurship

St. John's University
International Business Management

Please Note: Schools listed have self-reported concentrations as these that enhance the MBA with studies related to environmental and social impact management. In the "Quick Look" boxes, we have listed concentrations that we feel are most relevant. For clarification regarding the relevance of the reported concentrations to these issues, please contact the school.

MBA Concentrations

The Aspen Institute Center for Business Education's Alternative Guide to Global MBA Education

Sustainability and Business

University of Oxford
Social Entrepreneurship

University of San Diego
International Business

University of South Florida St. Petersburg
Corporate Social Responsibility
Forensic Accounting
International Business
Taxation
Managing Knowledge Resources

University of Stellenbosch
International Management

University of Western Ontario
Health Care

University of Wisconsin-Madison
Public and Non-Profit Management

Vanderbilt University
Environmental Management Studies
International Studies
Law & Business Program

Washington University in St. Louis
Organizational Leadership - General Management

Willamette University
Human Resources
Public Management
International Management

Yale University
Non-profit Management
Public Management

York University
Business and Sustainability
Business Ethics
International Business
Public Sector Management
Non-Profit Management
Health Industry Management
Arts and Media Administration

University of Calgary
Global Energy Management and Sustainable Development

University of California, Berkeley
Corporate Social Responsibility
Nonprofit & Public Management
Health Management
Global Management
Management of Technology
Entrepreneurship

University of California, Davis
Corporate Social Responsibility
International Business
Non-Profit Management

University of California, Los Angeles
Leaders in Sustainability

University of Cape Town
Business, Government and Society
Emerging Enterprises in a Developing Economy
Social Entrepreneurship
Emerging Enterprise Consulting
Social Marketing
Going Global: Doing Business in Emerging Markets

University of Colorado at Boulder
Sustainable Venturing Initiative

University of Denver
Values-Based Leadership
Not-for-Profit Management

University of Geneva
International Organizations

University of Jyväskylä
Corporate Environmental Management

University of Notre Dame
Entrepreneurship
Consulting
Management Development
Manufacturing Development
Marketing
Corporate Finance
Investments

Stanford University
Socially Responsible Business
Nonprofit Management
Government
Global Management

RMS Erasmus University
International Business
BSM (Business Ethics/Corporate Social Responsibility)

The George Washington University
Environmental Policy & Management
Nonprofit Organization Management
Strategic Management and Public Policy
Tourism & Hospitality Mgmt & Sustainable Destinations
Small Business & Entrepreneurship

The University of Arizona
Human Resources Management

The University of New Mexico
Policy and Planning

The University of North Carolina at Chapel Hill
Sustainable Enterprise
Entrepreneurship
Global Supply Chain Management
Real Estate

The University of Nottingham
Corporate Social Responsibility

The University of Texas at Dallas
Strategic Management
International Management

Thunderbird, The Garvin School of International Management
International Development

Tulane University
Public and Non-Profit Management

University of Alberta
Natural Resources and Energy
International Business
Public Management
Technology Commercialization

University of British Columbia

Please Note: Schools listed have self-reported concentrations as those that enhance the MBA with studies related to environmental and social impact management. In the 'Quick Look' boxes, we have listed concentrations that we feel are most relevant. For clarification regarding the relevance of the reported concentrations to these issues, please contact the school.

Joint MBA Degrees

The Aspen Institute Center for Business Education's Alternative Guide to Global MBA Education

Carnegie Mellon University
MBA and Public Policy and Management
MBA and Health Care Management and Public Policy
MBA and Civil and Environmental Engineering
MBA and JD

Case Western Reserve University
MBA and Master of Non-Profit Organization
MBA and Master's in Positive Organizational Development
MBA and Master's in Science and Social Administration

Columbia University
MBA and Master of International Affairs
MBA and Master of Science (Urban Planning)
MBA and Master of Science in Earth Resources Engineering

Cornell University
MBA and Engineering
MBA and Industrial and Labor Relations
MBA and JD
MBA and Asian Studies

Curtin University of Technology
MBA and MME (Natural Resource Management)

Dalhousie University
MBA and Master's in Engineering
MBA and Master's in Health Services Administration
MBA and LLB (Environmental Law)
MBA and Master's in Library and Information Studies

Dartmouth College
MBA and MALD
MBA and MPA
MBA and MSEL (Environmental Law)

Duke University
MBA and Master of Public Policy
MBA and Master of Environmental Sciences

Duquesne University
MBA and MS Environmental Sciences
MBA and MS Industrial Pharmacy
MBA and MA Social and Public Policy
MBA and MS Nursing

Monterey Institute of International Studies
MBA and MA International Environmental Policy
MBA and MA International Trade Policy
MBA and MA Translation and Localization Management
Master's International MBA program

National University of Singapore
MBA and Healthcare Management

New York University
MBA and MPA
MBA and JD

North Carolina State University
MBA and Masters of Microbial Biotechnology
MBA and Doctor of Veterinary Medicine

Pepperdine University
MBA and Masters in Public Policy
MBA and JD

Portland State University
MBA and Masters in Environmental Management

Rice University
MBA and MCE Program (Environmental Sciences)
MBA and MD Program

RMS Erasmus University
OneMBA

Saint Joseph's University
MBA and DO

Seton Hall University
MBA and MSIB
MBA and MS Diplomacy
MBA and JD

Stanford University
MBA and MA in Education
MBA and Master of Science in Environment and Resources
MBA and Master's in Public Policy
MBA and JD
MBA and MD

Emory University
MBA and JD
MBA and Master of Public Health Administration

Georgetown University
MBA and Master's in Public Policy

Georgia Institute of Technology
MBA and Public Policy
MBA and International Affairs
MBA and Environmental Sciences

Harvard University
MBA and MD
MBA and JD
MBA and Public Policy

HEC School of Management - Paris
MBA and Environmental Law
MBA and Environmental Economics

IESA (Instituto de Estudios Sup. de Administracion)
MBA and Master's in International Business

Illinois Institute of Technology
MBA and JD (Environmental Law)
MBA and MS in Environmental Management

Massachusetts Institute of Technology
MBA and Public Policy (MPP or MPA)
MBA and MS in Engineering

McGill University
MBA and MD
MBA and JD
MBA and International Masters in Health Leadership

MBA and MA Corporate Communication
MBA and MS Health Management Systems
MBA and MA Liberal Studies
MBA and MA Leadership and Liberal Studies
MBA and MS Taxation
MBA and JD
MBA and MS Accountancy

Please Note: Schools listed have self-reported joint degrees as those that enhance the MBA with studies related to environmental and social impact management. For clarification regarding the relevance of the reported Joint Degree to these issues, please contact the school.

Joint MBA Degrees

The Aspen Institute Center for Business Education's Alternative Guide to Global MBA Education

The George Washington University
MBA and MA International Affairs
MBA and JD Law

The University of Arizona
MBA and MS
MBA and JD
MBA and MS Natural Resource Studies

The University of North Carolina at Chapel Hill
MBA and Master of Regional Planning (MRP)
MBA and Master of Information and Library Science
MBA and Law (JD)
MBA and Master of Public Health (MHA or MSPH)

Tulane University
MBA and MD
MBA and MPH

Universidad de Los Andes
MBA and Master in Public Administration
MBA and Engineering and Environmental Management

University of Alberta
MBA and Forestry
MBA and Agriculture

University of British Columbia
MBA and Masters in Asia Pacific Policy Studies

University of Calgary
MBA and LLB
MBA and MSW

University of California, Berkeley
MBA and MA Program in International and Area Studies
MBA and MPH Program in Health Management

University of California, Davis
MBA and JD Environmental Law
MBA and MS Agricultural and Resource Economics
MBA and MS in Environmental Policy Analysis
MBA and MD
MBA and MA Education
MBA and MS Engineering

University of California, Los Angeles
MBA and MPP
MBA and Master of Urban Planning (MAUP)

University of Colorado at Boulder
MBA and MS in Environmental Studies
MBA and MA in Anthropology

University of Denver
IMBA and Master's in Global Finance, Trade, and Economic
Integration
MBA and JD (Environmental Law)
MBA and JD (Natural Resource Management)
MBA and MS

University of Geneva
International Organizations MBA & Master of Public Policy
MBA and Management of Public Affairs and International
Organizations
International Organizations MBA & Master's in International Studies

University of Jyväskylä
MBA and Renewable Energy Master's Degree Program

University of Notre Dame
MBA and Engineering
MBA and JD
MBA and Science

University of San Diego
MBA and JD
MBA and MS Nursing
ITESM MBA

University of San Francisco
MBA Environmental Management Program

University of Virginia
MBA and MA in East Asian Studies
MBA and JD

University of Wisconsin-Madison
MBA and JD
MBA and Master's in Land and Resources

Vanderbilt University
MBA and Master of Divinity
MBA and JD

Washington State University
MBA and Masters in Public Administration

Washington University in St. Louis
MBA and MS in Social Work

Willamette University
MBA and JD
MBA and BA
MBA and Certificate of Dispute Resolution

Yale University
MBA and MEM (Environmental Management)
MBA and MF (Forestry)
MBA and MA International Relations

York University
MBA and MFA/MA
MBA and Graduate Diploma in Business and the Environment
MBA and Graduate Diploma in Democratic Administration
MBA and Graduate Diploma in Arts & Media Administration

249

School Profiles by Region – U.S. Schools

The Aspen Institute Center for Business Education's Alternative Guide to Global MBA Education

Great Lakes Region

University	Business School	City	State
Case Western Reserve University	Weatherhead School of Management	Cleveland	OH
Illinois Institute of Technology	Stuart Graduate School of Business	Chicago	IL
Loyola University Chicago	School of Business Administration	Chicago	IL
Michigan Technological University	School of Business and Economics	Houghton	MI
Saginaw Valley State University	College of Business and Management	University Center	MI
The University of Michigan	Stephen M. Ross School of Business	Ann Arbor	MI
University of Notre Dame	Mendoza College of Business	Notre Dame	IN
University of Wisconsin–Madison	School of Business	Madison	WI

Northeast/Mid-Atlantic

University	Business School	City	State
Babson College	School of Management	Babson Park	MA
Baruch College—The City University of New York	The Zicklin School of Business	New York	NY
Bentley College	McCallum Graduate School of Business	Waltham	MA
Boston College	Carroll School of Management	Chestnut Hill	MA
Boston University	School of Management	Boston	MA
Brandeis University	Heller School for Social Policy and Management	Waltham	MA
Carnegie Mellon University	Tepper School of Business	Pittsburgh	PA
Columbia University	Columbia Business School	New York	NY
Cornell University	Samuel Curtis Johnson Graduate School of Management	Ithaca	NY
Dartmouth College	Tuck School of Business at Dartmouth	Hanover	NH
Duquesne University	John F. Donahue Graduate School of Business	Pittsburgh	PA
Georgetown University	Robert Emmett McDonough School of Business	Washington	DC
Harvard University	Graduate School of Business Administration	Boston	MA
Massachusetts Institute of Technology	Sloan School of Management	Cambridge	MA
New York University	Leonard N. Stern School of Business	New York	NY
Saint Joseph's University	Erivan K. Haub School of Business	Philadelphia	PA
Seton Hall University	The Stillman School of Business	South Orange	NJ
Simmons College	Simmons School of Management	Boston	MA
St. John's University	The Peter J. Tobin College of Business	Queens	NY
The George Washington University	School of Business	Washington	DC
The University of Vermont	School of Business Administration	Burlington	VT
University of Pittsburgh	The Joseph M. Katz Graduate School of Business	Pittsburgh	PA
University of Virginia	Darden Graduate School of Business Administration	Charlottesville	VA
Yale University	School of Management	New Haven	CT

Pacific Northwest and Alaska

University	Business School	City	State
Oregon State University	College of Business	Corvallis	OR
Portland State University	School of Business Administration	Portland	OR
University of Alaska Anchorage	College of Business and Public Policy	Anchorage	AK
Utah State University	College of Business	Logan	UT
Washington State University	College of Business and Economics	Vancouver	WA
Western Washington University	College of Business and Economics	Bellingham	WA
Willamette University	Atkinson Graduate School of Management	Salem	OR

School Profiles by Region – U.S. Schools

The Aspen Institute Center for Business Education's Alternative Guide to Global MBA Education

Southeast

University	Business School	City	State
Duke University	The Fuqua School of Business	Durham	NC
Emory University	Goizueta Business School	Atlanta	GA
Georgia Institute of Technology	College of Management	Atlanta	GA
North Carolina State University	College of Management	Raleigh	NC
The University of North Carolina at Chapel Hill	Kenan-Flagler Business School	Chapel Hill	NC
Tulane University	A. B. Freeman School of Business	New Orleans	LA
University of Florida	Warrington College of Business Administration	Gainesville	FL
University of South Carolina	Moore School of Business	Columbia	SC
University of South Florida St. Petersburg	College of Business	St. Petersburg	FL
Vanderbilt University	Owen Graduate School of Management	Nashville	TN
Wake Forest University	Babcock Graduate School of Management	Winston-Salem	NC

Southwest

University	Business School	City	State
Bainbridge Graduate Institute	Bainbridge Graduate Institute	Bainbridge Island	WA
California State University, Chico	College of Business	Chico	CA
Chapman University	The George L. Argyros School of Business and Economics	Orange	CA
Lamar University	College of Business	Beaumont	TX
Monterey Institute of International Studies	Robert L. and Marilyn J. Fisher Graduate School of International Business	Monterey	CA
Pepperdine University	George L. Graziadio School of Business and Management	Malibu	CA
Presidio School of Management			
Rice University	Jesse H. Jones Graduate School of Management	Houston	TX
San Francisco State University	College of Business	San Francisco	CA
Stanford University	Graduate School of Business	Stanford	CA
The University of Arizona	Eller College of Management	Tucson	AZ
The University of New Mexico	The Robert O. Anderson Schools of Management	Albuquerque	NM
The University of Texas at Dallas	School of Management	Richardson	TX
Thunderbird School of Global Management		Glendale	AZ
University of California, Berkeley	Walter A. Haas School of Business	Berkeley	CA
University of California, Davis	Graduate School of Management	Davis	CA
University of California, Los Angeles	UCLA Anderson School of Management	Los Angeles	CA
University of California, San Diego	Rady School of Management	La Jolla	CA
University of San Diego	School of Business Administration	San Diego	CA
University of San Francisco	School of Business and Management	San Francisco	CA

West Central

University	Business School	City	State
Iowa State University	College of Business	Ames	IA
University of Colorado at Boulder	Leeds School of Business	Boulder	CO
University of Denver	Daniels College of Business	Denver	CO
Washington University in St. Louis	Olin School of Business	St. Louis	MO

School Profiles by Region – Non-U.S. Schools

The Aspen Institute Center for Business Education's Alternative Guide to Global MBA Education

Africa

Country	University	Business School	City
South Africa	Rhodes University	Rhodes Investec Business School	Grahamstown
South Africa	University of Cape Town	Graduate School of Business	Cape Town
South Africa	University of Stellenbosch	Business School	Bellville

Americas

Country	University	Business School	City
Brazil	Fundacao Getulio Vargas, Rio de Janeiro	Brazilian School of Public and Business Administration	Rio de Janeiro
Canada	Concordia University	John Molson School of Business	Montreal
Canada	Dalhousie University	Faculty of Management	Halifax
Canada	McGill University	Desautels Faculty Management	Montreal
Canada	University of Alberta	School of Business	Edmonton
Canada	University of British Columbia	Sauder School of Business	Vancouver
Canada	University of Calgary	Haskayne School of Business	Calgary
Canada	University of Western Ontario	Richard Ivey School of Business	London
Canada	Wilfrid Laurier University	School of Business & Economics	Waterloo
Canada	York University	Schulich School of Business	Toronto
Colombia	Universidad de Los Andes	School of Management	Bogota
Mexico	ITESM (EGADE Monterrey)	EGADE	San Pedro Garza Garcia, N.L.
Venezuela	IESA	Instituto de Estudios Superiores de Administracion	Caracas

Europe

Country	University	Business School	City
Belgium	Free University of Brussels	Solvay Business School	Brussels
Denmark	Copenhagen Business School	Copenhagen Business School	Frederiksberg
Finland	University of Jyväskylä	School of Business and Economics	Jyväskylä
France	AUDENCIA Nantes	School of Management	Nantes
France	HEC School of Management–Paris	HEC School of Management	Jouy-en-Josas
France (and Singapore)	INSEAD	INSEAD	Fontainebleau
Netherlands	RSM Erasmus University	RSM Erasmus University	Rotterdam

School Profiles by Region – Non-U.S. Schools

The Aspen Institute Center for Business Education's Alternative Guide to Global MBA Education

Europe

Country	University	Business School	City
Spain	EADA—Escuela de Alta Dirección y Administración	EADA—Escuela de Alta Dirección y Administración	Barcelona
Spain	ESADE	Business School	Barcelona
Spain	IE Business School	Instituto de Empresa	Madrid
Spain	University of Navarra	IESE Business School	Barcelona
Switzerland	IMD—International Institute for Management Development	IMD	Lausanne
Switzerland	University of Geneva	HEC Geneva	Geneva
United Kingdom	Ashridge	Ashridge Business School	Hertfordshire
United Kingdom	Cranfield School of Management	Cranfield School of Management	Bedford
United Kingdom	Durham University	Durham Business School	Durham
United Kingdom	The University of Nottingham	Nottingham University Business School	Nottingham
United Kingdom	University of Bath	School of Management	Bath
United Kingdom	University of Oxford	Saïd Business School	Oxford

Asia and Pacific

Country	University	Business School	City
Australia	Curtin University of Technology	Curtin Business School	Perth, Western Australia
India	S. P. Jain Institute of Management and Research	Business School	Mumbai
New Zealand	The University of Auckland	The University of Auckland Business School	Auckland
Philippines	Asian Institute of Management	Washington SyCip Graduate School of Business	Makati City
Singapore	National University of Singapore	NUS Business School	Singapore

253

www.ingramcontent.com/pod-product-compliance
Lightning Source LLC
Chambersburg PA
CBHW080526220326
41599CB00032B/6217